STEVEN P. LOCKE

LITTLE LOCKE AND THE MIGHTY INDIANS OF 1975

iUniverse, Inc.
Bloomington

Little Locke and the Mighty Indians of 1975

iUniverse books may be ordered through booksellers or by contacting:

iUniverse
1663 Liberty Drive
Bloomington, IN 47403
www.iuniverse.com
1-800-Authors (1-800-288-4677)

ISBN: 978-1-4759-4345-0 (sc)
ISBN: 978-1-4759-4347-4 (e)
ISBN: 978-1-4759-4346-7 (dj)

Library of Congress Control Number: 2012915869

Printed in the United States of America

iUniverse rev. date: 9/4/2012

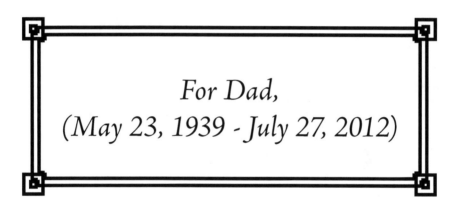

For Dad,
(May 23, 1939 - July 27, 2012)

INTRODUCTION

My father, who is the inspiration and much of the focus of this book, died three weeks before this manuscript went to press. I was fortunate to have read him several chapters aloud in our family living room. When I finished reading "The Game", the chapter on Pickerington, he had taken his glasses off and was rubbing tears from his eyes. I have decided to keep the last few pages of the book, including the coda, *Shadows and Memory*, unchanged. This is a story about time and place. When I was a boy I witnessed something extraordinary - a championship football season that for a brief moment captivated a small Ohio town. As the years passed I occasionally thought of chronicling the ten game campaign but had difficulty reconciling football - the process of becoming a team, athletic competition, the Xs and Os, and details of the various games - with *why* it was so important.

The *importance* assigned to football proved a conundrum. On the one hand, Eugene McCarthy's comment, "*Politics is like coaching football: You have to be smart enough to understand the game and dumb enough to think it is important,*" came to mind whenever I seriously considered a nuts & bolts book about gridiron experiences. And on the other hand, the reality of otherwise powerful men crying unashamedly in both victory and defeat, fans dressing from head-to-toe in team colors, painting their faces, arriving hours before games to eat and drink and discuss impending contests, journalists writing up the results in the newspapers, radio announcers describing the action for a vast audience of listeners, and the tremendous passion reserved for the game of football would indicate that it truly mattered.

Personally, the importance was not difficult to gauge as it determined the life of our family. Coaches who lose don't coach, not for long. My father's chosen profession meant that football counted in the Locke household, immeasurably. But why is football seemingly so important to everyone else who follows the sport? When my father retired following the 1991 football season I returned to Canal Winchester, Ohio to attend a ceremony honoring his tenure at the helm. At Weiser Field that evening I noticed subtle changes and it occurred to me that the importance of football in 1975 was somewhat different than it was nearly two decades later.

Thinking about it over that weekend I realized that if I was ever to write a book about the 1975 Canal Winchester Indians I would have to paint a portrait of the town and its people as it was at that time. In other words, why would anyone be particularly interested in details of football games that took place almost forty years ago if they didn't know who made up the team, where they came from, how they lived and who they were? And so through interviews and research I set about reconstructing a world that no longer exists. The result is *Little Locke and the Mighty Indians of '75* - a two-part book. Part one is an effort to bring the reader back in time to the second half of the twentieth century to rural central Ohio. How and where we lived, the music we listened to, the TV shows we watched, the politics and mores of the time, and a look at the local institutions - families, school, organized sports - that shaped the lives of the coaches and young men who made up the team.

Part two focuses on the ten-game season, how football was practiced and played, the grueling nature of two-a-days, my father's coaching style, the growing attention paid to the team as each victory led to ever more pressure to succeed the following week, and the town that followed and cheered them on in summer heat, driving rain, bitter cold and disappointment. Finally, I tried throughout to write from the perspective of the twelve-year-old that I was in 1975. In that way I hope to give the reader a sense of the wonderment, excitement and importance of the experience.

Steven P. Locke
Granville, Ohio
July 2012

PART I

LITTLE LOCKE

(Who we were and how we lived)

CHAPTER I.

MY ROOM: 1975

Asleep in the down of summer, at that light
Cricket's uplept, blinking their feet, and frogs
Trilled in their valley ponds.

(Joseph Langland - Aria for Flute and Oboe)

"Steven Paul Locke! Get down here this instant!" Summoned by all three names is universal-code for the parental hammer to fall. In my case it fell often but was exasperated when one of my friends – Greg Bruce – happened to be on hand for execution. Not that Greg witnessed an embarrassing scene but rather he learned my full name - Steven Paul Locke. At the time – 1975 – 'Pollock' jokes were all the rage for those of us about to enter junior high school; and the alliteration 'Paul-Locke' was more than close enough to 'Pollock' to merit weeks of torment.

The fact that I was even in my bedroom indicated malfeasance. As a teen I spent considerable time cloistered within its walls, but as a kid couldn't bear the confinement, disappearing before bedtime only when guilty of some heinous transgression. Unbeknownst to yours truly, therefore, and very much like the proverbial canary in the coal mine, an unexplained absence on my part actually heightened Mom's suspicions, facilitating her search for broken furniture, spilt paint or shattered glass.

My second floor bedroom was the first thing guests encountered when reaching the top of our staircase. The staircase itself was small; five steps to a landing - then left and up eight more to the top. An immediate right - my parent's room; a left led down the narrow hallway to the communal bathroom - the vital core of any dwelling containing one or more Lockes. Beyond the all-important family bathroom was the third and final bedroom in the house, and it belonged to my sister – Laura Susanne Locke (Which unfortunately didn't rhyme with anything).

The upstairs doors were made of dark pine; with round, scuffed and faded door knobs surrounded by scuffed and faded rectangular brass plates. The keyholes in the center of those brass plates resembled symbols denoting women's restrooms: round 'head' with the outline of a 'dress' descending from its center. I mention it because I loved playing with their keys - looking as they did in the eyes of a young boy like keys to some lost pirate's treasure chest.

The floors, made of narrow wood planking, were over a half century old in 1975. They creaked and groaned when trod upon, attracted great wisps of dust that settled into its many cracks and grooves, and had an unfortunate tendency to harpoon the unshod with an inexhaustible supply of splinters. Fortunately, Mom had been a battlefield surgeon in a previous life, keeping peroxide, alcohol, tweezers, needle and magnifying glass on hand in a trauma kit for immediate extractions.

When a splinter hit its mark she arrived on scene - having followed the screams - with the speed and dexterity of a MASH surgeon. Indeed, it was not uncommon, about once every month or so, for Mom to stretch one of us out on the couch, steady a throbbing foot propped atop a pillow beneath the reading lamp, and make a thorough examination of some grievous wound; coolly poking, prodding and exploring the soles of our feet for tiny wooden spikes.

My bedroom walls were white – as were all the walls in our house. Two windows, side-by-side, looked out from the western edge of the house, about four feet from the foot of my bed. Those windows dated to the 1920s, and were made of heavy glass containing subtle streaks and indentations. They didn't look or feel like lightweight windows found in homes today. Heavy to begin with, they were also difficult to open; their wooden frames expanding and contracting with the changing seasons. Left ajar without support they sometimes slammed shut with a tremendous thud.

Even closed the windows shook and rattled violently whenever jets from nearby Rickenbacker Air Force Base eclipsed the sound barrier; rewarding residents surrounding the base with reverberating 'sonic booms.' The Air Base was big business, and important to our local economy. In 1940 the US had only 36 large airports nationwide. With the world at war a massive airport building project commenced; within a year 457 new air bases were under construction, and Rickenbacker was one of those, though it started out in 1942 as Lockbourne Army Air Base.

Located 11 ½ miles from Canal Winchester, many Air Force families lived in nearby Groveport and CW. Primarily an air refueling facility, Rickenbacker served in North America's Strategic Air Command, (SAC) from 1951 to 1979; their jets and tankers were very familiar to area residents. Two of my best friends were Air Force Brats and the base was an integral part of our daily lives. Besides Rickenbacker's planes enhancing the general din, I periodically misjudged how far to pull down the window shutters. Heavy shutters like those are rare today but in the 1970s were common.

Coated in some weird wax-paper texture; attached by string with a small loop to move each shutter up and down; they were temperamental - possessing minds of their own. In fact, our shutters retaliated if not treated with kid gloves, shooting upward in an attempt to eclipse the speed of sound, spinning violently - round and round - until it got it out of its system. The window panes in my room were covered in yellow, lead-based paint that flaked off easily in thick malleable chunks when scraped with one's fingernails. Despite the window's appearance they were evidently made to last as we never had one break.

In the 1970s only 35% of American homes had air conditioning and the Locke Clan was not among that coveted minority. Without air conditioning or ceiling fans our windows usually remained open day and night during the summers. Mercifully, a great Mulberry Tree stood outside my bedroom window providing shade and relief from the sun. At night I would lie awake watching its branches move in the breeze.

Streetlights behind the Mulberry shone through its leaves; creating weird shapes that sometimes looked like the moon hiding within its canopy. Perhaps it was just the power of suggestion as the moon was big news in the 1970s. The continuing Apollo missions appeared simultaneously on all three TV networks. One year I even got a 'G.I. Joe Astronaut,' complete with plastic space capsule for Christmas. When you're a kid the world is truncated, closer; more immediate. Things like leaning against car windows on long trips in the back seat, experiencing the sensation of heightened inner-ear vibrations as your head jiggles against glass, are very real. To that end I spent most summer nights gazing out those windows imagining the moon and the men who walked upon it just beyond our Mulberry tree.

A small closet to the right of the windows housed Dad's ties, dress shirts and slacks. During the workweek, lying in bed in the early morning, half asleep and half awake, I'd watch him select ties from the tie rack hanging inside of the closet door. Always quiet, he stood there every weekday tying his tie before descending the stairs and going off to work.

At the foot of the back closet wall, beyond Dad's ties and clothes, was a tiny door; a sort of closet-within-a-closet used to access attic storage. And that tiny door impacted my imagination entirely out of proportion to its diminutive size. Only four years old when first moved into that bedroom my preternaturally agitated mind ran wild when considering that closet-within-the-closet. I therefore kept both closet doors shut tight. For many years no doubt whatsoever existed in my fevered little brain that some unspeakable evil lurked behind that spooky inner closet door.

Looking back it's comforting rationalizing the normalcy of a small boy fearing the darkness and cobwebs filling that tiny space; but alas I was not - and am in no way, shape or form - 'normal.' My overactive boyhood imagination conjured innumerable fiendish creatures behind that door. By age twelve, however, one is old enough to know better; unfortunately, an instructive example of my warped outlook dates to that period.

During the summer of 1975, the Locke Clan saw the movie *Jaws*; and to my sister's everlasting delight the Great White shark that so ruthlessly devoured residents of Amityville had relocated – in my mind - to Canal Winchester, Ohio. He lived – at least at night - in my closet. After seeing the film I seriously considered the closet capable of filling with water;

the Great White behind the door anxious to burst in, spilling into my bedroom to gnaw viciously on my slumbering, vulnerable, defenseless body. I was a weird little kid.

The trip to the Columbus' theater to see *Jaws* was in itself a big deal in our family. My sister Laura and I never wanted for anything but my family, like the vast majority of our neighbors and friends, didn't have much disposable income. We rarely went to the movies. When just three-years-old or thereabouts Mom and Dad took us to see *The Song of the South*, and I recall seeing *Winnie the Pooh* at the theater around the same age, but that was pretty much it.

Jaws, however, had become a phenomenon, being pretty-much all anybody talked about that summer. Most friends had seen it and my Uncle Phil - living in Bangor, Maine - phoned to say he was taking a hiatus from swimming in the ocean. Indeed, the film had entered the daily lexicon even in landlocked Canal Winchester, Ohio. When patronizing Bolenbaugh's Hardware Store to buy fishing lures the clerk, after espying an especially lethal jig asked, *"You gonna try to catch Jaws with that thing!"*

Despite repeatedly asking to see what all the fuss was about we had no luck persuading the folks to take us. At dinner one night, having asked if we could *"please, please,"* see *Jaws*, Dad responded in his usual fashion - he said nothing. Horace Greely's long-ago observation of President Grant - *"He has nothing to say and keeps on saying it all day long"* – was also apt for my father. But on this evening – after a time - turning his head and looking at me intently, he said, *"Listen, movies have changed from when I was kid. They don't show the shark, then the person, and later a fin swimming in fake blood. They show the whole damn thing!"*

Be that as it may, Laura and I were mortified (as only junior high-aged children are capable of mortification) at being the only two kids in Canal Winchester, Ohio - perhaps the entire country - who hadn't seen *Jaws* and loath to admit as much to our friends. We had pretty much given up when on the Friday before Labor Day weekend Mom and Dad descended the stairs in fashionable attire. As school teachers the folks dressed professionally September through June. Summer, on the other hand, was another matter and we knew something was up.

"Are we going to see Jaws?" Dad's economical rejoinder, *"Get in the car!"* couldn't have been clearer in the affirmative. We soon arrived on

Columbus's east side to see the summer blockbuster of 1975. Exiting our car the parking lot filled with the last group to see the film, and I distinctly remember them looking rather haggard. Inside, once the lights went down and the movie started, you could hear a pin drop. When the music signaling the next shark attack, *"Duh-dunt, Duh-dunt, Duh-dunt, DUH-DUH-DUH!"* reached a crescendo; the tension could be cut with a knife. Unfortunately, the shark attacks triggered a Pavlovian response in my bladder.

I had to urinate with extreme prejudice. Stephen Spielberg's mechanical Great White shark literally scared the piss out of me. At one point, while moving sideways past those seated to my left - on the fourth or fifth restroom trip - I heard a woman say; *"Now this is just getting ridiculous. That damn kid has something wrong with him!"* I felt bad but bladders and bowels reign supreme in the physiological hierarchy; it was out of my control. Emerging into the sunlit uplands of the parking lot following the film we discovered the shark got to Mom as well. She had chewed completely through the strap of her purse, carrying it by the severed band on the way to the car. It was a quiet trip back to Canal Winchester.

Little Locke, evaluating a beer can at Christmas

On the other side of my bedroom - to the left of the windows in the corner - rested a small wooden ladder. Dark brown and with two small hooks atop each post, it was once part of a twin bunk-bed set. Its six rungs served as shelving for my beer can collection. Like *Jaws*, beer-can-collecting was popular in the 1970s, at least in Canal Winchester, Ohio.

Several friends boasted collections of three and four hundred cans. In my particular case the obsession with locating and acquiring said cans began two years earlier in Fifth grade. Strolling through town, Pabst Blue Ribbon, Black Label, Stroh's, Schlitz Malt Liquor, Miller, Budweiser, Rolling Rock and Busch beer cans were easily salvaged from alleys, dumpsters and back yards.

Unfortunately, Mom's reaction to the new hobby was not positive. MOM: "*What are you doing with those?*" STEVE: "*I'm starting a beer can collection.*" MOM: "*Oh, for God's sake Steven Paul, I don't want those nasty things in the house.*" STEVE: "*Oh Mom, please! I promise I'll wash them out and it'll be really cool.*" MOM: "*Uh, huh.*" Despite her dim view she hadn't said no – a definite green light to ten year olds - and so the acquisition, cleaning and sorting of discarded beverage containers commenced in earnest. Neat, linear and alphabetically ordered on the rungs of my little ladder the beer-can-collection inadvertently exposed my growing and pronounced anal-retentive streak.

Dad's reaction was somewhat different than mother's. Glancing at the neat rows of cans he said, "*Cool,*" and then promised to help fill the rest of the ladder. "*I'll drink em, and you save the empties boy.*" As with everything else in my life – both then and later – fanaticism, in this case regarding beer-can collecting, reared its ugly head. Cans quickly multiplied exponentially as junkyards, trash bins, the banks of Little Walnut Creek, alleyways and parking lots were scoured for empties.

In Mrs. Gardner's fifth grade classroom a thriving black market developed in beer cans. We traded beer cans; evaluated beer cans, priced beer cans and carried on earnest discussions as to the merits of each can's size, future value and present worth. One student even purchased an entire collection; an action deeply frowned upon by those of us without the liquidity to do the same.

Wagnall's Memorial Library in neighboring Lithopolis, had a beer can collection book in circulation; and after checking it out repeatedly its worn pages were eventually committed to memory. Alas, no one in the family circle was immune from beer can collecting responsibilities. Aunts and uncles, grandma and grandpa, friends of Mom and Dad all kept their eyes peeled for unique, unclaimed beer cans.

At Grandma and Grandpa Riddell's in Middletown that summer, Grandma took us to lunch one day to Frisch's Big Boy. Sitting in the back seat with Laura - scanning the roadside for cans – one prized cylinder caught my eye. I yelled *"Stop Grandma, Stop!"* Immediately slamming on her brakes my terrified grandmother - convinced she'd hit someone or something – pulled off the road. *"Grandma, can you please pull into that parking lot? I see a beer can."*

Mom was none too pleased, but Grandma pulled into the lot and stopped. Jumping out, I grabbed an empty, slightly dented, 24 ounce, Colt-45 Malt Liquor beer can. Climbing back into the car my sister rolled her eyes before shooting a disdainful *'Harrumph!'* in my general direction. Grandma, sitting with her hand across her chest, kept repeating the words, *"Mercy, mercy child; lord have mercy."* Later, mother laid out explicit instructions not to do that while in transit - ever again.

The collection outgrew the ladder and so Grandpa Riddell spent an entire weekend building custom beer-can-shelves that eventually covered two walls. By the summer of 1975 it had grown into a handsome display containing well over 300 different cans of various sizes and colors. The crown jewel - a 132-ounce, gold and blue *Oktoberfest* beer can - rested dead center on the topmost shelf. Grandpa had surprised me with the can during a weekend visit. Reaching into a brown paper sack, he pulled out what looked like a small beer keg, placing it into my eager hands.

The memory of his handing me that can is clear to this day because it marked one of the few times when speechlessness fell upon the fountains of my great deep. Mute, silent, a literal cipher; beaming at the big gold shiny can, suspecting a hoax, a cruel joke. Perhaps a gag from some novelty-shop offered up to wrench uncontrolled emotion from a squat, slightly neurotic, hormonally challenged twelve year old.

Coming as it did from Grandpa Riddell, doubt should never have entered the equation. Indeed that genuine Oktoberfest beer can held great meaning not only because it came from Grandpa, but - more importantly - not a single friend or schoolmate had anything remotely like it. Besides the fishing pole Dad gave me for my tenth birthday, it was perhaps the most beautiful thing I had ever seen.

Grandpa Riddell's name was Edward, and he was an impressive man. Born September 5, 1919, in Whitehall, Kentucky he grew up continuously on the move through Indiana, Kentucky, Tennessee and Ohio. By the time he graduated from high school in 1935, he had attended seventeen different schools, never staying at any one more than five or six months.

His father, Speed Riddell, an itinerant house painter and something of a wheeler-dealer, kept his family on the road. Speed went where work led him toting his tools and family from job to job. Together with his wife Ella, they had three children, Edward, the oldest, Cora and Ruby. Like other young men of his generation – 'The Greatest Generation' - Grandpa Riddell survived the Great Depression and fought the Axis during The Second World War. In the spring of 1975, when constructing my beer can shelves, he was fifty-six years old. His life had been one of sacrifice and hard work.

Getting a hug from Grandpa Riddell. 1965

Standing six-feet, 1-inches tall, Grandpa had broad shoulders, black wavy hair, and hazel eyes. He smoked a pipe, which seemed to enhance the quiet dignity about him. On visits to his home repeatedly opening and closing his Zippo lighter proved irresistible. The sound it made, click-clack, click-clack was weirdly appealing. Grandpa would carefully watch my opening and closing of his lighter out the corner of his bespectacled eye; ten, fifteen even 20-times in a row. Having grown bored and setting the lighter aside Grandpa quietly picked it up placing it in his pocket; never once scolding or asking that I stop – no matter how annoying. To this day the slightly sweet aroma of *Half & Half* tobacco and the click-clack of a lighter remind me of him.

He entered the US Navy at twenty-six-years of age despite being married and having two young daughters. Grandma, Letta Riddell, spoke of sitting up late at night under a bare kitchen light, trying to create a private code in an attempt to elude government censors in their correspondence - so she might know exactly where he'd be and what he was doing.

Grandpa's place in our clan was of enormous import because of his mechanical skills, which the Riddell's possessed in abundance and the Locke's did not. If the car died, Grandpa could fix it; a TV set on the fritz, Grandpa could fix it; plumbing problem? Call Grandpa and he knew what to do; radiator problem? Grandpa could fix it. And when Grandpa fixed something, by God it stayed fixed.

He had a dry sense of humor that surfaced when watching TV. He enjoyed making wry comments, referring to an on-air klutz as *"a big ape,"* or perhaps a *"clumsy oaf."* After which he'd chuckle, and then take a drag on his pipe. Grandpa Riddell was very gentle and decent and had just given me the pride of my beer can collection.

By the time he built the bedroom shelving Mom's stance regarding beer can collecting had thawed. She even began to appreciate the myriad colors and designs, becoming an ardent ally in the acquisition of rare and new finds. When my folks entertained Dad always made a point of bringing guests into my bedroom to show off the beer can collection. *"I told the boy,"* he'd say, *"that I'd drink em and he could save the cans;"* and it never failed to draw laughter from guests. Standing by proudly admiring the adults admiring my masterpiece, I was ever ready and able to field questions about the origin of a can; where it was brewed; how it was acquired, etc.

My twin bed lay directly beneath the shelves. There were several small indentations on the wall beside the bed. Never able to fall right to sleep, studying the wall markings became a nightly activity before nodding off. One shape resembled a malted milkshake and, running my forefinger over it again and again, sleep overtook me wondering how it got there. Years later, when we moved across town, it hurt leaving it, like abandoning an old friend. Right of the closet sat the chest of drawers. My sequestered stash of one dollar bills - concealed inside a tube sock – remained hidden amongst ordinary socks beneath a Washington Redskins helmet-lamp atop the dresser.

Immense pride surrounded that lamp. It had been given to Dad at the annual gridiron banquet after his football team went undefeated - 10 and 0 - in 1970. Its lampshade was tan and coarsely textured; the helmet yellow/orange with an R-logo on each side trailing a tapered feather. As our school's sports teams were known as the Canal Winchester Indians, football helmet-lamps with Indian feathers represented the penultimate accessory for area fans - especially if the fan's father was the high school football coach.

Football is huge in Ohio, and it was big in my bedroom. The blanket atop my bed, part of an NFL bedding set, came replete with NFC and AFC team logos. On the wall across from my closet hung a poster of Charlie Taylor, wide receiver for the Washington Redskins. Next to the dresser hung a second football poster of the New York Giants attempting to block an extra-point by the Baltimore Colts; a third poster featured images of the Ohio State Buckeyes and several adages from central Ohio's great gridiron deity - Coach Woody Hayes.

Both Mom and Dad eventually earned master's degrees at Ohio State University and the Locke Clan bled scarlet and gray. Once, when Mom worked at Canal Winchester's Shade's Restaurant, Woody and some of his staff stopped in for lunch. She got a fix on the Buckeye Coach and pounced. Leaving the kitchen she approached his table and asked for an autograph. Woody smiled, took out a sheet of paper from his folder and wrote, "*Steve, work hard and come to Ohio State. Woody Hayes.*" That too made it on the wall of my bedroom.

Laura & Steve and empty fields behind our home on Waterloo St.

That small bedroom - my semi-private sanctuary - became a safe haven, the port in the storm when impending doom waited below. Guarded by an old dark pine door and containing the closet where Dad hung his clothes; the closet-within-the-closet to stir nighttime imagination; large windows with heavy wooden panes; flanked outside by the huge mulberry tree swaying beyond the glass.

The beer can collection, displayed and growing thanks to the family's collective effort; its hardwood floors - cold in winter, cool in summer - with its many hidden splinters. Adorned with football posters, football blankets, images and autographs of Woody Hayes; proudly displaying the much coveted football-lamp – all those accoutrements paid silent tribute to what mattered in my world at age twelve.

That was my room. It lacked television, radio and certainly a computer - some futuristic device known of personally only from *Star Trek* reruns. Even so the room was very much alive. At night in the summertime sounds of train whistles echoed beyond the fields behind our house; chirping crickets played unending, nightly orchestras, the heavy whir from vehicles passing below on Waterloo Street pierced the room every few minutes; parents yelled for kids to come inside, Rickenbacker's powerful jets periodically streaked across the night sky shaking the house; the swishing, rustling mulberry tree provided a diffuse breeze; flitting, weirdly illuminated fireflies danced outside the window screen and the smell of warm summer air all brought my bedroom to life.

During winter months - laying in bed at night - the sounds our furnace made rang especially loud. First, a familiar whoosh of air and then popping and groaning as it fired up to warm the house. One small floor register provided the sole source of heat in my room; on cold winter mornings, standing over it with a blanket wrapped about my body trapping its delicious warmth, it was greatly appreciated.

Bedtime came at 9:00 pm; never soon enough for Mom and Dad, always too early for Steve and Laura. Being high strung and hyper sleep eluded me long after turning in. After awhile, when eyes and ears adjusted to the darkness and quiet, dialogue from the TV playing downstairs could be clearly made out: "*The ABC Movie of the Week will return after these messages.*" Or, "*McCloud will return after this station identification.*"

One night in 1973, after hearing a commercial for *The Exorcist* the lamp atop the dresser remained on all night. The next night the mere memory of that demonic voice led me to fire up the lamp again; Mom eventually turned it off before going to bed. The following morning she asked about the lamp and I told her. Sympathetic, she patiently explained there was no such thing as the Devil; people had made him up long ago - before understanding the way the world worked. If lightning struck someone's home, or the harvest failed for example, it was interpreted to be the act of an angry God; murderers might claim the Devil had made them kill, etc.

Reassured, the lamp remained dark. A week or so later however, after listening to another eerie *Exorcist* commercial, the night light shone bright as ever. Exasperated, Mom turned to Dad and father stepped in to solve the problem. Reaching the landing of our stairwell the following morning Dad stood at the foot of the steps, (always a bad sign). Looking up sternly in my direction he said authoritatively, *"Steven Paul, if your mother tells me you've left your light on one more night I'm going to beat your ass! Do you understand me? There's no such thing as a Goddamn Devil. That's bullshit! Do you understand me? One more time and I'll beat your ass."*

As one might surmise father's parenting style was somewhat different from mothers. And it worked. Not so much for fear of getting spanked but because of the shame his scolding engendered. The thought that Dad saw me as timid – afraid of the dark - was unbearable. Opting to roll over and cover my ears during commercials the lamp stayed off. Nevertheless, the incident led Mom to refer to me as *"elephant ears."*

Laura especially delighted in implicating me for unauthorized after-hours eavesdropping; the typical indictment going something like this: MOM: *"How do you know that Steve? Where did you hear that?"* STEVE: *"You told me the other day at supper."* LAURA: *"Nu huh mom! He heard you talking last night. He lays there when he's supposed to be sleeping and listens to everything you guys say!"* MOM: *"Steven Paul Locke! Get up to your room this minute. You're not supposed to listen in on private conversations!"* Even upstairs in my pajamas, tucked in, I managed to get into trouble in my bedroom.

CHAPTER II:

OUR HOUSE

Our two story Sears Home had three bedrooms, one and a half bathrooms and a half basement. Slate gray, it sat atop a small rise that looked like a very substantial hill when we arrived during the summer of 1967. Sandwiched between a great brick home and a three story apartment building there had been no changes to the gray rental cottage over the years because the landlord wanted the house to remain the way it was. And it did. The owner, Mac Gayman, had turned Mom down when she first inquired about renting the place. He would not rent to anyone with kids, he said, and that was final.

As there were very few homes available in Canal Winchester, Ohio, within my parents' budget, Dad arranged to meet Mr. Gayman in private. We moved in two weeks later never having learned what had passed between them. Mr. Gayman was a large man who didn't say much, but sure kept his eyes open. He owned quite a bit of property about town; his family having lived in the area since Winchester's founding in 1828. Mac, his wife Thelma, and their twenty-four year old son, Bob Gayman, lived next door - immediately next door - with no more than ten or fifteen feet separating his brick house and the Sears' Home we were renting.

Kids everywhere! A gaggle on the porch at 106 E. Waterloo St.

Between 1908, Theodore Roosevelt's last full year as president, and 1940, when his nephew, Franklin Roosevelt, sought an unprecedented third term in the White House, Sears and Roebuck sold over 100,000 prefabricated house kits through their '*Modern Homes Catalogue*.' We lived in one such home at 106 East Waterloo Street in 1975. Ranging in price from $495.00 at the low end, and up to $4,115.00 at the highest, Sears Homes were shipped by rail in boxcars containing 30,000 numbered, precut pieces. Once the boxes were unloaded at rail yards it was up to homeowners to follow the leather-bound instructions included with the kit. Our house was built in 1922 as the town approached its Centennial, and since Canal Winchester had its very own municipal water system the Gayman's avoided the additional $23.00 cost for an optional Sears Outhouse.

We enjoyed a spacious front porch with rails on three sides, ideal for socializing, a porch swing and screen door. Two large windows fronted the house overlooking Waterloo Street. Mom's steel glider, part of her family for nearly thirty years and as heavy and indestructible as a tank, sat on the western end of the porch opposite the swing.

We spent a lot of time on that glider, rocking to and fro, dreaming about what we would include if we ever had enough money to build a house of our own, what the future held, and gossiping about the neighbors. Sometimes we just sat quietly watching the trees sway from side to side and the cars and bicycles rolling past. During the dog days of summer Laura and I occasionally slept on the front porch. The little house became stifling during heat waves and without air conditioning the second floor felt like a sauna. So we took pillows from our beds, spread sleeping bags upon the porch floor, and slept outside beneath the canopy of the Mulberry Tree.

Inside, the first floor living room was rectangular. The staircase was located to the right, and on the opposite wall there was a fireplace - which no longer worked. Against the back wall sat Dad's couch, though he wasn't home much to enjoy it. When he was, however, the couch was his. Stretching his long 6-feet, 2-inch frame across all three cushions, Dad would hold whatever book he happened to be reading in front of his face, occasionally peering over its spine to follow the action on TV. Speaking of the TV, it sat in the corner facing the couch. In 1975 televisions weren't the sleek, black, flat screened, hi-definition models prevalent today. They looked like other pieces of furniture in the home: large, brown, four-legged, and with grooves etched into the sides.

Although remote control devices were on the market in 1975, I was the 'clicker' in our house. My favorite chair - the 'Junk Chair' – sat close to the TV next to the picture window, and so the folks would say *"Steve, get channel 10 for me, would you please?"* when they wanted to see a different program. Turning the cumbersome knob that 'clonk, clonk, clonked,' as it rotated between channels the Locke's (and everyone else in town) could access NBC-4, ABC-6, and CBS-Channel-10. That was it. PBS was theoretically available but reception was usually too poor to pick it up.

Like channel surfing, proper reception became interactive as well. Sitting atop the TV, sometimes embellished with aluminum foil, rested the rabbit eared antenna which had to be adjusted just-so to get a good picture. Our antennae had a circular base out of which extended two rods that moved independently. Once an acceptable position was found, moving, bumping or any attempt to improve the picture with further adjustments was punishable by death. Well, not death, but losing the picture certainly led to verbal chastisement. *"Goddamn it Steven Paul!*

I just got it adjusted. Look at that crap! I can't see a damn thing. Move it back."

Although personally responsible for numerous jolts to the TV and its tiny topside antennae, the real culprit and most frequent violator of picture quality was our cat, *Blossom.* The TV set warmed the longer it ran and Blossom's favorite sleeping spot was located immediately next to the antenna. Every night at 9:00 pm, after Mom had us say goodnight, Laura lifted *Blossom* from his toasty spot - fluffy, coifed, snow white, spoiled-rotten *Blossom.* Grasping him under his front legs she would then say, "*S-T-R-E-T-C-H!*" On cue *Blossom* lengthened his body, instantly metamorphosing from coiled puff ball into elongated, albino tiger-cat.

Laura stretches Blossom after a nap atop the warm TV. Note the antenna.

The broad top of the TV also served as a platform for seasonal decorations: Pumpkins at Halloween, ceramic turkeys and pilgrims at Thanksgiving, plastic reindeer, Santa, and his sleigh at Christmastime. As for what happened on screen, tamer programming, at least for kids, reigned in 1975. Perhaps squalid fare existed on the dial for adults, but we rarely saw it. Limited to three channels, at school all day, in bed by nine, and subordinate to our parents' viewing veto, we were sheltered compared to the onslaught kids are exposed to today.

We watched *MASH, The Carol Burnett Show, All In The Family*, and on Friday evenings, my favorite lineup of the week: *The Six Million Dollar Man*, at 8:00 pm starring Lee Majors, followed by *Kung Fu*, with David Carradine, at 9:00 pm, and topped off at 10:00 pm, with *Kolchak: The Night Stalker*, starring Darren McGavin. Dad was gone Friday evenings and when his team played away, we stayed home. Although Mom skipped 'The Six Million Dollar Man,' she enjoyed 'Kung Fu' and 'Kolchak: the Night Stalker.' Laura, on the other hand, left the room almost immediately after *Kolchak* got underway, insisting it too scary and apt to cause nightmares.

On the far side of the living room beside the fireplace sat Mom's desk. At the back of the desk a small plastic clock ticked away, and Mom periodically glanced at it before announcing bedtime. Having observed this pattern, my nightly goal involved strategically placing foreign objects between Mom's chair and the chronometer, blocking her line of sight. Unfortunately, she caught on somewhat quickly and the practice was discontinued. Just in front of Mom's desk was the largest floor register in the house. Responsible for heating two rooms, it was a great, black monster of a register that also produced the greatest volume of noise when coming to life: pinging, groaning, and bellowing as heat escaped its grill. And damn if it didn't get hot – fire-hazard hot.

How hot is fire-hazard hot? Sometime during fourth grade, (age nine) Mom surprised me with a new pair of shoes. As I was walking home from school not long after receiving the shoes a raging tempest descended on CW - a downpour of Biblical proportions. Without an umbrella - no self-respecting 9-year-old boy from Canal Winchester, Ohio would be caught dead with an umbrella – a grand time was had by all as we 'Town-Walkers' jumped in every puddle, gutter, and standing eddy of water between Franklin and Waterloo Streets. I returned home completely drenched.

Once inside, disrobing commenced. Losing my shirt and grabbing a towel, I stood atop the living room register, heat pouring forth from below, warm and delicious. My feet were shoulder width apart and Mom was asking about my day. Laura - busily detailing how idiotic my behavior had been on the walk home - was first to spot tiny wisps of blue/white smoke rising from the floor. About to run upstairs and change my wet pants and socks, I too saw smoke and detected an odd, unfamiliar odor. The oily aroma accompanied by faint trails of smoke swirling gently past my face could mean only one thing. Looking down confirmed it: my shoes were melting into the grill and smoking at an alarming rate.

"Oh my God Look, Look at my shoes! Mom, help!" Startled, Mom asked, *"Are those your new shoes? Get off of the register! Get off of there!"* Her excited order to move triggered an inner alarm. That mild alarm turned to abject panic after realizing I could not move. The toasty warm, familiar register had morphed into a fiery, smoke belching cauldron of Hell. *"Mom, Mom! I can't move, I can't move! I'm stuck Mom! Get me off of here!"* She untied my shoes and escape followed. The great black furnace register, however, lost all of the trust we had built up over the years – never to be regained again.

Two bookcases formed either side of an archway leading to our dining room. We used the tops of the bookcases to display Christmas decorations, and the shelves were filled with Mom and Dad's college text books and a set of *World Book Encyclopedias*. Those bookcase doors also afforded another valuable lesson in Mom and Dad's differing parenting styles. To Wit:

Although forbidden to play with footballs, baseballs, or basketballs in the house, Mom cut us some slack during the winter months. One cold winter Sunday, standing four or five feet in front of the bookcase closest to Dad - who was stretched out on his couch watching football and reading - I began throwing a yellow rubber ball at the side of the glass case. Not hard, but with enough force so it bounced off the floor, against the case, back to the floor and up into my arms.

'Bop crash-bop-slap. Bop crash-bop-slap. Bop crash-bop-slap.' The ball landing, hitting and bouncing just feet behind my father's head. Being twelve and oblivious, it never occurred to me that the repetitive din might be annoying. Mom was not oblivious, however, and told me to stop. *"Why?"* *"Honey, you're doing that right behind your father; he's trying to relax and read his book. It's very distracting. If you want to throw the ball, go down in the basement or put on your coat and play outside."*

That made sense and I left the room without incident. A few weeks later - still being twelve and oblivious - the scene repeated itself, but this time without mother there to run interference. It's important to keep in mind no malice or defiance existed in my actions and I certainly was not trying to upset Dad. Heedless, unaware, oblivious – let's just say the preteen slamming the rubber ball behind his father's head was not the sharpest knife in the drawer.

Father's approach to obnoxious adolescent behavior differed markedly from Moms': Bop-crash-bop-slap. Bop-crash- bop-slap. Bop-crash-bop-slap. Bop-crash-bop-slap. *"Goddamn it! Stop that shit! If you throw that ball one more goddamn time I'm going to beat your ass!"* Dad wore glasses and when angry his face distorted in such a way as to lower the rims just below his pupils - which were now focused intently upon my shell-shocked frame. My legs shook involuntarily and my spinal cord felt as if it had fallen out of my ass. Dad then turned back to his book as if nothing had happened. I stopped – as had happened after Mom intervened – but this time made a mental note to discontinue throwing the ball in the house.

Our dining room - like the living room - was rectangular. A large picture window looked out on the backyard and in front of the window sat our dining room table. Suspended over the table, providing illumination, hung the original 1922 light fixture, since adapted with a long metal chain. Every time Dad pulled that chain, and I do mean every time, he said, *"And God said, 'Let There Be Light; There Was Light. And It Was Good'."* Behind the table at the center of the west wall of the dining room was Mom's antique buffet. She placed a soup tureen atop the buffet and Dad used its center cabinets to store booze.

Beside her buffet - mounted on the wall above Mom's Singer sewing machine - was the only phone in the house. Her Singer sewing machine was an older model with a brass wheel and large foot pedal on the floor. Mom pushed the pedal to and fro when mending clothes or making dresses. The black, rotary dial telephone had a long elastic coil so users could walk about while talking, and although we had a list of emergency numbers taped beside it, the model came without caller ID, call-waiting, or an answering machine.

On the opposite wall sat Laura's piano. Mom and Dad bought it secondhand after seeing an ad in the newspaper. Laura began taking lessons shortly thereafter. To the right of the piano, tucked into the corner, was the first floor restroom. Small - like a phone booth without the glass – it had a toilet, toilet-paper hanger and a single cord descending from above, attached to a bare light bulb. The dining room led to our kitchen which was brighter than the other rooms. The kitchen contained less wood, more linoleum, and had white cupboards, a white stove, and a white refrigerator.

We didn't own a dishwasher in 1975, and didn't get a microwave until we moved to Columbus Street two years later. Mom washed dishes after meals until Laura and I took over the chore, rotating every other night. The gas stove was a squat, solidly built workhorse with four top burners, an oven and grill down below. To fire up the stove, users first had to contend with a pilot light. A match was struck and placed next to the rim of a tiny, black metal hole located at the base of the oven; simultaneously the gas knob needed to be rotated just enough to ignite the flame. Too much gas resulted in frightful 'Kawhooooms!' while successful ignitions produced a hollow, thumping sound letting users know the stove had lit.

When Mom and Dad went out for an evening Laura and I were allowed to split a bottle of pop and make cheese crackers in the grill. Soda was a real treat in our home. Consequently, when green lighted to split a bottle we poured, compared and measured each drop with deadly seriousness. If Laura poured, for example, and her glass mysteriously held 1/1000 of an ounce more than mine, or vice versa, it was war. Cheese crackers, fortunately, ensured the evening had a festive quality about it. We made them together, standing next to the kitchen table, placing crackers on one of Mom's metal baking sheets; splitting slices of American cheese in quarters, covering each and every saltine on the tray.

Laura usually lit the grill, both because she was a protective older sister and because I was convinced the stove harbored a palpable degree of ill will - for humans in general and me in particular. Another heavy pine door opposite the stove opened to stairs leading to our half basement. A dank and dirty place, our basement was half cement, half hardened mud, adobe-like but dark brown with an ancient, defunct coal furnace sitting in a low lying area surrounded by a dirt floor. Here and there were old cylindrical blocks of granite, cobwebs, and two bare light bulbs. Dad kept paints down there along with his homemade wine. The washer/dryer sat next to our Kenmore freezer that Mom and Dad stocked annually with 'half-a-cow."

That was always an exciting time. Dad bought the beef from friends in Richwood, Ohio where he had begun his teaching and coaching career. Returning late from that trip every year - usually past 11:30 pm – he arrived home with two or three large cardboard boxes filled with steaks, ground beef, cube steak, hamburger patties, sirloins, Rib-eyes and T-bones wrapped in white butcher's paper. Mom and Dad spoke approvingly of the money they had saved and how long the beef would last. There is primitive satisfaction in a stocked larder – or Kenmore Freezer for that matter.

Not all basement memories, unfortunately, are so warming. *Rover*, my German Sheppard, was too large for our house and we eventually gave him to a good home. While we had *Rover*, however, it was my responsibility to clean up his twice daily constitutionals - which he deposited in our basement while the family was off at work and school. *Rover's* preferred spot was the dirt floor housing the decrepit furnace. The chore, always vile, became tedious over time.

A big strapping male German Sheppard, it followed that *Rover's* ordure was big strapping male German Sheppard excreta. Taking hold of each organic clump with paper towels, I would hand carry the offal up the basement steps, through the kitchen and into the dining room toilet for a well deserved flush. The monotony of this particular chore eventually got the better of me. Though justifiably proud of *Rover* being as prolific a shitter as any Locke who ever bore the family name; appreciation of this daily Turd Trek quickly vanished.

And then, during a routine sweep of the basement, several cylindrical granite blocks caught my eye. Large, accessible and hollow they appeared ideally suited for *Rover* refuse. The ever ubiquitous idea bulb lit atop my deformed adolescent noggin and the daily quota of Rover shit quietly made its way into the cylinders - no harm, no foul.

Unfortunately, Rover's capacity for defecating rapidly translated into several turd laden cylinders reaching their quota – and then some. Of course Mom eventually discovered the ruse. What really got her goat was not stuffing the cylinders with *Rover* turds but rather my lying about it – consciously and deliberating deceiving. *"Hell hath no fury like a mother scorned"* and scorned she was.

When exceedingly angry - irate, beside herself - Mom displayed an involuntary Horace Greely-like mannerism: raising her right arm before her body, pointing her forefinger directly at the target of her wrath, she trembled with rage before releasing the floodgates. In this instance she stood motionless, staring intently at her quarry with barely controlled disdain coursing through her little body - and then she cried havoc and let slip the dogs of war.

"*Steven Paul! This cement block is full of dog shit! Did you put it there? Did you? You better not lie to me again!*" Rhetorical inquiry made it worse as the mere mention of "lying again," convulsed her into further paroxysms of rage, reminding her aloud of my perfidy. "*That's right! Lying! Lying to me all week every time I asked you if you had cleaned the basement! I asked you right to your face if you cleaned the basement and you looked me right in my eyes and lied! Lied right to my face! Right to my face!*"

By this time the conflagration had brought Laura and Dad to the basement. There was nothing to be said in my defense - I was busted, caught brown handed as it were. Talking - learned through bitter experience - only made things worse. Unfortunately, the appearance of Dad and Laura meant Mom had to explain what happened, and as she told the tale her ire ignited anew.

Dad's advice - once he deciphered from his ranting wife that I had lied - was succinct and to the point. "*Beat his ass! Patty, you don't have to put up with that shit. Beat his ass!*" That was pretty much Dad's solution to childrearing, (no pun intended) and waver in the approach he did not. Indeed, before being sent off to elementary school he informed me, "*Steve let me tell you something. If you get in trouble down there, if one of your teachers has a problem with you, I want you to know I've already told them to beat your ass. Do you understand? You do what your teachers tell you to do, and if you don't, it's your ass.*" I believed him.

The scene was so tense, the outcome so assured, that Laura - sister, sibling, nemeses, and sole rival for parental affection and attention - actually came to my defense. "*He's my brother and I love him; don't spank him.*" Unfortunately her selfless act only made the contrast between us that much starker, and her pleas for clemency fell on deaf ears. Father's admonition was duly followed and thenceforth the basement cleaning proceeded the way it should have. The truth shall set you free, though somewhat sore of ass.

It's important to note there was never any abuse in our home. Dad was in no way menacing or intimidating. He was, however, a man - like the father's of my friends - and when one knowingly lied or misbehaved there were consequences. Indeed, the men in town, at least those we knew, were not touchy-feely, in-tune-with-their-emotions types.

Consequently, a distinct division existed between men and their world, and the world their children inhabited. That division is blurred today. It was crystal clear in 1975. Grown men in Canal Winchester had first and certainly secondhand experience with the Great Depression, and nearly all of them had served in the military; many having fought in WWII, Korea, or Vietnam.

A substantial number served at nearby Rickenbacker Air Force Base. They smoked cigarettes, chewed tobacco and told bawdy jokes in hushed tones beyond the range of nosy youngsters. When kids ventured too close they were more likely than not to hear, "*Go play and let the grown-ups talk.*" The adults in town certainly weren't all 'working-class-heroes,' but when their kids lied or got out of line they responded the way Dad did, opting not to spare the rod.

The interior walls in our house were made of sheet plaster - a type of plasterboard predating today's sheetrock or drywall. On the second floor, bedroom ceilings on either end of the hallway sloped downward following the roofline. As a result available headroom along the back walls was considerably less than that in the front of the bedrooms. A narrow hallway running north/south connected the second story rooms.

An original 1922 radiator sat against the hallway wall, mute in summer, boisterous during winter months and an excellent obstacle with which to stub one's toe in the darkness. The second floor bathroom lacked shower facilities but our porcelain tub came complete with four legs, brass handles and rubber stopper. Dad showered at the high school but to me and Laura showers were unchartered territory – some futuristic contraption seen only at grandma's house.

Laura's bedroom ceiling sloped at an angle and one large center window looked down upon Waterloo Street. In 1975, Laura Susanne Locke was thirteen years old. She had large green eyes, curly brown hair and excelled at piano, singing, academics and drawing. Yet the distinguishing characteristic that most defined Laura in the summer of 1975 – the dominant trait in fundamentally describing her – had to have been her devotion to, ardor for, infatuation with, adoration – nay - pagan idolization of - Donny Osmond. The girl had a bad case of 'puppy-love.'

Laura Suzanne Locke, circa 1970

Though small by today's standards, Laura's bedroom contained more Donny Osmond paraphernalia than the Osmond Brother's Museum in Branford Missouri. Indeed, within its claustrophobic confines she dedicated, (committed) herself to covering every available space with images, song lyrics, posters, paintings, magazine articles, drawings and any and all erstwhile representations of the toothy Mormon crooner she could lay hands on.

It was a veritable teen-queen's shrine and disturbingly reminiscent, in its degree of obsession, of the beer can collection down the hallway. Mom took to referring to Donny as 'Scrawny Osmond,' and we all teased Laura a bit, but her bedroom looked cool - in that time and place - plastered from top to bottom with devotions to Donny. Of course, at the end of the day, Mom was no doubt relieved the object of Laura's devotion was as tame, wholesome and unobtainable as the virile vocalist from Utah.

Off the first floor kitchen leading to the back yard, an attached, small, screened-porch with a concrete floor was used primarily for storage. Screen doors led from the kitchen to the porch and from the porch to the back yard. Large metal springs not only returned the doors forcefully to their frames but also made loud, distinctive slamming sounds every time we used them. One distinct memory of that back porch relates to childhood maladies.

Both Laura and I suffered from allergies. Pollen gave us problems but dust especially set us off and our fifty year-old Sears' home was exceedingly dusty. So dusty in fact that we both received weekly allergy injections from Doc Burrier; that is until Mom decided she was tired of expensive office visits. It occurred to her that she could save both time and money by administering the allergy shots herself, and so asked Doc Burrier for medical clearance to expand her thriving splinter removal practice.

Doc Burrier

Our family physician – Dr. G.W. Burrier – agreed; bringing Mom into the examining room to bequeath standard AMA hypodermic knowledge. Doc Burrier must have been about forty years old at the time. Standing approximately five feet, 9-inches tall and balding, he was fleshy and more closely resembled a baker than small town doctor. Bespectacled, mustachioed and a sideline-fixture during Dad's football games, he conducted annual team physicals for Canal Winchester's athletically inclined, and treated injured players during football and basketball season. Doc Burrier moved and spoke deliberately, had a pleasing smile and gentle way about him.

That was the conventional wisdom before his 'shot lesson,' anyway. Despite familiarity with Doc Burrier, the one-on-one injection tutorial to enhance Mom's surgical skills was, for me at least, downright brutal. When we were little Laura and I didn't cry or carry on at the doctor's office. Mom did a good job prepping us for the experience.

She talked about what a fuss some kids made over the smallest procedures, how ridiculous it was to act that way, and equally ridiculous that parents allowed it. She spoke of the pride she felt when we listened quietly to the physician and did what was asked of us, and of how much faster and easier exams went when we did.

So when Doc Burrier asked me to climb on the examination table and roll up my sleeve, I did as instructed. That week's shot - my shot - lay on a tray next to the table, and I eyed it closely. Before administering it, however, Doctor Burrier spoke earnestly to Mom about needles, medication, dosages and what steps to take in case of a bad reaction. At last he got round to the shot, which was usually one quick sting endured stoically week after week. On this day, unbeknownst to his naïve and soon to be incredulous patient, Doc Burrier sought to demonstrate to Mother Nightingale what *not* to do when administering injections.

Raising the medicinal spear - and in a dry, dispassionate, clinical voice - he held forth: *"You can't be timid Mrs. Locke. You don't want to stab him, but you need to apply enough force to insure the injection takes."* At this point Doc Burrier broke the epidermis, but just barely. *"See that, that's not going to get it done,"* he instructed Mom as she looked on. Thinking to myself; *"What the hell? Did he really just do that?"* Doc withdrew the hypodermic and prepared to demonstrate the proper technique. I felt a sense of relief as he began to carry out his usual spiking of my upper arm, but alas it did not end there.

Doc Burrier gave me another shot but again refrained from injecting the medication. The needle penetrated into my triceps. He stopped for the second time in his tutorial, looked at Mom, and then continued his lesson: *"See that Patty? Be very careful you don't break the needle off in the arm; don't ever do this."* '**This**' being moving the syringe to the left and then to the right – back and forth, up and down. *"This is about as far as you dare go,"* he demonstrated. By now, focusing entirely on pain management, I concentrated solely on biting my lower lip, trying not to cry. Finally, satisfied Mom understood, he at last forced the plunger down and withdrew the lance from my throbbing arm.

It meant a lot to boys my age to be perceived as tough - chips off the old block. The worst epithet in my circle of friends in Canal Winchester was 'Sissy.' Painfully aware of this I jumped off the table smiling at Mom. Before leaving Doc Burrier said, *"Thank you Steve;"* Mom added, *"Yes, thank you son."* Outwardly, I basked quietly in the moment, presenting an unfazed mask of serenity and manliness to those about me. Inwardly it was different: *"AHHHHH! AHHHHH! Are you out of your fucking minds?! Ouch! Ouch! Ouch! Dear God you cruel, heartless bastards! AHHHHH!"*

The connection to the back porch was our allergies. Despite Mom's administering weekly shots, Laura and I gagged and hacked our way through hay fever season and especially during winters after the house was shut up. Laura suffered her worst allergic episode during Christmas-break, 1974/1975. Mom and Dad had brought home a real pine tree for Christmas and we dutifully strung lights, hung bulbs, sipped eggnog, listened to Christmas Carols and topped the tree with a star. And all the while Laura nearly choked to death.

The tree had set her off, and though Mom hoped her immune system would adjust, it never did. After three days of incessant coughing Laura was informed we had to get rid of the tree. She began to cry. When Laura cried tears flowed in cascading torrents, her body shook uncontrollably and her anguish was deep and abiding. The scene was too much to bear, and Mom resolved the Lockes would have their cake and eat it too. First, after the family had gone to bed, she removed everything from the tree - no easy task considering how over the top our annual tree trimming. Bulbs, ornaments, lights, tinsel, garland, candy canes, and the plastic star that sat atop the now forlorn tree were dislodged, disconnected and unfastened.

Next, she dragged the gargantuan evergreen through the living room, dining room and kitchen - leaving pine needles and stray tinsel as she went. Somehow she managed to wrestle the tree through the kitchen door leading to the back porch, setting it up in the icy December air by the dim glow of a naked light bulb. Lastly, she brought up the artificial tree from the basement, removed its varied pieces from the box and assembled, strung lights and decorated it before we woke the next morning.

And so my strongest memory of the screened, cement back porch is the year it displayed the bronchial busting Christmas tree. We made decorations at the kitchen table, hung ornaments while wearing coats and hats, strung popcorn and ran to the door every morning to admire the tree. Standing before the forlorn fir Laura would say, *"Good morning Christmas Tree, we didn't forget you."*

Unlike residential neighborhoods today, there wasn't rows and rows of tract housing behind our home. There wasn't much of anything. Our backyard stopped where it met a narrow alley. Beyond the alley cornfields stretched into the distance, framed on either side by a tree line and an old rust covered wire fence. East of the cornfields leas of grassland allowed me and Greg Kinard to shoot our bows and arrows without fear of hitting anything. North of the cornfields - a considerable distance from our backyard - ran the tracks of the Hocking Valley Railroad where we picked blackberries in August.

The back yard was small. Double clotheslines connected two cross-shaped iron posts about thirty feet apart where Mom dried clothes and bed linens with wooden clothes pins. Ten square slabs of concrete lay parallel to the clothesline and Mac Gayman's big brick house. Mom walked up and down the cement slabs on washday with her basket and pins, hanging clothes or taking them off the line. In the far corner next to the alley sat a large, 55-gallon drum used for leaf burning – and much else. Unfortunately, in 1973 the State of Ohio passed the 'Open Burning Law', which banned the practice. But up until its enactment my family, like everyone else on our street, burned leaves in the backyard every autumn.

Behind the houses of Waterloo Street beneath clear black skies, neighbors clustered about fires ridding themselves of piles and piles of autumn leaves. The smell had a romantic quality to it - sweet and intoxicating. Blue white smoke rose above the drums, quickly disappearing into the darkness, but the pleasing aroma lingered; intensifying or diminishing with the winds. There is something primitive and deeply satisfying about fire. Especially on cold October nights surrounded by family and friends, watching flames flitter and flick in the darkness, listening to leaves crackle and pop, smelling the sweet aroma of leaf-smoke. We lost something by banning autumn leaf burning.

Laura and I played in the backyard with neighborhood kids. 'Freeze tag,' 'Hide and seek,' 'Wiffle ball,' and 'Red rover' come to mind. Standing in two opposing lines of three or four kids each we'd chant, *"Red rover red rover, send Laura right over,"* and Laura - or whomever happened to get called - charged the enemy line of locked arms and hands trying to break their chain. 'Ring around the rosy' was another favorite though none knew it a relic of medieval plagues. *"Ring around the rosy, a pocketful of Posey. Ashes, ashes we all fall down!"*

By age twelve we no longer played much in our backyard. During winters we built snowmen but junior high started an hour earlier than elementary school, and organized sports, friends and homework assignments pretty much steered us away from our childhood stomping ground. Besides taking out the trash every week and mowing the lawn, our little backyard became a place less traveled.

And so our house in 1975 was a two story, three bedroom Sears home with a slate roof. There was no garage - Dad parked on the street. We had one rotary telephone. The stairway's banister provided railing for hanging Christmas cards every year. The living room, dining room, kitchen and back porch were exceedingly small by today's standards.

Though the fireplace did not work, the first floor register burned with the heat of a thousand suns. There was a half basement where I met my Waterloo, a full bathroom on the second floor sans showers, half a bathroom on the first floor and a small backyard beyond which lay cornfields and the Hocking Valley Railroad.

Each room holds many stories and memories. Today the Sears house at 106 E. Waterloo Street is still standing, closing in on its centennial anniversary. Our landlords - Mac and Thelma Gayman - died long ago and the property went to outsiders after their son, Bob, committed suicide in 1977. In 1975, two years before we left or even knew we'd leave, it was the center of the known universe.

Chapter III:

OUR STREET

Waterloo Street runs east/west across Canal Winchester, bisected north/ south by High Street through the center of town. Growing up, Waterloo Street was the absolute hub of our solar system, as it was for all the kids on the block. We were vaguely aware that other streets, towns and even states existed elsewhere, but were in no way familiar or remotely interested in them.

It was a busy place. Indeed, one of the biggest differences between the early 1970s and the second decade of the 21st century is the dearth of kids playing outside. Kids were everywhere in our neighborhood: hanging out of trees, riding bikes, cutting through yards, playing tag, roaring up and down sidewalks on Big Wheels, competing in pickup basketball and baseball games and - every so often - fighting one another.

Shockingly, those fights were real, complete with swinging fists, kicking feet, smatterings of blood and plenty of cursing. CW's elementary playground was a crucible where rites of passage involved knockdown, drag out brawls, and the same held true on Waterloo Street. For Mary Matyac, moving to Canal Winchester in 1972 was a shock, *"I had never seen a real fist fight before we moved there,"* she recalled. *"At Canal even the girls were known to give each other black eyes. And pickup basketball games sometimes ended with blood on the court. It was a tough place."* It seemed no matter what we did, it usually took place outside. Neal Seymour, about to begin his junior year in high school in the summer of 1975, and personifying the typical Winchester adolescent, recalled how he and his friends spent their time.

Mary Matyac

"*We were always playing some kind of ball,*" Neal explained. "*Running in the fields; we were always playing in the fields. Sometimes the cops came by because we were playing basketball until 10:00, even 11:00 O Clock at night. We spent a lot of time at the pool; and of course Little League baseball was big. It was a big thing playing under the lights on the diamond by the concession stand. Nobody wanted to go home when the weather was good, there was too much to do.*"

Dale Burrier, Doc Burrier's son, concurred; "*On Trine Street, it was a death sentence if we had to stay inside. My friends, Randy Lewis, Mark Raines and Carl Swartz used to go down to the train station and bug the station master about stuff and when he wasn't looking put pennies on the tracks to be flattened by the C&O. We'd walk the old canal bed all the way to Baltimore/Carroll . . . halfway to Groveport and ride our bikes to Millersport. From the time school let out until our parents made us come in for the night we were getting into something we shouldn't or playing ball.*"

Hear! Hear! After arriving home from school early afternoons, my primary goal in life was to get outside as quickly as possible. Changing clothes with breakneck speed every kid on Waterloo Street raced outside promising to return by 'supper time.' And not only did kids converge immediately on Waterloo Street after school, *lots* of kids converged on Waterloo Street immediately after school.

Multitudes of them, from large families. A veritable host unto themselves - pitted daily against legions of moms conspiring and communicating behind their backs. For example: the Winlan family living directly across the street had four kids - Jerry, Terry, Diane, and Jimmy-John. The Shirks, residing at the corner of Waterloo and Trine, had four kids, Rick, Terry & Kerry, (twins), and Michelle.

The Ensley family two doors down had five children - Misty, Jay, Julie, Brody and Hugh. The Zerby's also had five kids - Mike, Michelle, Pat, Kerry, and Ty junior. The Jordan's, who moved to Canal Winchester in 1972, had seven kids - Scott, Ty Jeff, Linda, Julie, Susie, and John. And the Cook family, one block over on Columbus Street, had nine children.

Thank God for the fabled Cook fecundity because Tom Cook – the youngest of the brood – played a major role in my childhood development, teaching me new and ever more odious cuss words. No fool, Tom burned the candle from both ends, admonishing underlings not to use toxic verbiage in front of churches. *"You'll go to Hell if you swear in front of church,"* Tom instructed, adding; *"It's true! Don't cuss in front of a church or you'll end up going straight to Hell!"* At that those in our group knowingly nodded in grave agreement.

Rick Shirk, two years my senior, became my best friend on Waterloo Street. The oldest of three brothers, Rick was a tough kid - not a bully - but hardnosed. His Dad, Richard, was a carpenter, drove a truck, owned lots of tools, and was forever working on cars, mini-bikes, trucks or some other mechanical device. Rick's mom – Margaret – stayed home, ran the house and raised her kids.

Rick, tall and lean, had sandy brown hair and brown eyes. He loved baseball, camping, girls, fishing and corny jokes – not necessarily in that order. His interests coincided with mine on a descending scale in that my baseball skills were sadly lacking. Rick on the other hand was quite good. He had a great arm, hand/eye coordination, excellent feet and was a solid hitter. When paired with his young friend in sandlot baseball, however, his heart sank.

My best friend, Rick Shirk, between twins Terry and Kerry and sister Michelle

Baseball was incredibly popular in the 1970s, and the Cincinnati Reds were the best team in the Majors at mid-decade. When kids on Waterloo Street got together to play a few innings most aspired to be Jose Concepcion, Joe Morgan, Johnny Bench, Pete Rose, Ken Griffey or one of the other players that made up the *'Big Red Machine.'* And as with so many other kids across town, Little League Baseball occupied a prominent place in our summer activities.

Little Locke, the world's all-time worst LL baseball player.

Canal Winchester had three baseball diamonds located behind the high school. On game nights a round robin of little league ball clubs occupied each one of them. Stands were full, parents lined the perimeters of the ball fields in folding chairs - equipped with coolers and bug spray - and the concession stand behind Diamond One busily served hot dogs, Coca-Cola, popcorn, peanuts, and candy bars to fans and ball players alike.

Only Diamond One, closest to the school parking lot, had night lights, which were turned on at 8:00 pm. As dusk settled and families from the other two diamonds worked their way toward their cars they'd often stop to watch the last game of the night, swelling the ranks of onlookers. The constant hum of *"Swing batter, swing batter, swing hum batter swing,"* filled the air, broken only when someone got a hit and the crowd erupted in one great roar.

It was quite a spectacle and at times unnerving for little leaguers - especially if athletically challenged. Rick loved it, dragging me to the diamonds so he could throw, hit, catch pop ups, field grounders and run the bases. Though my love of the Reds was unshakable - our family hailed from the Cincinnati area - actually playing baseball was another proposition entirely. Despite an inability – some might say disability - to hit, catch and slide, and my general disdain for Little League Baseball generally, the value CW placed on America's past time determined how those in my age group spent their summers.

Baseball was important. Rick, my best friend, loved baseball; most other kids on Waterloo Street shared his passion for baseball, and so I too played baseball. Every year, after only a few practices, little league coaches resolved to place me in deep, deep, deep roving right field where the least harm could come. And there, far from the immediate action on the ball diamond, night after night, dressed in polyester pants, long colored sox, black cleats and ball cap, listening absentmindedly to teammates chanting *"Swing hum batter, swing hum batter, swing hum batter swing!"* my mind wandered further afield – even more so than usual.

At twilight, alone in my little world, I wondered what in the Hell I was doing at the end of an empty field with a buzzing, malleable, mini-swarm of mosquitoes hovering about my head. The athletically challenged coach's son desperately wishing he liked playing baseball; failing that, my imagination transported me to the CW swimming pool where Becky Seymour screamed helplessly to be rescued from ferocious undercurrents in the deep end.

It was usually about this time that a "pop-fly" came my way. I'd call out, *"I got it, I got it,"* run beneath the ball, and then watch helplessly as it hit the ground beside me, bounced off my glove or sailed over my bewildered head. That failure was immediately followed by collective groans from the crowd and incessant screaming from teammates. *"Throw it Locke! Throw it! The Play's at second! Throw it!"* Clearly, baseball was not the fulcrum around which friendship with Rick Shirk revolved. Rather, it grew from a shared love of fishing.

From my earliest memories I can still recall Dad taking our family fishing – on weekends, spring breaks and summer vacations. He had grown up hunting, trapping and fishing, and though Mom dissuaded him from shooting or trapping animals, Dad continued fishing streams, creeks, ponds, lakes, even the Atlantic and Pacific Oceans. In fact, some of my first sentient recollections are of falling into the wash on family fishing expeditions.

During the summer of 1975, Rick and I carried on the angling tradition, making our way to Little Walnut Creek nearly every day. A brackish, shallow, meandering stream about a mile and a half south of Waterloo Street, we referred to the Little Walnut as 'the crick,' and tramped back and forth to its banks with our fishing poles, tackle boxes, and stringers all summer, sometimes twice a day.

Typical outings began at Rick's house. Leaving Waterloo Street we walked south on Trine Street, past the Canal Kitchen Pizzeria and an ancient concrete dike left over from the Ohio/Erie Canal. The dike looked out of place and lonely, the last of its kind standing in town. Crossing Columbus Street we cut between houses before picking up a gravel lane. The gravel thinned the closer we got to the creek; grass growing down the center of the lane as it wound through a corn field.

About 100 yards from the creek's tree line sat an abandoned car. Forlorn and decrepit with unfamiliar, rusted levers, shattered glass windshields, chunks of foam protruding from what remained of the upholstery, half its frame sunk into the earth, and partially obscured by tall grass. It looked very much like the car in which Bonnie and Clyde met their doom, having been thoroughly peppered over the years with bullet holes. Which was hardly surprising given the number of kids in town that owned firearms – rifles, pistols, shotguns and in some cases all three – while many of the men had amassed virtual arsenals in their homes.

While spending the night at Tom Cooks' house, for example, he took me into his Dad's 'gun room' to show off the Cook family weaponry: Winchester rifles, Colt revolvers, smooth bore muskets, six-shooters, a gun safe, firearms behind glass, mounted on the walls and leaning in the corners, etc. In our own home Dad kept a 22-caliber pistol and three rifles, and most of the kids Rick and I knew owned guns. Consequently it was not uncommon to approach the Little Walnut amidst the sounds of small arms fire.

Younger kids owned BB guns - I got mine at age ten - and Bolenbaugh's Hardware Store did a brisk business selling those little yellow tubes packed with BBs. Every so often the *Times* ran a story detailing the sporadic BB maimings along Little Walnut Creek or in the fields behind the high school - urging gun safety. Those warnings were far too little and much too late for the old car - we shot the Hell out of it on more than one occasion.

Having reached *'the crick'* we negotiated its steep banks through high grass, ticks, jiggers, sticker bushes and the occasional broken root to the water's edge. Sand bars and little pebble covered islands became objectives; leaving our tackle on the bank we waded into the Little Walnut and began casting, fishing without live bait. Once in awhile we dug up worms but it was less hassle to use lures, tying new ones on the end of our lines as need arose.

Rick and I constantly compared the contents of our tackle boxes. If Rick acquired a fluorescent glow-in-the-dark bobber more readily visible at dusk, I began a quest to acquire a fluorescent glow-in-the-dark bobber more readily visible at dusk. And if Dad gave me a rubber toad lure with a lone fish hook whose legs mimicked the actions of an amphibian moving across the surface of the water; Rick's life became incomplete until he too obtained a rubber toad lure with a lone fish hook whose legs mimicked the actions of an amphibian moving across the surface of the water.

Our plan that summer was to impress the folks by putting on a grand 'fish fry.' We spoke earnestly of inviting neighbors, family and friends while cleaning our catfish, rock bass and blue gill. In the meantime we carefully packed the fillets in zip-lock freezer bags, eventually accumulating enough frozen fish to open a Mrs. Paul's Fish Franchise. Alas, the 'grand fish fry' attended by admiring family, neighbors and friends never took place, though Rick and I ate enough of our catch to put us off fish for years to come.

Two weeks before school started a new family took up residence on Waterloo Street. Their arrival came to my attention via the sounds of applause from Rick's front porch. Five or six neighborhood boys were staring intently at the new neighbors, clapping thunderously every few seconds. Joining the group, deep understanding washed over me. While moving men lugged furniture into the house a fifteen year-old girl performed back flips, handstands, cartwheels and a variety of erotic, gymnastic exercises on the front lawn.

It wasn't that we hadn't seen female gymnasts before, nor was there a dearth of young girls on Waterloo Street. Rather it was the shape of this wondrous new arrival that captivated her hormonally imbalanced audience. From our vantage point on Rick's porch there was no doubt that this gymnast, this new girl, this divine gift from the outer world, was preternaturally talented. No small, prepubescent training bra for her – whoever she was. No, this voluptuous maiden had real, fabulous, American breasts. They were large, heaving, beautiful, full, ample, shapely, magnificent breasts. And with each handstand, back flip and cartwheel the amorous affection in our appreciative hearts grew exponentially. To Hell with lures and fish fries, Aphrodite had arrived - on our street – she to whom the good Lord in his infinite wisdom had been so obviously generous, now lived and breathed amongst us. God was truly great.

The Zerby Clan - whose father Ty was an officer in the US Air Force - followed their Dad to CW when he was assigned to Rickenbacker AFB. (God Bless the USAF!) Yet another military family, the Zerby's had lived all over the country, relocating whenever Mr. Zerby was transferred, consequently they had never stayed at any one location more than two or three years. There were seven Zerby's in all. Captain Zerby, his wife Connie, the three boys, Mike, Pat and Ty Junior, Michelle, (the most talented gymnast God ever did sit down on his big blue orb), and Carrie. Tight knit and Catholic the Zerby kids were a rough bunch; no doubt a prerequisite moving as much as they did. Pat Zerby, the second son, was exactly my age. We became close friends as junior high school got underway.

The older boys on Waterloo Street – three to four years older - were larger than life in our eyes. Their leader, Carl Swartz, was an early childhood hero of mine. Carl sported beach blond hair and brown eyes, was solidly built and routinely flashed an ornery, mischievous grin. Ironically, his mother – Lois – once rang our doorbell to inform Mom that she had, on more than one occasion, heard me 'swearing.' Specifically, using the word 'shit,' a bit too liberally. Having overheard most of the hushed and earnest conversation, I was terrified the hammer would fall. But relief unexpectedly followed when I heard Dad laughing and Mom asked only that an awareness of surroundings influence my ever expanding vocabulary. Knowing much of my repertoire had been gleaned from Dad, she explained there were times and places for inappropriate language and the Swartz's home was not one of them.

The episode's irony stemmed from the fact that Carl's hero like status derived, in part, from his well developed fluency in profanity. It was Lois's youngest son who imparted the timeless, sentimental ode that

- had Mrs. Swartz known of it - would have most likely brought Carl's childhood to a premature conclusion. Standing astride our bicycles on Columbus Street, Carl held forth: *"Mother fucking, titty-sucking, two-ball bitch, Mother in the kitchen making red-hot shit; father in hell; brother in jail; and sister on the corner saying pussy for sale."* It was, at age nine, quite simply the most beautiful poetry ever encountered, and the next few days were spent memorizing and pleading with Carl to repeat it.

In 1975, painted traffic lines on east Waterloo Street were nonexistent, it was rather just black and gray roadbed, the tar surface bubbling on hot summer days. In spring, when the rains came, Waterloo and Trine Streets nearly always flooded. One year water rose so high that small boats navigated both streets as well as the field behind the Shirk's house. After hard rains gutters on our block welled up and water rushed along the sides of the street on its way to the sewage drains. Kids walked barefoot against the flow, some playing in its rivulets with plastic boats, others' making mud pies.

Rick's house, at the corner of Trine and Waterloo Streets marked the

Canal Kitchen Pizzeria

end of our block. Waterloo's homes gradually gave way to businesses as our street neared its intersection with High Street in the center of town. The only business on Trine Street was the Canal Kitchen Pizzeria. Mr. Cook, Tom's Dad, ran it, which gave Tom Cook enormous clout in our circle of friends. Watching Tom, or one of his brothers, casually walking home with two or more pizzas, piping hot in clean white boxes, filled us with the utmost reverence and awe.

Housed in a squat, brown building the Canal Kitchen Pizzeria did booming business - especially on Friday and Saturday nights. Inside bakers wearing white T-shirts worked behind a four foot counter beside the Vulcan pizza ovens. The pizzeria was small; bordered by the Cellar Lumber Company on one side, and an empty gravel parking lot on the other. Heat constantly radiated from the block building as if from hot coals. Mr. Cook greeted patrons, checked pizzas and ran the cash register. Four plastic chairs situated around two tables, topped with napkin dispensers and red tin ashtrays made up the 'dining room.' The only other amenities were the soda cooler and cigarette machine with its clear plastic pull knobs.

Next-door, half the Cellar Lumber Company's property consisted of a fenced yard where long white sheds housed great piles of wood. Men in jeans and ball caps drove pickup trucks in and out of Cellar Lumber from the moment it opened until closing time. They were always in a hurry, entering the store in a rush and then leaving minutes later with dead bolts, post-hole-cutters, hinges, chain saws, hack saws, routers, nails, and lumber.

Like Canal Kitchen, Cellar Lumber seemed alive. The constant buzz of table saws and the pungent smell of burnt wood permeated the place. Flatbed lories pulled in and out of its chain link gates, men walked back and forth from the lumber yard to the front office all day, and the air about the place contained a fine sawdust mist that settled on the skin, hair and clothing of anyone who moved within its confines.

Cellar Lumber also marked the end of 'Our Street.' After that, moving west on Waterloo, past the Shirk's, the Zerby's, the Canal Kitchen, and the lumberyard, it was no longer our block. Kids were different and unfamiliar up the street, houses turned to businesses and downtown Canal Winchester was a different place entirely than the familiar haunts of East Waterloo.

Although memories of Waterloo Street are pleasant and nostalgic - close friendships, pretty girls, the smell of burning leaves, the sound of train whistles on the Hocking Railroad, kids on bicycles and delicious Canal Kitchen pizzas - Waterloo Street was not an idyll. It could be a tough place. Fistfights, wrestling matches, screaming, crying, wrecked bicycles, spankings, being sent to one's bedroom and the bruised egos that result from surviving childhood were as much a part of Waterloo Street as fishing in the Little Walnut.

At Canal Kitchen one of Dad's high school football players - who didn't get the playing time he felt he deserved, and whose parents had written Dad a detailed letter listing his many personal and professional shortcomings - stood outside the pizzeria nightly denigrating my father. Every time I passed by or stopped in to pick up a pizza he'd yell, "*Hey Locke! Tell your old man he sucks!*" All summer the corner of Waterloo and Trine echoed with such embittered sentiments: "*Hey Locke! Tell your old man he sucks!"* Sometimes, for added flair, he'd add *"Fucking sucks!"* Other than that, he stayed on message.

On another occasion, around the same time, either a frustrated football player or an angry student went far beyond verbally abusing the coach's son. Awake in bed, watching shadows cast from our Mulberry Tree and trying to fall asleep, a sudden and violent *Bang!* brought me sitting upright in bed. Moments passed, and nothing else happened. Assuming a car or truck had backfired, I tried to go back to sleep. The following morning three Canal Winchester Police officers were standing in our living room; one prying a bullet slug from the front door.

For the most part, however, Waterloo Street was a wonderful place to grow up. There were lots of kids to play with and moms to supervise. We rode bikes, went fishing, played tag, hide-and-seek, *Ring-around-the-Rosie* and pickup hoops - spending as much time as possible outside. There were plenty of empty fields to explore, barns and sheds to rummage through, and the Little Walnut Creek to wade. Swing sets stood in nearly every other yard and there were endless opportunities to get in trouble – which was Rick's fault.

CHAPTER IV:

WINCHESTER, OHIO

"The Past is a foreign country; they do things differently there."

(Leslie Poles Hartley)

My hometown, obviously, did not spring forth from *Mother Earth* in 1975 complete with roads, sewers, schools, churches and businesses. The summer of my twelfth birthday the town was nearly 150 years old. Originally Winchester, Ohio it owed its birth to 'progress' and the innate American desire for wealth. In 1827, the area that now makes up Canal Winchester was heavily forested and sparsely populated. Just a few hardscrabble farms dotted the landscape, one of which belonged to a farmer named Reuben Dove.

Mr. Dove, however, was not a happy camper as his property stood in the way of '*internal improvements*' and development. The Ohio-Erie Canal was slated to traverse Reuben's wheat fields, eventually cutting a swath through his meadows and destroying his crops. This Mr. Dove would not abide. As a free citizen in a free country, he determined to fight 'city hall.' Problem was, there was neither a city nor a hall, just dense woods, Little Walnut Creek and a few isolated farms.

Frustrated by his inability to stop the planned canal from bisecting his farm, Mr. Dove made up his mind to sue the State of Ohio. At this point some of his workmen recommended an alternative. Rather than sue the state, Mr. Dove and his fellow farmers ought to plat a new town to take advantage of the coming canal traffic. According to **_The History of Madison Township_**, a workman opined, "*We believe there will be more money in laying out a town than in trying to collect damages from the state.*" And on that note a town to make 'more money' was born. Reuben and his fellow farmers christened their new village 'Winchester,' as Mr. Dove's father hailed from Winchester, Virginia.

Roads being what they were in the area - narrow, potholed ribbons of mud - the Ohio-Erie Canal, begun in 1825 at Licking Summit in Newark, Ohio, was a godsend to local farmers. Allowing faster - up to four-miles per hour - shipment of agricultural goods to market than hauling produce overland, the canal opened markets previously unreachable. It is difficult to overestimate the importance of the canals. The new transportation system eventually reduced overall distribution costs in the Midwest by 87%.

Canal Boat winding its way through Winchester, Ohio

In 1830, the year before the canal reached the town it birthed, prices for local farm products were as follows: Wheat ran 37 ½ *c* a bushel. A cow with calf cost $9.00. Eggs were 3 *c* a dozen. Flax was 1*c* a pound. Beef, 2 ½ *c* a pound, and butter set patrons back 6 ¼ *c* a pound. When the canal finally passed through Reuben Dove's old wheat field in 1831, it immediately connected Winchester to Newark, Columbus, and Circleville. Prospects for the upstart little village looked bright.

By the mid 1830s Winchester, Ohio boasted one tavern, one grocery store, a log and frame grain warehouse, one tannery, one hotel, a stable and three mills – sawmill, woolen mill and flourmill. In Ohio's heartland unfettered, free market capitalism thrived. Like modern billboards lining today's highways, Winchester's newly erected stores were strategically placed to face the towpath side of the canal, advertising their wares on large signs, listing prices and goods passing boatmen could not miss.

The canal itself bisected Winchester, running slightly north/west to south/east through the center of town. Bridges were constructed across High and Washington Streets tall enough to accommodate passing canal boats below and wide enough for townsfolk and wagons above. Besides transporting surplus crops the canal served area residents in a variety of innovative ways: required by law to be four feet deep along its entire course it became an ideal swimming hole during summers and an excellent, solid, ice skating surface most winters. When fires struck (occasionally at 'lamp-lighting-time') the canal provided a reliable source of water in the very heart of town. Farmers were also known to water herds when the canal's water level was high enough.

Despite being a catalyst in founding the town, and having beneficial uses to citizens, its heyday was brief. The first canal boat passed through town in 1831. By 1869, Winchester's first train depot was completed, and the railroads made Ohio's network of canals obsolete by the second half of the 19th century. The last barge passed through town in 1901, though the canal hadn't been a vital means of transportation for some time.

When in 1900 the State authorized spending to maintain the canal's upkeep the Winchester *Times* took exception; editorializing that Ohio was *"pouring money down the same old rat hole."* Clearly, the canal's importance had faded into history well before the twentieth century got underway.

The *Time's* description of the canal as a *"rat hole,"* was certainly apt. Even before the canal was drained in 1911, residents used it as a dump. As World War I began in Europe during the summer of 1914 the last stretch of canal running through town was finally filled, an outdated relic of the past. It is interesting to note how readily new technologies were embraced, only to be discarded a generation later when further advances in engineering made them untenable.

The canal of 1831 gave way to the railroads, which lost some of its passenger traffic to the interurban line, which in turn eventually lost business to the automobile. As the horse and buggy gave way to automobiles the streets upon which they ran were eventually paved. Prior to that, Canal's thoroughfares had to be wetted down twice a day to keep the dust under control. In 1873 wood planking, compacted mud and loose gravel gave way to Winchester's first cement sidewalks. Mounted messengers gave way to the telegraph in 1849, and the telegraph to the first phone line in 1882. Wood burning stoves and family hearths gave way to coal stoves, and eventually to gas heat, once Canal's first gas lines were installed in 1900.

Watering the streets to keep the dust down.

In 1905 - just four years after the last barge meandered through town - the Scioto Valley Transportation Company constructed a depot at 20 S. High Street for its interurban rail line. Connecting Columbus to surrounding communities, the CW Interurban ran from the state capital to Obetz, Ohio, where it split in twain. One line ran south to Chillicothe, while the second stopped at Canal Winchester before moving on to Lancaster. The depot, built of slate-colored brick with a crimson roof, saw a lot of traffic. Scioto Valley rail cars were electrified, traveled up to sixty mph, and carried both freight and people. The line operated from 1904 until 1930.

Last run of CW's interurban. Sept 20 1930

Change was constant - the degree and breadth of which may be surmised by looking at some of Canal Winchester's businesses lost to history: Lamp-lighting stores, dress makers, basket makers, teamsters, blacksmiths, gunsmiths, weaving looms, cooper stores, harness shops, saw mills, woolen mills, grist mills, tanneries and the telegraph office, to name just a few. And before the advent of radio, television and mass communication, Canal Winchester boasted numerous social organizations that have also vanished in time.

The CW Literary Society, for example, formed in 1840 and comprised of *"any respectable male person,"* challenged members by posing - and then answering – some of society's thorniest questions. Examples, as recorded by society member George Bareis in 1847, are listed below. *"Has the African more reason to complain than the Indian?" "Does the newspaper press produce a salutary influence?" "Is climate the cause of the different varieties in the human species?" "Ought females to be equally educated with males? "Resolved, that all laws making distinction on account of color should be repealed." "Resolved, that foreign immigration should be prohibited."*

From its birth in 1828, to the last decade of the twentieth century, Canal Winchester remained small. In 1850 its population reached three-hundred and fifty. Fifty years later, in 1900, the town boasted 667 citizens. Seventy-five years after that – when Laura and I walked its streets - we were two of just twenty-four hundred residents, most belonging to large families (although 'large' is certainly relative in historical terms).

As prodigious as the Zerby's, Ensley's and Jenkins were in begetting five children per family in the 1960s, Floyd and Beverly Jordan bringing forth seven little Jordan's in the 1960s and early 1970s, and as fruitful as Mr. and Mrs. Cook were in bequeathing to posterity nine offspring in the 1950s and 1960s, their efforts pale in comparison to the stupendous fertility of Winchester's 19th century clans.

According to George Bareis, author of the **_History of Madison Township_**, the Boyer family had, by 1832, seventeen children. One might conclude John Boyer - besides deriving pleasure from making baskets and barrels - had an overdeveloped fondness for bringing little Boyers into the world. But according to Mr. Bareis, that was not necessarily the case as he assured readers in 1902 that seventeen children was *"not an unusual number for those days."*

Canal Winchester has been referred to as both *'Winchester'* and *'Canal Winchester.'* And that is because the town's name formally changed in 1841, thirteen years after its founding, when Winchester obtained a post office. *'Winchester'* is therefore correct for the years 1828 to 1841 and *'Canal Winchester'* from 1841 onward. As Ohio boasted six *'Winchesters'* when the post office arrived, residents wanted to distinguish their community from the other five. At various town meetings consensus could not be reached regarding a new name. Both *'Pekin'* and *'Carlisle'* were considered - and rejected. The post office, fortunately, in a moment of clarity, solved the multiple Winchester conundrum by affixing *'Canal'* to *Winchester* - which both paid homage to the town's historical origins, and made it immediately dissimilar to the other Winchesters in the state.

Despite myriad changes to its physical makeup, the town that came to life during a rearguard action to save Reuben Dove's wheat field remained an agricultural enterprise. Phone lines, gas lines, concrete sidewalks and reliable banks improved life for area residents - but the business of Canal Winchester was farming. Glaciers had deposited nearly a foot of rich loam across two thirds of Ohio before receding after the last ice age, and the top soil about CW is as fertile as in any part of the state.

CW postcard

The fields surrounding the town, provided the right quotient of sun and rain, consistently produced bumper crops. In the late 1960s and early 1970s my friends and I occasionally rode our bikes out of town on grand adventures. Sometimes pedaling to Lockbourne to climb the locks of the old canal, accoutered with backpacks laden with sandwiches and pop. We might also take on an additional challenge if someone hinted we weren't man enough to bike seven or nine, or thirteen miles to some mysterious central Ohio destination.

Whatever the reason for departure, as our determined little gaggle cycled beyond the safety of town we were immediately engulfed in seas of corn, wheat and soybeans as far as the eye could see. Which wasn't, incidentally, very far. Most of us sat astride stubby, Huffy bicycles, which came standard with "banana seats", sissy bars, rubber handle grips, multicolor streamers, and circular chrome mirrors mounted on the left handlebar.

Though only four years old when we moved to Canal Winchester in 1967, memories of local farmers coming into town on Saturdays remain vivid. They struck me as tough, hardened men. Their faces were ruddy and weather beaten, like the old ball caps many wore sporting *John Deere, Red Man, Mack Truck, or STP* logos. The farmers never seemed to move inside the crosswalks but rather crisscrossed Waterloo and High Streets bent forward, like they were walking into a storm. They entered and exited the banks, Zeke's Barbershop, the Wigwam, Shade's Restaurant,

Conrad's Market and Bolenbaugh's Hardware Store, utterly oblivious to the urbanites in their midst.

In the late 1960s, before the enormous reduction in the amount

of physical labor required of most Americans, people still bore scars and deformities earned from living in a less settled age. It was not uncommon to see men in town with pronounced limps, eye patches and missing appendages. Canal Winchester's village handyman, Bob Miller, for example, known to locals and kids about town simply as "Bob", had but one digit on his right hand. Bob constantly ran everywhere, from one business to another, and from odd job to odd job. He swept sidewalks, shoveled driveways, replaced

Bob Miller, CW handyman and jack of all trades

streetlights, painted municipal property and picked up after horses during the annual Labor Day parade.

Slightly retarded and grizzled, he had difficulty speaking clearly and was forever in motion – as if the utmost emergency beckoned him forward. Kids in town often yelled, *"Hey Bob! Thumbs up!"* Or, *"Hey Bob, give me one!"* whenever he dashed past, flashing the thumbs up sign and adding a dose of derision to his already heavy burden.

The Waterloo/High Street Axis

The point where Waterloo and High Streets intersected marked the epicenter of Canal Winchester. On its four corners sat the Canal View Pharmacy, Conrad's Market, the CW Municipal Building and Alspach's Barbershop. Outside Conrad's Market men loitered about a petrified tree stump and a long wooden bench. It was here that old timers - some missing fingers from battling combines or chain saws - sat whittling and spitting tobacco in the afternoons.

The High - Waterloo Street Axis 1956

Their wrinkled, slightly yellowed fingers methodically removed books of papers from bib overalls to roll cigarettes, drew on pipes to smoke, or spat chewing tobacco onto the sidewalk and into Styrofoam cups. Chewing tobacco was a popular pastime in the 1970s, not only in Canal Winchester but nationally. Big league ball players, rodeo riders and TV pitch men 'dipped.' Yet even in an era of prevalent tobacco use it was obvious that "chewers" marched to the beat of a different drummer.

Their need to spit - indoors and out, constantly and in public - screened off the overly sensitive from their ranks. Let's just say that, as a group, they were somewhat oblivious to the niceties of the world around them. Equipped with spitting receptacles, bulging back pockets - a wallet in one and a folding pouch of chewing tobacco in the other - and the ever-present bulbous deformity protruding from the side of their face, they were not hard to miss.

Red Man, Mail Pouch and *Beech Nut* chewing tobaccos, among others, were sold at Super Duper, Conrad's and Canal View Pharmacy. Loose leaf and aromatic, chewers loaded up by unfolding a tobacco pouch, carefully grasping three fingers worth of leaves, tilting their heads slightly askew to meet the approaching collage, and pushing the succulent treat between *"their teeth and gums."* And though they chewed, gnawed and spit almost everywhere they found themselves, it was the tree stump and wooden bench in front of Conrad's Market where so many of their tribe congregated. It marked the geographic center of town.

In 1975 two traffic lights operated in Canal Winchester. A fact Nebraska move-in Craig Cox found noteworthy; "*The town was so small. Our school in Nebraska had almost 3,000 kids just in 10th through 12th grade. I couldn't believe we had moved to a town small enough to only have two traffic lights.*" One of those traffic lights hung above the intersection of Washington and Columbus Streets adjacent to the schoolhouse.

It was necessitated at that location in order to keep motorists from maiming school kids on their way to and from class. And it ensured the safety of the bus fleet constantly transporting students, athletes, cheerleaders and the band to various field trips, musical competitions and sporting events. Canal Winchester's second traffic light operated at the intersection of Waterloo and High Streets, where the old-timers sat outside Conrad's Market.

Lifelong resident Steve Crist agreed with his new classmate about Canal's diminutive size. "*CW,*" he said, "*was a really small town where everyone knew each other. We used to ride bikes, swim at the pool, and all the kids and parents went to school or sports functions year-round because that's pretty much all there was to do.*" Steve's cross-town teammate, Rick Ross, likewise remarked on Canal's insularity: "*Back then – in 1975,*" Mr. Ross remembered thirty years later, "*CW was like Mayberry, the ultimate place to grow up as a kid. You knew everybody. There weren't a lot of activities available, but we just entertained ourselves; riding our bikes, hanging out together at the pool and DQ, and having sleepovers just about every weekend.*"

Perspective, of course, is in the eye of the beholder; whereas longtime residents saw beauty, new arrivals thought the town somewhat odd. Craig's older brother, Gary Cox, remarked; "*It was really small. I thought it was weird that the only 'hangout' was the Dairy Queen, and that the only thing to do was 'go cruising in cars.' Even the phone man knew who I was before we arrived in town. When he hooked up our phone he told me all about myself – at least what he had heard about me and my family. It was definitely a small community.*"

Besides two traffic lights, Canal Winchester boasted two grocery stores. Conrad's Market, owned and operated by the Conrad family since 1938, and Super Duper, which opened in 1961. Super Duper operated at 152 W. Waterloo Street, nearly three quarters of a mile from the center of town, out of a blunt, square, masonry and sheet-metal building fronting a row of large glass window panes.

The larger of the two groceries, Super Duper provided shoppers a paved parking lot while Conrad's, though its prices were slightly higher, enjoyed the better location. And the stores were decidedly different. They looked different, smelled different, offered different products and outfitted employees in different uniforms, unlike the dreary uniformity of today's virtually indistinguishable mass national chains.

Super Duper

While today's communities – large and small - share a mind numbing sameness, businesses being virtual replicas of large grocery chains or franchised fast food restaurants constructed over and over in town after town; in 1975, neighboring communities like Carroll, Groveport and Pickerington, Ohio were unfamiliar territory to Canal Winchester residents. Each offered its own unique set of groceries, bars, jewelers, pharmacies, restaurants and gas stations - no two exactly alike. They were, in many ways, self contained little kingdoms unto themselves.

In Canal, Conrad's Market boasted two checkout lines, two cashiers,

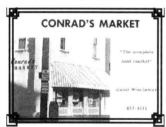

Conrad's Market

two mechanical cash registers, two conveyor belts and two baggers standing at the end of the lines. Every year CW's Kindergarten class took a field trip to Conrad's because it was such an important local business. After walking through town holding hands Kindergarteners entered the store and took the dime tour. Cash registers clanged and chimed without today's electronic touch pads, printing out paper receipts for customers from a roll inside the machine.

In the 1970s, besides receipts, grocery stores rewarded customers with rows of green stamps after every purchase over a certain dollar amount. "*S&H Green Stamps*", sometimes called "*Green Shield Stamps*", could be redeemed for items in the *Sperry and Hutchinson Catalogue*, which listed an array of products and indicated the number of stamps needed to purchase each item. In the 1960s and early 1970s the *S&H*

Rewards Catalogue was the largest circulation publication in the United States.

Mom saved those little green stamps religiously. After amassing rows and rows in her booklet, we'd look through the catalogue together, discussing whether we really needed something or should continue saving for swankier items. Nearly every shopper exiting Conrad's and Super Duper had coils of green stamps hanging out of their paper grocery bags. At its height S&H issued three times as many stamps than the US Postal Service.

Before scanners, grocery clerks were forever stamping cans and boxes with purple ink from stainless steel price punchers. Indeed, part of the shopping experience was listening to the familiar and intermittent '*cu-punch, cu-punch, and cu-punch*' as stock boys priced foodstuffs. This barely noticed background noise occasionally exploded into a cacophonous din when Conrad's or Super Duper received a new shipment of canned goods.

The stock boys kept the price punchers in holsters on their hips, wielding them with the speed and dexterity of western gunslingers. Faced with an entire case of canned corn store clerks erupted in sustained assaults which reverberated down the aisles: '*cu-punch, cu-punch, cu-punch, cu-punch, cu-punch, cu-punch, cu-punch, cu-punch, cu-punch, cu-punch, cu-punch and cu-punch!*'

Choices in grocery bags were limited to paper, and payment was by check or cash, not credit or debit card. None of this slowed down my mother who wrote checks faster than any human being before or since. The pen may indeed be mightier than the sword, but Mom wielded hers like a Samurai warrior. She would whip that baby out of her purse with lightning speed, fill out the check with a flourish and return it to its lair at least as fast as today's shoppers run cards through an ATM scanner.

Super Duper being more modern had electric, automatic doors – one of the few businesses in town to have such a convenience in 1975. Entering, shoppers were confronted by a large, metal framed bin where empty glass pop bottles were returned, entitling depositors to a discount voucher. Behind Super Duper's first of three checkout lines in the summer of 1975, stood Mike Matyac in his apron, working as a bag boy. Once, while waiting in line with Mom to pay for groceries, he asked me a question that caused my face to turn six shades of red. Mr. and Mrs. Matyac, for reasons known only to themselves, sired four children and christened each with monikers beginning with the letter 'M,' - Mary, Mark, Mike and Matt. Mary - the oldest Matyac - was beautiful. Although five or six years older than my group of friends, every twelve-year old boy in town deeply appreciated her long brown hair, olive skin, athletic body and dark brown eyes.

And every Matyac was like that in his or her own way. Each possessed a superb physique to carry them through life. Mary looked like a model and Matt, the youngest, looked like Arnold Schwarzenegger while still in sixth grade. Although not personally acquainted with the Matyac's - none were exactly my age or in my class - in a town the size of Canal Winchester I certainly knew who they were.

Which brings us back to Mike Matyac and his infamous question - he made an inquiry regarding one of Mom's feminine hygiene products. It was an uncomfortable topic for me at that age, what with being a squat, distracted, body-obsessed, overly self conscious twelve year old entering puberty. Standing next to Mom and Laura in the checkout line, absentmindedly daydreaming while Mike bagged groceries, young Mr. Matyac picked up an enormous box of tampons, leaned over, looked me in the eye and asked, *"Are these for you?"*

Some common grocery prices in the summer of 1975 were as follows: milk averaged $1.57 a gallon. A loaf of bread cost shoppers .36 cents, a Hershey Bar was .15cents, a six-pack of 12-ounce Pepsis ran .88cents, an 18-ounce box of Kellogg's Cornflakes set shoppers back .46 cents, and a 15-ounce package of Oreos was .89 cents the summer Mike Matyac tormented me at Super Duper. The median income in the United States was $14, 816.00.

Minimum wage that summer was set at $2.10c an hour. New cars off a dealer's lot averaged $4, 225.00 nationwide. Gasoline was .44 cents per gallon, and a McDonald's hamburger cost customers .30 cents. The price of gas, .44 cents a gallon, was a frequent topic of conversation amongst the men outside Conrad's Market, and nearly everyone else in town at the time. It was considered by most an outrageous, unreasonable sum, inflated as it was by the lingering effects of OPEC's 1973 oil embargo.

Besides two grocery stores, Cellar Lumber and several Pizzerias, Canal Winchester boasted the usual businesses found in most small towns: two restaurants, three banks, an auto parts store and garage, a hardware store, barber shop, jewelry store and Laundromat. And there were two gas stations - Sohio and Esso - both located on Waterloo Street, neither of which remains today.

The Sohio station, located downtown at 18 W. Waterloo Street across the road from the CW Bank, was a hub of constant activity. Today's service stations offer multiple pumps located beneath expansive overhanging canopies that shield customers from the elements; patrons refuel their own vehicles, pay with plastic and can purchase damn near anything inside the attached minimarts.

Not so in 1975. Perhaps the biggest difference is the absence of the constant *"DING," "DING,"* echoing off the pavement every time vehicles crossed the long rubber signal hose. Those *"DING," "DINGS,"* were loud, sonorous and unrelenting - alerting station attendants that customers had arrived. It never stopped during business hours and rang after hours as well. Walking, riding our bikes or zipping past Parker's Sohio with the windows down in the car the chiming 'pings' were audible forty yards away.

The Sohio opened downtown in 1954 and was later purchased by Hollis Parker in 1960. By the summer of 1975 his grandson, Dave, ran the station. Dave Parker - in his mid-twenties in 1975 - was handsome, athletic looking and always flashing broad smiles.

With dark brown hair and a perpetual tan he looked like a movie star. Customers didn't exit their vehicles after pulling into "self-service." Rather, the signal hose rang; an attendant emerged from the garage, approached the car and said something like, *"what'll it be?"* The patron responding, *"Filler up, will you Dave? And can you check the oil."*

Four pumps meant that only four vehicles could refuel at once. There wasn't an overhanging canopy above the pumps shielding sun and rain - which goes a long way in explaining Dave's perpetual tan. There also wasn't much of a store; just a two door garage for auto repairs and a small office with a counter and cash register. In front of the counter sat a metal rack filled with road maps of Ohio, a pop machine, cigarette machine and gumball machine. Parker's Sohio was Spartan and utilitarian, and always busy.

Dime Day at Winchester Auto Parts

Winchester Auto Parts, located next to *Parker's Sohio* and separated only by a porous hedge, operated out of a large, rectangular brick building that took up the rest of the block. Multiple bays with massive automatic doors faced Waterloo Street, each equipped with car lifts, mechanics, pneumatic hoses, tool chests, various auto parts and an assortment of tires. The central office also faced the street and sported a huge storefront window.

It was a noisy enterprise. The sounds of drills, compressed air, hammers, revving engines and salty talk echoed from its confines; especially during summers when the big bay doors remained open all day. The men working there were a rough lot, and nearly always covered in oil and grease. Today numerous television programs are dedicated to rebuilding old cars and NASCAR is hugely popular - yet viewing interest seems to have an inverse relationship with hands on experience.

Don Hartman Inc. Infamous site of the stolen soda saga.

In the mid 1970s a lot of Canal Winchester's residents still worked on their cars, raced cars and talked – incessantly - about cars. Car talk - that tortuous, indecipherable foreign language spoken between the mechanically inclined - served as a second language across town: at the NAPA Auto Parts Store, Cellar Lumber, Bolenbaugh Hardware, both gas stations, the Canal View Bowling Alley, the parking lot of the Canal Kitchen Pizzeria and most certainly along Waterloo Street in front of Winchester Auto Parts.

Unfortunately, Dad's mechanical deficiencies and disinterest were bequeathed to his son. To compensate, mimicking his head nodding technique seemed to work best when unavoidably caught in 'car-talk' crossfire. While men with blackened hands used words like '*manifold*,' '*fuel-line*,' '*cam(s)*,' '*carburetor*,' '*pistons*,' and '*4-barrel*' Dad gravely and knowingly nodded in agreement. It became a useful tool in my repertoire as well and nods of understanding are employed to this day when a mechanic attempts to explain the mysterious workings of the internal combustion engine.

At Winchester Auto Parts mechanics often worked on tire rims in front of the shop. Stopping with friends one summer afternoon we stood quietly in an arc, watching while two men swung sledge hammers as a third held the rim. It was hot, the mechanics were covered in oil and grease and sweat. One of them counted aloud, above the din, providing cadence as his coworkers beat the frame.

Eventually one of the hammers missed its mark; landing flush on the thumb of the man holding the rim. The men swinging sledgehammers stopped, several kids in the group gasped and the injured mechanic rose to his feet. He calmly held his thumb out, looked at it, turned his hand to the left and then to the right, wiggled the thumb two or three times and then began to laugh.

How could someone laugh at something like that? He laughed along with his coworkers. No screams, no tears, no walking about shaking his hand. It had to have hurt but he showed no sign that it did. After a few moments he squatted back down on his hams, took hold of the metal rim and started counting again; the other's raised their sledgehammers and resumed pounding away as if nothing had happened. Men really were like that when we were growing up in Canal Winchester.

Memories of the Winchester Auto Parts building itself are not nearly as inspirational. In the front office - just inside the door - sat a *Coca-Cola* machine. Red and white with a long, rectangular glass door running up and down its left side that – once open - provided access to a column of icy cold bottles of soda. At age six, in 1969, having stopped with a group of friends to get a bicycle tire patched, the oldest kid in the group discovered he could remove bottles of Coke without putting change in the machine.

His excitement was palpable and infectious; we began chattering amongst ourselves in hushed tones about duplicating the daring feat; getting our hands on a 'free' bottle of pop. *"Pretend you're putting a dime in the slot, then open the door and pull on the third bottle from the top. It's easy!"* With such exacting advice to guide us, having already succumbed to the 'herd mentality' - and without a hint of subtlety - we approached the machine one after the other, feigned a deposit and yanked three more *Coca-Colas* from their moorings.

Unbeknownst to us a customer had witnessed the whole thing. She walked up to the counter, whispered in Mr. Hartman's ear, returned to her seat, sat down, crossed her legs, gripped her purse and watched the unfolding dragnet with grim satisfaction. Mr. Hartman was a tall, quiet man with pepper colored hair, heavy glasses and a uniform shirt with his name sewn above the right breast pocket. He looked at us intently, came out from behind the counter and asked if we had paid for our drinks. Overcome by hot flashes - waves of panic and terror raced through my body. Within seconds every one of us confessed.

Only seven or eight seconds elapsed after my admission of guilt before the tears rolled. Mom and Dad taught me never to steal; never take anything of Laura's, nothing from her room, or even borrow something without first asking permission. Outside our home it had never occurred to me to steal anything. In the auto parts store, however, none of that training, the ethical considerations and moral lessons impressed upon me during the first six years of life entered my mind. I went along with the group and now stood crying in the front office of Winchester Auto Parts with an unwanted bottle of cold pop.

Mr. Hartman sent us home to bring back 10c apiece; failing that he'd call our moms. Being the only member of the group sobbing as we raced down Waterloo Street; the oldest boy, the 'ring-leader' of our criminal enterprise, pulled me aside and told me to stop crying *"like a little girl,"* explaining we could still avoid getting into trouble. *"Nobody say nothing! You got it? Don't say anything. Stop crying Locke! When you get home get a dime from your piggy banks and everybody promise to keep your mouths shut."*

At that a faint glimmer of hope impressed itself on my disturbed little mind. What waited to be 'impressed' upon my round little ass if Mom or Dad found out was abundantly clear. Entering the front door and running upstairs the most desperate, intensive search for a lone dime ever undertaken in North America got underway. Mom, sitting at her desk in front of the black floor register, said not a word.

While rifling through my sock drawer that changed. The familiar and dreaded, *"Steve, what are you doing? Are you looking for something?"* soon echoed in my ears. There were no dimes in the sock drawer, none on the floor and not a single coin in the little dish beside Dad's bed where he nightly placed his watch and spare change.

The search became frantic; there wasn't a stray coin in the entire house. It was at that point when inspiration struck - ask Mom for the dime - just ask her; she won't know what you need it for. Maybe I just want a candy bar. It was so simple. It never occurred to me she might *ask* what the dime was for. So I asked, and when I did she turned her head slowly, looked me in the eye and asked, *"What do you need a dime for?"*

At first no words came; then tears and futile attempts at explaining my unfortunate circumstances amid incoherent blubbering. Just a few slurred words into my explanation the phone rang - and I knew for whom the bell tolled. It was Mrs. Ensley; the only bright spot being someone else had cracked first. It wasn't much consolation however, as Mom talked into the receiver staring evermore intently at my convulsing, wretched little frame.

At last she set down the receiver. 'Q.' *"Steven Paul, did you take a bottle of pop without paying for it? Answer me! Answer me right now!"* 'A.' *"Yea."* 'Aftermath.' *"Get up to your room! Get up to your room! You get up to your room this instant!"* She continued yelling as I raced up the stairs - sobbing, deeply ashamed; slightly unhinged and utterly doomed. *"We didn't teach you to steal! You don't steal! When your father gets home it's the first thing I'm going to tell him when he walks in this door! Do you hear me?"* Mom routinely handled discipline as Dad was almost always working, so her final broadside was unmistakable in its dark and foreboding intent.

Having lain down in bed, still sobbing - Mom yelled up the stairs, *"Steven Paul, get down here right now."* Damn, she's too angry to wait, I'm going to 'get it' right now. (*"Get it"* was big on Waterloo Street. At least two or three times a day friends warned or admonished, *"Ah, you're going to 'get it!'"*). She stood at the foot of the stairs holding a dime in her hand. *"You take this to Mr. Hartman right now. Don't stop for anything else. You take this dime to Mr. Hartman and you tell him you're sorry for what you did and you get back here as fast as you can! Do you understand me?"* I ran down the street arriving at the store just moments after my fellow thieves made restitution. They were now crying en masse, but we said nothing to one another.

Running back up Waterloo Street my father's car was nowhere in sight; as it turned out it was not Dad I needed to worry about. Whether her maternal eruption stemmed directly from my stealing, lying about the dime, the fact neighbors would learn of my perfidy, that Mr. Hartman and those he worked with knew Dad, or simply that Mom's inner rage boiled beyond her capacity to contain it in the time it took me to run to Hartman's and back we may never know.

Perhaps it was all of the above? Whatever it was my first willful act of juvenile delinquency resulted in the greatest ass whipping of all time. The comedian Sinbad – having deliberately sassed his mother while his Dad was out of town – remarked on the punishment his mother meted out, *"If I knew then what I knew now; oh my God; I turned round and my momma stood over me, standing 6-feet10-inches tall, cape blowing in the wind and a big W on her chest for whipping!"*

It appeared much the same way in Canal Winchester in 1969 as Mom's wrath had altered her appearance as well. She used to say she had to spank me to "keep me alive." Impulsive, distracted, and incapable of caution or forethought there is probably a lot of truth in that. On this day she determined to keep me alive with extreme prejudice.

Reentering the house Mom stood in front of the great black floor register, her feet shoulder width apart; instead of a dime she now held two yardsticks in her hand; gripping them the way Black Beard handled a cutlass. My heart stopped and the spinal cord fell out of my ass. *"Turn around and bend over Steven Paul!"* I'd taken whippings from Mom when she used a lone yardstick - her instrument of choice when saving my life - but never before saw her wielding two. Whack! Whack! *"Don't you ever steal again! You don't take things that don't belong to you! Do you understand me?"* Babe Ruth had nothing on my mother. She could have played in the big leagues if permitted to swing those yardsticks; her face red with rage lining up the next whack. Spare the rod my ass!

As any kid who's ever taken a spanking knows, questions are strictly rhetorical. Unfortunately, at age six - still a novice – answering seemed an act of self-preservation. *"I understand! I won't ever do it again!"* This of course led my enraged mother to incorporate those very words into her ass-assaulting Jihad. *"Your God damn right you understand"* – Whack! – *"You better never, ever, ever steal anything again!"* – Whack! – *"I bet you'll understand now!"* – Whack!

The following year while in second grade, Rick Kriegal and I got in trouble in art class for painting one another. Mrs. Weiser, our art teacher, was out sick and the substitute had a difficult time keeping tabs on 30 seven-year-olds armed with paints. It didn't take long for Kriegal and I to realize - seated as we were in the back of the room – that we were gloriously unsupervised. We quickly found ourselves pitched in a ritualistic, hand-to-hand, full-contact paint dual. Unfortunately, arch nemeses Tammy Rawn wrote our names down; providing them to Mrs. Robinett, our homeroom teacher, with a detailed account upon our return.

When we admitted guilt she announced to the class the importance of treating substitute teachers with respect and how disappointed she was in the way the entire class had behaved – especially Steve Locke and Rick Kriegel. She called Kriegel and me to the front of the room; ordering us to turn around and lean against her desk to be paddled. Mrs. Robinett's paddle hung on the side of the 'teacher's closet' for all to see, a visible and for the most part effective deterrent. Removing it from the hook the class sat deathly still as Mrs. Robinett walked behind us.

Shaking, trying desperately not to cry in front of the others, the paddle fell. She had 'spanked' me. *"That's it? That's all you got? You've got to be kidding!"* I thought to myself. Compared to Samurai Mom it wasn't even a practice swing. Of course, such sentiments were best kept unexpressed. On Dime Day the spanking – amazingly - failed to soothe Mom's savage breast. Scrambling up the steps she yelled behind me, *"You think that hurt? Wait until your father gets home! He's going to give you something to cry about!"*

Damn! Having just taken the worst spanking of my life the only positive had been surviving it – that it was now *behind* me, (no pun intended) only to learn there was more to come? The next two hours, alone in my room, were nerve wracking. I stared at the tiny milkshake shaped indentation etched into my bedroom wall and listened for the car. When Dad got home he parked on the street. The sound of his closing car door, followed by clearing his throat - a nightly cough announcing his arrival - was unmistakable, even from the second floor bedroom.

Quiet followed. Mom was telling Dad what had happened, relaying the entire seamy sequence of events to a powerfully built ex-marine who stood six-feet, 2-inches tall and weighed over 220 pounds. His footfalls grew louder on the stairs. Sitting on the edge of the bed facing the door, it opened; he walked in stoned-faced. *"Mom tells me you stole a bottle of pop downtown today. Is that true?"* ("Yes"). *"Then you can't be trusted to go downtown without us because you're a thief."*

That hurt worse than the spanking. ("Oh no Dad; I'm not, I'm not"). *"Yes you are,"* he replied. Expecting to get spanked again Dad instead sat next to me on the bed. Rubbing his hand across my back he finally said: *"Boy, you know better than to steal. I don't care who you're with or what they're doing, if your friends steal something, you get the hell out of there. Do you understand?"*

We sat there side-by-side for maybe a minute before Dad stood up, walked to the door, turned around and remarked, *"Boy, I'm going to give you some advice. You better never steal anything ever again. And you by God better start listening to your mother - or she's likely to kill your little ass."* It was the best advice he ever gave me.

Haircuts and Candy

Across Waterloo Street and up the road - two buildings down on South High - was the CW Bank. It had originally opened in 1887; prior to that investment capital came via local grain merchants who extended small amounts of specie against land, crops and draft animals. The bank's entrance faced South High Street, but its drive-through, added in 1964, ran down West Waterloo Street. In 1973 the Central Trust Company purchased the bank, though folks continued to refer to it as the Winchester Bank for at least another decade.

The Canal Winchester Bank.
Courtesy Canal Winchester Area Historical Society

Two expansive windows looked out on South High Street allowing tellers inside a bird's eye view of downtown. Behind the tellers an enormous mural stretched across the upper wall. Entitled *'Winchester on the Canal,'* it featured bright reds, yellows and blues; rendering High Street as it appeared in 1887. Despite the artist's questionable and dubious background – he hailed from Pickerington, Canal Winchester's archrival north of Route 33 – James Huffman's mural depicted South High Street's 1880s businesses; children clad in overalls and straw hats, the old draw bridge over the canal and plenty of lush green trees and blue skies.

Winchester on the Canal.
This mural covered the wall behind the tellers at the CW bank

Abutting the CW Bank the Wigwam Restaurant did a thriving business; and next to the Wigwam sat Paul 'Zeke' Alspauch's Barbershop – think Floyd's Barbershop in Mayberry. Before he became a barber Zeke Alspauch had batted his way to the New York Mets' top minor league affiliate in Buffalo. In our small, sports-crazed Midwestern town that experience carried a lot of weight.

Zeke's shop sported two chairs, two mirrors and ancient creaking floors. The building where he groomed Canal's male clientele was erected in 1837, though the first barber didn't start cutting hair at that location until 1887. Zeke's baseball celebrity drew customers and coupled with low prices, decent haircuts and plenty of local gossip there weren't many lulls during workdays.

Lehman Building

Zeke's Babrbershop

He had purchased the two chair shop in 1969 and usually worked with another barber. Trim with dark hair and black mustache Paul Alspauch stood about six-feet tall and wore thick-rimmed glasses. Like the bank tellers, Zeke surveyed his domain from two square, well placed windows - one looking out on South High, the other on West Waterloo. While the women at the bank enjoyed a wider view across High Street, Zeke's two strategically placed portals allowed for maximum observation.

From his corner lair Mr. Alspauch became all knowing and all seeing in downtown Canal Winchester. The latest gossip, bawdy jokes, sporting news, local politics, weather patterns, town business, school levies and the scourge of communism were all fair game. Zeke cut my hair just once; Mom usually cut it, insisting it a waste of hard earned money to pay for haircuts when she could do it herself. That lone trim and frequently accompanying friends, however, acquainted me with the barbershop.

It was a very masculine environment; a de-facto segregated enclave of maleness seldom breached by females. The only time women ever stepped foot in Zeke's was to drop off kids. Even little boys of three and four came in with their Dads. And conversations reflected that. Fishing – hunting – baseball - and boxing dominated discussions while *Field &*

Stream, Popular Mechanics and *Sports Illustrated* provided the reading material. Once, while sitting with friends, I overheard an older man in bib overalls say to another - matter-of-factly - *"You know Jimmy it's the damn niggers who's prejudiced!"*

That comment notwithstanding, racial animosity wasn't something that touched our daily lives. Growing up in CW in the 1960s and 1970s we weren't exposed to anyone other than those who looked and spoke exactly as we did. From the time we moved to Canal Winchester in 1967 until HS graduation and joining the military in 1981, Canal Winchester, Ohio was overwhelmingly white.

Nor did we see Blacks or Hispanics when visiting Bloom Carroll, Teays-Valley, Circleville, Lithopolis or Sugar Grove. Small Ohio towns between Columbus and Lancaster were comprised of white Americans who, as a former presidential speech writer has written, *"spoke the same language, watched the same three TV networks, listened to similar music, read the same books and magazines; ate similar foods and worshipped – for the most part – the same God."*

We weren't completely isolated from the wider world and its racial tensions because of television. Mom cried every time TV news flashed images of Blacks being hosed, beaten or attacked by German Shepherds; and those images, together with her reaction, had a lasting impact. Both Mom and Dad thought racial discrimination inane and did their best to instill a sense of fair play - the need to emphasize the individual, not the group – in both of us.

But we weren't 'Holier-than-Thou' either. Racial jokes were pervasive in the 1970s and told and re-told across town, especially at school. Poles, Irishmen, Hispanics, Asians and Blacks were all 'fair game.' It wasn't unusual to hear older women in town say things like, *"Eenie, meenie, minie moe, catch a nigger by the toe, if he hollers let him go, eenie, meenie, miny moe."* At recess kids often barked, *"Fight, fight a nigger and a white. White don't win I'll jump in!"* It should be noted that Canal Winchester wasn't a cauldron of bigots; the vast majority of its residents didn't talk that way. But plenty did; and despite an absence of minorities there was never an absence of racial slurs - it was part and parcel of the culture of the time.

Military families especially seemed to carry particular animus towards Blacks and were veritable fonts of racial jokes and epithets.

While playing at a friends' house in the summer of 1975, for example, we ran inside to get a drink of lemonade when the tail-end of a television commercial announced; *"We are an equal-opportunity employer."* To which my friends' military father wryly commented, *"Why don't you just tell the truth and say, 'We hire niggers.' "* Mary Matyac, who moved to Canal Winchester from Worthington the summer before her freshman year in 1972, recalled: *"A big shock to me, coming from an integrated upper middle class suburb, was that there were no black or Hispanic students at CW. I had never heard the term "nigger- lover" until we moved there."*

Though slavery had been forbidden in the Northwest Territory, Ohio, like many northern States, passed 'Black Laws' in the first half of the 19th century. Designed to discourage Black settlement in Ohio the various statutes specifically forbade free Blacks from voting, attending public schools or testifying in cases involving white Americans. Basic civil rights, equality of opportunity and changing attitudes, therefore, was an evolutionary process.

The climate of toleration had improved between the town's founding in 1828, when Blacks were legally discriminated against, and the summer of 1975, when the legal framework of oppression had been dismantled and replaced with verbal ridicule. And the climate has improved further still between 1975 and 2012.

Across the street from Zeke's Barbershop and Conrad's Market was the Canal View Pharmacy; where Doc Burrier's prescriptions were dispensed. Opening in 1951 and operating for nearly a quarter century in the heart of downtown CW, the pharmacy had added a credenza and a small brick wall to support it by 1975.

Though primarily a dispenser of prescription medications; kids most valued its supply of wiffle balls and bats, plastic handcuffs, toy guns, squirt guns, silly putty, Slinkies, yo-yos, and seasonal trinkets. During Halloween room was set aside to shelve plastic vampire fangs, white tubes of fake 'blood,' rubber spiders and snakes, and a fairly respectable assortment of masks.

The Canal View Pharmacy

At Christmastime the same shelves were laden with stockings, candy canes, antler ears and elf hats, while Valentine's Day saw bags of cards, red and pink heart shaped boxes of chocolates and plastic roses. Easter witnessed a profusion of stuffed bunny rabbits, plastic Easter eggs, chocolate Easter eggs, hollow chocolate Easter bunnies for rookies and solid chocolate Easter bunnies for chocoholics.

In 1975, at age twelve, the true epicenter of the Pharmacy was not the toy shelves, or the medicine counter; but rather the multi-tiered candy display. Candy's importance in the lives of children cannot be underestimated; kids in town knew the exact price of candy bars, bubblegum and every other sugary confection. Blow Pop lollipops, for example, were 5 cents apiece. A square of Bazooka-Joe Bubblegum was 2cents; while Snicker Bars, Zero Bars, Clark Bars, Hershey Bars; Zagnuts, Chick-o-Sticks, Mars Bars, Three Musketeers and Milkyways cost juvenile shoppers .15 cents each.

And some of the candy marketed to kids in the 1970s mirrored the larger adult world of the time. Candy cigarettes, for example, were big sellers. If a confectionary tried to sell candy cigarettes to 'children' today merchants would wind up in reeducation centers - a veritable Gulag Archipelago run by America's nicotine police. But in 1975 both sugar and bubblegum cigarettes were widely available, as were bubblegum cigars. The cigars were wrapped in clear cellophane, and once the wrapper was discarded they didn't last long. The sweet flavor of bubblegum tempting the taste buds was too delicious for most kids to resist and the perfectly formed cigar became an unrecognizable wad in a matter of moments.

The bubblegum cigarettes, on the other hand, came in boxes that could pass for the real McCoy; containing 20, individually wrapped rods in white paper. Though realistic, they were impractical. Once the novelty of pseudo-smoking wore off kids were left with gum sticks embedded with soggy paper and the unpleasant and time consuming task of removing saliva saturated wrappers from the gum itself.

Likewise, sugar stick cigarettes came in realistic looking boxes and were by far the best of the child-luring, fake smokes on the market. Each cigarette had a weird, pronounced texture – a pattern etched into it – and was comprised entirely of molded, compact glucose. The piece-de la resistance - the candy-makers crowning effort at authenticity - the ends of each cigarette were dipped in red dye giving them the appearance of being 'lit' at all times.

Along with fake cigarettes the Pharmacy offered *Snicker Bars, Reese's Cups* and *M&Ms* – plain and peanut. *Boston Baked Beans, Sugar Daddy Pops, Jaw Breakers, Cherry Heads, $100,000 Dollar Bars, Lemon Heads, Apple Heads, Laffy Taffy, Pop Rocks, Pixy Sticks, Necco Assorted Wafers, Atomic Fireballs, Wonka Tart N Tiny's, Tootsie Rolls, Wax Lips, Clark Bars, Baby Ruth's, Almond Joys, Butter Fingers, Chunky Bars, 5th Avenue Candy Bars, OH Henry Candy Bars, Pay Day Candy Bars, Good & Plenty, Heath Bars, Hershey Bars, Junior Mints, Milk Duds, Mounds Bars, Chuckles Candy* and more.

The irony of selling sugar delivery systems and fake cigarettes to children in a branch of the health care system was lost on all concerned. Also lost to time is the Canal View Pharmacy. Competition from large chains like CVS, Kroger and Walmart proved daunting and it went out of business in the 1990s. The building that housed it on the corner of High and East Waterloo Streets is used today for office space - and is no longer a hub of communal activity.

South High Street

The store immediately next to the pharmacy must have been jinxed because different businesses set up and disbanded there in a never ending cycle. At one time or other it served as bakery, hair salon, gun store, antique shop and tackle shop.

When a bakery opened next to the pharmacy in 1971 the Locke Clan heartily approved. Conrad's and Super Duper carried boxed, powdered, chocolate and glazed doughnuts, though that was about it. But the new bakery offered fresh, gooey, jelly-filled, custard-filled, cream-filled, glazed, sprinkled, sugar-dusted, delicious, wonderfully-smelling, full size American doughnuts! While it remained in business Mom sent me downtown many a Saturday and Sunday morning to buy a baker's dozen.

CW had a popular jewelry store - Shaw's Jewelry - located between the ever changing storefront and Shade's Restaurant - at 9 South High Street. The owner, Damon Shaw, residing on High Street since 1956, had operated the jewelry since 1947. Shaw's Jewelry was nearly hospital clean. Entering through the large front door sonorous chimes rang out alerting the proprietors that a patron had arrived. Their glass display cases were always immaculate despite kid's leaning against them with grimy hands while looking at the shiny baubles. It certainly wasn't a designated kid location - except when Mom's birthday rolled around or at Christmastime when we went to look at pins and broaches. Shaw's had a monopoly in the jewelry trade in Canal Winchester, did well and is still operating today.

Shaw's Jewelry

One store down from Shaw's Jewelry – the next to last business on South High Street – was Shade's Restaurant. Mom worked there for two years before going back to school. Her job offered Laura and me occasional access to the kitchen – *The Promised Land of Milk and Honey* - to say hello or help out shelving mayonnaise jars in the walk-in refrigerator. But much, much more importantly, Mom's association with Shade's Restaurant meant she frequently brought home hamburgers topped with colorfully tasseled toothpicks.

Shade's Restaurant, where Mom worked before returning to school

Back in the day - as discussed above - we rarely went out to eat. It wasn't something we did more than three or four times a year and even then we ate somewhere like BBF, Burger King or McDonalds. We consumed plenty of hamburgers at home but that was different; we had to make those ourselves, on our stove, using white toast, mustard and ketchup. Most unpleasantly, we had to clean up afterwards.

'Real,' restaurant made, greasy, cheese-covered, sauce-dripping hamburgers with lettuce, pickles and tomatoes - and topped off with a multi-colored, tasseled toothpick - were an absolutely awe inspiring sight. Nothing made my heart go pitter-patter more than Mom walking home from Shade's toting Styrofoam hamburger boxes. Despite the occasional free burger, and access to the kitchen for me and Laura, working at Shade's Restaurant definitely wasn't Mom's dream job.

Watching TV one evening she began crying. She sobbed uncontrollably, saying over and over again, *"I'm 34-years old and I make salad dressing in a diner."* She sat at the end of the couch, head in her hands, weeping and repeating that phrase. *"I'm 34-years old and I make salad dressing in a diner."* Dad sat next to her, rubbing his hand across her back *"Patty, it's OK."* He assured her in soothing tones. *"It's OK Patty."*

Under normal circumstances Dad referred to her as 'Trish,' or 'My Chief-Of-Staff.' If the phone rang, for example, and friends requested his company he'd say, *"Let me ask my Chief-Of-Staff."* When 'Patty' entered the lexicon it was usually serious. Having at last calmed her down Dad asked, *"Why don't you go back to school? I'll help with the kids and you can go back to school, get your license and teach."* Mom countered that it was too expensive. Dad parried with his usual subtle approach: *"Bullshit! We'll go* down to the bank tomorrow," he insisted. *"We'll take out a loan. I'll watch the kids and you can enroll at Ohio State."*

The idea of losing access to Shade's hamburgers would be shocking to my system but a worthy sacrifice considering how unhappy Mom was in her job; but father watching Laura and me? That was a horse of a different color. The striking – nay glaring - difference in parenting styles - the lack of wiggle room when it came to the old man - raised serious doubts in my mind about mother furthering her education.

Having shot down finance as a stumbling block Mom countered, *"I'm 34 years old!" By the time I finish the program I'll be 36 or 37."* It was quiet for a moment and then Dad delivered the coup de grace: *"So what?"* he said. *"You'll be 36 or 37 anyway. Why not turn 37 and do what you want?"* That solid reasoning allowed Mom to give Shade's Restaurant notice and pursue a career that held real meaning for her.

Back on South High, an alley separated Shade's Restaurant from the last business on the East side of the street – the Huntington Bank. Ranging over a large corner lot once occupied by two private homes and the Freeman Hotel, the Huntington Bank opened in October 1964, just three years before Dad accepted the head coaching position at CW. We didn't bank there but the Huntington's parking lot was magnetic to skateboarders, cyclists and roller skaters.

The Huntington Bank

Directly across the street from Huntington Bank the Dwayne Spence Funeral Home saw to Canal's dearly departed. The funeral home was very grand looking, constructed of brick and trimmed in white - very stately, even regal in appearance. Despite the grandeur it gave me the willies. Thoughts of death overwhelmed me – even as a kid - and the idea of embalming, dressing, applying makeup and combing the hair of the dead before positioning them for display was too creepy to contemplate.

Dwayne Spence Funeral Home

The last two locales worth mentioning on South High Street were the Police and Fire Departments and Winchester Laundry and Dry Cleaning. The Village Police Department was somewhat bigger than TV-Land's fictional Mayberry's – but not much. Unlike Mayberry, North Carolina, Canal Winchester, Ohio in 1975 was a real place with real problems. Indeed, according to Carroll and Steube's **_Canal Winchester Ohio: The Second Ninety Years_**, "*In the 1970s problems revolved around curfew law . . . youth gathered far and wide to drink beer sold from trunks of cars, profanity, disorderly conduct, suspected drug dealing, and littering of private property existed.*"

Besides dealing with stolen bikes, traffic accidents, speeding, break-ins and the problems cited above - CWPD's internal dynamics were a veritable Peyton's Place of intrigue, gossip and maneuver. The year we arrived in CW, 1967, Ken Griffin became Canal Winchester's first chief of police. Four years later, in 1971, one of his deputies – Robert Miller – leveled a series of formal charges against his boss. Chaos ensued: the department split into hostile camps - those supporting the chief and those who sided with the Young Turks. The anger and animosities within the department spread into the wider community after Deputy Miller publically accused his boss of malfeasance. Two council meetings, both of which turned into hostile showdowns, were held to deal with the charges, the second a marathon meeting taking more than six hours. When Chief Griffin refused to resign the town council fired him. Shockingly, soon thereafter Deputy Miller became CW's second chief of police.

Chief Miller had broad shoulders, stood nearly six-feet-four inches tall, sported close-cropped grayish brown hair, was always clean shaven and had a meaty, round face. He was also quite plump, slightly obese in fact. Though not at first. In the mid-1960s and early 1970s he was heavy but managed to carry it well on his large frame. By 1975, life behind a desk, and sitting long hours in patrol cars had greatly enlarged his once girlish figure.

Kids called him '*Chief Boob*' and he epitomized - in physical appearance anyway - the small town, overweight, doughnut eating, slow moving hick Sheriff. Of course, no one called him '*Chief Boob*' to his face. He was too imposing a figure. His deputy officers were a busy lot. They spoke to kids at school; patrolled football games and parking lots outside sporting events; performed thankless, difficult and often dangerous jobs; continually cruising the roads, alleys and byways of Canal Winchester.

The fire and police departments shared the same building in 1975; a square brick structure with wide bay doors for the fire engines; two benches out front allowed volunteers to sit and relax in the evenings. Unlike the paid village police force, firefighters were nearly all volunteers - and it had been that way from the beginning.

CW's fire department dates to 1878 and its first captain - Reverend Davis – ran a company of volunteers using horse drawn hooks and ladders. Ten years later the department dissolved leaving a lone employee to maintain equipment and ring the fire bell – 3-chimes - at 9:00 pm, signaling to the town it could tuck itself in for the night.

It took a fatal fire that claimed the life of a small child in 1941 to prompt the village to reestablish a reliable fire department – made up once more of volunteers.

Three decades later, in 1972, Canal hired two fulltime firemen. Like most communities CW saw its fair share of conflagrations over the years; and the men who volunteered to fight them worked hard to protect friends and neighbors. That said, it is worth noting that the men who volunteered absolutely reveled in it; the 'type' being can-do, busybody, slightly self-important, gossip-loving He-Men.

Even as kids we recognized the swagger and confidence. Like our policemen they visited school; spoke to us about fire safety, dressed in firefighting uniforms - complete with rubber boots, fire hats and axes – and we looked up at them in awe. In our sleepy hamlet nothing made police and firefighters happier – nothing on God's green earth – than sounding their numerous sirens. Whether such enthusiasm is widespread or peculiar to CW, sirens blared early and often in our little corner of the world. The sounds of ear-piercing, high-decibel alarms filled the breasts of our emergency service personnel with great joy.

Antecedents for such continuous rackets were abundant. In 1932, for example, lightning set off the town siren at approximately Midnight – well after unsuspecting residents had gone to bed. And it apparently blared nonstop most of the night; terrifying the sleep-deprived who awoke convinced they were in the midst of a firestorm of Biblical proportions. When not cranking sirens the volunteers cleaned fire trucks, continually checked gear or sat about the benches on South High Street, talking and waving to passersby. During summertime Dad would put the top down on his convertible and when passing the fire station would honk the horn, receiving a chorus of 'Hey Coach, Coach! All right coach!'- In reply.

Canal's fire trucks were painted bright red and snow-white, with gleaming patches of chrome diamond plating that sparkled in the sun. Unfortunately some misguided policy during the 1970s led fire departments to change those colors to puke-green, and alter the sound of the sirens to 'modernize' their emergency vehicles. Apparently 'sophisticated' Europeans used puke-green fire trucks while INTERPOL sirens screeched like braying asses: eeee-oooooh, eeee-oooooh, eeee-oooooh, eeee-ooooh and eeee-ooooh.

That proved to be enough for bureaucrats looking to their cousins across the pond for guidance. Why any American governmental entity would look to Europe as a model for anything was beyond the average resident of Canal Winchester to fathom; and after vociferous complaint proper colors and siren sounds were eventually restored.

Finally, Winchester Laundry and Dry Cleaning stood next to the police/fire station at 28 South High Street. When we moved to town Mom and Dad didn't own a washer or dryer so the Laundromat became an important weekly destination; though Laura and I hated laundry day. Faced with two choices – coming along or tagging along – we spent what felt like an eternity at the Laundromat until Mom finished the wash.

Accompanying her to the humid, airless, extraordinarily loud confines of Winchester Laundry and Dry Cleaning was like getting sent to your room. The building, constructed of concrete blocks, had been designed by sadists. During Ohio's oppressive summer heat-waves its heavy wooden backdoors were kept open, ensuring an adequate supply of oxygen inside the hazy, stifling, stagnant sweatshop. A barebones operation it had one cash register; two long rows of machines on either side of the room, with washers on the left, dryers on the right, metal shelving above the washers for laundry detergent; and a *Coca-Cola* machine identical to the one in Hartman's Garage. Every glimpse of that infernal pop machine induced Vietnam-like-flashbacks to the ass-whipping-of-all-ass-whippings meted out by my mother – now standing quietly folding clothes.

The Winchester Laundry & Cleaners

For kids - at least this kid - it was pure hell. We weren't allowed to act up, we weren't allowed to go out front because of traffic on High Street; we weren't allowed to go out back and play in the gravel because cars were continually pulling up to the rear entrance; playing on the floor was Verboten because we got in the way of other customers, and as the *Coca-Cola* machine was inherently evil I gave it a wide berth throughout our interminable stays.

It was a huge deal when Mom and Dad bought their first washer and dryer. Today I don't think twice about washing a load of dirty clothes. But the introduction of those timesaving, Laundromat-avoiding, modern marvels of domestic tranquility led the entire Locke Clan downstairs to observe our shiny new Kenmore Dryer when it buzzed to signal the completion of the first wash.

There were numerous other businesses in CW – banks, restaurants, the bowling alley, for example. But those listed above should provide readers with a flavor of our town circa 1975. By age twelve I had pretty much grown up with these establishments; it seemed they had always been there and always would be. They represented the Waterloo/High Street Axis, giving shape and meaning to the only world most Canal Winchester kids my age knew.

CHAPTER V:

EDUCATION

"A school is where they grind the grain of thought,
And grind the children who must mind the thought.
It may be those two grindings are but one . . ."

(Howard Nemerov –
September, the first day of school)

The 2012 CW School District is comprised of two Elementary Schools, an Intermediate School and High School housed in several different building complexes in various locations across town. In 1975 students used one, all-encompassing brick building that had been added to over the years; serving every student in the district - Kindergarten through 12th grade. Fortunately, small town Canal Winchester – despite legions of kids running up and down Waterloo Street - had a fairly small enrollment.

The seniors who played football for Dad in the autumn of 1975, for example – the Class of 1976 - graduated ninety-four students. The year before that, the Class of 1975, numbered seventy-eight seniors. By contrast, in 2011 the district graduated two-hundred and twenty-two students – compared to 1975 an increase of 139%. Both Laura and I began Kindergarten in the newest wing, and years later when we received our diplomas on the cinder track surrounding Weiser Field, we had taken all of our classes inside the same building.

It was an old school and quite small considering its mandate. Nebraska move-in Gary Cox was stunned after his first tour of the building. "*Canal was microscopic,*" he remembered shaking his head. "*Compared to some of the schools we attended across the country; I couldn't believe grades K-12 were under one roof. There were only three hallways in the high school; the gym was so small, I didn't know when a 'backcourt' could be called during basketball. The weight room was tiny; in fact all the facilities were tiny. We had to go through the elementary school area to watch game film.*" Unbeknownst to Mr. Cox, the building he found so small in 1975 was much larger and vastly improved from its predecessors. The structure Gary used during his senior year in high school was actually the town's fourth public school building.

Winchester's first formal schoolhouse operated just fourteen years - 1834-1848 – before students outgrew the space; it later sold at auction for the princely sum of $29.50.

Two new buildings were constructed - in 1848, and 1851, respectively - to accommodate the burgeoning student population and keep the sexes apart. Sexual apartheid – school policy from 1834 until 1855 - kept Winchester's students rigorously segregated. Boys occupied the North school while girls attended classes in the South building; mimicking the larger North-South divide about to tear the country asunder.

CWHS under construction

The foundation of the building we used in the 1970s was constructed in 1861-1862, and its first students entered the four-room facility about the time Lee and McClellan squared off at Antietam, Maryland. The value Winchester's residents placed on education can be seen in their willingness to invest ever-larger sums on schools: while the original brought $29.50 at auction, those built in 1848 and 1851 cost well over $600.00 each, and the modern, four-room 1862 schoolhouse set taxpayers back $2,360.00.

One of the primary textbooks used in Winchester's first school was the King James Bible. Heat was provided via coal-burning stoves. Teachers earned approximately $18.00 monthly and the curriculum stressed reading, writing, English grammar, philosophy, geography, arithmetic and geometry. When we attended in the 1970s the Bible was no longer used as a textbook; we did, however, start each school day reciting the pledge of allegiance and the Lord's Prayer.

The 1862 structure became known as the South building after a new school was erected just north of the original in 1906. Twenty years later, in 1928-1929, the two wings were connected by a center section. The Elementary School was attached in 1957 and further modernized in 1968. It served Kindergarten-sixth grade students while the older structures – including the auditorium and gymnasium - served students 7th through 12th grades.

Speaking of the elementary school, it was the nicer of the two wings. Compared to the brick, iron, mortar and plaster that darkened the older building, K-6 was modern, brightly lit, carpeted in the 1968 attachment and stylish. From 1968 to 1974 only one spanking marred my elementary school record – the paint duel with Kriegel – but warnings were routine occurrences.

Once during fifth grade, for example, I attempted to re-enter school at breakneck speed following recess, and collided unintentionally with another student. We weren't supposed to run and Mrs. Cheney, a sixth grade teacher with a ferocious reputation, took me by the shirt and slammed me against a brick wall. Back in the day teachers grabbed kids without fear of legal repercussion; the practice expediting interrogations.

Mrs. Cheney was slender and petite with yellowish hair worn in a stylized 'do.' She wore pant suits and was known to wield the paddle on occasion. And she was divorced, which was still somewhat scandalous in the early 1970s. Her steely reputation among students stemmed not from physical stature but rather her overall demeanor and intensity with which she carried herself. *"What's your name!"* she barked after the collision. *"Steve,"* I muttered. *"Steve Who?"* she demanded; her eyes narrowing; focusing intently upon my deer-in-the-headlights mien. *"Steve Locke."*

When the name 'Locke' left my lips Mrs. Cheney involuntarily relaxed her grip, her eyes widened in startled disbelief. Thinking – momentarily – I might catch a break because Dad was the high school football coach, Mrs. Cheney continued her queries. *"You're not Laura Locke's brother are you?"* she asked. (Laura - the show-off, national honor society, honor roll, honor student, teacher's pet, older sister form hell, evil sixth-grader in Mrs. Cheney's class - had struck a crippling blow without even trying) Oh the treachery.

"Yea," I replied. At that her stern features softened into a sorrowful gaze and she seared two words into my prepubescent psyche: *"What happened?"* It was a question uttered by a woman whose head was slightly atilt and who looked sadly perplexed – as if the creature before her could not possibly be related to the delightful little girl in her class. Electing not to respond, the opportunity of Mrs. Cheney's momentary shock and confusion allowed me to sidle along the brick wall and escape up the cement steps leading into the building before the shock wore off.

The following year, mysteriously assigned to Mr. Will's sixth grade class instead of Mrs. Cheney's, warnings nevertheless continued my way. Mr. Will was the only male teacher in the elementary building. His father, Milton Will, had also taught and coached at CW for over thirty years. Standing five-feet, 10-inches tall, lean with sandy brown hair, Mr. Will wore glasses and dressed immaculately in suit, vest and tie. He had delicate fingers slightly yellowed from smoking cigarettes and liked to roam the classroom while we worked at our desks, sometimes stopping to squeeze the back of a student's neck – sometimes affectionately, other times to get his or her attention.

Mr. Will was good natured and a good teacher. As junior high basketball coach he gave every 6th grade boy with future dreams of scoring hoops in front of cheering fans reason to tow the line. Speaking of boys, it was perhaps thirteen or fourteen of that tribe who were scolded

– 'warned' if you will - by Mr. Will for our 'immaturity.' The class had gone stag after Mrs. Cheney absconded with the sixth grade girls in the spring of 1975 – taking every last one of them in a massive gaggle to parts unknown.

For precisely what reason this was done our erstwhile female classmates never divulged, although 'the boys' suspected it had something to do with the dark, mysterious workings of the female body. Whatever the reason Mr. Will ended up with a baker's dozen of eleven and twelve-year-old boys facing his desk once a week on warm spring afternoons.

He usually kept us busy filling out worksheets, reading, or working on a writing assignment. Anyway, one such afternoon we were sitting quietly, working at our desks, when a shoulder tap got my attention – the universal nonverbal adolescent-signal indicating communication is desired while under surveillance. "At 3:05 *drop your pencil, everyone's doing it, pass it on.*"

In front of the classroom, Mr. Will was reading; behind me the mini herd of preadolescent males scattered about the room were clearly visible, the absence of girls having opened up the space considerably; each and every one of them smiling wryly. I turned around, checked on Mr. Will and then tapped the shoulder of the kid in front of my desk; whispering "*We're all dropping our pencils at exactly 3:05 – pass it on.*" Fulfilling my male, peer pressure induced duty of solemnly passing on the communiqué' I turned my attention to the wall clock.

Enduring the countdown was tedious but it also allowed for reflection. '*Why in the hell are we dropping our pencils at the same time?*' Unfamiliar with this particular caper I nevertheless continued to eye the big round wall clock. Those clocks were set just a tad differently from room to room; and no matter the differences kids in each class knew the exact position required for dismissal – or recess, lunch, music and art class for that matter - to the nanosecond.

Every wall clock had a minute hand, hour hand, and, most importantly - a red second-hand. We were watching that red second hand like hawks; tick, tick, tick. The tension was unbearable. Were we really going to go through with it? What could Mr. Will do? He's not going to spank *all* of us - would he? At last the long gray minute hand tocked to 3:04.

The red second hand moved on, inexorably, second-by-second – moving around the clock face. It moved upward now, toward the very top;

tick, tick, tick - TWELVE! The long gray minute hand-tocked to 3:05 – X-HOUR – the moment of truth had arrived - pencils away: Clink, clatter - quiet. Laughter ensued, giggles and then quiet once again.

The *gravity* of the prank was suddenly clear; (pun-intended). In that quiet classroom our pencils had made a lot more noise than anticipated. Unfortunately the ensuing silence was that much starker. Everyone was looking down at their worksheets, only glancing up occasionally at Mr. Will to read his facial expression; wishing the damn girls hadn't abandoned us. It was their departure after all that had led to operation pencil-drop. Mr. Will stood up behind his desk, emotionless, looked out across the room and growled, *"Pick em up!"*

He failed to see the humor in our carefully synchronized endeavor. In fact he was as angry as we'd ever seen him. Teachers are talkers and Mr. Will was no exception. At this moment, unfortunately, he was icily quiet. Rather than warn us he turned and walked deliberately toward the teacher's cloakroom. *"He's not – he can't spank all of us. Oh shit!"* was one of the thoughts racing through my mind. Just as in Mrs. Robinett's second grade classroom, Mr. Will kept a long wooden paddle hanging astride the teacher's cloakroom - the ultimate symbol of authority.

That Instrument of Order - cut and forged no doubt in an ancient fire - had a classic shape, perhaps twenty-inches long - and resembled frat house paddles. It sported a shiny lacquered finish and hung forever vigilant, foreboding – like the Sword of Damocles suspended above our collective heads - capable at moment's notice of ruining anyone of our days.

Not all teachers displayed paddles; several didn't 'believe' in paddling. These nonbelievers were usually younger staff who practiced educational 'New-Thinking' in which self-esteem is paramount; never hit a child, every student is precious. The philosophy was popular at teacher colleges in the late 1960s and 1970s and eventually found its way to CW. It was a school of thought much admired by the student body – especially sixth grade boys watching Mr. Will move toward the teacher's cloakroom.

University proponents of New Thinking philosophy were thoroughly unfamiliar with Steve Locke, Rick Kriegel, or twelve-year-old boys in general. Mr. Will knew us well and therefore did not subscribe to the notion that we were in any way, shape or form, precious – at least not at the moment. Grabbing the paddle didn't necessarily mean spankings would ensue. Mr. Will sometimes just walked up and down the aisles with his paddle; taking it down when angry to make a point. The clincher was whether or not he got a 'witness.'

In order to paddle kids at CW, wood-wielding educators were required to have another teacher, or administrator, observe. This ensured sufficient cause existed to paddle offenders; and protected the deliverer of the blow from accusations of abuse. By sixth grade we knew bluff, rather than paddling, depended on the presence of said observer; after removing the paddle from its peg Mr. Will walked out the door to locate a witness.

His absence allowed bitter recriminations and accusations to begin in earnest: *"Nice job! Asshole! Real good;" "Shut up." "You shut up!" "Gonna make me?" "Yea, I'll make you." "You and whose army?"* And on it went until Mr. Will reentered the room. Mercifully, Mrs. Cheney's departure with the sixth grade girls meant the other two 6th grade teachers had departed in her wake. Fifth graders were on the playground at that moment – along with their teachers. Glory Hallelujah! Time spent searching for his witness allowed Mr. Will to think better of paddling all of us; he stormed back into the classroom and launched a verbal salvo of immense wrath.

"That's the most immature stunt I've ever seen by sixth graders! If you ever do something like that again every one of you is going to get his butt beat! Do you understand me? The only reason I'm not spanking every single one of you right now is because I couldn't find a witness. The girls in this class are certainly more mature than its boys I'm sorry to say." It was a close call. For the remainder of the afternoon, even after the girls returned, we gazed at our worksheets as if they were the most important documents ever written.

Elementary school was a fun time. We put on annual Christmas pageants with every class singing in the high school auditorium before family and friends. We marched through town every Halloween -1st graders in the lead and 6th graders bringing up the rear - dressed in an array of Frankenstein, Dracula, Werewolf and Witch costumes. Year after year we watched Disney educational films, took fieldtrips, blew off steam during gym class and daily outdoor recess; colored, finger painted and sang our lungs out in the music room. In my case, elementary school drew to a close in the spring of 1975.

Once the glorious 'fish fry' summer of 1975 came to an end the prospect of leaving the familiar, bright haunts of CWES for the larger, raucous, intimidating brick and mortar structure that was CWHS – inhabited as it was by large, raucous, intimidating teenagers - was daunting to say the least. And the most striking difference between elementary and Jr. High School was the abolition of recess.

Since First grade we had enjoyed three scheduled recess breaks a day: a short 15-minute burst at 10:15 am; a marvelous 35-minute extravaganza after lunch and another 15-minute break about an hour before the end of the school day. Not so in seventh grade. That was the first obstacle barring a smooth transition. The second obstacle was changing classes nine times daily. In sixth grade we changed classes for math, science and social studies, but simply had to walk across the hall. We spent the majority of our day in homeroom.

Seventh graders, by contrast, gathered in homeroom for morning attendance and then proceeded forth to different rooms and different teachers in math, science, history, English, physical education, art, music and shop. The most profound difference between elementary and seventh grade, however, involved an across-the-board time change. Never a morning person, I firmly believed afternoon Kindergarten – running from 12:35 to 3:30 pm - the most appropriate schedule and one that would truly work in the best interests of students.

Elementary School began at 9:00 am and ended at approximately 3:30 pm. In Junior HS, in what most new seventh graders considered institutional child abuse, the school day began an hour earlier. According to these new draconian rules students had to be in homeroom by 7:30 am – an inhuman, ungodly hour known only to milkmen, paperboys, night watchmen and certain branches of the US Armed Forces.

On our first day of junior high in the autumn of 1975, the entire student body assembled in the high school auditorium for an assembly. Built between 1928 and 1929 the auditorium had a six-hundred seat capacity. Rows of connected wooden chairs filled the space; heavy metal springs kept them upright until one was lowered for use. When assemblies came to an end or a basketball game concluded and the audience stood, a cacophony of 'whack,' whack, whack, whack, whack, whack . . .' reverberated throughout the acoustically sensitive room.

The bottom half of the auditorium sloped slightly downward toward the stage and basketball court. The balcony, where upperclassmen congregated, stretched halfway over the lower seats where the younger students huddled. To say we were intimidated on our first day, sitting clustered in tight formation directly in front of the proscenium; would be an understatement. Not only were we lowest on the collective totem pole, we were positioned with the entire eighth grade and high school population behind us. My seventh grade cohorts and I dared not turn around. Even the densest kids knew not to unnecessarily draw attention to themselves; and so we stared intently at the stage.

At last Mr. McCann, CWHS principal, walked on stage and began speaking. Bill McCann was a tough old cob. That adjective recurs throughout these pages, but in a town like CW authority figures needed some hard bark on their frames. Canal Winchester didn't have an assistant principal in 1975; Mr. McCann handled student discipline, faculty, parents and staff.

The kids called him 'Zeke,' and it was an affectionate moniker; though not one spoken directly to the high school principal. *"Everyone called him 'Zeke,'"* junior Neal Seymour recalled, *"though not to his face. Once, when the Year Book had been dedicated in his honor, Mr. McCann received the award in the auditorium at an all-school assembly. When it was handed to him, without looking at the audience, he turned and said, 'Zeke thanks you.' The whole place lost it."* Despite his role as disciplinarian, most students liked him. *"He was a class act,"* recalled senior Rick Ross.

CWHS Principal William McCann

Varsity cheerleader Peggy Fox went further, saying, *"Bill McCann was one of the most wonderful human beings I've ever known. I first met him as a tot, when our families were neighbors. We all had so much respect for him as our principal; and a lot of love for him on a personal level. I miss his sense of humor, he always made me laugh."* William McCann stood approximately six-feet, 2-inches tall; was solidly built, always clean shaven; sported silver hair and had a dignified Roman nose.

His words were brief that morning – welcome students, do what you're told. At that he turned to exit stage-left and the spring loaded chairs began their cacophonous instrumental as the auditorium seats sprung upright. We lowly seventh graders were unceremoniously forced from the safety of our enclave into the wider environs of the old school. The stage upon which Mr. McCann had just addressed the student body was actually an extension off the north edge of the basketball court - an additional ten feet that marked the 'out-of-bounds' portion of the playing area and doubled as a stage.

In order to transform itself from hoops court to stage an enormous, velvety maroon curtain was pulled into place by hidden ropes and pulleys. Sitting in the auditorium, audiences could see both sets of stairs leading to the proscenium on either end of the dais. Every banquet, pep rally, musical performance, play or school-wide assembly saw CW students carefully - very carefully - ascending those few steps – to receive an award or join friends already on stage.

Perhaps the greatest fear universally shared at CHWS was that of tripping and busting one's ass in front of an all-school assembly. On rare occasions when some unfortunate clod did lose his footing the merciless din that arose immediately from the student- audience was unrelenting, loud and mortifying. Having born witness to such misfortune even the wildest kids slowed and crept up those few steps like Kwai Chang Caine moving methodically across rice paper.

On the far side of the stage and across the basketball court stood an entire wall of concrete bleachers. Like the stage, the bleachers were accessible via steps on either end. CWHS's cement stadium was unique and definitely not for the faint of heart. Spanning the rear of the gymnasium end to end, it looked like a series of hillsides under cultivation in Asia – square tier upon square tier ascending nearly to the gymnasium rafters. And their mud brown color didn't add much to their aesthetic quality either.

Facing this monstrosity from the court below was like looking up at an earthen Mayan temple with an anachronistic electronic scoreboard mounted on the adjacent wall. During basketball games opposing teams hunkered down on opposite ends of the cement bleachers along its front row – next to steps providing easy access to the court. The front row also accommodated three game time officials.

Beneath the Mayan Tiers on the hardwood.

Seated in metal folding chairs behind a narrow rectangular slab of wood bolted to the railing and used as a makeshift table; the athletic-apparatchiks occupied the best seats in the house. They kept score, recorded substitutions, maintained a running tally of fouls and operated the game clock. Most importantly they controlled the buzzer, which engendered an involuntary, 'Pavlovian' response every time they laid into it.

The gymnasium took a continuous beating. Besides formal athletic competitions, physical education classes were held there for every student 7-12 who moved through CWHS between 1929 and 1977. Lunchtime 'intramurals' saw hundreds of screaming seventh and eighth grade kids running to and fro, making out on the Mayan tiers, beating the hell out of one another and generally losing their collective, hormone addled minds. There was almost never a time when one group or another wasn't in the gym.

Its ceiling must have been one hundred feet high. Suspended from its lofty heights hung big incandescent lights that made low humming sounds when first turned on. Here and there plaster fell from walls revealing small patches of what looked like rusting chicken wire. The basketball court itself sported yellowed hardwood floors with sporadic dips and dead spots - whose locations were advantageously known only to the Canal Winchester Indians. In both 1974, and 1975, CW fielded excellent basketball teams, making game night something special.

The Varsity played on Tuesday and Friday nights during the regular season, and it was pitch dark by 5:30 pm in the Midlands that time of year. Outside of school during cold, dark winter evenings, everything stood still, quiet and bleak. Folks kept hands buried in their pockets, vapory breath condensed with every exhalation as hoops fans braved Ohio's arctic air on the way to the gymnasium. Once inside, however, a warm, brightly lit, completely different world revived the senses.

The bleak outer landscape was replaced by a maroon & white sea of humanity. And it was loud. Raucous fans, screaming cheerleaders, the "*thwack, thwack, thwack*" of bouncing basketballs; popping corn, the pep band's drums and horn sections, unruly children darting about, intermittent buzzers sounding play or timeouts, all combined into the cacophonous chorus of well-attended high school basketball games.

Varsity cheerleaders lined the steps of the Mayan tiers on either end of the bleachers beside their teams; racing onto court at halftime and timeouts to lead the crowd in rousing, whooping hurrahs. And they put their ample, healthy American lungs into it: "*Shoot-Two;*" *clap, clap;* "*Shoot-Two!*" *clap, clap; Shoot-Two!*"

When not on the floor they initiated verbal sparring matches with their female counterparts. Challenging the visiting cheerleading squad's womanhood with "*We got spirit, yes we do! We got spirit how bout you?*" Naturally such challenges had to be met, and visiting squads duly shot back the same rhetorical cheer; before long entire sections of fans were screaming, "*We got spirit, yes we do! We got spirit how bout you!*"

Cheerleaders were very much appreciated in those bygone days. Prior to the Internet and satellite TV the most glamorous females we ever saw walked the runways during Miss America contests on our flickering black & white TV screens. Just as lovely, fortunately, as that group of unobtainable beauties – at least in seventh grade male circles were - CWHS cheerleaders. Though dimly aware we weren't supposed to view them as sex-objects; they were unquestionably the sexiest objects ever observed by twelve year-old boys in Canal Winchester, Ohio in 1975.

Clad in pleated maroon skirts, maroon socks, maroon underwear and white turtleneck sweaters emblazoned with big maroon '*W*'s' stitched across lovely bosoms; sporting feathered hair, big smiles and ample applications of red lipstick, they rivaled Aphrodite herself. Standing on the yellowed hardwood beneath the incandescent lights, the smell of leather and sweat heavy in the gym; those lovely young lasses provided the perfect counterpoint to flying elbows, hairy armpits, enraged coaches and shrill whistles.

Running onto court to execute cheers they threw one another high into the air, performed cartwheels, leapt before doing the splits, and kicked their legs high in unison – imbued as they were with 'team-spirit.' All of which was watched intently by little girls in cheerleading outfits; proud parents; brothers & sisters, boyfriends; hoops fans and prepubescent, slightly drooling twelve-year-old boys.

During the winter of 1976/1977, CW indoor sports moved to a state-of-the-art gymnasium housed in newly constructed athletic facilities about a half-mile north of the high school. And the new gymnasium was truly impressive; it was larger, cleaner, and had better hardwood floors – the whole enchilada. But those final few winters in the old gymnasium, with its leaky roof and great concrete stands - where half the town tried to squeeze into its bleachers – created a more immediate and emotional experience than what awaited future players and fans.

Both the 1974 and 1975 basketball teams surpassed the one-hundred point mark in several ball games. When the score reached ninety, CW fans - en masse - would stand on their feet. When the magic number hit 100, the place erupted. Showers of maroon & white confetti fluttered down to the gym floor; the pep band blasted Rare Earth's '*I Just Want to Celebrate*' and the cheerleaders took to the floor to mark the milestone.

Outside the all important gymnasium was the first of three long corridors. Two trophy cases stood near the entrance to the dreaded office of the principal, and CW's classrooms were located off all three hallways. During summer and Christmas breaks janitors waxed the floors to a shiny gleam - which never lasted long. Hundreds of lockers lined the first and second floors. CWHS ran on nine, 45-minute class periods, and after every bell two hallways' worth of clanking, slamming puke-green locker doors contributed to the general din. Although not exactly sentient, it's fair to say CWHS's one great school building was truly alive nine months out of every year.

Canal Winchester High School, autumn 1975

Chapter VI:

FACULTY & STAFF

In 1975 the Canal Winchester school district employed approximately thirty-five teachers - grades 7-12. They were a busy lot. Administrative staff, maintenance personnel, cafeteria workers, teacher's aides and bus drivers all pitched in and slogged it out, but it was those thirty-five teachers that worked most closely with the students.

The superintendent in 1975 was C.A. Miller. Stocky and powerfully built Mr. Miller was an ex-Marine, ex-teacher and ex-coach. He was also quite shrewd. For example, C.A. owned a *Cadillac* but never drove it in town or parked anywhere near school. Rather, he continued to drive an old, beat-up station wagon to work; parking it out front of the offices and using it when attending football, basketball and baseball games.

C.A. took Canal's athletic programs seriously, as junior Neal Seymour remembered. *"One year at Thursday football practice Coach Locke is hot because the field hasn't been mowed. I mean it hadn't been mowed in awhile and we had a game the next night. Anyway, about that time we saw a guy on a tractor at the far end of the field in a shirt and tie. This guy's mowing the field; we couldn't figure out who it was until Coach says, 'Hell, that's C.A.' It made it seem like what we were doing was pretty important."*

*Superintendent C.A. Miller congratulates Jeff Black
on scoring 1,000 points in four years. 1974.*

Whereas the majority of elementary teachers were female the opposite held true for grades 7-12. Coaching staffs for football, basketball, baseball and track necessarily required a minimum of seven to ten male teachers. And so the kinder, gentler, more patient, and certainly more understanding atmosphere of grammar school disappeared in the masculine environment of grades 7-12. Some of the more memorable staff members of the 1970s are described below.

Librarian Jim Butts preferred – indeed, insisted on - the title, '*Media Center Specialist*;' which, together with his rather unfortunate surname, left him open to quite a bit of whispered ridicule. Mr. Butts was compactly built, bespectacled, stood about 5-feet, 9-inches tall; wore ties every day and had a full head of blazing red/orange hair. He was an excellent librarian: meticulous, organized, thorough – just what one might expect from a libr . . . er, media-center-specialist. Mr. Butts maintained a mental image on the locations of every item in his library, and used the term '*Shhhhh!*' at least one-hundred and fifty times a day.

Mr. Butts amid his books

The Social Studies Department was manned by William Lake, Dan Brisker and Jerry Jones; all three taught fulltime; coaching at least two sports each. Mr. Brisker coached varsity basketball and was good at it. He was what one had to be in order to succeed in coaching – fanatical. He lived and breathed hoops. *"Brisker was always talking basketball,"* one of his starters recalled. *"I mean, the guy just loved it; Brisker was always finding different things to try out."*

Head basketball coach and Athletic Director, Dan Brisker.

On one occasion, ill with flu; running a temperature well over 100' and with the attendant aches, pains and miseries common to the affliction – Mr. Brisker nevertheless drug himself to school; spending the day gagging, coughing, hacking, vomiting and devouring aspirins - prostrate on the couch in the faculty lounge while fellow teachers covered his classes. That night, however, he was front and center at tipoff, his mind intently focused on winning the game as his Indians ran onto the yellowed hardwood.

Bill Lake taught eighth grade American History and coached junior high football and basketball. The '*Great Lake*,' - as obnoxious 8th graders were wont to call him - was tall, thin armed and sported a mustache. He was slightly pear shaped, his hips wider than his shoulders, and sported a small paunch.

Mr. William Lake.

When he got worked up in class, or angry at basketball practice, the right corner of the '*Great Lake's*' mouth secreted a white puss-like liquid which clung to both upper and lower lip; expanding and contracting with every utterance. Its emergence, like the proverbial dead canary in the coal mine, alerted students and athletes that his blood was up. Well aware of this anatomical anomaly the '*Great Lake*' kept a handkerchief handy in his rear pocket so he could wipe his mouth when the need arose and soldier on.

Mr. Jones – Jerry Jones - taught seventh grade Ohio History – though using the term 'taught' is somewhat generous. It is more precise to say he 'talked' about many things, and occasionally Ohio History was one of them. Jerry Jones was the youngest member of CW's teaching staff in 1975. With dark black hair, hazel eyes and a trim, athletic build he was a hit with the student body. "*Jones was a good sport,*" recalled one of his students at the time. "*He had a boyish face like Paul McCartney. Jones looked a lot like Paul McCartney.*"

It is fair to say Mr. Jones was an enthusiast – of life, food, books, cars and especially women – and he immersed himself into all endeavors with great relish. He loved camping and fishing; working out and telling tall tales. Dad nicknamed him '*Mordecai,*' after the character Mordecai Jones from the 1967 movie *The Flim Flam Man.* In the movie George C. Scott plays a con artist who winds up in a series of epic car chases with his nemeses the sheriff - played by Harry Morgan - in hot pursuit. Like his big screen counterpart, Canal Winchester's very own Mordecai Jones loved to race cars as fast as they would go – whether to the grocery, high school or the movies.

Jerry Mordecai Jones.

Mr. Jones could be quite charming and many an adolescent female at CWHS swooned when he walked past. As with everything else Jones loved to eat. Not only did he eagerly scarf whatever was placed in front of him, he whimpered aloud while doing so. Mom fed Dad's younger coaches on occasion and used to roll her eyes listening to Mordecai devour chili; moaning and whimpering with delight. Eventually he'd hand her an empty bowl and ask for another.

Fellow teacher Dave Lewis described Mr. Jones this way: *"Jones? Man I hated him. Even when Jerry got to be 35-years old he still looked like he was fifteen. He had the baby face, you know. All the girls and all the mothers and everybody loved him."* According to Lewis, Jerry and his wife Jenny underwent a metamorphosis of sorts after arriving in town. *"When he first came to Canal Jerry was married and he had a family and he and his wife were, I mean, neither one would say shit if they had a mouthful. Neither one of them drank, it was unbelievable. I mean they were right out of Ozzie and Harriet. Jonesy was nice looking and very enthusiastic."*

The metamorphoses placed Mr. Jones in several precarious positions. The amorous attraction he engendered in women was eventually reciprocated, despite having a wife and two children. Once, at a weekend coaching clinic in Canton, Ohio, Mordecai made friends with a delightful young woman who turned out to be rather generous with her favors. Mordecai vanished; didn't make a single lecture and couldn't be located until they departed for home Sunday afternoon.

Fond of storytelling, Coach Jones did not subscribe to the notion lovers don't kiss and tell. He told. As a result of this encounter Dad and Coach Lewis decided to 'use Jonesey,' as they put it. Their scheme involved asking a female friend to write a missive to Mordecai; appearing as his Canton mistress. In the letters she explained that she planned to drive down to see him at the next football game; and that – ominously - she had a big surprise!

The mysterious epistles had the desired effect – Jones swallowed it hook, line and sinker. After receiving the second missive an ashen Mordecai approached Dad in the teacher's lounge and asked for advice. Clutching the letters, he kept shaking his head and repeating, *"Surprise? What surprise? God she's not pregnant is she? What surprise? What surprise?* The following morning he read one of the letters to Coach Locke and Coach Lewis before school began. Not to worry, his erstwhile buddies told Jones, they'd help out by 'running interference;' keeping his unwanted date from making contact with the missus.

Unbeknownst to Dad and Coach Lewis, Mordecai had determined to come clean, confess to his wife and let the chips fall where they may. Exiting early from football practice Jonesy drove home slowly - a first - rehearsing his confession speech while en-route. He had one of the letters in his left hand when he noticed the Columbus postmark. That last minute observation kept the entire episode a practical joke and averted a domestic tragedy – at least for the time being. He hit the brakes, did a U-turn on route 33, crossed the grassy median and put the pedal to the medal. Dad & Lewis were in a darkened film room with the football team, evaluating their next opponent when the double doors burst open revealing an enraged, animated, irate, Jerry 'Mordecai' Jones. Football players, sitting about the floor on either side of the projector recoiled when the doors slammed against the cement walls with a tremendous crash!

"*Locke! Lewis! You mother fuckers! I'll get you! I'll get you if it's the last thing I ever do!*" And with that he was gone. As debased as the culture has become in the first quarter of the 21st century; and as crude and profane as high school football players often are, they were not accustomed to hearing anything like that from one of their teachers in 1974. Locke & Lewis, on the other hand, were on the floor, laughing so hard they couldn't quite regain their composure. At the same time stunned football players were asking, '*Coach, what was that?*' '*What was that about coach?*' '*What's the matter with Coach Jones?*' "*Is everything OK? "Is Coach Jones alright?*" Fortunately for Mordecai his secret was safe with his 'buddies.'

Jerry Jones was also softhearted, as one of his football players recalled: "*What I remember most about Coach Jones,*" Kurt Swiger explained, "*was freshman year. I told him I wanted to play running-back even though I had always been a lineman. Coach said he really needed me on the line and I figured that was that because that was the response I had always been told. Well,*" Kurt smiled, "*he surprised me the next day in practice by putting me in the backfield. It was the only year I played running-back and I still appreciate him for giving me that opportunity, even though I don't know what changed his mind.*"

"*In class,*" remembered varsity cheerleader, Peggy Cox, "*Mr. Jones used to carry a baseball bat around. He used it to add emphasis to his storytelling; and his favorite song was Maggie May. I don't know why I remember that*"

Mrs. Thomas - Sue Thomas - was CW's physical education teacher. Slightly buck-toothed with thin, shoulder length brown hair, Mrs. Thomas looked and acted the way one might expect a high school gym teacher to look and act. She had fairly broad shoulders, a somewhat bulbous behind, wide hips and powerful legs. She wasn't fat, but rather powerfully built. Once or twice a year Mrs. Thomas came to work wearing a dress and heels – and she looked beautiful. But most days she wore maroon sweat pants, white T-shirts and spoke in a masculine, authoritative voice: "*All right line up! Dodge Ball. You wanna go boys against girls, or pick teams?*"

Sue Teach Thomas

Mrs. Thomas coached girls' basketball and softball and her players liked her a great deal. Her athletes addressed Mrs. Thomas as '*Teach.*' '*Hey Teach, can I go to the library?*' '*Teach, what time is practice tonight?*' A CW Indian through and through Sue Thomas attended all the football and basketball games sporting maroon and white hats and colorful CW pins, and she was a permanent presence in the gymnasium.

Mrs. Hartman – Ginny - was high school secretary and the only person in the building who actually knew what the hell was going on at any given time. Even before first bell her job entailed managing the ever-growing tide of humanity passing through the offices, classrooms and corridors. In addition to dealing with teachers, students, parents and administrators she took care of daily attendance slips, announcements, typing, teacher mail, copying and answering the phones.

Secretary Ginny Hartman

It's interesting how ideally suited so many teachers and staff were to their particular positions, because Mrs. Hartman – like Sue Thomas in physical education and Jim Butts in the libr . . . er, media center – 'looked' the way she ought to have looked, as if they'd been typecast. Her hair, already graying in 1975, sat high atop her pate' in a circular motif and she wore big, round, Elton John glasses attached to a chain about her neck. When Ginny Hartman smiled it lit up the room but you sure didn't want to cross her.

Once, during the second or third week of 7th grade Mrs. Woodward, our English teacher, took sick leave and Mrs. Hartman swung by to drop off some papers for the substitute teacher. Ginny noticed Greg Bruce, one of my best friends, sitting against the wall - evidently, she correctly surmised, for making the sub's life miserable. Mrs. Hartman decided on the spot that his attitude was somehow subversive. Looking him in the eye she said, *"You, come with me." "*What did I do?*" "I said come with me. Right Now!"*Greg knew that baiting substitute teachers was one thing, and pissing off Mrs. Hartman was another. He dropped his defiant edge and followed Mrs. Hartman dejectedly down the hallway.

Greg Bruce

On another memorable occasion Ginny got upset at a school board meeting. *"Ah, she was pissed,"* Dad recalled years later with a grin. *"The meeting got heated. Several parents and board members were shouting over top of each other. They usually followed protocol but this time things really did get ugly for a few minutes. Anyway, when it calmed down Ginny says, 'If this ever happens again I'm not coming back!' And it's quiet after that and then from the back someone said, 'You Promise?' God Ginny was pissed."*

Mr. Baker - David A. Baker - directed Canal Winchester's marching band, taught students nearly all the musical instruments and organized, drilled and led the band – whether marching on parade, at a contest or sweeping across Weiser Field. 'Bakes,' as his musicians fondly referred to him, was a man in perpetual motion - and one of the most popular teachers at school. His enthusiasm and competence were infectious, and students certainly admired and respected him.

Mr. David Baker

Bill Willison, for example, spoke for nearly all of Mr. Baker's students when he said, "*If I had years I couldn't put into words all the good things I remember about David Baker. He was fair, honest and diligent; funny, caring, giving and spent countless hours away from his wife and family to help us.*" And Mr. Willison's characterization was not unique; fellow offensive lineman Bill Griffith said this about Canal's band director: "*Mr. Baker was/is a rare and excellent talent that comes along once or twice in your lifetime. He was such a motivator of young people in music; he was just outstanding in every way. We loved him.*"

Approximately 5-feet, 10-inches tall, 'Bakes' had thin black hair parted to one side, a high forehead and aquiline nose. He was bespectacled and fond of wearing turtleneck sweaters under that 1970s fashion relic, the 'leisure suit.' "*Mr. Baker just cared so much,*" recalled trumpet player Judy Haffey. "*He took a real interest in us – not just as members of his band but as people. He really allowed us to enjoy music.*"

His annual band camp, held at Ohio University in Athens, was both an opportunity to put in some hard work and have a good deal of fun. Driving or hitching rides with Mr. Baker or assistant band director Kevin

Peters for the sixty-mile trip, the CWHS Marching Band descended on Ohio University, took up residence in campus dorms and practiced continuously on the Bobcat's football field for a week. According to trumpet player Judy Haffey – who remarked that at that time *"Band was my life"* – a good time was had by all.

"At night we'd tape newspapers across the doorways of our band mate's rooms," an enthusiastic senior recalled; *"in the morning they'd open up and see nothing but papers and masking tape; or we'd build pyramids out of pop cans right next to their doors so that when it opened the cans would come crashing down!"* Mr. Baker and Mr. Peters were obviously underpaid.

After camp broke the band marched in the 1975 Bexley Fourth of July Parade; (Where Judy Haffey once passed out from heat exhaustion) the Orient Band Concert; the Millersport Sweet Corn Festival and Canal Winchester' Labor Day Parade. All this *before* classes even started. Once school did get underway they performed for the football team toward the end of practices. On game nights they played before, during and after football games and marched at halftime. Throughout the autumn of 1975 they participated in contests, finishing a close 2nd that autumn at the Athens Band Contest and winning the Zanesville competition outright. That success was no accident. *"We had inspections before every football game,"* recalled one dedicated musician. *"Mr. Baker had us line up outside the band room and he'd look at every one of us, a uniform inspection."* A senior trumpeter concurred, *"We wore black shoes with white spats, high top hats, white gloves, maroon jackets with an overlay bib that hooked to the side and it had to be perfect for Mr. Baker. I remember many nights using* Brasso Polish *to shine my trumpet for inspection."*

The award-winning CWHS Marching Band

That fall, in addition to their usual repertoire the band mastered two pop tunes by the Doobie Brothers, 'Long train Running,' and 'Celebrate.' When football practice wound down on Thursday evenings - the day before the big game - the band assembled in the end zone and played both songs for their classmates. Gathered in the fading autumn light; attired in T-shirts and bell-bottom jeans - football players in shorts, torn jerseys and their football helmets - the evenings crisp and cool; renditions of 'Celebrate' and 'Long Train Running' stirred the heart.

Seventh graders were required to take shop class for one nine-week term, and it was taught by Mr. James Roth – Jim to his friends. Mr. Roth held a Bachelor of Science and Master of Arts from Ohio State University in Industrial Arts and Mechanical Drawing. His class was generally popular because students weren't required to sit still at a desk, take notes, or study for tests. Shop was held in the bowels of the building where the sounds of sawing, drilling, hammering and the occasional yowls of accident victims could not unduly disrupt sober, academic pursuits.

The big man himself - Mr. Roth – had lost the top half of his pinkie finger in Shop one year; doctors being unable to reattach it. My father certainly didn't endear himself to Mr. Roth, when, after the latter's return from the hospital Dad held out his hand and said, *"Welcome back Jim baby! Give me four and a half."* Coach Lewis described Jim Roth as follows: *"Oh, he, he was a lookalike – a dead ringer - for Fidel Castro. Uh, just picture Fidel Castro and that's Jim Roth. He was crazy."*

Coach Jim Roth

According to Coach Lewis, Mr. Roth enjoyed showing movies in class - *"and they weren't Bob Villa films either,"* Lewis remembered laughing. Roth recruited his teaching colleague to bring his physical education classes down to Shop on 'Movie Friday's.' *The Knute Rockne Story,* among others from the old *Profiles In Courage Series,* held students rapt attention. What the films had to do with mechanical drawing Coach Roth never divulged, but they did leave his students with a greater appreciation of classic American films. Lewis concluded, *"Roth could pull that stuff off but I would get busted."*

Mr. Roth was different: smart, funny, and with a slow, deliberate way of walking. He seemed to live somewhere other than where he happened to be at any given moment. As junior high football coach he did a lot of scouting and film work. Old black and white photographs of Mr. Roth confirm Coach Lewis's physical description; the resemblance to the Cuban dictator is obvious. He had Fidel's dark shaggy beard, bushy mustache, black hair, dark eyes, and body type.

Though Coach Roth had a laidback air, enjoyed showing old movies on Fridays, loved a good joke and comically resembled the Cuban dictator, students mistook his congenial nature at their peril. *"When we were in junior high school,"* recalled former student-athlete Neal Seymour, *"some kids were fighting and Roth stepped in and broke it up. The only problem was one of the kids wouldn't stop. So Roth grabbed him and put him up against the foam pads beneath the basket in the old gym. When the kid still didn't back off Roth lifted him up about four feet off the ground and held him out in front of him until he stopped. Right then everyone knew not to mess with that Fidel Castro guy."*

Dad, Coach Lewis, Brisker, Jones, Roth, Thomas and Lake, spent day after day in the classroom and on the practice fields, basketball courts and baseball diamonds. They watched game films; traveled all over central Ohio by school bus, scouted rivals, and strove to please parents, fans and their student-athletes. In our home we never saw Dad until 7:30 pm. or later. On Fridays he coached the varsity football game; never getting home before 11:00 pm. Saturday mornings he reviewed game film, and later attended junior-varsity football games. Saturday nights he scouted opponents and Sunday met with his coaching staff to 'game-plan' for the following Friday. Like the other coaches at CWHS, it should be noted, he was doing exactly what he loved; it was a deeply rewarding profession.

As noted previously, Canal Winchester High School was small, rural and rough around the edges, but it was home, as student Mary Matyac explained in our interview. *"I was the worst clarinet player in the band. Braces and being tone deaf didn't deter me. Mr. Baker didn't get paid a dime extra to try to teach me trombone or the drums. He finally settled on alto clarinet so that I didn't have to be last chair for four years. Almost every teacher at Canal had that quality of being willing to get to know the students. Worthington offered better equipment and a much more diverse curriculum but only two of my teachers could say hello to me by name when we passed in the hall. In Canal Winchester even the chief of police greeted me by name and gave me either a hug or a pat on the back when he saw me."*

INTERLUDE:

The Ghost of the 'Lew-I'

Physical education teacher and coach David Lewis has been frequently mentioned despite leaving CWHS after the spring of 1975. Coach Lewis came to CWHS in 1971; taught physical education, was an assistant football coach, and head baseball coach. He eventually became the football team's defensive coordinator. Coach Lewis looked, according to Dad, exactly like the kid on a *'Dutch Boy'* paint can. An apt description, for he was fairly squat, muscular, had ruddy cheeks, intense blue eyes, and sported a shock of wavy yellow hair that refused to lay flat atop his head.

Head Baseball coach and defensive coordinator, Dave Lewis.

'Intense' was also apt for his overall personae. Like Dad, he was a fanatic – pretty much about everything he did. When hired in 1971 he filled the roll Dad had held at Richwood High School when he started teaching and coaching in 1963 – young, enthusiastic, closer in age to the kids he taught and coached – and well liked by his students. Coach Lewis was a great storyteller and a student of both baseball and football.

Born in 1949 in Columbus, he says he became 'hooked' on football in the fifth grade – 1959 – when friends took him to an Ohio State football game at the Horseshoe. Coach Woody Hayes' Buckeyes had won national championships in 1954 and 1957, and were a resurgent power in the land when ten-year-old Dave ascended the stadium stairs and gazed out on the panorama for the first time *"I got hooked,"* he later admitted, *"I mean I just thought it was the greatest thing. I loved it; you know, the color, the pageantry, the whole thing."*

Graduating from high school in 1967 he enrolled at Capital University the following autumn, and played for the Capital Crusaders football team. That he was an offensive guard and defensive linebacker goes a long way in explaining his ardent personality. Between his freshman and sophomore years, he took a job at the Wonder Bread Bakery in Columbus; working less than twenty-five feet from the giant ovens. *"I was always close to that oven,"* he noted in our interview, *"and it was hot! I mean it was miserable and I remember looking at those poor guys who were lifers there and thinking, I've got to study!"* The realities of what awaited those who failed to study - factory work or perhaps a stint in Vietnam – provided ample motivation and he graduated in the spring of 1971.

Interviewing shortly thereafter at CW, both the principal and district superintendent explained to the aspiring teacher the importance of small town athletics; asking bluntly if he could deal with the pressure that came with coaching. He assured them he could. After fielding a series of questions Mr. Lewis thought he was on the verge of signing his first professional teaching contract when C.A. Miller unceremoniously pulled the document from his grasp.

Looking up from the spot where his contract had been he locked eyes with the superintendent, who said solemnly: *"David, before you sign this contract I want you to take it home and think about it carefully."* The "Lew-I's" sky blue eyes widened as he listened to the earnestness in C.A.s voice: *"You have never coached before. You have always been an athlete. You have never been on the other side. There is one thing I want you to know: As superintendent I'll fire you before you get me fired!"*

Coach Lewis suddenly felt uncertain about teaching at Canal Winchester High School, but C.A. wasn't finished. *"The baseball program* has got to get turned around, it's been a thorn in my side for years and I'm not going to have it cost me my job. So remember, before you sign that contract, that it will cost you your job before it will cost me mine." The "Lew-I" drove back to Columbus feeling a bit shell shocked and wary of ever returning to Canal Winchester.

That evening he made several phone calls. After speaking with teaching mentors and former high school coaches, he decided to take the job. They explained it to him this way: *"Dave,"* his former high school football coached advised, *"There's an honest superintendent. You can work for him. It's the sons-a-bitches, the ones that all they do is talk about 'Education this and Education that - and then fire you because your under .500 as a coach. Those are the son-of-a-bitches you don't want to work for. The guy sounds honest."*

With that Lewis joined the faculty of CWHS. Assigned to coach two sports and teach fulltime, his new contract awarded him $7,900 annually – or $303.84 every two weeks. Despite Lewis's short tenure at CWHS, his imprint was lasting. He liked to tell his athletes, *"If you want something bad enough, you can reach out there and take it."* His passion and intensity rubbed off on players; Lewis's junior-varsity football team was unbeaten and un-scored upon during his final season in 1974 and he never gave C.A. Miller cause to fire him as baseball coach.

Dave Lewis was also a loyal friend to Dad. Young, ambitious coaches, hired as assistants, often bridle at the limitations placed upon them. But Coach Lewis was dutiful to both Dad and his program, and spent a lot of time at our home socially. Together they fished and hunted morel mushrooms; drank beer, watched old black & white movies and talked sports. After moving to CW Coach Lewis met and fell in love with Mary Jo Drumheller. They married in 1971, but by 1974 had divorced.

Dad helped Dave through that difficult time, later recommending him for his first head coaching job at Bishop Ready High School. On the other hand, Dad didn't miss everything about Coach Lewis once he had left. Sharing a small coaching office where staff changed clothes before practice, the *"Lew-I"* felt the need to leave "presents" for his coaching mentor. During his free period Lewis would go down to that office to relieve himself, which was standard-operating-procedure for a lot of the staff. Most teachers found it difficult to lecture students wearing suit and tie and then sit on a toilet, pants about their ankles, trying to relieve themselves in front of their charges after class.

The coach's office, therefore, became a popular destination for Jones, Brisker, Lewis, Roth and Locke. But it was Lewis who thought leaving un-flushed turds marinating in the bowl an ingenious idea. Indeed, not only did he opt not to flush, he expedited the fermentation process by turning the small heater next to the toilet on high before shutting the office door.

Dad failed to recognize Lewis's plot for what it was the first time it happened. Finding the door closed; the furnace running and an un-flushed turd in the commode - he figured someone just forgot to flush. Having failed to catch on even after the third offense, Lewis, passing him in the hallway, mercifully asked, *"Did you enjoy your gift?"* The light bulb at last lit, and the identity of the phantom shitter was known.

Revenge, of course, is a dish best served cold. Coach Lewis recalled his comeuppance: *"Oh my God,"* he began, *"it's like the sixth or seventh game of the season and practice is hum-drum, slow, and Locke says 'we have to do something to get practice going, we've got to get the kids jacked up.' So we started arguing in practice,"* at the memory of which the *"Lew-I"* smiles. *"It was always a classic,"* he continued, *"the varsity was going to move the ball down the field and my JV-team was going to stop them."*

"We'd blow the play dead and then start in at each other; 'He was down right here!' I'd yell, and Locke would bark, 'No he wasn't - he was not! His knee wasn't down!' And we'd argue back and forth and the kids would pick up on it and I'd go back to the defensive huddle and say, 'God damn it! I don't care if he is the head coach you guys know that's cheating!' and within a few moments both sides were tearing into each other full bore and practice had gone from mundane to fever-pitch." Coach Lewis, laughing now, explained how their staged confrontation morphed into revenge.

"So we were really getting after it one practice, and, uh, back then we used to shower with the kids; and so we did our thing during the scrimmage and we come in after practice and I go in and I'm taking a shower. And I hear Mike in the coach's office and its sounds like he's tearing the place apart. And I'm thinking to myself, 'what in the Hell is going on in there?' Well," (Laughter) *"I come out of the shower and I just put my towel on and Locke walks out of the coach's office with his starter pistol."*

"He was the track coach and he had a starter pistol in his office; well he walks out with it – and let me tell you it looks like a gun to me – and he says, 'God-damn-it Lewis I'm sick of your shit!' And then BAM BAM, BAM! (Laughter) Were the kids down there? "Oh yea, they were in the shower and were hitting the ground. Guys in the locker room are running and guys in the shower are dropping for cover."

"And it's like, oh man, my heart stopped and you know; I had to go back into the shower so I could clean the shit off my leg. I mean, I got shit running down my leg, (laughter) and he just thought it was the funniest thing in the world. Two years later, my last year, he got me again, only this time I was taking a dump when: BAM! BAM! BAM! (Laughter) I mean he is sick!"

It wasn't all fun and games with Coach Lewis, though, as student athlete Kurt Swiger recounted years later. Kurt played both football and baseball and got a full dose of the *"Lew-I's"* intensity in action. "He definitely had a temper," Mr. Swiger began. "After losing a baseball game to Berne Union in the spring of 1975, he lost it big time. Coach started screaming and ranting and throwing things. We started running bases and then moved to the track. Lewis was just waiting for someone to quit so he could flip out again; Carl Swartz did. They both started screaming at each other – face-to-face – for minutes. This was good news for the rest of us: we quit running and left. Coach Lewis was too busy screaming at Carl to notice."

According to Dad, however, Kurt Swiger - Carl Swartz's adolescent contemporary - may not be the best character witness for "The Lew-I." During a football scrimmage with Colonel Crawford in 1973, Kurt Swiger and Coach Lewis shared an encounter neither would ever forget. "Oh my God," Dad began the tale, still laughing at the scene over thirty years later. "It was one of the funniest things I ever saw, Lewis was beside himself, I mean, I thought he was going to have a stroke. We're scrimmaging Colonel Crawford, and you gotta remember back then coaches weren't allowed on the field - that changed a year or two later, but we were on the sidelines; after the varsity had played, our reserves took the field just before half."

"Now keep in mind," he continued, "the reserves were freshman and sophomores for the most part with very little experience working together as a unit. And because CW was such a small school, they had to learn more than one position. Anyway, Colonel Crawford took the ball on their 30 yard line - there were no punts - and begins its first offensive drive. With the JV on the field I stepped back and let Lewis run the show. On 1st down, Crawford runs a dive play up the middle and it goes ten yards, easily ten yards. Lewis screams, 'C'mon Ron! Where are you?' "Ron was the middle linebacker and was standing right beside the Lew-I on the sidelines."

"I'm standing a few feet to the right and rear watching this, OK," Dad says with obvious glee. "And Ron says, 'I'm right here coach.' "Lewis looks to his right, and there stands Ron." **LEWIS:** 'Why aren't you in there?!' **RON:** 'I twisted my ankle.' **LEWIS:** 'Tom! Tom! Where's Tom?' "Tom alternated at middle linebacker." **TOM:** 'I'm right here coach.' **LEWIS:** 'Why aren't you in there? Why aren't you in there? Get in there!' "As Tom's sprinting toward the huddle Lewis is yelling at the kid, talking to himself, 'Why hell yes! Hell yes they can get first downs up the middle against ten men with no middle linebacker!'

The memory of Lewis's frustration animates Dad's re-telling. "I mean, this was their first play; Lewis is calling defenses exactly eight seconds and there's no linebacker. So as Tom runs to the huddle another kid playing defensive end figures he's coming in for him and trots to the sideline. And Tom, seeing the kid who plays defensive-end leave, forgets during those twenty yards from the sidelines Lewis's instructions to play linebacker, and takes over at defensive end. So Lewis's got two defensive ends to one side, ten men and no linebacker!"

"Crawford runs its second play, and bam, another easy 15 yards right up the middle!" At this point Dad's laughing so hard we stop the interview for a moment. "God, I was losing it, and Lewis is pissed! He's yelling, 'God damn-it! God damn-it! God damn-it! Where's Dan? Where's Dan? God damn-it!' "Dan also played some defensive end and Lewis grabs him by the facemask, and the Lew-I is red-faced, his eyes are bulging and he's nearly in poor Dan's helmet, when he draws a deep breath, and talks real slow."

LEWIS: 'Dan, I want you to get in there and play defensive end. Tell Tom to move to linebacker. You go to defensive end, tell Tom to move to linebacker. You got it?' **DAN:** 'Got it Coach.' "You're not going to believe this, but I swear to God, Dan lines up at right defensive end! Canal has two right defensive ends, one left defensive end, 11 men on the field with no middle linebacker. Crawford runs its third plays and it goes right up the middle for another 15 yards! Lewis is going Berserk!" **LEWIS:** 'Time out! Time out! Time out God damn-it! Time out!'

"Now you gotta remember that the rules said coaches couldn't go on the field, they had to remain on the sidelines; only one player could come confer with the coach - and none of them wanted to leave the safety of the herd. Lewis is apoplectic! He screams, 'Swiger! Kurt Swiger! Get over here!' "Kurt Swiger," Dad continued, "was a really bright kid, a really smart young man - and he wasn't stupid. He leaves the huddle but stops a good 15 yards from Lewis, not wanting to risk life and limb. Lewis, seeing this, is incredulous and starts in on him." LEWIS: 'Swiger! Are you a straight-A student? Are you a straight-A student?'*

"And Swiger looks spooked, man. He's not sure where this is going but doesn't want to give the wrong answer. He just nods in the affirmative.." LEWIS: 'Then go out there, grab Tom by his fucking facemask and drag his ass to middle linebacker!' *"Thank God we were fifty miles from home,"* Dad said shaking his head. *"The F-word wasn't exactly accepted in polite society back then. Especially from molders of American youth. It must have rattled poor Kurt something awful because - and you're not going to believe this - he grabs Tom and moves him to the other defensive end spot."*

"I swear to God. We line up, and the look on Lewis's face; oh my God. Canal's reserve defense has two right defensive ends, two left defensive ends and no linebackers. Crawford runs up the gut for 9 more yards. He grabs a kid named John, and he's no longer screaming; he desperate, pleading." LEWIS: 'Please John, I'm begging you, go out there, tell Dan to come here and tell Tom to move to linebacker. Got it?' JOHN: 'Got it coach!.' *"So John runs onto the field, but Dan doesn't come off. We've got 12 men; two defensive ends on the left, two on the right, and a middle linebacker. All four defensive ends were broken down in defensive end stances, and they kept looking at each other."*

"The refs never call us for too-many-men on the field, and Crawford's coach called a sweep. With 12 guys and two defensive ends we stuffed them for a loss. Undeterred, their coach called another sweep to the other side. Again, the refs didn't notice our 12th man, and with two defensive ends they lost more yardage. And our reserves ended up winning - without a middle linebacker! But that scene between the Lew-I and Swiger, with Kurt refusing to near the sideline, God it was one of the funniest things I've ever seen."

Coach Lewis was intense, passionate and driven; but no longer part of the Canal Winchester School District. The "Lew-I" accepted the head coaching position at Bishop Ready High School after the 1974/1975 school year.

Chapter VII:

CWHS - THE WAY IT WAS

Located beneath the school, Canal's concrete walled weight room had a dungeon-like quality. The door - of course - had been painted maroon and the room white. Inside it was basically a hollowed square of cement blocks. A Universal weightlifting machine occupied the center of the room and along its outer edges were scattered the newfangled free weights. On the wall Dad painted the names of athletes who had bench pressed 200, 250 and 300 pounds, and gaining such recognition under the 250-Lb-Club, for example, became an important accomplishment in weightlifting circles. Near the exit Dad painted a poem he had written:

Breathe a little deeper, love a little stronger
Push a little harder, work a little longer
Though winning is joy and losing is sorrow
Live each day as if there is no tomorrow
For the worst hurt of all is what 'might have been'
And you will not pass this way again.

The bowels of the school were essentially concrete catacombs. Long corridors framed by cement blocks led past the weight room, junior high locker room, and elementary art room before finally emerging into the lighted hallway outside the high school locker room. Sited directly below the Kindergarten, the locker room was Spartan and utilitarian;

having been designed with destructive adolescent males in mind. It also possessed a distinctive smell, different from other parts of the school and one that lingered year-round. The combination of sweat, mildew, toilets, shampoo, athletic tape, talcum powder, *Ben Gay* and the residue of youth lingers still.

The locker room's cement floors had to be negotiated with some finesse, especially after football players donned cleats. About once a day during the gridiron season someone would bust his ass and be subjected to immediate, unmerciful ridicule. Players consequently trod gingerly on their way into and out of the locker room. On entering, to the immediate left was an equipment room where helmets and shoulder pads were stored in the offseason. Also on the left was a long, rectangular chalkboard where Dad drew up plays and formations.

Five wooden benches bolted to the floor took up the center of the room. Players sat there before games and at halftime but used them sparingly during practice weeks. Fifty orange lockers lined the walls. The coach's office – of 'Phantom-Shitter' fame – had two square glass windows that looked out on the showers and taping table. Behind the showers were three urinals and two commodes. The shower room was square; its floor patterned with hundreds of tiny blue and gray tiles.

Cheerleaders showed up on game days to decorate lockers; using maroon and white crape paper, posters and even balloons during homecoming week. Sweethearts of various players also arrived to decorate their beaus' lockers. This practice was an important rite in the CWHS mating ritual. Photographs, candy, stuffed animals and balloons all made their appearance inside the lockers, but the most important item by far was the 'private note.'

A pregame love letter of sorts, in which decorator's might simply indicate interest by writing, *"You're an awesome player! Good Luck! Beat those Tigers!"* If, on the other hand, the decoratee was in a serious, long term relationship, he might expect a lengthy, amorous epistle. On occasion players received '*Dear John*' letters – which, as one might imagine, didn't do much for their mental state prior to football games.

CWHS was a noisy place. Old pipes popped and pinged, band instruments were continually being played, the voices of hundreds echoed in the halls, lockers were forever opening and shutting, shrill whistles carried on the air, class bells rang every 45 minutes and the long yellow school buses constantly pulled in and out of the parking lots.

Mr. McCann and the faculty spent a good bit of time separating overly affectionate lovers. The bowels of the school leading to the locker room proved to be a particular hot spot. Out of sight from prying eyes the basement corridors afforded numerous dark recesses and hideouts for those wishing to get better acquainted. At least once or twice a week a beaming young man and his red faced female companion emerged from the basement with a staff member not far behind.

The cement bleachers in the gymnasium, especially the top row, also served as a 'make-out' point. Every day during seventh grade intramurals, for example, Becky Seymour, - cute, redheaded, brown-eyed Becky Seymour - was locked in the arms of Walter Ball. Having had a crush on Becky since fifth grade their daily encounters certainly didn't elevate my opinion of her companion - Damn that Walter Ball!

The balcony on the opposite side of the court and accessible from the second floor was also a popular romantic destination. Couples set up shop away from the hallway entrance on the far side of the projector room, thereby obscuring passionate embraces from intrusive, curmudgeonly staff. *"Break it up!'* was the usual admonition to cool the ardor of the overly amorous - but alas it didn't do much good.

Canal Winchester's adolescent males, when not beating the hell out of each other, were beholden to a primordial, biological mandate: to couple with as many nubile young females as physiologically possible. Unfortunately that mandate is at odds with societal conventions. This was especially true in 1975.

Four years earlier, in 1971, the Canal Winchester School Board unanimously approved guidelines forbidding pregnant students from taking part in the district's extracurricular activities - sports, band, student council, graduation ceremonies etc. To ensure that the rules were fairly administered the same restrictions applied to the lecherous lads responsible for the impregnations. As it turned out the backlash against promiscuity engendered a backlash against the backlash, and two years after enacting the 'Maroon Letter Policy,' it was abolished. Once again, in the spring of 1973, pregnant females were entitled to plod across the stage at commencement.

Notwithstanding town elders frowning on young romance, the decision to loosen the rules was probably for the best. Young men and young women are genetically programmed to seek each other out. Gary Cox, for example, found CW's sexual mores quite advanced for the time; *"I was a virgin when we moved to CW,"* he recalled. *"But I had this horny love affair with a girl who was in the band's rifle/flag corps. One time we were driving in my car to go see her boyfriend when she just started putting her tongue in my ear. I pulled the car to the shoulder as fast as I could and laid her right there with the engine running. God I loved Canal Winchester."*

Denims, flannel and T-shirts dominated the fashion scene. Farm kids wore boots and jeans to school; and when Future Farmers of America (FFA) held meetings the hallways became a sea of blue and gold corduroy jackets. Mary Matyac recalled the culture shock of moving from an upper class, Columbus suburb to Canal Winchester: *"My first day at CW,"* she remembered, *"I found out you could feed popcorn to the mouse who lived in the hole in the corner of the study hall. And missing class for the county fair was ok if you had livestock and you were expected to miss class for the harvest."* FFA's leader, Howard Siegrist, had a Bachelor of Science and Masters of Science in vocational agriculture from Ohio State University. Kids called him *'Siggy-the-Piggy,'* and Mr. Siegrist's features and slight lisp encouraged the sobriquet.

Looking more like a math teacher or CPA than an outdoors, jack-of-all-trades vocational agriculture teacher, he combed his thin black hair to one side over a head resembling an orb. Wearing heavy, black 'Clark Kent' glasses, sporting a slight paunch and speaking with the aforementioned lisp; Mr. Siegrist was forever walking about with his shirt hanging out and slacks tucked into muddy boots, accentuating his odd appearance.

Industrial Arts, Howard Siegrest.

His disciples, most of whom transferred to the Joint Vocational School after sophomore year, were a tough lot. Mr. Siegrist's future farmers represented a distinct subdivision within the student body: According to prevailing adolescent wisdom there were jocks, (tracksters, golfers, football, basketball & baseball players); nerds, (kids taking advanced math, chemistry courses and belonging to the chess club).

Band-fags, (an unfortunate label assigned to young men who failed to partake in physical tests of courage); hoods, (the small but enduring minority of drug taking, class-skipping, cigarette smoking, dope toking, alienated stoners); and 'Siggy the Piggy's *Shit Kickers* , who arose early to feed livestock, wore muddy boots and blue corduroy FFA jackets to school.

Eventually ridicule and derision became too much for Mr. Siegrist and he left teaching; but in 1975 he hadn't yet reached his tipping point. The staff who remained year after year embodied a small, hard core of veteran teachers – seemingly permanent fixtures at CWHS; and though students didn't necessarily like all of them, they learned to respect them – sometimes the hard way.

While that small core remained steadfast numerous teachers came and went: some retiring, others taking higher paying positions in different school districts, others leaving on their own terms to enter entirely different professions. Kids being kids, some teachers left without ever looking back; because they couldn't handle – or control - their students.

One such unfortunate educator was Elizabeth Tewksbury, who taught high school English at Canal Winchester in 1972. On one occasion during her brief tenure, while walking down the third floor hallway, Dad heard a group of students raising hell in one of the classrooms. They were unruly, loud and getting louder. He quickened his pace and strode forcefully into the room to find out what was going on.

"*I walk in there,*" he said, "*and the kids are going nuts and there's no teacher. So I bark in a stern voice, 'Sit down! Sit down right now and knock it off!' You know, and the kids jumped back in their seats. 'Who's class is this?'*" he demanded, and one of the students said, Miss Tewksbury's. Figuring that she had received an important phone call or perhaps had become ill, Dad made his way toward the desk. "*So I ask where she went,*" he continued, "*and the kids point to the desk. I'm thinking what the hell? Why are they pointing to the desk? So I bend down and look under the desk. And there's Tewksbury, on the floor, almost in a ball and she's holding a book. She looks up at me and says, 'I just had to get some peace and quiet!' *".

Kids at CW, like kids pretty much everywhere, were quite adept at spotting weakness - and teachers like Miss Tewksbury didn't last long. Unfortunately for Miss Tewksbury, it wasn't only students who perceived her timidity. "*She was squirrely man. Bless her heart,*" Dad opined thirty years later. "*She was high strung, nervous, always worried about something. One time the superintendent planned to observe several classes and the 'Tewkes' comes into the teacher's lounge and she's frantic. I'm in there with the 'Lew-I' and she explains how she'd worked all night on her lesson plans and is terrified.*"

Laughing, he continued, "*So she's in there running around like a chicken with her head cut off and so I said to her: 'Don't sweat It Tewkes; our superintendent is pretty easygoing. I've been here five years and the only thing C.A. ever reprimanded me for was fucking the cheerleaders.'*" Laughing hysterically now, Dad concluded, "*Oh man, it blew her mind. She stopped and looked at me, just staring blankly, and then she shrieked and ran out of* the room. *And I look back and Lewis is on the floor, literally on the floor. He was lying on the couch and had rolled off and is on his stomach beating the floor. God we laughed till we cried"* As much as he enjoyed relating Miss Tewkesbury's tale of woe, his favorite part of the story is that after leaving CW she became a professor of education.

For students life in Canal Winchester revolved around the old schoolhouse at 300 Washington Street. To us it seemed as permanent a fixture as the big Maple Tree on its front lawn. Most kids had no idea that the old wing dated to 1862, or that the gymnasium was constructed in 1929; we didn't know how much money teachers earned; that coach Lewis was fond of leaving organic presents for my father; or that the maroon & white colors we sported so proudly originated with the 'Violet Guards,' who wore white pants, violet shirts and drilled every month between 1844 and 1846.

Nor did most care; our school was the center of the known universe because we spent most of our time there. Her three stories, long hallways, puke green lockers, decades-old classrooms, and the brick façade was a home away from home. With the exception of June, July and August, the majority of our early lives were spent within its hallowed halls.

Chapter VIII:

THE POOL

The Canal Winchester Pool, twenty-one years old in the summer of 1975, opened in the spring of 1954 at 180 Groveport Road. An empty field lay south of the pool across Groveport Road in the hazy summer distance; a parking lot to the west; an alley north and another large lea on its eastern edge. In the pool's parking lot oily tar used to patch cracked and crumbling blacktop bubbled on hot summer days, and bi-weekly tests of manhood required piercing them with one's fingers.

An old rusted cable sagged between sawed-off telephone poles marking the lot's boundary; and grassy medians separated cars. The pool itself was shaped like an upside down letter L. The south (bottom) end was three feet deep, gradually increasing to a depth of five feet at its north edge. The square (top) - known as "The Deep End," – measured 10-feet in depth with a steep grade connecting it to the rest of the pool.

Three life guard chairs and a sea of cement surrounded the pool, and the entire facility was enclosed

A summer day at the CW Pool

by a ten foot fence. Once the gates opened at noon, a lone diving board on the edge of the Deep End became the pool's focal point. Dad managed the pool over the summers to earn extra money; hiring lifeguards, changing filters, vacuuming the pool, adjusting chlorine levels, expelling trouble makers; and ensuring that a good time was had by all.

In my humble twelve-year old opinion, Dad's summertime vocation meant that he had reached the pinnacle of success. Accompanying him early in the mornings I braved the cold waters to vacuum the bottoms and search for lost coins. At noon the high pitched whine of CW's siren signaled kids across town that the pool was open for business, though a line had usually formed well before that hour. Old Glory waved from a flagpole at the entrance. Inside, swimmers scampered on the wet concrete, while from a wooden bench outside the chain link fence observers watched those frolicking within.

Mrs. Ulrich – Jean Ulrich - manned the entrance. She knew nearly everyone in town. Mrs. Ulrich had snow-white hair, wore stylish ladies glasses and was kind to all. In August, she bought the pails of blackberries I gathered along the railroad tracks, and baked homemade pies. And she knew how to handle kids, especially boys. Her oldest son, Jim, was about to enter his junior year in high school in 1975. How such a sweet, considerate, kindly women could have spawned such a wild man God only knew.

From September to June Mrs. Ulrich worked in the school cafeteria, and then spent her summers manning the gate at the CW Pool. Both locations were prime gathering places for kids, and it may have been that Jean purposefully opted for positions that kept her in close proximity to Jim. He wasn't a trouble maker, just wild. He played third base on the varsity baseball team and was an Ohio Scholastic Scholar. A non-scholar myself, Jim nevertheless came to my attention, becoming, during the summer of 1975, an early philological hero.

Thin and wiry, he had wavy blond hair parted in the middle. His dark eyes were piercing and intense; when unsupervised by his mother, Jim took on a decidedly un-scholastic demeanor. Once, while playing pickup basketball on the 'Chamberlains' – an outdoor court with eight-foot baskets – just weeks before school started, Jim excoriated his teammates for fouling and 'cherry-picking.' Sitting alongside Tim Priser on the swings next to court we watched and listened, hoping to get a chance to play. Ulrich wore gray shorts and a gold crucifix; long blond hair clung matted to the back of his neck from sweat, and he had peeled off his

T-shirt. Anyway, after getting fouled he yelled, "*Watch what you're doing - fuck wad!*" The word 'fuck' was ubiquitous despite its cachet as the worst thing young men might utter. Its pairing with 'wad,' however, sounded unimaginably vulgar; after calling his opponent a 'fuck wad," Ulrich spit disdainfully on the asphalt and dribbled the ball down court.

Wordsmith and personal hero, Jim Ulrich.

It sounded so exquisitely dirty - it was wonderful! The dirtiest insult ever uttered. Once the initial awe wore off I commenced planning for the right situation to repeat it. Unable to share my new phrase at home the unveiling would have to premiere at the CW Pool. Canal Winchester's swimming pool, ironically, didn't offer much room for actual swimming. Instead kids threw pebbles and pennies and then dove to retrieve them; tossed waterlogged Nerf balls back and forth over the unsuspecting; swam through one another's legs; vied to see who could hold his breath longest under water, splashed each other unmercifully, and played tag and hide & seek amongst the throng.

Another popular favorite involved descending beneath the water line, belting out some word or phrase, and then resurfacing, challenging friends to decipher the bubble-filled enunciation. Rick Shirk and I opted to go swimming just days after Jim Ulrich had shared his delightful prose, so naturally I had to try it underwater, almost the moment we entered the pool. There's something about water pressure - slight as it is just below the surface - that creates disharmony in one's ears. Words uttered below – BLUE - for example – sounds more like Whooaaaghh!

Despite this difficulty I asked Rick if he could tell what I was going to say under water. Rick said OK, and counted – *"One, two, three!"* At three we drew breath and slid beneath the waves. After allowing a few bubbles to escape - facilitating sinking - my eyes fixated on Rick; having calculated for depth, distance, current and drag I bellowed: *"Fuck Wad!"* which sounded like *"Bhwooguh Wouadouagh!"* in Aqua-speak. At the surface Rick wiped his eyes and said. *"I have no idea."* Disappointed I translated - *"Fuck Wad."* Rick looked at me for a long moment; leaned in, smiled and then began laughing. Abruptly he asked: *"Where'd you hear that?"* I confessed I got it from Jim Ulrich. He laughed some more before shaking his head and adding, *"That fucker's crazy!"*

The pool's concession stand was packed during breaks. Two lines formed immediately; swimmers fueling up on burgers, hotdogs and fries; apple pies, Chico-Sticks, Snicker bars, M&Ms, Reese's Cups, Sweet Tarts, *Cocoa-Cola*, Mountain Dew and every other sugary treat not recommended by local dentists. Once, Laura and I asked Mom for money to visit the stand. She replied *"No. We come to the pool to swim not to eat. If you want to eat we'll go home and you can eat. If you ask again we're leaving."*

A typical day at the CW pool started at noon and ran to 5:00 pm, whereupon we gathered up our bikes and raced home for supper. 'Supper' is a relative term. A peanut-butter & jelly connoisseur with free reign of the kitchen, my summer suppers often consisted of two PB&Js, Nestles chocolate milk and chips – if we had them. The speed with which said peanut-butter & jelly sandwiches were assembled is shocking in retrospect. It is probably fair to say Nestle' Chocolate Quick; Wonder Bread, Jif and Smuckers owed much of their financial success in the 1970s to my fondness for their products.

With dinner in hand it was time to watch *The Big Valley*. While Nick, Heath and Jarred Barkley battled the forces of evil around Stockton, California – stoically suffering Victoria Barkley's (Barbara Stanwick) mandatory, moralizing nightly speech to any who dared cross her brood – I sat transfixed; absent mindedly devouring my meal.

When the show ended at 6:00 pm its episodic theme music sent me into paroxysms of joy. *The Big Valley! Duh duh-duh/duh - duh/duh, duh/ duh. The Big Valley; duh, duh, duh/duh. Na, na na na na/na. Na na na na na na/na. The Big Valley . . ."* That music, lighting some weird primordial fuse, triggered involuntary spasms sending me over the edge: dancing, spinning about the room, jumping up and down on the couch. This bizarre behavior was Mom's cue to send me back to the pool. Sometimes Laura went with me, but I returned nearly every night, staying until the 9:00 pm closing.

The pool was also Canal's primary summer location for the sexes to mingle and strut their stuff. When Sandy Hays and Cindi Hunter walked into the pool, for example, the collective behavior of the young men inside changed the moment they were picked up on "Maledar." Postures improved, poses were struck, muscles twitched and millions of years of evolutionary biology involuntarily kicked in.

Whispering and laughing commenced. One afternoon I was sitting behind junior-to-be Gregg Wright, who had just moved to town, when he said of Sandy Hays - to no one in particular - *"Damn she's got a nice body. Mmmm, Mmmm Good."* Staring at the object of his desire like a dog ogles a bone, another admirer replied, *"Fuck-N-A! She's fine."*

Sandy Hays did indeed posses a shapely form. Her dark brown hair, olive skin, bubbly personality and penchant for wearing white bikinis served her well. Cindi Hunter, a year older than Sandy and poised to enter her junior year of high school in the summer of 1975, was an absolute knockout. Indeed, when God Almighty created Cindi Hunter He spent an inordinate amount of time on the lass, bestowing upon her every conceivable physical attribute.

Cindi Hunter, the object of Little Locke's adolescent admiration.

Not surprisingly, Cindi Hunter was a varsity cheerleader. With long, sandy blonde hair, brown eyes and an hourglass figure, she looked like Raquel Welsh – at least to me. Ah, to be young and alive in 1975. On the transistor radios that summer the following tunes were played in heavy rotation: *Love Will Keep Us Together* by the Captain and Tennille, *Rhinestone Stone Cowboy* by Glen Campbell, *Philadelphia Freedom* by Elton John, *Lyin' Eyes* by The Eagles, *Jive Talkin* by the Bee Gees, *Black Water* by the Doobie Brothers, *Shining Star* by Earth, Wind and Fire and John Denver's *Thank God I'm A Country Boy*.

A few swimmers, including yours truly, habitually stayed late. Occasionally, however – perhaps five or six times a summer - the last few swimmers departed early; when that happened Dad called home, telling Mom and Laura to get ready for a car ride. From 1972 to 1977 our family car was a 1972 Plymouth Barracuda convertible, and my father loved to drive it in the annual Labor Day parade, waving at the crowds lining the route. It took only a few minutes to escape town; and between CW and nearby Lithopolis, Pickerington, Groveport and Lancaster, Ohio lay a sparsely populated land dotted with farmhouses, barns, ponds, silos and the occasional rural tavern. Dad fancied himself a 'pathfinder' and enjoyed nothing more than turning onto some unknown road in order to 'discover' where it came out. Finding one he'd slow down to give us a better chance at spotting deer. By the time we turned for home the corn and hay fields were alive with thousands of lightning bugs; chirping crickets and katydids. One night, navigating the roundabout way, we drove all the way to Lancaster. Compared to Canal Winchester, Lancaster is hilly, and we ascended several steep inclines before pulling the convertible to the side of the road.

We sat above Lancaster as dusk ebbed to night, Laura and I looking about from the back seats, smelling the cool evening air, listening to the sounds of night. After several moments Dad said: "*God Patty, I look out at all the beautiful lights and just wish I could live forever.*" Mom didn't reply but the comment stayed with me.

Watching my father I came to realize that he spent countless hours with his football, basketball and track teams because he genuinely loved coaching; he worked at the swimming pool not just to earn extra money, but because he enjoyed swimming, soaking up the sun and being with people; he delighted in tramping the woods hunting morel mushrooms in the spring, fishing every summer and relished – as he put it – "*going bye, bye.*" He organized camping trips, 'Boonie-stomping-expeditions' into Ohio's hinterlands as well as family vacations; read everything he could get his hands on; taught himself to paint and play guitar; made homemade wine and beer in our half-basement and signed up for Karate classes at age 40. He really did bestride Canal Winchester like a colossus. Roger Hanners said of him in our interview, "*Locke? He was a 'Good-O Boy'; an enthusiast. He ran the CW pool over there for years. There was always a line of folks stopping by to talk to him. He really liked people.*"

CHAPTER IX:

PARADE

To this day Canal Winchester's largest community event is the annual Labor Day Parade. It has taken on a life of its own over the years growing into a three-day festival complete with musical acts, dancing contests, vendors of every sort, dunking machines, food stands, pole climbing contests, punt-pass-and-kick contests, sack races and grandiloquent speeches by local politicos. It begins bright and early on Saturday morning and concludes on the first Monday in September with a tumultuous procession through the streets of town.

CW is no stranger to fairs and parades, sponsoring many over the years. Agricultural fairs were especially important to the town's economic history and were held annually with only intermittent disruptions. Besides dancing, music and the usual speech-making, the 1909 Agricultural and Art Fair, for example, boasted a merry-go-round, Ferris wheel, livestock exhibits, pie baking contests and a marching band. Likewise, Canal Winchester went all out in 1928 celebrating its Centennial. Yet even the Centennial celebration paled in comparison to the Labor Day Parades of the 1970s.

Actually CW was somewhat tardy adopting Labor Day as its largest festival. New York City's Knights of Labor first celebrated Labor Day in 1892; Congress declared it a legal holiday in 1894, but Canal Winchester didn't adopt it as an annual celebration until 1960 – and it did so then primarily for economic considerations. Rather than watching residents skedaddle to parts unknown to celebrate the achievements of the American working man, why not keep them – and their money – at home.

With that in mind CW held its first Labor Day parade in 1960. Fifteen years later it was the single biggest event of the calendar year. Live bands performed downtown, square dancing and disco dancing contests were held in the Huntington Bank's parking lot and – starting in 1962 - an annual beauty pageant was staged to select 'Miss Canal Winchester.'

Seemingly half the town assembled in the high school auditorium to watch the pageant crown both '*Tiny Miss CW*' and '*Miss CW*' with faux-diamond tiaras, bright sashes and bouquets of roses. Winners rode atop convertibles; waving to the throngs lining the streets on Labor Day – doing the same in other area parades: Reynoldsburg's Tomato Festival; Circleville's Pumpkin Show and Millersport's Sweet Corn Festival. They also had their pictures taken for a feature in the *Times* newspaper.

Not long after CW started celebrating Labor Day high school students began a tradition of their own – 'Freshman Initiation.' Strictly a student affair it was never sanctioned by school officials. Upperclassman had decided that incoming freshman needed to endure a hazing process before entering the hallowed halls of CWHS; they gave them one - subjecting those on the lowest rung of the pecking order to a series of initiation rituals.

Naturally, what started as good spirited fun degraded over the years into ever-crueler acts of physical and emotional torment; those with bullying streaks now had license to target unwary kids, even warning them not to show their faces in town. Rather than forcing freshman to wear their shirts inside out, or spend the day walking backwards, initiations devolved into mud baths, covering freshman in paint; splotching hair with glue, abducting them to be driven outside of town and marooned; or unceremoniously throwing them into Little Walnut Creek. Worthington transfer Mary Matyac recalled her first encounter with the practice in 1972: "*At the labor day parade the seniors were hazing the freshman. I lied and told the guys I was a sophomore. I don't know if Mr. Baker, the band director, told them or if it was Bill Willison but I was held down by five seniors in front of a crowd of spectators and literally covered with shoe polish from my head to my toes. I had to beg someone I barely knew to let me go shower at her house. We had school the next day.*"

It finally got so out of hand that parents demanded it be stopped, and shortly thereafter 'Freshman Initiation' was duly sacked upon penalty of suspension. In 1975, however, it was a common sight to see incoming freshman painted from head to toe, walking about with matted, disheveled hair or, more often than not – running for their lives from upperclassman. Saturdays and Sundays of Labor Day weekend were busy morning to night, but merely prelude to the great Monday parade signaling summer's end.

By noon on Labor Day chairs, blankets, coolers and clusters of people merged into one snaking wall of humanity along both sides of Waterloo, Trine and Columbus Streets. Each year different blocks entered floats, and like everything else in town it became an intense competition.

In 1975 East Waterloo Street entered a giant cardinal - Ohio's state bird - sitting atop a wagon covered with paper, flowers and tinsel. Work got underway during evenings in the barn behind the Winlan's home. An enormous frame of chicken wire – curiously resembling an enormous chicken-wire frame – eventually took on ornithological dimensions after slatherings of paper machete and several coats of red paint were applied. The larger the cardinal grew the greater the apprehension of getting it through the cross-buck hayloft doors on the second floor. Fortunately it was successfully lowered onto a wagon below and driven through town to the delight of its proud creators.

E. Waterloo Street's Cardinal float just prior to the parade.

Besides floats, there were bands from Canal, Bloom Carroll, Pickerington, Millersport and Groveport. No matter whence they hailed marchers wore shorts and T-shirts to compensate for the early September heat and played almost continuously from the starting point until arriving at the high school nearly an hour and a half later. Majorettes goose-stepped and percussion sections boomed and thumped as they paraded through town.

Reminders of the not-so-distant past - a cavalcade of horses - clip-clopped through town while Jerry Winlan and his brother Terry trailed behind toting wagons and shovels. Both wore signs that read *"Super-Duper-Pooper-Scooper"* and when steaming horse-apples disappeared into their receptacles the crowd belted out hearty cheers. Following the horses and Winlan brothers were the antique cars. Henry Ford's black Model-Ts lead the way; drivers beaming with pride, their children throwing hard candy and bubblegum to kids along the route. Kids sometimes pumped their arms as the old cars crept closer triggering a cacophony of delightful sounding horns. 1926 Model-T pickup trucks were also painted black, but as the fleet rolled on vibrant colors began to appear. Red 1931 Model-A Roadsters, Green 1936 Plymouth two door Coups, and yellow, brown, cream and gold 1957 Studebaker Golden Hawk 285 Paxons.

Convertibles were popular parade vehicles and made excellent platforms for beauty queens and politicians desirous of getting noticed. 1957 Thunderbird convertibles, 1961 Buick Le Sabre convertibles, 1964 Mercury Monterey convertibles and Dad's 1972 Plymouth Barracuda convertible rolled through town carrying mayors, school board members, policemen, fire chiefs and a bevy of nubile young beauties. The 1969 Corvette Stingray was a huge crowd favorite. No other automobile looked anything like it.

Behind the automobiles came the really big vehicles: red and chrome fire trucks occasionally blasting their sirens; emergency vehicles of every size and description doing likewise; giant, bright green John Deere tractors and combines towering over the biggest floats, looking far too tall and wide to fit safely on the streets; antique tractors and even Semi truck cabs detached from their loads.

Little Locke prepares to ride in the Labor Day Parade.

Every September Mr. Babbert - Ernie - dressed from head-to-toe in his clown suit, which was noticeably incongruous considering his vocation the other 364 days of the year. Mr. Babbert, or E.C. to friends and business associates, owned and operated E.C. Babbert Inc., which produced reinforced concrete pipes, concrete box culverts, 3-sided culverts and concrete bridge systems. A friend of Dad's, E.C. was a "man's man" with wide hairy forearms, compact stocky frame, broad forehead and a receding hairline.

Mr. Babbert's behemoth cement mixing trucks were a staple of life in CW, and E.C. looked like the company's tough, owner-operator ought to have looked. On one memorable occasion he proved the look fit his temperament. Driving on the outskirts of Canal Winchester three college age students had sped up as E.C. tried to pass their vehicle; denying him the opportunity to get around their car. So he followed them for miles – tailgating and blasting his car horn - eventually forcing the car over. Though alone, E.C. launched into a frightening harangue; demanding to fight *"the little bastards."*

"You think that God Damn shit's funny? I'll fight all three of your little asses right now! Let's go you sons-a-bitches. Right now! God damn punks! I'll fight all of you right now let's go!" Caught off guard by this ferocity, the

137

shaken driver backpedaled for all he was worth; *"Sir, what's the matter?"*
I don't want to fight you. Why are you upset?"

E.C. would have none of it; wearing a white T-shirt and holding
some sort of rubber/wire hose in his right hand he continued breathing
fire. *"Bull shit! When I tried to pass on Diley Road you sped up you stupid
son-of-a-bitch. You think that shit's funny. It's real fucking funny trying to
get someone killed! Let's go you sons-a-bitches! I'll fight all of you right now!
Let's go!"* Nearby when the showdown took place I was stunned by the
confrontation - the person about to kill three strangers was not only a
friend of Dad's but dressed as a fun-loving clown every Labor Day. Yet
here he was, willing – nay, anxious - to fight not one, not two, but three
young men half his age.

Fortunately the cowering, submissive protestations of innocence at
last gentled Mr. Babbert's condition. *"Sir, I wasn't trying to do that. I didn't
even know you were trying to pass. We don't want to fight you sir."* With that
E.C. turned, opened his car door, looked back contemptuously and said,
"Fucking punks!" before driving off, his tires spitting gravel and kicking
up dust.

On Labor Day weekend 1975, E.C. strolled down Waterloo, Trine
and Columbus Streets waving happily, blasting the unwary with a
squirting flower pinned to his lapel and throwing handfuls of candy
to little kids. Besides E.C. Babbert other proud men – members of the
VFW, Lion's Club and Kiwanis Club - marched in the parade, together
with standard bearers waving Old Glory and Ohio's State flag, civil war
re-enactors, ROTC squads and surviving veterans of the Bataan Death
March.

VFW members roamed the streets all weekend handing out poppies
and collecting funds for disabled veterans and VA hospitals. Mrs.
Gardner, one of our fifth grade teachers, besides having us recite the
US presidents in chronological order, insisted we commit to memory
Colonel John McCrae's poem about the 1915 Battle of Ypres - *In Flanders
Fields.*

In Flanders Field the poppies blow,
Between the crosses, row on row,
That mark our place; and in the sky,
The Larks still bravely singing, fly,
Scarce heard amid the guns below,

We are the dead.
Short days ago,
We lived, felt dawn, saw sunset glow,
Loved and were loved and now we lie,
In Flanders Fields.
Take up the quarrel with the foe,
To you, from failing hands, we throw,
The torch, be yours to hold it high,
If ye break faith with us, who die,
We shall not sleep, though poppies grow,
In Flanders Fields.

Too young to understand the magnitude of the catastrophe that nearly destroyed Europe's civilization in the first half of the 20th century, we were nonetheless able to discern the reverence and respect elders paid to soldiers on parade. Glen Lions worked as a maintenance man at CW high school and had survived the Bataan Death March, and captivity in a Japanese prisoner-of-war camp. He spoke once or twice to students about his ordeal, though preferred not to. When he marched past with other members of the VFW a hush fell over the crowd, adults and older kids placed hands over hearts, and every year without fail Mom cried.

Mr. Gene Lyons at the Podium.

Although illegal to walk public thoroughfares with open alcoholic beverages, no law prohibited parade watchers from imbibing within the confines of their porches, yards and homes. And when the parade ended revelers filled the streets in an exceedingly happy mood. From both sides of Canal's Streets it looked as if Moses had led his Tribe through the Red Sea only to have it crash in upon itself as parade watchers filled the roads. There was much catching up to do.

Laura and Cousin Missy Smith and Little Locke
march in the Labor Day parade.

Besides reunions and rekindling old friendships a great deal of attention was paid to cuisine. Like Thanksgiving and Christmas, Labor Day *grew* into a holiday largely dedicated to gluttony. Across town charcoal grills, gas grills and barbecue pits smoked like bonfires; charring hamburgers, hotdogs, chicken and bratwursts. Consuming mass quantities of 'Fair-Food' also represented an important part of the Labor Day experience. The moment the last float came to a stop behind the school, homemade pies, ice cream, cinnamon & sugar elephant ears, soft pretzels, buttered popcorn in red & white bags, warm peanuts, taffy, cotton candy, burgers, hot dogs, corn dogs and sugary beverages were ingested with gusto

Every year Dad introduced his coaching staff and varsity football team to crowds gathered at Wesier Field. The school had an ancient, wooden 'stage' that was moved in front of the bleachers prior to introductions. It sported as many splinters as my bedroom floor and sloped to one side on the cinder track. Players and coaches sat along the stage, standing when introduced; moms and dads applauded, while wives and girlfriends cheered for boyfriends and assistant coaches.

"I remember," junior Neal Seymour recalled, "*one time at Labor Day's Meet-The-Team, Coach Jones – Mordecai Jones – introduced one kid named 'Phil' as "Feel;' then proceeded to announce that 'Feel' was from Mexico. The whole place, everyone in the stands, just lost it. That was always a big deal for the football team and it seemed like nearly half the town showed up for meet the team.*"

I was sitting in the bleachers when Dad put the 1975 starting offense on stage; he spoke briefly about the seniors and he changed formations a few times - explaining what each might do out of various sets. An older lady sitting across the aisle said, "*Well I understand that. They moved around. And then they moved back!*" At which everyone nearby laughed, agreeing that the mysteries of football formations were best left to coaches.

As the coach's son I had learned that was a minority view. One of the great joys of rooting for a football team is complaining – bitterly when losing - about play selection, formations, defensive coverage, time management and every other decision made by the head coach. Unfortunately, what is thoroughly enjoyable for fans is not much fun for the coach's families. It bothered Mom so much – to hear people denigrate her husband in the stands – that she stopped attending football games after the 1972 season.

Coaches have to have thick skins to survive. Once, out of curiosity, I asked Dad what he thought of people calling him names while he coached. To my surprise he laughed; answering by relating one of his favorite football stories: "*Ah, Hell! You can't let it bother you,*" he said smiling. "*I remember during the 1970 season, Canal Winchester hadn't had an undefeated team in its entire history – not once. I'm in my fourth year as head coach and we go undefeated. We win all ten games and by the end of the season the place is packed every game.*"

"Anyway," he continued, "*once the last game of the season was in the bag I was trying to get all the kids into the game; especially seniors who worked hard for me and might not have had a chance to play much. So I'm calling timeouts, making substitutions, and we're up by three touchdowns; it's my first undefeated season as head coach, it was so exciting, the place is going wild and I forgot how many timeouts I'd called. I'd used them up, but forgot, and so I call timeout for a fourth time and get penalized. It's quiet for a sec, when I hear this voice yell, 'Hey Locke! Nice call you Dumb Ass!'*"

Laughing, he finishes the story; removing his glasses and wiping his eyes before concluding; "*We go 10 and 0, and I get called 'Dumb Ass' moments before the entire team is marched through town for a parade. You just can't let that shit bother you.*" And he didn't. Although it's somewhat easier not to '*let that shit bother you*' when you're winning. Whether he won or not, it infuriated Mom to hear fans belittle him. Fearing temper might get the best of her - and for her own sanity – she opted to stay home on football Friday nights.

That didn't mean she missed the games. When CW played Mom listened to Roger Hanners call the contest on WHOK AM radio. Placing the transistor above the bookcase next to her desk for better reception she would pace to and fro, across the big black register, stopping occasionally to yell at announcers or scream something like, "*Run, run! Damn it! Run!*"

When CW played at home, Mom not only listened to the radio, but also developed a fairly reliable system of gleaning information during and after the games. By leaving the front door open game sounds could be faintly heard through our screen door. What tipped her off definitively, however, was whether or not the visitor's school bus was raucous or quiet as it rolled down Waterloo Street toward Route 33. When she was nervous the skin on the ends of her fingers pealed and bled; a condition she contended with her entire life but one that was especially acute during football season.

Before bedtime most evenings she would apply an ointment Doc Burrier had prescribed on her fingers and would then wrap them in cellophane - but it never did much good. When games were too close for comfort she'd kill the radio, spending the remainder of the evening glancing at the screen door, awaiting the visitor's school bus to reveal who won. Sitting in the stands Mom had forsaken on Labor Day held plenty of powerful emotions for me as well. One of our neighbors; sitting a few rows behind me, said Dad would have been fired long ago if not for one of his assistants. That he never taught players anything and wasn't much of a football coach. It's a constant for coaches and their families.

When Dad concluded his presentation players would drift onto the cinder track and head into the bleachers; while the bands that marched in the parade made their way to the grandstand to perform. Each ensemble did their best to outplay its predecessor, giving the crowd a free, live concert on the last day of summer vacation. Before Labor Day festivities formally ended patrons were treated to several contests requiring unusual sets of skills; including climbing a greased pole with fifty dollars wedged at its height; corralling squealing, slippery, slimy, terrified pigs inside a circular pen; and throwing baseballs at a bulls eye in an effort to soak some poor soul suspended over the tank of a dunking chair.

The dunking chair spilt various occupants throughout the weekend, but on Labor Day heavy hitters climbed aboard. Teachers, coaches, politicians and beautiful women made their way onto the dunking seat to raise money for the boosters. Crowds grew about the apparatus, roaring in support of the pitchers. Fifty cents bought three balls - hurled at the bull's eye located at the end of a lever; it was a cash cow as would-be Big Leaguers - standing no more than ten feet from the target - hit the mark time and again.

Labor Day festivities at last came to an end late Monday evenings when we collapsed in front of the TV to watch Jerry Lewis's Muscular Dystrophy Telethon. It ended every year with Jerry tearfully singing 'You'll Never Walk Alone' from the musical, Carousel. Like the end of the telethon, the conclusion of Labor Day festivities felt bittersweet. Despite the upheaval, excitement, great food and pageantry of the three-day extravaganza - none of it forestalled the end of summer vacation. An entire new school year waited on the morrow.

Families and friends said farewell, out-of-town visitors packed up and left, fire pits burned down to glowing embers, darkness descended and the familiar quiet reasserted itself outside our house on Waterloo Street. When we awoke the following morning and dressed for school the cleanup across town had begun; the glorious summer of 1975 was over.

CHAPTER X:

MICHAEL ERROL LOCKE

My father was born in Chester, Illinois on May 23, 1939 to Norman and Leora Locke. The youngest of two, his older brother – Phil – had arrived in 1937. Dad's middle name, Errol, was Leora's tribute to Errol Flynn, whom she found particularly handsome; admiring his larger-than-life, swashbuckling personae. It turned out to be an appropriate moniker; her second son eventually possessing some of the big screen actor's charm and good looks. Unfortunately for Mike and Phil that middle name was pretty much the only indulgence Leora allowed to popular culture.

Leora Locke with her sons, Philip, holding a stick, and Michael.

On the contrary; the Locke household was filled primarily with religious instruction and books – lots and lots of books. Norman Locke, 'the old man' as he was affectionately known, was something of a wild man whom Leora Mosiman did her best to tame. When Mom first started dating Dad, for example, her Aunt Elizabeth, asking about her love life, was positively horrified when informed by her niece that she was dating Norman Locke's spawn: "*I saw my Aunt Elizabeth,*" Mom recalled, "*and she said 'Who are you going with these days?' And I said Michael Locke. And she got this terrible look on her face and said, 'Locke? Oh my God! Not Norm Locke's son I hope!*"

Born in 1912 in Indiana, Norman fought – boxed – for prize money across the Midwest under the ring name, *Curly Chik*. He had also spent time in jail before meeting and falling in love with the small, dark haired Mennonite girl he determined to marry. Leora, on the other hand - quiet, intellectual, deeply religious - could not have been more different than the six-foot, red haired hellion pursuing her.

Norman Locke in his Sunday Best.

Despite being near complete opposites, one from the other – love - being blind, led them to the altar and later to child-rearing in 1937 and again in 1939. Norman Cyril Locke, with curly, reddish/brown hair and twinkling blue eyes was impulsive, fiery and a consummate storyteller.

Nothing pleased him more than swapping tall tales in darkened bars, drinking Pabst Blue Ribbon beer, munching on red husk peanuts and ending his evenings with a big, greasy, tavern hamburger wrapped in wax paper before heading home. By the time Dad came along in May of 1939, Norm worked as a machinist at Shartle Brothers Machine Company in Franklin – a small town in Southwest Ohio situated along the Great Miami River.

Norman and Leora Locke.

That fast flowing river - harnessed after several mills were constructed along its banks - provided the power to saw timber and grind grain in Franklin. The mills led to the growth of the waterwheel industry; and later, when Norm and Leora arrived in Franklin, paper mills employed a majority of its citizens. When Dad came of age he too worked long, hot hours at the mills – which he despised.

Norm served in the US Army during the Second World War; stationed at Hickam Field – now Hickam Air Force Base – on the big island of Hawaii. During that posting he finagled his way into a sweet assignment - Bob Hope's official driver and escort - driving him about when the crooner arrived with the USO to entertain troops in the Pacific theater. According to Norm they hit it off immediately.

Predictably challenged on the veracity of his tale in a neighborhood tavern after the war, Norm retrieved a folded piece of paper from his wallet, led his drinking buddies to a pay phone and dialed the number. Although razzed while dialing and faced with a setback after an unknown female answered the phone, he was quickly vindicated when Mr. Hope accepted the call. At that point the boys in the bar took turns saying hello to 'Bob;' furiously patting the now famous machinist on his back.

Like her husband, Leora Mosiman was born in 1912; but came into the world a bit further north; Guernsey, Saskatchewan, Canada. She was twenty-seven when her second and last child was born. Unlike her husband, Leora was a devout Mennonite and practicing Presbyterian who believed sincerely in the Divinity of Christ and endeavored to abide by His teachings. For Phil and Mike that meant reading the Bible and attending church twice weekly. When they rebelled Norm did not spare the rod and back to church they went.

Reading, however, was not limited to the Bible. Literature deeply influenced and shaped both boys, representing the defining characteristic of their home. Leora had attended Bluffton College, earned her Ohio teaching credential and taught both English and Latin at nearby Springboro High School. She was fluent in French, and, indeed, English was her second language. When Mom first met Leora she was the only person on either side of the family who'd been to college. Leora read the Bible as Holy Scripture, but also as literature and knew its great stories by heart. She absolutely loved to read; devouring every book she could get her hands on; as did Norm.

Not only did Leora read the classics - she read and re-read them with her English students - discussing them at length, toting books to and from school every day. Her love and enthusiasm for literature was instilled in her children at an early age. The first time Mom laid eyes on Dad – in first grade during the autumn of 1945 – he already wore reading glasses and had his head buried in a book. And so it went at home, where all four Lockes read the classics, comic books, murder mysteries, novels, biographies, histories and science fiction.

Although Leora taught Latin and English and the four of them appreciated literature, it was a rough and tumble world outside their front door. Mike and Phil grew up in two worlds: at home, where both parents valued education and the sincere, deeply religious impulses of their Mennonite mother held sway; and the masculine, competitive, often gritty environment beyond where Norman and his youngest son, Michael, felt most comfortable.

Like other kids in their neighborhood the Lockes climbed trees, rode bikes, went fishing and hunting, ran trap-lines in local creeks, picked blackberries along railroad tracks and collected pop bottles to redeem at local grocery stores. *"Mike was a real outdoors guy,"* Mom recalled, discussing their first few dates. *"I never went through a cornfield in my life until I started going out with him. And going fishing, I had never been fishing before and that's the kind of thing he liked to do. He would bait our hooks before we started necking."* She concluded with a smile.

According to Dad, Phil, AKA *"Doody,"* – being two years older and equipped with an inexhaustible supply of roguish capers – was the brains of their youthful outfit; devising mischievous stunts Dad and his buddies duly carried out after receiving instructions. The sobriquet –'Doody' - dates to March 1948 when *'The Howdy Doody Show'* debuted on NBC, airing five times a week between 5:30 and 6:00. Phil – who turned eleven that July – was, by popular consensus, an eerily uncanny, spitting image of Doody himself.

Mike and Phil Locke, 1943.

Howdy Doody was a TV marionette with bright red hair, a fixed ear-to-ear smile set across a face marked with 48 freckles – one for each state in the union in 1948. He starred in the hottest kid show on television. *'Buffalo Bob'* Smith hosted and led off each episode with a rousing rendition of *'It's Howdy Doody Time'*. Buffalo Bob asking the audience: *'Say kids what time it is?'* To which they replied: *'It's Howdy Doody Time!'*

"It's Howdy Doody Time . . .
Bob Smith and Howdy Do . . .
Say Howdy Do to You . . . So kids let's go!"

Phil didn't mind his newfound fame as the living embodiment of Howdy Doody and the name stuck. Even Phil's teachers preferred the adopted nickname. Sixty years after the show first aired my father still refers to his older brother as *Doody*, or 'Uncle Doody'. Phil, however, wasn't always as kind as his small screen alter ego - especially when it came to his youthful sibling. In fact, he enjoyed nothing more than seeing Michael in distress; and to that end devised multiple strategies to induce it.

At school, for example - while sitting across from Dad at a work table in the library – Phil would yelp in pain, and then glare accusingly at his sibling; the teacher or study hall monitor on duty invariably looked in their direction. At that point Phil would let out another yelp, grab his shin in mock agony and demand his brother stop kicking him.

Despite Dad's protestations of innocence and anger over being duped – which Doody relished as any older brother would – Phil prevailed, becoming so adept at using his punk kid brother that Dad made a point of avoiding him entirely after first bell. Both young men tested the other, occasionally engaging in knockdown, drag out fist fights when their parents weren't around to stop them. They also fought neighborhood rivals from time-to-time and endured well-deserved, intermittent 'whoopuns' from their father.

Norman Locke meant what he said and expected his boys to listen. One evening while eating dinner Norm asked his youngest son to chew with his mouth closed. A few moments later, when it became obvious proper masticating etiquette was not forthcoming, and he had not been listened to – without saying a word – he swung his left arm striking Dad across the chest; knocking him and his chair to the floor. Norm continued eating his dinner. When Dad resumed his place at the table he chewed with his mouth closed.

The Lockes. Norman, Leora Mosiman Locke, Philip and Michael. 1947

Despite having two steady incomes the Locke's were relatively poor - and had been so for quite some time. Norm had started a tax accounting business with a partner. After working steadily for three years, landing several clients and building a respectable portfolio Norm arrived at work one morning to find his partner gone - and their bank account emptied. Skipping town, he was never heard from again. When the dust settled Norm was cleared of any wrongdoing or liability for the crash; he nevertheless determined to repay those who lost money. And he eventually did, though it came at a high price.

Phil earned an academic scholarship in mathematics, but his younger brother, it was decided, would have to find employment after high school. Entering Franklin High in the autumn of 1953 Dad hoped that he too might attend university after completing his studies. During his senior year, however, Leora was diagnosed with cancer. The disease and debilitating expenses that came with fighting it - closed the door completely on higher education.

Graduating in May 1957 he found a steady job; enlisting in the United States Marine Corps. With three HS friends – Roger Dwyer, Earl Eversole and Bob Bowling - they signed up before commencement, flying across country to San Diego, California just a few days after graduating.

INTERLUDE:

GO TELL IT TO THE MARINES
Don't-don't-don't-don't-look at what's in front of you.
(Boots-boots-boots-boots-movin' up an' down again);
Men-men-men-men-men go mad with watchin' em,
An' there's no discharge in the war

Try-try-try-try-to think O' something different –
Oh-my-God-keep-me from goin' lunatic!
(Boots-boots-boots-boots-movin' up an' down again!)
There's no discharge in the War!

(Rudyard Kipling – BOOTS Infantry columns)

Considering his initial reaction to Boot Camp the support system provided by his classmates proved pivotal in surviving the early trauma of Marine Corps indoctrination. Despite his sometimes gritty upbringing Dad was Leora's youngest – her baby; the blue eyed, curly-haired, handsome young man attractive enough to win adoring oohs and aahs from her friends. She found him irresistible; and treated him that way. The Marines did not. After arriving at Camp Pendleton and being unceremoniously shorn of his curly locks, he was immunized, examined roughly from head-to-toe, provided a set of uniforms, a steel bucket, and a sea bag to tote his belongings, and then marched to his billet.

The world in which Dad grew up was an ugly, scarred, roiling mess. Four months before his birthday in May 1939, Hitler's armies swept through Poland; the Second World War erupted, completing the European and civilizational suicide begun in 1914. When it ended in 1945 warfare had entered the atomic age.

In 1948, the year *Howdy Doody* premiered on NBC, the state of Israel - established in Palestine - found itself immediately besieged, existing from its inception in a perpetual state of war. That same year the Soviet Union blocked allied access to Berlin leading to the Berlin Airlift. In 1949 Mao's communists came to power in China; in 1950 North Korea invaded South Korea and in the US President Truman announced the nation's intention to construct Hydrogen Bombs.

In the Franklin, Ohio School District – like school districts everywhere across the United States - students were instructed to '*Duck and Cover*' in case of an atom bomb attack; bomb shelters and public fallout shelters were constructed throughout the 1950s; in 1952 Whittaker Chambers published **_Witness_** detailing Alger Hiss's trial and communist activities inside the US; Julius and Ethel Rosenberg were executed in 1953.

In the summer of 1957, the United States Marine Corps prepared 'boots' diligently for combat - with the expectation of conflict in mind. Sleep deprivation is central to that preparation. Indeed, lack of sleep is the underpinning to the Corps' introduction of stress to the lives' of its newest members - and Mike Locke did not appreciate it.

"*It was the hardest thing I'd ever done man, let me tell you.*" He recalled in our 1999 interview. "*They'd run us ragged all day: barracks inspections, bunk inspections, rifle inspections; PT (physical training), pull-ups,*

PFC Michael Locke, Autumn 1957.

push-ups, running the obstacle course; marching to the rifle range. It never ended. It was constant because when we thought the day was over it wasn't.

Night after night we'd slog back to the barracks dead tired and I'd pray the last couple miles, 'Dear God, please. Please let the barracks be OK; please not tonight.' And we'd walk in and the bunks and lockers were turned over, our gear and uniforms were scattered all the hell all over the room and its past midnight and we'd have to have it perfect and back in order by 4:30 AM."

Dad was less communicative at Camp Pendleton. During the first week of boot camp he refused to speak unless signaled out by drill instructors. He ignored bunkmates and other boots, and refused to speak to Bob, Earl or Roger. Not even during chow or before lights out would he design to speak. Mike Locke was an angry, pissed off eighteen-year-old: at his predicament, his decision to enlist in the Corps in the first place, his friends, his drill sergeants and anything else remotely associated with the military.

Asked about overcoming his taciturn demeanor he replied, *"Hell, you get numb. You have to if you're going to get through it. You suck up your guts and keep moving."* The phrase, *'Suck up your guts,'* is a Marinecorpsism – part of the special, salty language unique to that particular branch of the armed forces – and just one of many his football players became familiar with in years to come. Despite the initial shock, Dad has consistently maintained his experiences in the Marine Corps were some of the most important of his life.

Boot Camp lasted twelve weeks in 1957; after receiving the coveted Eagle, Globe and Anchor emblem, four weeks of additional training followed at the Marine Corps Infantry Training Regiment. It's fair to say Dad enjoyed his time in the Corps. It gave him the discipline so desperately needed by young men; humility and the desire to do something else with his life. He took up boxing in the Corps, becoming sparring partner for Tom Adams – the onetime golden gloves champion of St. Louis, Missouri.

Though destined to become friends, their first encounter was not auspicious. After exchanging heated words – Private Locke being painfully unaware Tom Adams was a golden gloves champion - Dad manned-up; exchanging blows with his erstwhile adversary to determine top dog in the barracks. He awoke on his bunk an hour later unable to move his jaw. When sparring with Tom Dad simply could not connect, never laying a glove on him - except once. Having brought his right hand all the way back from Mississippi, Dad landed a right-cross flush on his jaw. Tom shook his head and said, *"Nice shot Locke,"* and then continued sparring as if nothing happened.

"That blew my mind man. I hit him as hard as I ever hit anyone in my life and he looks at me and says 'nice shot Locke?' I dropped my gloves and looked at the guy in disbelief." The experience was a learning one. A few hours later Corporal Adams explained how much the punch really staggered him; pointing out the importance of never showing you're hurt in boxing. Dad eventually related the incident to his football teams; describing his inadequacies as a boxer he imparted the lesson that no matter how hard they might get jacked-up on Friday nights, it's tougher on opponents

–psychologically - to feign indifference and run back to the huddle as if nothing happened.

Private Locke's MOS (military occupational skill) was radio relay. And as Marines - then as now - spend their tours of duty in the field or at sea, reliable communications between units is vital. Communicating in the field prior to the information revolution required setting up multiple radio relay stations that enabled line officers and NCOs to talk with one another. Connected by miles of wire and usually situated on high ground the stations were constantly being set up, tore down and relocated based on the demands of the mission.

With his M-1 Garand Rifle by his side, Pvt. Locke drove 1/3 quarter ton trucks equipped with generators and telephone lines; setting up radio relay stations from hilltop to hilltop across the open ranges of Camp Pendleton, California. Having once reached an assigned destination his crew aligned the relay station to pick up and transfer signals; making sure the generator hummed along without interruption.

After setup it was smooth sailing - Dad and his buddies lolled about in the California sun until ordered to relocate. *"It was beautiful,"* he recalled, *"We'd set up on top of a mountain, well I suppose just a foothill in California, outside San Mateo and we could look down across the Pacific Ocean and Route 101. It was just unbelievably beautiful."* Unfortunately, downtime for energetic teenage Marines leads to trouble - and Dad's crew was no exception. One particular mission ended with a bang that nearly landed Private Locke in the brig. With the radio relay station in position Dad noticed their particular location was near the front line of one of Camp Pendleton's abandoned rifle ranges; and that quite a bit of un-spent and unexploded ammunition lay scattered about.

Within minutes of this discovery they were removing gunpowder from ammo casings and depositing fine black powder into a discarded coffee can; one Marine hit the mother-load when he located an old Bandelier. Little by little their fine grained pile of gunpowder began rising up the insides of their would-be bomb canister. *"You couldn't believe it man."* Dad said laughing, *"We dug about a four-foot hole with our entrenching tools after we got the coffee can filled and stuck it down there; then it dawned on us the damn thing might blow our asses up – it was a hell-of-a-lot of gunpowder. "*

'So what'd you?' "Well, we didn't want to be too close to all that powder," he continued, "so we pulled a shit-load of hollow reeds that Pendleton's hillsides were lousy with and filled those with gunpowder. That took awhile. It looked like a big straw sticking out of the hole when we finished but it was loaded with gunpowder." 'Weren't you scared about getting hurt or getting in trouble?' "We were too young to worry about getting in trouble; we were excited about our bomb, so we spent another half hour laying a line of powder – a cartridge at a time – leading from our bomb to the truck."

'Did it work?' "Yea, well we waited a few minutes. Maybe it wasn't the best idea. Then we thought, 'What the hell' and lit the sumbitch! And it worked. Man, it was right out of James Bond the way that powder-line burnt. It was like something from TV. It hit the reeds and then, oh my God! Kaa-Boom-Kaa-Blooie! It was like we were under enemy attack. Half the God Damn mountain blows up; dirt flies everywhere - up, out, down – it hit our truck so hard it sounded like shrapnel. And being the dumbasses we were it never occurred to us that we'd end up cutting our telephone wires."

'So you lost communication?' "We were out of communication immediately but didn't know it. And then about ten minutes later, after the dust had started to die down, I look down the hill and here comes a group of Marines, following our wire line, picking it up and following it toward our station. And out in front is the Chief Master Sergeant and he's red-faced, watching what's going on with his hands on his hips.

"That's when we worried about getting in trouble - and oh my God was he pissed." 'What happened when they got there?' "The Master Sergeant asked what set off the explosion and of course we lied like hell! 'We don't know Sarge; we were checking the generator and the damn hillside just blew up.' We said." 'Did he believe you?' "I doubt it," he concluded with a smile.

The Locke brothers played chess as kids and were good at it. Unfortunately, at Camp Pendleton Dad made the mistake of playing - and checkmating – officers who challenged him to matches. "They didn't like that shit," was his colorful way of describing the outcomes. That is somewhat of an understatement.

Indeed, college educated officers in the USMC, fancying themselves military tacticians and strategists; were not the least bit amused when beaten in chess – repeatedly – by an eighteen year old PFC from Franklin, Ohio. If that wasn't bad enough Private Locke wrote a tongue-and-cheek doggerel regarding the crimson complexion his opponents adopted once checkmated. For haughty usurpation and lack of respect he was quietly ordered out of his bunk one night; stood up in front of a group of offended officers, and punched repeatedly in the stomach.

Antecedents

Mom – Patricia Anne Riddell in her youth – spent the summer of 1957 writing Dad long letters and processing water bills for Franklin's City Government as an entry level typist. Born July 14, 1939, mother - christened Patricia - was the eldest of Edward and Letta Riddell's two daughters. Ed worked for General Motors before serving in the Navy during World War II; and at Westinghouse Electric after the war. Letta ran the house on Maple Drive and did so with an efficiency and attention to detail worthy of an engineer's wife. Born Letta Carpenter in 1921 she married Ed Riddell at age sixteen. Like her husband she grew up poor.

With brown, shoulder-length hair and a solid frame Letta Riddell wore dresses everyday of her life; stitching them by hand with patterns and cloth purchased at the Hancock Fabric chain store in Cincinnati. She wore spectacles that hung about her neck on a chain; and loved music, babies, gardening and especially her home.

The Riddells. Letta Carpenter Riddell, Edward, Nancy and Patricia 1945.

Letta was none too fond of the military as it had snatched Edward from her in 1943, leaving her alone with two small children. She used to say, *"We've fought for every country in the world except our own."* And could never reconcile her love for Country with its practice of sending its young men abroad to be maimed and killed. Letta Riddell was a staunch Roosevelt Democrat who said of Republican Party candidates: *"I don't vote for crooks."*

Although staggered over the course of a workweek she dutifully swept and vacuumed floors, made beds, washed laundry – which included carrying heavy baskets from house to clothes line where they dried in the sun – sewed dresses for Patricia and her younger sister, Nancy; hemmed, darned socks and started every meal by peeling a 'mess' of potatoes. As a result Letta Riddell was the fastest potato peeler in the annals of human history.

It was Letta who drove fifteen-year-old Patricia to the Franklin Theater to meet Dad on their first date in 1955; a sold out performance of *'The War of the Worlds.'* Dad later admitted selecting the film with an ulterior motive in mind - the frightful Martians wreaking havoc on screen afforded him the opportunity to chivalrously hold his date in the darkened theater. Six months into his enlistment PFC Locke returned to Franklin, Ohio to propose. Christmas Eve 1957, among twinkling Christmas lights, he knelt on bended knee and asked Patricia Riddell to marry him.

Franklin HS student, Patricia Riddell, 1955.

Mom, AKA Patricia Riddell, 1956.

They wed seven months later at the Franklin Presbyterian Church while Dad was on leave in July 1958. With financial as well as time constraints the newlyweds sped to Niagara Falls for their honeymoon.

Wedding Day, July 15, 1958. Mike and Pat Locke,
Phil Locke and Nancy Riddell.

It didn't go well. Stuck in traffic, unable to move forward or turn around, aware the clock was ticking - he was soon due back at Camp

Pendleton - the groom exploded. According to Mom, who began crying shortly after his eruption commenced, father's stint in the Marine Corps had vastly expanded his vocabulary of profane terms - and he used every one of them to berate fellow motorists.

For his part, Dad couldn't understand why his justifiable anger over a traffic jam should upset his new wife? He wasn't upset with her. Nevertheless, the angrier he got, the harder his new bride cried; and the more she wept the angrier he became at the stalled cars in front of and behind them. "*Oh my God, it was awful,*" she remembered forty years later. "*I truly thought you're father would start a riot. It scared me because people could hear him and he was screaming and we were just sitting there on the road and he was yelling things like, 'Move your God damn car you dumb son-of-a-bitch!' at the top of his lungs. I cried and cried and by the time we got there we had to turn around and go home. It was just awful*"

"*It was a stressful time,*" she continued, "*we were using a borrowed car because we didn't have any money; and your father was on call because of the Suez Canal Crisis and I was frantic about that. As soon as we got there he had to check in incase his unit deployed. It was just awful.*"

Despite the inauspicious beginning they were in love and anxious to start their lives together. He surprised her in letters detailing his desire to become a teacher - like his mother. When his time in the Corps ended he'd take out a loan, go to college and find a teaching job somewhere close to his wife's family. Honorably discharged in 1959 – he had enlisted for two years when the Corps offered shorter enlistments to increase its ranks – Dad hitchhiked home from San Diego, California to Franklin, Ohio.

The young couple put Dad's plan into action. Norm drove them to Bluffton College – Leora's alma mater, and where her uncle was once president of the college - in Northwest Ohio; cosigning a student-loan for his youngest son. Founded in 1899 by the General Conference Mennonite Church, Bluffton College covers 234 acres along Little Riley Creek; its sylvan campus is quiet and picturesque.

The Mennonite connection paid off. One of Leora's former professors helped them purchase a trailer belonging to a graduating senior named Chet Foreaker. Blue, tiny – 30-feet long and eight-feet wide - and situated on an empty lot next to campus; the newlyweds purchased their first home for the princely sum of $500.00, moving in soon thereafter. A few days before classes started Norm returned with some of their personal items; later taking a walk with Mom along Little Riley Creek. Most students and incoming freshman had arrived on campus and the commons was a beehive of activity.

Mom started crying; Norm asked what was wrong? She said she felt left out; that she'd like to go to school too; that it was difficult to see all the excitement and kids her age going to college and not be part of it. Norm listened patiently, comforted her as best he could and continued on with their walk. No one in Mom's family had been to college, and women of Letta's generation expected daughters to marry, have children and run their homes.

Mom planned to work while Dad went to school and later, if future children didn't keep her from attending, she'd enroll. Feeling guilty for burdening Norm, Mom tried to forget the whole thing. Two days later there was a knock on their trailer door; opening it she found herself staring at Norm. *"My first thought was that something was wrong. Maybe there had been an accident or someone was sick,"* she said later. Everyone was fine, it was just that Norm loved surprises - and especially loved his daughter-in-law - so he smiled and handed her an envelope stamped with Bluffton's College Seal.

'What is it? What's the matter?" Mom blustered. *"It's a student loan,"* Norm replied, *"so you can go to school too, Patty. It's all taken care of."* And with that, as with so many things in her life, she began to squall, falling into her father-in-law's arms. Dad studied science; biology, health, psychology, anatomy and took prerequisite education courses, to earn his teaching certificate. Mom signed up for elementary education courses along with the usual fare of Humanities studies.

At Bluffton College attendance at 'Chapel' was required, participation recorded, and both Patricia and Michael Locke duly took part in daily services. For Dad it wasn't a welcome respite. After eighteen years of mandatory religious instruction he harbored resentments. To his mind the idea of 'God' was probable, but the notion He possessed myriad human qualities – *"I am a jealous God"* – struck him as absurd. Never a professional atheist, he nevertheless resented those who considered themselves 'Holy' and came to look upon religion as a means to control people.

Enrolled at a university founded by Mennonites, he found himself at odds with many of its practices. To compensate he used humor as a coping mechanism. Two examples bear this out: Education majors working on teaching certificates were assigned student-teaching duties in local school districts. To get there, he and one of his Marine Corps buddies shared rides with 'Harold,' who – according to Dad – was thoroughly, devoutly and piously 'Holy.'

"Harold was a religious fanatic. In every way, and in everything, I mean everything," he responded in our interview when asked how Harold's holiness manifested itself. *"I mean if I'd say, 'How are you today Harold?' He'd say, 'One is as one does, Leviticus 3-13."* (Laughter) *I mean, you'd ask him if he was happy about getting an 'A' on an exam and he'd say, 'Whosoever exalts himself shall be humbled. And whosoever is humble shall be exalted."* Harold had an unfortunate tendency to look down upon the unwashed, sinning rabble - so Dad went out of his way to supply Harold with ammunition.

"I remember your poor little mother," he explained with a grin, *"arriving home one night after class and saying," 'There's this boy on campus and I don't know how to say this but he looks at me funny. I get the feeling he thinks I'm dirty.'"* - *"Oh God, your father,"* - Mom added, jumping in to give her side of the tale. *"I'm walking across campus with my books and this boy looks at me with the most disgusted look I've ever seen."*

"He sneered at me like I was sick, it really bothered me. So when I got home I asked your Dad about it." In their tag-team recounting Dad picked up the narrative: *"She says this boy looks at her funny and I'm thinking, 'Oh Shit!' because Tom Eddinger, we rode together to student-teaching with Harold and made up lies about our families to make him happy."* At that Mom rolled her eyes while her husband forged ahead. *"Anyway, we told Harold that on Friday nights we all met and we'd throw in our car keys or house keys in a bowl, turn off the lights and everybody would grab some keys and go home with somebody else's wife."*

And he believed you? *"Oh; of course! Harold wanted to believe that shit. He was a typical religious fanatic - he thought the worst of everyone. And your poor little mother, she's going – this guy keeps looking at me funny. But we couldn't resist lying to Harold cause God he'd suck it up. We made Harold happy – the fanatical little bastard."*

On another occasion Dad took it upon himself to enhance the cultural richness of Bluffton's campus via art. Growing up, especially after Norm's business partner absconded with their assets, both Locke boys painted Christmas windows during the holidays to earn extra money. Phil, an accomplished artist, taught Dad – who continued seasonal painting well after Laura and I had graduated from high school.

At Bluffton he kept his water colors in a wooden crate, together with an old rag and a stack of Christmas cards used for ideas and inspiration. Dad painted freehand from the inside of buildings, filling entire windows with Santa's, reindeer, holly leaves with bright red berries, snowmen and Christmas trees. His holiday scenes stood out because he filled every inch of store windows with copious amounts of white paint; transforming the panes into shadowy, snowy Christmas landscapes.

Having warmed the cockles of his soul one autumn evening with bourbon, Dad located his paint set. Departing without telling Mom his destination, he disappeared into the darkness, heading for the campus water tower. The tower loomed over Bluffton's students, readily espied anywhere on campus. As such it became an irresistible target for Dad and his chums to share their gifts with Bluffton's 'Holy.' A three man-job – lookout, paint transporter and artist –they rendezvoused at the tower's base; ascending its ladder with visions of religious frescos dancing in their heads.

Dad painting a Christmas scene at home.

Given the size of the water tank, the mural's intended objects needed to be much larger than store window reindeer; and so he took his time; painting enormous symbols – Hieroglyphics, as he was wont to call them. The following afternoon Dad ebulliently strolled across the quad, reacting with as much surprise as his classmates at the unusual series of symbols sprawled across the water tank.

The first figure was a giant CROSS; the great rood fitting nicely with campus attitudes – despite the defacement of property - leading many students to believe the symbols were some cryptic statement of faith. Next; an emblematic FISH – another Christian symbol – followed by a DIAMOND, the first mysterious, non-Christian ideogram in the sequence. Next to the diamond was what looked like a SHOVEL? And beside the shovel some sort of draft animal, perhaps a DONKEY or MULE? Finally the string concluded with an enormous, round, red TOMATO.

To his delight, the hieroglyphic riddle became the talk of campus. The more students pointed toward his mural, inquiring of their professors its puzzling meaning, the wider the smile stretched across his face. For only Mike Locke, the lookout and the paint hauler knew the meaning behind the strange symbols: **Holy**, **Mackerel**, **Sapphire**, **Dig** the **Ass** on that **Tomato**. Midway through the mural's first day's debut the trio revealed its hidden code to select classmates.

Having graduated high school, served in the USMC, married his high school sweetheart and successfully completed his first year of college, Dad was ecstatic - and terrified - when Mom returned from the doctor's with news she was pregnant. He was on track, moving in the right direction and about to become a father; but his mother, Leora, was losing her battle with cancer.

Eating lunch in the school cafeteria one afternoon, drool began to dribble down the side of Leora's face. It went unnoticed until one of her teaching colleagues pointed it out; and she realized that she couldn't feel anything. "*Somebody said something to her,*" Mom recalled. "*And she had numb areas. It came through behind her ear; a big open place and she had to stop work and stay in bed.*"

Despite the initial scare Norm determined he and Leora would fight and 'beat' the cancer. Unfortunately, no matter how hard they fought, how many doctors they saw, or how diligently Leora prayed, the cancer continued to spread. By the time Mom announced her pregnancy in 1960, Leora - forty-nine-years old at the time – had been battling the disease for two years.

When doctors in Franklin offered no hope; Norm drove her over seven-hundred miles to the Mayo Clinic in Minneapolis, Minnesota. The prognosis in Minneapolis was dishearteningly identical to the one back home. Doctors could not check the spread of Leora's terminal, inoperable cancer and so she and Norm returned to Ohio – a twelve hour drive alone in their car.

The disease ate away and disfigured Leora. Her bright, sensitive eyes lost their light, her dark brown hair turned white and her cheeks and lips sagged. "*Both her mouth and eyes looked like they had been grabbed and pulled down.*" During the illness, having on one occasion willed herself out of the house, she dropped the family mail at Franklin's Post Office only to have three boys – who saw Leora sitting alone in her car – yell, "*Witch! Witch! It's a witch!*"

She returned home unable to stop crying, Mom remembered, "*She just cried like her heart would break.*" When Norm learned what had happened he got in his car, drove back to town in a rage, and cruised slowly up and down Franklin's streets looking for his wife's tormentors.

"He was just beside himself; even when she was crying Leora was trying to tell him, 'No, no. Don't do it. It's not their fault.'"

For her youngest son the pain his mother endured was unbearable. Grateful his time in the Corps and at Bluffton removed him from the scene of so much suffering, he nevertheless thought of her constantly; answering every phone call with dread. Leora knew she would die but wanted to live long enough to see her first grandchild. Mom was due November 1960 and Leora clung to life hoping she might hold her grandchild at least once.

Mom and Dad set up a small nursery to one side of the trailer. Already student-teaching as part of an early classroom instruction program, she began to 'show.' And once she did her student-teaching days were unceremoniously terminated; pregnant teachers being strictly verboten in 1960. The closer Mom got to her due date, the more Dad grew panicked that he was about to become a father. His studies weren't complete; his wife couldn't work with an infant child at home and despite working four days a week at Bluffton's College book store, he still needed another two years worth of classes before graduating.

He did everything in his power to accelerate graduation; taking as many courses as Bluffton would allow. Working fulltime over semester break at Maxwell Paper, he also took evening classes. Through that long hot summer Leora steadily worsened; by autumn she was in agony. *"She begged Norm to kill her,"* Mom remembered in hushed tones, *"She was in so much pain."* At last, on November 11, 1960, Patty Riddell Locke went into labor; Dad drove her to Bluffton Community Hospital in a borrowed car and then called home to tell Leora the news.

On November 12, 1960, at 12:42 am, Nancy Elizabeth Locke arrived. She weighed 8-Lbs, 2 ½ ounces; measured 21-inches long and was named after her mother's sister. She died at birth; the umbilical cord wrapped about her neck had strangled her to death. Men didn't accompany wives during labor in 1960; rather they paced waiting room floors; glancing nervously at doorways and wall clocks. When the nurse informed Dad his daughter was dead his first thought was of 'Patty.'

The following day, November 13, 1960, a memorial service was held for Nancy Elizabeth; attended by her parents, maternal grandparents – Ed and Letta Riddell – and Norman Locke. Leora was too sick to get out of bed. Twenty-one days later Leora Mosiman Locke succumbed to cancer. She was forty-nine years old. Dad sat quietly on Norm's couch weeping into his hands.

After Leora's funeral Mom and Dad returned to Bluffton. Removing himself from Franklin helped somewhat, as did keeping busy with coursework; but for Mom especially, the trailer - filled with baby toys and an empty nursery - haunted her. Returning to Franklin over Christmas break Mom stored the baby items at her parent's home; Yuletide festivities that year were dreary, somber, nearly unbearable affairs. On one end of town, the house at 65 Skokiaan Drive - where Leora had read to her sons - stood gloomy and dark; the silence only occasionally interrupted by the shuffling feet of her widowed husband.

On the other side of town at the Riddell residence, Letta gathered up Christmas presents intended for Nancy Elizabeth and placed them out of sight. Mom and Letta and Nancy cried intermittently and in torrents day after day while Dad took long walks in the icy December air. Two months later, during the first week of February 1961 - when Dad at least no longer felt numb - Phil arrived in Bluffton unannounced to tell his kid brother their father was dead.

Norman Cyril Locke had said repeatedly that he couldn't live without Leora. He didn't want to overcome her death. According to Mom, *"They had a lot of trouble in their marriage, but he adored her. And he had exhausted himself taking care of Leora; he was a mess so he checked into the hospital."* Norm entered Grandview Hospital in Dayton in extreme pain brought about by acute pancreatitis on February 3, 1961 and died two days later.

When Norm's mother, Clara Locke, stopped by the hospital to check on him he was nowhere to be found. *"It was a two-person room and so she asked, 'Where's Norman Locke?' And the other patient just blurted out: 'Oh, he's dead.'"* The cause of death was listed as 'Shock.' In just over four months his mother, father and daughter had died. He was twenty-one years old. The losses had a profound impact on my father. Death was indifferent; it struck down young and old alike - indiscriminately, without remorse or pity. Life − his life − was in no way guaranteed. It should thereafter be lived hard, at full-tilt - to the nth degree.

His outlook didn't develop into a selfish 'live-life-for-today, who cares about tomorrow' attitude; but became rather a sober awareness that the meaning of life is that it ends. My father never made a very good victim;

for the rest of his life he kept tilting forward into the storm; starting with those long walks across Franklin in the winter of 1960. There was method, as it turned out, behind the perpetual motion we observed in him as children. He became a living maelstrom; moving incessantly, outrunning death.

Besides teaching fulltime and coaching three sports, he planned camping and fishing trips, ran the CW pool, scouted CW's football opponents, earned his master's degree, painted store windows at Christmastime, hunted Morel mushrooms every spring, taught himself to play guitar; how to make homemade wine and brew homemade beer. He studied Karate, lifted weights and jogged; attended all of CW's school functions, went to hockey matches and coaching clinics; and after collapsing on his couch in the evenings read books until he was too tired to go on. Much of that pace and continual striving can be traced to the shock of losing his baby daughter, mother and dad in the winter of 1960/61.

On July 21, 1962 Laura was born – a healthy, beautiful baby girl – she was a joy and a relief. The previous nine months had been nerve wracking. But the delivery went well; three days later they brought her home to the trailer, at last putting Nancy's nursery to use. The following spring Dad graduated from Bluffton with a degree in science education. Concerned he wouldn't find a teaching job, and with Mom pregnant once again with yours truly, he had begun the process of becoming a secret service agent.

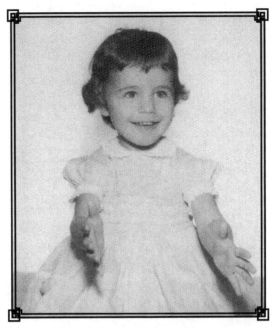

Laura Suzanne Locke.

With a college degree, and having served in the USMC, Dad was a promising candidate. He had already advanced through several stages of the government's secret service process. Mom, on the other hand, didn't want him taking a job where he'd have to carry a gun; fortunately, he was hired to teach science and senior biology at Richwood High School in June 1963, before toting loaded firearms became an issue.

Richwood, Ohio is located 34 miles Northeast of Columbus along Route-4 between Marion and Marysville. Mom happily put the trailer on the market and began packing for the 57-mile trip from Bluffton to their new home: A rental house located on Rural Route 3, the new place was definitely a step up from the cramped confines of the trailer.

From a single, rectangular tube at the edge of Bluffton's campus, they moved into a white, four-bedroom farmhouse with a first-floor master; double French doors and screened-in-porch. And their new abode looked out on 160-acres of rolling pastures, furrowed fields, meandering creeks, wood rows and fertile meadows. Not long after relocating the heavens aligned on June 23, 1963, marking my entry into the world and completing the Locke Clan's nuclear family.

Steve Locke.

The farm was a going-concern; with livestock, barns, grain silos, an old tool shed and quite a bit of farm machinery. The owners - the Wiley's - worked it fulltime, living less than a mile down Rural Route 3. They rented the house out while Mom and Dad were responsible for paying utilities, mowing the lawn, shoveling sidewalks and getting the Wiley's their rent-money on time. Laura and I did our part by waving to John Wiley whenever he drove by the screened back porch on his big red tractor.

Atop John Wiley's tractor on the Richwood farm, 1965.

Like CW, Richwood was a small, conservative Ohio town that took its local sports teams seriously. New teachers, no matter the location, are usually fairly nervous during their first weeks in the classroom – the proverbial 'Baptism of Fire' - and Dad was no different. He spent long hours that summer preparing lesson plans and reading the textbooks assigned to his classes.

Richwood' head football coach - Fritz Drodovsky – sat in during teacher interviews earlier that summer because he needed an assistant football coach and wanted to look over the candidates. Like all applicants Dad was asked if he would coach. He answered in the affirmative – despite having absolutely no coaching experience. Fortunately, he and Fritz hit it off during the interview; what Dad lacked in experience he'd make up through study and hard work.

Fritz Drodovsky was as Germanic as his name implied; heavyset - not fat - but big, beefy and square; he had a round, meaty, slightly Slavic face, blue eyes and close-cropped muddy blonde hair. On appearances alone it would have been easy to picture Fritz leading a Panzer Division across Europe for the Whermacht.

Fritz' wife, Betty, explained how anxious she was for football season to start each autumn as she feared Fritz's backside would permanently attach itself to their living room furniture over the summer months. Like his new assistant coach, Fritz Drodovsky was not big on manual labor. Indeed, Fritz didn't like to mow lawns, paint houses, clean gutters, shovel snow or work in the garden – he preferred soft couches, air conditioning and floating about his backyard swimming pool - both feet dangling in the water, hat pulled slightly over his eyes, a cold beer firmly in-hand.

Once football season began, however, Fritz underwent a metamorphosis no less dramatic than moth-to-butterfly, and his alter ego - Coach Drodovsky – took center stage. The laidback, easygoing German shopkeeper of June, July and August faded from memory and a dedicated, serious, slightly fanatical Teutonic high school football coach emerged – much to the chagrin of his Mid-Ohio League opponents.

Besides preparing for his teaching assignment Dad assisted Richwood's varsity squad during two-a-day football practices; coaching junior high football once classes began. Both experiences were invaluable in his new profession. Working with older, more capable athletes gave him a feel for the possibilities, granting a learning curve while he became familiar with the offensive and defensive schemes used in Fritz' system; coaching junior high ball put him in charge of a team for the first time, wielding authority over the group – and responsibility for any shortcomings.

Getting twenty-five 7th and 8th grade boys – many of whom were playing organized sports for the first time - ready to face eight different football teams complete with refs, cheerleaders, scoreboards, fans and curious onlookers was no easy task. They needed to get in shape; had to understand their offensive plays and various defensive assignments, taught fundamental tackling, blocking, kicking and throwing skills, and learn sportsmanship - how to handle both winning and losing.

Young coaches also receive their first taste of dealing with parents. For every mom and dad aware of their offspring's athletic limitations, there are three or four who firmly believe their child is God's Olympian gift to the sporting world; and that coaches – incomprehensively - are deliberately misusing Junior's talent. Despite the challenges Dad realized fairly quickly he'd found his calling; thoroughly enjoying both coaching and teaching.

As one of Richwood's youngest staff members it was important Dad demonstrate mastery of the subjects he would teach and earn his student's respect. And he did, though it wasn't easy. His first day teaching senior biology, for example, proved somewhat more primal than he anticipated. *"Ah, man you wouldn't believe it,"* he said of his first day on the job. *"I spent something like six hours preparing that first lesson plan; I knew it backwards and forwards and was ready for any question the kids might have. So I'm standing up there in my suit, writing on the chalkboard, talking away."*

Describing that long ago first day, he pretends to straighten his tie, clears his throat and assumes the mien of an authority figure. *"Anyway, the classroom was down in a basement and behind the teacher's desk, in the area where I'm lecturing, is a window that I can see through but the kids can't. Thank God! So I begin the lesson and it's going pretty well and for whatever reason I glance out the window. And two feet on the other side of the window two dogs are fucking!"*

You've got to be kidding me? *"No. I swear to God! I'd of liked to have died man. I mean they were going at it. And I looked at them for a second, and my mind goes blank. And then one of the girls asks, 'What's the matter Mr. Locke?' I turned to look at that kid and must have looked like a dear in the headlights."* What'd you say? *"Oh, I recovered – just barely - and said I'd lost my train of thought and continued on. But those fucking dogs – no pun intended,"* (laughter) *"went at it for 30 minutes. I made damn sure the kids stayed in their seats until the bell rang. I'd a liked to have died man!"*

Two days later, in the same classroom, his rookie teaching skills were once again put to the test. *"It's the third day,"* he continued, *"I'm up there talking and I've got one of those old chairs with the handle on it where you put one elbow on it. And I'm talking and there was a guy sitting right in the front row and right behind him was this girl – I didn't even know all their names yet. So behind the guy was this girl and she was sitting there looking at me and she went – Bllaaagh! - And threw up all over this guy's head.*

(Laughter) *I mean, she never said 'I'm sick,' or 'Can I go to the bathroom,' she never turned her head. She must have been looking at my face,"* (laughter) *"I don't know, but she barfs all over this guy – he's screaming 'You dirty whore!' – And there's barf and the other kids are sliding their chairs out of the way and it's my third day!"*

During his first year at Richwood - coaching three sports - Dad earned $4,300 - or $477.00 monthly for nine months; *"My first year,"* he recalled, *"I was junior high football coach, junior high basketball coach and assistant track coach – and I loved it. I loved all the coaching. I loved* the teaching too. *I really enjoyed it; being a ham, running off at the mouth up in front of class. I enjoyed the kids and coaching."* He would sometimes comment of his chosen profession, *"It beats the hell out of working for a living."* After the USMC, and summers at Maxwell Paper teaching and coaching didn't seem like work.

On another occasion at Richwood - again while in the middle of teaching - came a knock on his classroom door. Teachers, then as now, often sent messengers when unable to leave students unattended. So he hears a knock on the door; *"and I go over and open the door and there stands Bonnie Bell, a junior high student, with a folded piece of white paper. So I say thanks and take the note but Bonnie says, 'Mr. Pouterri said I had to wait for you to read it.'"*

Who's Pouterri? *"Ah man. He was this crazy son-of-a-bitch I coached and taught with. Good guy, but crazy as hell."* Did you suspect something? *"No not really. I mean, my mind was on the lesson at hand and next thing I know I'm in a conversation with Bonnie Bell, and so I never had time to think he was up to anything. So anyway, I thought it kind of odd he wanted her to stand there while I read it but I opened it up quick because I needed to get back to my class. And I open it up and it says: 'Hey Locke, have you ever seen tits this big on an eighth grader before in your life? Mr. P.'"*

You're not serious? Oh my God what if she had opened it? *"I know man,"* he said shaking his head. *"I stood there for a second with my mouth hanging open. Folded the note, put it in my pocket and told Bonnie to tell Mr. Pouterri I said thank you. And when I saw Pouterri at practice after school he was rolling man, just laughing his ass off, asking if I got his note. God he was a crazy son-of-a-bitch!"*

By his fourth year at Richwood Dad no longer wanted to be an assistant coach. He liked Fritz Drodovsky, but felt he understood the game well enough to throw his hat into the ring and apply for a head coaching job. He also knew he wanted to work in a small town like Franklin or Richwood. With that in mind he unfolded a State of Ohio road map, spread it across the dining room table and proceeded to circle fifteen to twenty small schools in red ink. He penned an introduction letter, made copies and posted them forthwith.

One of those schools held an annual invitational track meet Richwood participated in; and he made a special point to mail one of his letters to their superintendent - C.A. Miller. During the spring of 1967, Dad brought Richwood's Wildcats to the Milton Will Invitational Track Meet in Canal Winchester, Ohio. The invitational lasted all day and included as many as fifteen different high schools. C.A. Miller – Canal Winchester's politically astute superintendent - was busy roaming the infield, schmoozing parents, speaking with students and chatting-up various coaches from visiting schools. When C.A. met Dad he introduced himself and the two snuck off to C.A.'s office to conduct their interview in private.

C.A. took a shine to Dad; and the basis for that attraction turned out to be the United States Marine Corps. C.A., fortuitously, had also served in the Corps, and since that time came to believe American kids were soft. The superintendent also confided he was under considerable pressure due to the dismal state of the district's football program. In the course of their conversation he outlined - in great detail - just how dreadful the 1960s had been for his Indians.

Since 1960 every season ended with a losing record – save 1963 when they broke even, 5-5. 1960, (2 -8); 1961, (3-7); 1962, (3-7); 1963, (5-5); 1964, (2-6-1); 1965, (1-8). Most depressingly, during the preceding autumn's campaign, the Indians finished dead last in the Mid State League, (0-8-1); losing the final game of the 1966 season 74 to 6. The football program had become an embarrassment – an albatross about C.A.'s neck - and no superintendent - no matter how politically astute – could survive an entire decade in a small, sports crazed town with a record like that.

The losing had to stop. The next coach had to understand the game of football; eliminate Canal's culture-of-losing; have a thick skin; possess the ability to motivate kids; and coach the football team to more than five wins. The interview ended with a hand shake and both men returned to the Milton Will Invitational. Two weeks later Dad got a call from C.A. According to the superintendent he had narrowed his search to two candidates, himself and Mike Locke – and C.A. admitted he definitely did not want the job.

After four years in Richwood moving was not easy. It meant uprooting the family, relocating to another small Ohio town where they didn't know a soul. Mom would have to give up the farmhouse, and the 160 acres that went with it to reside in a tiny; three-bedroom Sears home fifteen feet from retired owners who didn't want to rent to a family with kids. And if the football program did not turn around, her husband would end up getting fired like the previous coaches.

On the other hand, with Laura about to begin Kindergarten the timing was right. Dad wanted to be a head coach and Mom wanted what Dad wanted; so he accepted the job and talked Mac Gayman into renting his house. It was a scary time – he had gotten what he wished for – a football program. He alone was now responsible not only for wins and losses, but un-sportsman-like play, poor academic performance, uniforms, conditioning, game plans, the junior high and JV programs, dealing with parents, boosters, game time decisions, halftime adjustments, assistant coaches and a thousand other tasks that come with the territory.

It suited him to a Tee. Theodore Roosevelt once remarked that the best way for a man to live his life is to engage in some great struggle holding real meaning for him; to be consumed in a fight that matters. My father found that. He was one of those few, fortunate people who knew exactly what they wanted to do in life and was able to do it. And the underlying drive that would sustain him throughout three decades of coaching was unquestionably raw, naked – nearly all-consuming - competitiveness.

Indeed, despite his penchant for corny jokes and sad country ballads; the easy, elongated strides of his gait; the white belts and white shoes he donned because "good guys wore white"; and his oft-masked soft heartedness; he was more than anything else absolutely, implacably competitive. He wanted to win at everything – pickup basketball, golf, euchre, chess, and especially on the football field. He detested - with every fiber of his being – losing and played to win.

There is a story regarding quarterback John Elway's fierce competitiveness that comes to mind: When John Elway's backup the last couple years of his NFL career – Bubby Brister - beat the Bronco starter in a game of billiards, Elway sold his pool table the following day. Apocryphal or not, that mindset is no doubt what propels successful people to the top of their fields; and Dad – for better or worse – had it. For instance: When playing pickup basketball he once broke his hand after punching the brick wall in the school gymnasium. He had missed a shot costing his team the game.

He took up golf in the mid-1970s; playing at Homestead Springs where he became close with the owner –Buddy Rainier. Buddy was older; had lost a son in Vietnam and Dad, having lost his father in 1961, enjoyed something close to a father/son relationship with Mr. Rainier. Despite Buddy's patient golfing instructions Dad once returned from the links without his driver. After two tee-shots went awry he heaved the offending 1-wood down the fairway – propelled by a litany of epithets. It landed in a small pond, disappearing forever into its muddy depths.

He liked playing euchre, primarily because it didn't require mental exertion and he enjoyed breaks from his responsibilities. When partnered with Phil they devised several slogans reflecting their card playing philosophy: *'Obnoxious in defeat, unbearable in victory!'* was one of their favorite maxims. When the cards didn't fall his way, however, he was decidedly unpleasant to be around. Once at Christmas, after taking a trick, he grabbed my arm because he hadn't been able to see the card. After several losing hands he abruptly stood up and said, *"I can't stand it!"* *"I can't stand it!"* and then stormed away from the card table.

Phil, a mathematics professor at the University of Maine, once challenged his younger brother to a chess match during one of our family vacations in the Pine Tree State. Despite having plans that day, Dad sat opposite Phil staring at pawns, rooks and knights for eleven hours; whereupon he checkmated his older brother. They never played again. The last example occurred while on vacation in Tennessee. We had rendezvoused with my aunt's family, spending the week fishing, swimming and camping in the Smokey Mountains.

At our campsite a long, heavy rope hung from a huge Birch tree. In the evenings after fishing all day, kids scrambled up the Birch, taking turns swinging out over the lake and jumping into the water. My cousin Missy ran track in Middletown, Ohio; a good athlete, Missy was perhaps a 7th or 8th grader at the time. On our first evening in camp Dad helped me grab the rope following Missy's leap; before I swung away he said, *"That was a pretty good jump. But you don't want to let her beat you. Really swing into it and get some air under you."*

Once he issued this challenge beating her jump was important to me as well. Up to that point, however, it had never occurred to me. Granted, I was never the sharpest knife in the drawer - and never much of an athlete - so perhaps my disinterest was atypical. But it struck me at the time as indicative of his personality. He didn't turn around and announce to the group Steve would jump higher than Missy; and after I did he never said a word, but it was important to him that his son compete and win – whether anyone else knew a contest was afoot or not.

So when C.A. Miller hired Mike Locke to coach Canal Winchester's woeful, downtrodden football team he had unknowingly enlisted one of the fiercest, most aggressive, stridently competitive human beings alive to his cause. He was 28-years old.

CHAPTER XI:

LITTLE LOCKE IN 1975

"My father rests behind a hedge,
Bard of my storied childhood,
And in the fading half-light of ambition,
Wanting and having merge . . ."

(Linda Pastan – In the Walled Garden)

I was born June 23, 1963 – five months prior to President Kennedy's assassination in Dallas Texas. Laura and I were only eleven months apart and spent every waking hour together – an arrangement she would have preferred to alter. According to my beloved mother yours-truly was the ugliest newborn in the Dayton Hospital. *"Oh my God!"* she said, *"There were all these beautiful babies behind the glass in the maternity ward and people were looking at you, pointing and saying, 'look at that baby, look at that redheaded kid.' You were scrawny and long with bright red hair and you were moving your arms and legs - you looked like a spider."*

If that doesn't bring tears to your eyes – what could? As a little kid I enjoyed climbing trees, riding atop tractors with the owner of our Richwood home, John Wiley, and playing with our German shepherd. Dad worried about my masculinity, as I was continually surrounded by Mom, Laura, Cousin Missy, Grandma Riddell and my Aunt Nancy.

Every time I'd breathe funny two women jumped to my aid, whisking me away from potential harm.

To compensate for this feminization Dad took an overly He-Man approach when dealing with his boy. As he stood 6-feet, 2-inches tall and weighed over two-hundred pounds, he frightened me. When I'd fall down or skin a knee he'd bark, *"Shake it off Locke! Get up! You're alright!"* Eventually I took to crying whenever he entered the room; which seemed to prove his point. Exasperated he'd say, *"Keep crying and I'll give you something to cry about!"* And the cycle continued.

At some point Mom intervened; warning Dad that if he didn't speak softly, hug me and stop trying to ensure I'd be tough; she'd leave, taking Laura and me with her. Dad hadn't grown up in an overly affectionate family; though he certainly loved me, he didn't know exactly how to show it. As it turned out he needn't have worried about my handling adversity. Childhood – in my case - became an endless series of physical traumas. Mom and Dad came to believe I was 'fearless;' chasing cows about the corral while still in diapers, climbing across rooftops, ordering stray dogs about - the typical rough and tumble farm boy. Mom used to say she had to spank me to keep me alive because I lacked the 'fear gene.'

Actually, nothing could've been further from the truth. All parents have an abiding and irrational love for their children; and what Mom and Dad saw as my absence of fear was in reality an absence of brains – caution, forethought, being even remotely sentient. From the first moments of consciousness I dwelled in a world of my own – completely - and with only minimal interruption. Once I recognized that herding cattle, climbing roofs and taking food from stray dogs was dangerous, I desisted. It just took me a lot longer to figure things out than it did the typical child.

That lack of awareness, and the resulting slew of injuries led our family doctor in Richwood to suspect child abuse; I was continually rushed to his office or the nearby hospital. At age two, I reached for the Iron on our ironing board. It fell on my left hand. Being too small to lift it, the Iron burned my third and fourth fingers down to the bone. The following year my right hand got stuck in an empty soup can with a half-opened lid. Laura decided to assist in the removal, yanking my wrist and freeing the appendage. The fingers of my right hand were forced across the jagged lid – nearly slicing them off.

Because I dislocated my shoulder almost weekly the family doctor showed Mom and Dad how to reset it in order to avoid the expense of an office visit. Having noticed that our German shepherd, whom I dubbed "Noonie", growled and snapped when I tried to take his bone, I put on a pair of Dad's gloves to see how hard he could bite. Mom had warned me not to take his bone or disturb him when he ate, but I liked the sensation of getting bitten through my gloved hand.

At Grandma and Grandpa Riddell's, while the grownups talked in the kitchen, I went into the garage, climbed into grandpa's car and pressed the cigarette lighter. When it popped it didn't appear hot; the inside of the lighter was white and not red. Surmising it didn't work unless the car was running I pushed my right index finger into its base until it reached the heated coil - finding that it did indeed work when the car wasn't running.

One day, not long after we moved to Canal Winchester, I cut Laura's grapefruit for her, ignoring her protestations that Mom or Dad ought to do it. Moments later, bright red blood began spreading out from the base of the grapefruit like ripples in a pond. Mrs. Ensley drove us to Children's Hospital in Columbus where doctors reattached my index finger. On and on it went. In each instance my injuries resulted from being brainless; or more fairly, of living not so much in the world peopled by those around me, but in my own, unique, separate universe. Grandma Riddell used to tell mom, *"Patty, that boy won't live to be an adult. You'll never get him through."*

Incongruously, I was also a worrier; at an early age whispering whatever I intended to say before saying it aloud. Perhaps Dad had been right to doubt my masculinity, since I inherited from Mom a pronounced capacity to sob. For example: when the networks aired *The Wizard of OZ*, without fail I excused myself as Dorothy prepared to leave OZ; saying her tearful farewells to the Tin Man, Cowardly Lion and Scarecrow.

The first couple times it happened I announced that unquenchable thirst was driving me from the room. I ran to the kitchen, pretending to drink chocolate milk; while in actuality I stood with the glass in front of my face squalling beside the refrigerator. When Lassie injured her paw, Frosty melted in the greenhouse or our neighbor shot pigeons off the roof of his house, you could bet your ass I was weeping uncontrollably.

Of course, even as a distracted youth I understood there was a time and place for emotional displays – and the CW playground was not one of them. Indeed, recess at Canal Winchester Elementary was Like Mutual of Omaha's Wild Kingdom – a veritable survival-of-the-fittest. Every day, at least one knockdown, drag out fight would break out, and when it did a gauntlet of fight fans would immediately encircle the combatants.

During recess in first grade Trent Shaw, Randy Gohagen, Ray Spence, Dean Ray, Danny Haynes and an inexhaustible cadre of sandlot toughs beat the living hell out of each other and anyone else who got in their way. Thirty years later my brother-in-law, Jeff Jordan, who had moved from Worthington to CW as a fifth grader, recalled the cultural shock he had felt after arriving – and surviving recess - at his new school, *"Oh my God it was like entering the Dark Ages,"* he groaned.

No doubt 'Dark Ages' is an exaggeration but one that aptly captures the playground dynamic at the time. Not only were there daily spats but at least once a week the buzz would begin about 'a big fight.' No matter what grade the antagonists, the male half of the student body were in attendance to cheer, jeer, root, critique, berate losers and congratulate victorious pugilists when the dust had settled.

While the hard asses pounded each other, Rick Kriegal and I played 'Army' – stalking across vast expanses of playground and then shooting each other with imaginary rifles, for which we supplied our own, unique sound effects. We played tag, kickball and dodge-ball; mastered the monkey bars, tossed footballs back and forth and even used the swing sets on occasion; but never once did we demonstrate even the remotest desire to pummel our classmates.

My favorite sport was basketball; due to accompanying Dad to the gym Saturdays and Sundays while he played pickup hoops. He gave me a basketball and I dribbled alone, shooting baskets in the multipurpose room. Dad easily spent three hours at the gym both days and as a result my dribbling skills excelled. It was during this period that I received one of the few compliments for doing anything remotely athletic. The young men waiting their turn to take the court would say things like, *"Damn, look at that little kid dribble the basketball!" "How long you been playing kid?" "Watch this kid, Man he can dribble the shit out of that ball."*

Older kids – Dad's high school football players - called me '*Little Locke*' from the beginning. Receiving attention from older kids and being called a name I had never heard was confusing, but once in town with Dad it became clear why I was being singled out. Teachers are recognized in the communities where they work and when in town can expect – indeed count on - kids saying hello or yelling from across the streets. Yet it was unbelievable the amount of attention Dad received.

Somehow he was different from my friend's fathers; he was constantly stopped, patted on the back and had his hand shaken vigorously. While Rick Shirk's Dad might have friends stop him and say, "*Hey, Dick how are you?*" my father was never called Mike, but rather 'Coach.' At Super Duper, Conrad's Market, Canal View Pharmacy, the CW swimming pool, on the streets – everywhere we went someone honked their horn and yelled, "*Hey Coach Locke!*"

Men slapped Dad on the back saying things like, "*How's the team looking this year coach?*" "*Who's going to be you're QB next year coach?*" "*How the Hell you been coach?*" "*Did you see the Buckeyes Coach?*" And always, over and over if Canal lost a football game, "*What happened coach?*" In retrospect it was like being in the entourage of a rock star – which surely sounds like an exaggeration – but everyone, everywhere, seemed to know him, wanted to talk to him and treated him as someone special. Motorists honked car horns upon sighting him; yelled and waved when we gassed up at Parker's Sohio; and accosted him in grocery aisles – occasionally glancing my way and asking, "*How are you Mike?*"

Kids on Waterloo Street – when they were young – believed their fathers to be the best men in town. The Ensley kids, Rick Shirk, Carl Swartz and Terry Winlan repeatedly argued over which of their fathers was toughest, richest, fastest, the smartest - and in what ways. I never said much during those debates, for I already knew that my Dad was really the toughest, richest, fastest, smartest and certainly most famous man in town.

We were a close family; despite rarely seeing Dad. Being the only son of a successful coach in a small town had a number of advantageous perks. I got to see and hear adults – seen and heard elsewhere exclusively as authority figures – with their guards down. When we went camping and fishing, Mr. Jones went along, and I listened to his conversations; what he thought about certain student-athletes – and what he thought of academically poor students. Coach Lewis tramped through the woods hunting morel mushrooms with our family, and I was able to observe another side of him – one not apparent to the rest of the student body.

At the dentist, doctor's office, and pharmacy people treated me well. They'd ask, "*Are you Mike Locke's boy? How is your Dad? Are you going to be a football player when you grow up?*" "*Are you going to coach football like your Dad?*" Despite being christened *Steve*, and called *Little Locke* by the older kids in town, I was often referred to as 'Mike.' And as much as I enjoyed the attention, I tried never to abuse the advantage. Indeed, one of my greatest fears at school was being accused of favoritism. Classmates had no way of knowing that Dad's first words to my teachers every year were: "*If he gives you any trouble. Beat him! Beat his ass – you have my full support. I won't have a kid of mine acting up in class*"

It took until high school to realize there was nothing I could do or say to change perceptions. For example, during sophomore Spanish class we reviewed a weekly quiz aloud on Thursdays, and one week I did quite well. The next day, however, I bombed the written test. Mrs. Zanner – Elisa Zanner from Honduras – was, shall we say, somewhat unconventional, and when the quizzes were handed in at the end of class she looked at my score with surprise and said, "*Esteban! What happened? You did so well yesterday in the review? No, no, no! I will change the C to an A.*"

She had her favorites and up to that point I hadn't qualified, but gratefully accepted the upward adjustment in my grade. The following Monday, toward the end of Spanish class, a fellow-sophomore named Kathy said, "*Man my mom was pissed at you this weekend!*" I didn't much know Kathy's mom and Kathy wasn't someone in my orbit of friends, though she was always very nice. Surprised I asked why her mom was angry, "*Because you got an A instead of a C on the Spanish quiz because of your Dad, that's why. It's not fair!*" Though the accusation was inane, I knew it wouldn't do any good to point out that Dad couldn't – and wouldn't – ask another teacher to change my grade.

As a seventh grader I had no choice but to take science from Canal Winchester's 7th grade science teacher – Mr. Locke. The science room had three rows of long black tables accommodating two students each; allowing for dissections, lab work and other scientific experimentation. The science teacher's desk was extra long and bolted to the floor. It had a built-in sink, electrical outlets and an area for Bunsen Burners. Beside the blackboard were two props - 'Plastic-Removable-Body-Part-Torso-Man' and the schools lone Skeleton-on-wheels.

Science teacher, Mike Locke, explaining the mysteries of the human ear. 1975

I sat in the rear of the room, middle aisle – the last possible desk - with Rick Kriegel. On the first day of class Dad pulled me aside and said, *"You've called me Dad your whole life so it's OK to call me Dad in class."* This provided momentary relief in an awkward situation for an awkward twelve-year-old; and I appreciated Dad's kind words. Immediately thereafter I felt overwrought concern that my classmates saw the exchange and would suspect that he had imparted information privy only to his son.

Dad entered class smiling almost every day, and then loudly uttered the only Spanish phrase he knew – compliments of Mrs. Zanner - *"Que-Pasa!"* He liked showing Disney science movies on the school's communal projector – though it was often necessary for Mr. Butts to thread and start films for him. Entering a classroom and discovering a projector the first thing students focused on was the size of the reel. Big reels meant big breaks and no work that day; small reels usually meant that a pop quiz would follow the film.

As he worked through the seventh grade science textbook Dad stood beside 'Plastic-Removable-Body-Parts-Man' day after day, holding up the heart and discussing its valves; likewise the kidneys, lungs, intestines, etc., patiently describing some mysterious anatomical system to his captive, seventh grade audience. He also made ample use of the mobile skeleton and would often put a joke-question on a quiz or test: "*Q. True or False. A Greasy Burger is the result of a Barfo-tropism?*" Or 'matching:' 'Starsky' in one column, 'Hutch' in the other.

My father had an easygoing teaching style, and kept students busy from bell-to-bell. His demeanor was surprising to some – including yours truly – in that it seemed to contradict the striding, authoritarian football coach persona. My surprise stemmed from the fact that I spent more time with my father as his seventh grade student than I ever spent with him at home.

He was able to do all that – the educational films, physical presentations, lighthearted jokes and banter - primarily because when classroom rules were broken he paddled offenders. Because he followed through with corporal punishment he only ended up paddling one or two kids annually – usually at the beginning of the school year. And though frequently hearing students say they loved Dad's class, I also heard the obverse from those he'd punished.

Once, during lunch of the second week of 7th grade, I sat my tray atop the aqua-colored folding table, climbed over the attached bench and sat down to eat. Across the aisle, Kent Long, whom I'd known since third grade, took a seat, looked at me intently and said: "*I hate your fucking Dad! I fucking hate him!*"

Kent Long wasn't in my science class; and I had no way of knowing he'd been paddled by my father. But there it was. Rick Watson, on the other hand, was in my science class, and after he too became a recipient of corporal punishment meted out by my father, Rick shared to those around him that he also "*Fucking hated*" my Dad. Canal was a tough place, and there were kids who routinely crossed the line, but it was difficult to hear those things about your father.

CWHS didn't have a vice principal in 1975, so a great deal of discipline devolved to Mr. McCann, who had a well earned reputation for wielding the paddle. Students in the old wing knew that in addition to Mr. McCann and Dad, Mr. Lake, Mr. Jones, Mr. Brisker, and Mr. Peterson - even Miss Thomas and Miss Ralph - all swung the paddle when they deemed it necessary. "*The first time I saw one of the boys bent over on the gym floor to get paddled while we sat in the bleachers,"* recalled Mary Matyac, *"I almost fainted. Coach Locke, Mr. Brisker and Mr. McCann were accepted by all to be the paddlers. Female teachers would threaten disruptive students with a visit to one of the three and everyone knew what that meant. Howard Siegrist threatened nearly every day to paddle someone but no one took him seriously. I don't think he ever actually paddled anyone. I did once see him throw books at Mark Meadows and then throw a desk at him. I think Mark had unbolted his chair or done something equally disruptive. Mr. Peters tried to paddle a student in study hall my junior or senior year, but the boy took the paddle out of his hand, broke it in two, and threw it out the window. Only coaches and the principal were intimidating enough to get away with unchallenged paddling."* Sensitive to the sufferings of classmates like Kent Long, my loyalties nevertheless rested with Dad, and it hurt to hear him denigrated.

I found solace in humor. Indeed, by the time seventh grade began in the autumn of 1975 my skills at making people laugh were well honed. This came easily to me and reflected the weird and idiosyncratic way I observed the world; a view not always shared by family or friends. Both Mom and Dad were storytellers, as was Grandpa Riddell. As kids we had listened intently to their tall tales. Dad loved bawdy jokes, corny jokes, one-liners and even convoluted riddles if the payoff was funny.

On weekend fishing excursions Dad told jokes wholly unsuitable for the fairer-sex. He'd say something like, *"Now don't tell your mother I told this joke, but . . ."* When he did so, it made me feel like 'one of the guys,' reinforcing the notion that some things were just not meant for the ladies. I was an auditory person for whom every joke, nuance and punch line stuck. This came in handy on the playground.

On our ride home from one especially long Saturday fishing trip Dad stopped at a tavern outside Lancaster, Ohio. We sat on leather stools at the bar, waiting for our hamburgers and fries. Swiveling back and forth on my seat I watched him drink his beer. In that particular establishment he sipped *Stroh's* while I took an occasional swig of *Coca-Cola*. It occurred to me Rick Shirk's Dad detested *Stroh's Beer*. In fact he referred to it as 'Panther-Piss' – which Rick and I thought the funniest thing in the world. Rarely alone with my father, feeling awkward during a long silent lull, I asked, *"Dad do you like Stroh's beer? Because Mr. Shirk says it tastes like Panther Piss."* He looked at me in apparent disbelief, took a swig from his frosty brew and then gently explained the facts of life: *"Beer's like women boy. It's all good, just some of its better than others."* Unfortunately that adage struck me as immensely profound – and with the aforementioned auditory skills, I committed it to memory. At home a week or so later, and without the slightest notion it might not be well received, I blurted out, *"Beer's like women mom. It's all good, just some of its better than others!"*

"Oh for God's sake Steven Paul, where did you hear that?" she demanded. *"Dad told me on the way home from our fishing trip."* Unaware it compromised the Old Man; I had forgotten about it until our next excursion. Alone in the car a few miles from home he looked over and said, *"By the way; for God's sakes don't repeat to your mother things I tell you on our fishing trips; like beer being the same as women - God damn boy!"*

It's worth mentioning, what with being the coach's son; that my physical makeup in 1975 didn't meet prevailing small town 'expectations.' Most youngsters are self-conscious about their bodies and I was no exception. Offspring of coaches, however, are held to higher standards, especially in regard to athleticism.

It certainly isn't a fair assumption. Even to a brain dead twelve-year-old the logic didn't hold up. Wilt Chamberlain's kid, for example, could be expected to inherit an athletic gene or two. But just because Woody Hayes' coached the Buckeyes didn't mean his son – Steve Hayes - would be an athlete or play football at Ohio State. Nor did it follow that I might be any more athletic than the next kid. But alas, such reasoning did not hold.

I had won a couple swimming races as a 1st grader, but those feats constituted the beginning, middle and end of my athletic accomplishments. Though not mentally slow, physically - once out of the friendly confines of the CW Pool - I slowed to a crawl. By age twelve I was plodding, almost always worried about something, generally uncertain and absolutely glacially ponderous. President Lincoln once commented on General McClellan that he had what the rail-splitter referred to as *"a case of the slows."*

In my case the affliction was terminal. As a result, from the time I started missing pop-ups in Little League baseball, through the first years of 'Pee-Wee-Packer' football, Canal Winchester's youth coaches and volunteers expressed utter dismay at my non-existent athletic abilities.

For example, the high school football team began practice as soon as Dad emerged from the locker room and blew his whistle; with that signal the entire team jogged a quarter-mile lap around the track before ascending a small knoll to start calisthenics.

The men coaching pee-wee football did the same, beginning each practice with a mandatory lap. And the head football coach's son finished not fifth from last, not 3rd from last, but dead last. Sometimes Rick Kriegal showed up wearing farm boots and ended up in the final spot, but nine out of ten practices that dubious distinction was mine alone. Predictably, Dad came home one evening and said to Mom, *"Guess who was the very last pee-wee football player running the warm-up lap?"* Mom said nothing so Dad graciously volunteered the answer: *"Your son!"*

My face reddened as he went on, *"Hell there were little kids running ahead of him!"* At that he looked at me and warned, *"If you want to play football you're going to have to work harder. I know you're not fast but you ought to at least be in the middle of the pack, Middle-C."* Middle-C, I thought to myself. I can make Middle-C. It's embarrassing finishing last; let alone being the coach's son and finishing last - I'd run harder on the morrow.

Worry, my constant companion, consumed me that night and the next day. I secretly vowed to find the ever elusive 'Middle-C' at practice. When the whistle blew I ran as never before. Breathing mightily through a soggy plastic mouthpiece; the football helmet encasing my head bouncing up and down with each stride, rhythmically thumping the top of my skull, shoulder pad straps digging into my armpits; the foam padding tucked into my football pants growing heavier and heavier with each successive step, I chugged awkwardly around the enormous cinder track.

At last, having pushed my ungainly, pre-pubescent ass to the middle of the pack I began glancing over my shoulder every few seconds to see if Dad, who was coaching atop the hill, was observing my achievement. When we later lined up for stretching the 'Pee-Wee-Packer' coach rapped my helmet with his whistle – producing horrific, reverberating concussions within its shell – and said, *"I can't believe you're the coach's son and you're out there jogging in the middle. Come on Locke! You ought to be out front!"*

Likewise in Little League baseball; after striking out, missing pop-ups, or failing to slide properly into home plate, I'd hear; *"Can you believe he's the coach's son?"* Once, when several of us were lifting stacks of mats in the gymnasium following intramurals, Mrs. Ralph, our 7th and 8th grade math teacher, noticed my struggles and remarked, *"I'm surprised Pat Zerby's carrying so much more than you. I thought for sure you were stronger than Pat, being the coach's son and all."* And so it went.

Along with lowered expectations, junior high school offered a wide range of humiliations - like the advent of acne taking up residence upon one's face. Waves of energy and raging hormones coursed through the veins - making it difficult, if not unbearable, to sit still. Forced to inhabit that weird space between childhood and young adulthood, we endured the unrelenting onset of puberty, in my case working through all of those changes at school in front of my parents while classmates looked on.

As Canal Winchester's staff and students prepared to attend the first Friday night varsity football game of 1975 it would be fair to say that I was quietly the team's most ardent fan. Tickets were on sale all day on Fridays during the season. Mrs. Thomas set up folding tables decorated with maroon and white bunting outside the principal's office; along with programs, buttons, pom-poms; plastic footballs and other CWHS athletic department items. Most of it sold by the end of lunch period.

It irked Mom that Laura and I had to pay to attend football games our father coached. In charge of the bills she watched every penny, and felt that her husband, especially in regards to coaching, was grossly underpaid. She once added up all the hours he spent coaching: traveling to and from games, running coaching meetings, game-planning with his staff, watching endless reels of game film, scouting opponents, attending clinics, and then divided said hours into his coaching salary. When the quotient came to .23 cents an hour she ran the numbers a second time. The result was the same.

With this knowledge at her disposal she walked into the athletic director's office unannounced one afternoon, cornering both Dan Brisker – the AD - and Mr. McCann – the principal. She stated her case - the principal and AD readily agreed – and Mom reported that we need no longer purchase football tickets. Laura, self confident and in complete accord with the arrangement, had no problem serenely striding past the ticket booth Friday nights, skirting the long winding line of parents and football fans to rendezvous with chums inside the gate.

For me it was awful, but not because Mom was wrong. It was clear, even to my distracted, adolescent self, that Dad lived at the school, and poured his heart and soul as well as a good bit of his disposable income into the program. But showing up to football games, the biggest event of the week in our tiny community, and drawing unwanted attention to myself by ditching while everyone else waited in line; walking past the ticket booth without paying, epitomized the exact type of preferential treatment I desperately wanted to avoid.

To skirt the issue I took to showing up early, blending-in and hiding until enough spectators filtered through the gate to emerge unnoticed into the growing throng. For away games I just bought tickets with my own money. Thus demonstrating un-preferential, working class solidarity with my peers. This was not exactly throwing myself on the barricades, but it captures my makeup at the time: worried, insecure, emotional, self-conscious and uncertain. Later, in high school, having grown taller, stronger and surer of myself, confidence and self-assuredness took root – but in junior high I was a pustule.

I stood five-feet, six-inches tall with bushy brown hair, hazel eyes and slouching shoulders. I watched *The Six Million Dollar Man*, *Kung Fu* and *Kolchak the Night Stalker*; *Flippo the Clown*, *MASH*; *The Brady Bunch*, *F-Troop* and *All in the Family* on TV. My favorite food was pepperoni pizza. I had a crush on Raquel Welsh and Shirley Jones – Mrs. Partridge from the Partridge Family.

Little Locke, Pat Zerby and Rick Kriegel,
annoying Laura and her friends, autumn 1975

At Canal Winchester, Linda Jordan had caught my eye, though I never dared to tell her so. As a good student, lousy athlete, obnoxious brother, adored grandson, and seldom-seen nephew, I wore many hats. I was a fanatical beer can collector, plodding runner, avid fisherman, animated joke-teller and momma's boy. My best friends were Rick Kriegel, Pat Zerby and Greg Bruce who knew me as 'Steve,' Others' knew me as 'Little Locke.' In my heart I was simply the coach's son, and his football team's biggest fan.

Dad talking to Captain Bill Allen on the sidelines.

PART II

AND THE MIGHTY INDIANS OF '75

"Seventeen, no great event
he says. He glides past us
with undisturbed intent.

He would photograph well
easing into the jeep
whose military shell
he painted red to cover
the old green wounds,
that war long over.

This boy, this innocence,
Brown, summer muscle
Flexed without pretense.

There are no mysteries
for him. The winter branch
always leafs into light.
Supreme biology.
His days shine with chance.

I follow his car in mine.
Dust rises from our road.
Three months without rain,
Already some of the pines

I planted a year ago
are dead. When we reach
the highway, we go
apart. Always the wrong time

To tell my son what I mean.
He doesn't see my wave.
When I was seventeen
I didn't look back either."

(Christopher Brookhouse)

Chapter XII:

CANAL WINCHESTER FOOTBALL

In the autumn of 1974, for the second time in Dad's eight-year tenure as Canal Winchester's Head Football Coach, his Indians won every game; compiling a perfect 10-0, record. When Dad took over the program in 1967, the Indians hadn't recorded a winning season since 1959. In 1970 they went undefeated for the first time – ever. Though Canal Winchester had fielded its first football team in 1909, during the ensuing 61 years it had never once gone unbeaten.

The town relished the 1970 accomplishment. The final victory that year ignited an impromptu parade through the streets of Canal Winchester. Fire trucks and ambulances with blaring sirens led the way. The CW Marching Band wailed away on brass instruments and pounded drums, while the football team, parents, cheerleaders and coaches followed in the wake. At the banquet that November Dad and his staff were showered with gifts, trophies, US Treasury Bonds and repeated, thunderous applause.

According to Coach Dave Lewis; *"If you were in school at CW in the early 70s and you weren't in the band or an athlete on one of the teams, there wasn't much to do. I mean seriously, I mean coming to the football game on Friday night was it!"* Warming to the topic Coach Lewis offered an example, *"Hey, the town went nuts after winning it all in 1970, but look what happened to the reserve squad in 1972 or 1973. Our JV team played Pickerington's JV team during the eighth game of the year and it's on a Monday night. Our JV team was undefeated and un-scored upon and Pickerington's JV team was unbeaten. We played Monday night at Pickerington under the lights to a packed stadium."* It was packed on a Monday night for JV's? *"Absolutely, a Monday night JV game and its packed. Roger Hanners radio station, WHOK even broadcast the game. A JV game! Leading late in the game we stopped them on a goal-line stand with 30-seconds left when Rick VonSchriltz intercepted a pass in the end zone. And the place erupted. You would have thought we'd won the NCAA National Championship! Canal's fans went nuts, ran onto the field, picked up players, kids were hugging each other it was unbelievable."*

That underclassmen received that much adulation after winning a reserve football game, gives some idea of the enthusiasm generated by the unbeaten 1970 team. An unblemished season proved a difficult feat to duplicate; over the next three years Dad's teams went 8-2, in 1971; 6-4 in 1972; and 8-2 again in 1973. When lightning struck a second time in 1974 and the Indians won all ten games, CW had become one of the top football programs in the Mid-State League.

After eight seasons Dad had won 63-games, lost 14 and tied once; winning 82 percent of the time. That success raised expectations in town and from the moment the 1974 season-ending banquet concluded, Dad was asked repeatedly if the Indians could go undefeated two years-in-a-row. It didn't look promising. Of the 36 varsity football players on the 1974 squad, grades 10-12; twelve had graduated in the spring of 1975 – one-third of the team. And though every HS football program loses its senior class each year, the twelve departing Indians included the program's three-year starting quarterback – Jeff Black.

Jeff was one of those special athletes that only come along once every ten or fifteen years in small communities. He stood five-feet, 9-inches tall, had a low-center of gravity, was solidly built, and appropriately, given his surname, had jet-black hair. By his senior year he'd quarterbacked the football team to an undefeated season; reached 1,000 points in basketball, and received full-scholarship offers from both Harvard and Ohio State University to play baseball.

When he reached the 1,000-point milestone in basketball during the winter of 1974/1975, he did so at home on Canal's yellowed hardwood court, whereupon C.A. – the consummate small-town politician – promptly stopped the game, exited the stands, walked onto the court, took the microphone from the scoring-table and gave a rousing speech hailing Jeff's prodigious athletic accomplishments.

Jeff was a certified local sports hero – Media Center Specialist Mr. Butts even put his picture on the cover of the Class-of-1975 Year Book - and when the *Times* ran a pre-season article on August 27, 1975 profiling the new team, its headline read: '*Black replacement eludes CW.*' Jeff had also handled all the Indian's kicking duties – punts, kickoffs, field-goals and extra-points. With his departure Canal lost a veteran quarterback, the team's entire kicking game and a beloved sports celebrity.

The other eleven graduating seniors would also be sorely missed. The Indian's tri-captains: Jon Kemmerling, John Robinett and Tom DeLong, each received All-League honors in 1974; and defensively both run-stopping tackles – John Hays and Jerry Bayer - left gaping holes to fill on the team - and on the defensive line. So dominant had been these two defensive tackles that not one of Canal's final five opponents had managed to score a single point in 1974.

John Hays, the taller of the pair, resembled an all-American life guard. He was handsome, chiseled seemingly from an ancient Greek quarry, and flashed a bright, infectious smile. Standing six-feet, 2-inches tall, broad shouldered, with a lean waist and wavy blond hair, John Hays bench-pressed three-hundred pounds as a 15-year old sophomore. Cheerful and optimistic, he later became a Baptist Minister.

Jerry Bayer was his alter-ego – Lex Luthor to John's Superman. A diametrically opposed evil twin separated from his fellow lineman at birth. Jerry Bayer exhibited a brooding, swarthy mien with thin, jet-black hair, slightly sloping shoulders and gray eyes. He was thick as a tree-trunk and strong as an ox. According to Dad "*Jerry Bayer had the most devastating forearm I've ever seen in all the years I coached.*"

Linemen lost to graduation, Jerry Bayer and John Hays

According to coaches and players alike, Mr. Bayer was an incredibly physical, hardnosed defensive lineman, earning All-Ohio honors in 1974. According to Matt Hartman – a junior linebacker in 1974, Jerry Bayer was the more dominant of the two down linemen. *"We lost two of the best defensive tackles probably that ever played there,"* he related in our 1999 interview. *"John Hays was great but Jerry Bayer would absolutely punish people. We'd sit there and watch films just to laugh and see how far he could hit people into the air."*

Coach Lewis, who had at least one story for each of his former players, concurred: *"We put our best defensive linemen to our defensive left, which matched up with opponent's right offensive line. Jerry Bayer was tough. We were taking charge of a game against Berne Union, 1974, when Jerry was a senior. The kid across from Jerry, Berne's offensive right tackle, was all-Ohio as a junior in 1973. He was a good ball player. So I went up to Bayer on the sideline and said 'Jerry how are you doing? How are you doing out there?' And he said he was 'holding his own.'"*

Coach Lewis leaned forward in his chair describing the exchange, his anecdote building; *"And I said, 'Jerry! You can't just hold your own! This kid was all-state last year! Your goal is to be all-state! You have to kick his Ass!"* At this point Coach Lewis is fully-animated. *"I said, 'Jerry do you want to make all-state or almost all-state?' You've got to kick his ass!' And Locke, who has heard the whole conversation, walks over and he grabs Jerry Bayer by his*

198

face-mask, turns him around and Mike said, 'Jerry Bayer! I told everybody you were going to be an all-state football player! And you by God better be an all-state football player or I'm going to kick your ass!'

"Mike's got him by the shoulder pads and he's right in Jerry's face and he yells, 'Jerry Bayer, you get out there and kick that kid's ass!' We had gotten Jerry so jacked up you would have thought it was the first Super Bowl. I mean he went out there and destroyed this kid. This poor kid from Berne Union is out there, he's having a good game and all-of-a-sudden he lines up against Jerry Bayer and Bayer's wild-eyed and absolutely out of his mind! And I swear to God because the play was on our sideline, on our hash-mark, Jerry was left-handed and he cranks this forearm and jacks this kid and this kid's knees buckled! He stunned him. I'm telling you as God is my witness, this kid was stunned. It was done and that kid was done – and Jerry Bayer got enough votes in 1974 and made all-state."

And now, in 1975, Jerry, John, Jeff and the rest of the seniors were gone, out of the program, receding rapidly into gridiron lore. With so many skilled players departing, it seemed highly unlikely that Canal Winchester would complete another undefeated season, just as they had failed to complete a second perfect season in 1971. This time, besides athletes, Coach Lewis had also left. So along with his quarterback and kicking game, both tackles, the tight end and left guard; both defensive corners and his starting safety, Dad lost the best coach he'd ever worked with.

Be that as it may, in the spring and summer of 1975, those interested in CW football – which was pretty-much everyone he crossed paths with – stopped to ask, "*Who's going to be your QB next year coach? Who's going to be your fullback next year coach? Who's going to be your defensive coordinator next year coach? Who's going to be your quarterback next year coach? Who's going to take over for Jeff Black next year coach? Who's going to be your QB next year coach?*" "*Are you going to win em all again this year Coach?*"

At the end of each season since 1967 his teams had voted for the following year's three captains, and it was these tri-captains who led the first round of player-only conditioning drills in early August. Dad believed that delegating responsibility for conditioning strengthened the squad, improved leadership skills and built team-work. When August arrived three brawny young men made an annual pilgrimage to our house on Waterloo Street, sat down with Dad, discussed various conditioning drills and inquired about where they could procure footballs, kicking tees and helmets.

The 1975 captains were Gary Griffith, Bill Allen and Mark Hartman. Both Mark and Bill were linemen – and looked the part – Gary Griffith, on the other hand, more closely resembled a male model. Known affectionately as 'Froggy' since 1968, he had straight, platinum blond hair; piercing blue eyes, a roman nose and a lean muscular physique quite attractive to the opposite sex.

1975 -Tri-captains, Mark Hartman, Bill Allen, and Gary Griffith.

His classmates bestowed the nickname "Froggy' upon Gary sometime during 4th grade when he returned to school after battling a strain of influenza that had temporarily rendered his speaking voice raspy and much lower than before the illness. Kids - universally sensitive, caring and understanding – immediately dubbed him 'Froggy' because, according to Matt Hartman, *"He sounded like he had a bull-frog in his throat. I mean, it was hilarious, it sounded like the poor guy had swallowed a frog."* The name stuck.

Besides athleticism and good looks, Gary Griffith was fleet of foot, one of the two or three fastest kids in the entire school, and excelled in both football and track. *"Froggy was probably the most talented player we had,"* junior halfback Steve Crist remarked, *"he was extremely competitive and when he glared at you with those blue eyes you knew he meant it."* In a way, Gary's natural gifts – he was handsome, fast, agile, chiseled and popular – could be seen as something almost owed him, a sort of cosmic compensation for all the difficulties in his personal life.

He came from a large family and though he lacked for nothing in the way of food or shelter, the Griffith's, like a lot of families in Canal Winchester, didn't have much disposable income. During Gary's sophomore year in high school his youngest brother, Tony, was struck by a car in the center of town. At first it wasn't known whether he'd even survive, and when Tony did pull through the accident left him permanently disfigured, somewhat cross-eyed, with a slight speech-impediment and life-long learning disabilities.

Tony's accident further stressed an already fractured family. Though Gary had spent his entire life in Canal Winchester, his parents, who divorced late in 1974, both decided to relocate. His senior year looming, *Froggy* faced the prospect of having to finish high school elsewhere, amongst strangers. Heartbroken he spoke to Dad, who listened sympathetically and then moved to keep him an Indian.

Dad approached long-time CW resident Roger Hanners and spoke to him about Gary. Mr. Hanners, an enthusiast of everything Canal Winchester, had been the Jeff Black of an earlier generation. An outstanding baseball player, he had eventually made it to the Major Leagues, playing for the New York Yankees. In 1975 Mr. Hanners, serving as ambassador from an earlier era, called Canal's football games for WHOK AM radio. Not long before his death Roger Hanners spoke of how he came to temporarily 'adopt' Gary Griffith.

Sportscaster and local sports star, Roger Hanners

"It came about because of Coach Locke. Gary's family was having some difficulty. They were splitting up and Gary didn't want to leave, he would have been a junior. And uh, my two boys were gone and Mike said, 'Why don't you take in Gary Griffith? He's a great young man.' Wearing gray coaching shorts matching his gray hair and mustache, Mr. Hanners paused, sat forward in his chair, took a sip of iced tea and added, "I had to talk to my wife about it. We'd been living alone for only two years at the time and had just gotten somewhat used to it."

So let me get this straight. A coach approaches you out of the blue and asks if you'll take in a kid you don't really know? "Yea, your Dad did. And the wife and I thought: if we can help this young man, then we should do it. So I talked to Gary after the Labor Day parade. He stopped past after their football workout and said he'd like to stay with us." Was it awkward? "Yes, at first. But it was one of the best things we have ever done for someone.

Gary turned out to be one of the finest young men I ever met; he was our son, not a stranger."

At that Roger smiled, leaned back in his chair, shook his head with obvious pride and concluded, *"It worked out extremely well, because Gary wasn't sure where he was going or how bad he wanted to go to school – that type of thing. And he ended up never missing a day of school his senior year, was a captain of the football team, and we talked him into going to college. And you know what? Gary went to college and graduated with honors."*

So when Canal's three football captains showed up in August 1975 to talk to Dad, Gary Griffith was among them. Conditioning drills were held on the eastern edge of the football field - Weiser Field - commencing with the traditional lap around the quarter-mile cinder track. Prior to workouts players gathered about the field's lone telephone pole which housed a fuse box used to fire-up the field lights. Milling about, waiting to begin, upper classman were cocky and vocal, sophomores cautious and freshman self-defensively mute. Self-preservation demanded fourteen and fifteen year-olds watch their tongues; especially with full-contact drills just days away.

After calisthenics seniors led the team through running drills. Dressed in shorts, T-shirts, white-tube socks and football cleats; sprinting went according to class rank. Standing on the goal line Mark Hartman barked, *"On one, on one! Set, Oklahoma Hut"* and the seniors raced to the forty yard line; followed shortly thereafter by juniors, sophomores and freshman. Yet no matter how much running took place during summer conditioning, it paled to what awaited them during 'Two-A-Days.'

CHAPTER XIII:

HELL, AKA TWO-A-DAYS

August in the Midlands is brutally hot - sweltering. By noon during the eighth month Ohioans may easily discern shimmering heat waves twenty yards out in almost any direction. And the heat is stifling, almost an assault upon the body. To avoid heat stroke, heat exhaustion and dehydration, two-a-day football practices were held from 8 to 10 am and 6 to 8 pm, Monday through Saturday, until the onset of formal classes brought them to a merciful end.

While non-football players surely dread the end of summer and the beginning of the academic school year, football players – conversely - mark the first day of school on their calendars as if it were Christmas morn. *"Have you ever been to war?"* is how one Canal Winchester football player thought of two-a-days thirty years later.

Kurt Swiger, senior cornerback, remembered how workouts began: *"Practice always started with Coach Locke walking from the locker room. Everyone would just stare in his direction and wait for his whistle. Then, the whole atmosphere changed to everyone screaming and running our first lap."*

Kurt Swiger, senior cornerback and tight end.

Gary Cox, another senior cornerback, similarly described the abrupt attitude adjustment, *"After we donned the pads and got through calisthenics practice became more intense, then more solemn."* Completing their warm-up lap the team ascended a small rise behind the home stands, beneath the press box and overarching bleachers. Class rank again determined position on the sloping incline; tri-captains faced south to lead the group; seniors made up the row closest to the top of the grade, followed by juniors, sophomores and finally the lowly freshman, who assembled under the bleachers at the base of the hill.

Jumping-Jacks, push-ups, and then hamstring stretches were followed by neck-strengthening exercises in which one player would get on all fours, press his helmet against the thigh of his partner while working both sides of the neck, and finish by pressing his head upward against cupped hands. During groin-stretching players sat upright, both feet pulled in toward their torsos, their hands wrapped about their cleats gently stretching the groin, knees pushing downward. Cadence for this particular stretch abandoned numbers in favor of *"Ooh-Aahs, Ooh-Aahs"* in low, guttural voices.

The verdant, summer grass on the incline gradually succumbed to the army of cleats; eventually morphing into clumps of hardened clay as two-a-days wore on. During morning practices the grass remained wet and slick with dew; subsequently uniforms became wet and slick with dew - and sweat. While football players stretched atop sodden earth, the coaching staff walked up and down the ranks, stopping to speak with individuals or help those without stretching partners. During evening workouts they tossed footballs about while the team loosened up.

Mornings were indeed solemn, and in some ways forlorn. During evening workouts at least, once players' parents got off work, they headed for the bleachers to watch practice from on-high. The added attention helped, especially when accompanied by daughters, cheerleaders and female band members; at which point the pace and intensity of practice quickened. During morning drills there were no such audiences.

Misty, late-summer dawns are prominent features of the Ohio landscape; at the early hour when Canal's football players arose for breakfast and morning practice, chalky, ethereal mists shrouded the empty fields about town. As two-a-days stretched one into another - blocking, tackling and hitting one-another atop the wet, muddy earth - practicing with ever more tired, stiff and aching muscles - whatever charms the workouts may have held vanished along with Augusts' early morning haze.

When the final callisthenic was completed Dad blew his whistle to signal the commencement of *"snake drill."* Dropping to the ground seniors started the effigy: first, Gary Griffith fell flat on his belly, face-down. Then Mark Hartman hurdled over him, then Bill Allen ran over both Gary and Mark, to flop down and wait for Bill (Wee-Willie) Willison, who high-stepped his three prone teammates and hit the deck; and on it went until lowly freshman began running the horizontal gauntlet.

For freshman snake drill was particularly nerve-wracking. As the youngest, smallest and weakest members of the team it behooved the hell out of them not to accidently step on teammates; at the same time, the moment the last freshman in line began to high-step through the accordion of players, seniors rose up from behind attempting to catch them. It wasn't uncommon to see panic-stricken frosh racing in terror through the snake, older tormentors in hot pursuit; gaining and yelling as they closed in.

The lower one's class rank, the less popular the drill. Lying on the ground – wet, muddy, unforgiving ground – players had no defense against misplaced cleats; backs, fingers, forearms, hips and – ignominiously – the buttocks were routinely mangled. When a grounded player suffered a gashed finger, for example, primitive howls could be heard followed by avowals of retribution; *"Smith, you cock-sucker! I'm going to kick your ass you son-of-a-bitch;"* The threat pushing Smith to his top-most-speed so that he could flop down and disappear into the body of the snake. What it did for practice, however, was immediately catapult the slow and steady warm-up - where damp and dull morning aches were uppermost in player's minds - to an intense, violent blood-sport where the senses were suddenly alive.

Atop the rise behind the bleachers sat a two-man, and a seven-man sled; both became heavier and harder to move as practice wore on. When the snake drill ended Dad blew his whistle and coaches barked assignments: *"Quarter backs and running backs with Coach Locke; secondary and receivers with Coach Jones; linemen in the pit with Coach Roth. Let's go let's go! Hustle up!"* And the team broke into its constituent parts. Though seemingly endless, two-a-days actually lasted just over a fortnight, with the first scrimmage scheduled only ten days after practicing in pads began. With that in mind offensive and defensive alignments were taught as quickly as possible.

Morning workouts usually revolved around offense; evening practices spent more time on defense. Either way it was tough on everyone, even captains, as Gary Griffith recalled; *"The second and third day of contact practice in pads we were always so sore. You had a hard time getting out of bed, let alone playing ball."* But play they did. While quarterbacks Scott Jordan and Gregg Wright took snaps, handed off to running-backs, rolled out, and threw to tight ends and receivers; linemen remained mired in mud.

As its name suggests, 'The Pit' did not attract athletes who ordinarily scored touchdowns, dated homecoming queens or got their pictures in the Canal Winchester *Times*. It was, rather, aptly named for the location where big, beefy offensive and defensive linemen battled each other at close quarters. Players formed two opposing lines; those in front got down into three-point offensive and four-point defensive stances just a couple feet apart.

Defenders kept their backs to the coaches, because during football games they'd never know the offensive 'snap-count.' Offensive linemen knew the count and so looked intently at Coach Roth, waiting for his hand signals. Pointing, for example, to his right and then holding up two fingers Coach Roth would want O-lineman Bill Allen to block D-lineman Mark Hartman to his right on the count of two.

Coach Roth was laid back, good-natured and well-liked. But once in the pit players glared at him with fierce intensity, watching his every move. "*Set, Oklahoma, hut, hut!*" At that both linemen fired into the other with as much raw force and violence as they could generate. Grunting accompanied the collisions, and as the battles in the mud progressed, linemen in both rows yelled encouragement until Coach Roth blew his whistle and the next two linemen entered the pit.

Blockers weren't allowed to use their hands in 1975, so it was important they fire out clasping their own jersey, elbows extended outward like wings to 'hook' their opponent. They tried to position themselves on the opposite side of the defender from where they needed to drive him; finally they needed to stay low to retain leverage, and always – always - keep their feet moving. Failure to do all of the above meant losing the individual battle, getting corrected by the coaching staff and increasing the odds against winning a starting spot.

Unlike offensive linemen defenders could use their hands, thus compensating for not knowing the exact snap-count, or which way the play was going. Once an offensive lineman moved, defenders could throw the blocker to the ground, jack him with a forearm, or 'Bear Roll' in place making their nemesis miss his block. Though the pit usually hosted those whom collegiate commentator Keith Jackson called 'The Big Uglies," it wasn't exclusively reserved for linemen; everyone needed to know how to block and tackle.

At times lines leading to the pit comprised the entire team, both rows beginning with seniors and descending to freshman. That way, seniors weren't tackling sophomores; they tackled other seniors, while freshman tackled other freshman. Players waiting their turn counted places from the front of the line, using that number to determine their adversary; sizing him up before entering the pit. This was helpful to know; drills in the pit were not for the faint of heart.

According to senior linebacker and fullback Matt Hartman, hitting one-another was a much-loved past-time at Canal Winchester. "*We had some big hitters. I mean everyone loved to 'pop' people. Garry Griffith, Neal Seymour and my brother were all big hitters. I mean I loved to pop people!*" Of course the degree to which any one athlete enjoyed contact varied from man to man; linebackers – like Matt Hartman – might not be the best gauge to measure its popularity, well-known as they are for possessing somewhat skewed personalities. Junior cornerback Craig Cox, for example, one of the fastest men on the team in the autumn of 1975, remembered 'popping' people somewhat differently.

Matt Hartman, senior fullback and linebacker.

"*We had to go all out. There was no loafing,*" he recalled. *We would run a ball carrier verses a tackler in the pit. One day Matt Hartman ran me over. I mean, he actually ran over me – running on my chest as he went by and even tried to step on my head! I grabbed his ankles as he was running on me and eventually tackled him while he was dragging me out of the pit.*" Great quantities of testosterone and adrenaline pumped through players, and, at times, fear.

*Craig Cox, junior cornerback
and one of the fastest athletes on the team.*

To reduce the impact at the point of contact - thereby reducing the risk of injury - tackling practices in the pit began with both runner and tackler lying on their backs, looking up at the blue August sky. At the whistle ball carriers spun around, taking two or three short strides before tacklers laid into them and wrestled them to the ground. Another whistle ended the confrontation and the next two opponents entered the pit to lie on the wet grass.

When blocking and tackling drills were over practice shifted to the seven-man and two-man sleds. Linemen ran to the two-man sled, formed two lines and waited their turn to drive the damn thing across the fruited plain. Coach Roth or Coach Jones - sometimes both at once - stood on the sled clasping its rusted iron handles, adding to its weight. *"Drive until you hear the whistle! Drive until you hear the whistle! Here we go! Set,"* Coach Jones barked, *"Ohio, hut, hut!"*

Bill Griffith – no relation to Gary – played left guard. He and Mark Hays, AKA 'Bay Hays' (John Hays's younger brother), got into their three-point stances, looked intently at the pads before them - as if they had insulted their mothers - and fired into them on the snap-count. Once contact was made the sled moved slowly across the wet grass, rotating away from the lineman pushing hardest; guaranteeing that both young men gave their best effort.

The linemen dug their cleats into the mud, sweat dripping onto their faces from inside the heavy helmets, breathing heavily through plastic mouthpieces, While Coach Jones and Roth drove them on. It didn't take long for a linemen's legs to feel like lead weights. On occasion one of the two lost his footing, falling face first onto the ground while his partner soldiered on. Sled drills built endurance and teamwork.

After tackling, blocking and sled work Dad blew his whistle somewhat longer than usual, signaling the morning's first break. A lone water spigot across the cinder track and attached to the rusted wire fence enclosing Weiser Field served the entire team. The tap stood out against brown posts and wire fencing; a bright, chrome-colored, gleaming spigot. When water breaks began, half the team raced down the practice-hill to crowd around that singular oasis. Its water pressure was quite high and most of the players quickly soaked themselves with its powerful stream before drinking their fill. Break lasted only 10 to 15-minutes and was much needed. Some players sat in clusters; others sprawled on the ground, using helmets for pillows. Those momentarily discarded helmets scattered across the field gave the appearance of a sea of upended turtles on their backs.

Recovery time was fairly short. The old saw, *"Youth is wasted on the young,"* no doubt contains a healthy dose of envy; for there surely aren't many demographics as strong or physically resilient as seventeen and eighteen year-old football players. Indeed, within five or six minutes of rehydrating, juniors and seniors formed impromptu lines and proceeded with the annual *'mud-slide'* contest. The grass of the practice field had seen better days. Pierced by hundreds of cleats during nearly two weeks of two-a-days, it gradually became ground down, uprooted, matted and in places transformed into slick, muddy bogs.

And as practices took place atop a hill, it wasn't long before some anonymous football player took advantage of Earth's gravitational pull; hurling himself head-first into an expanse of mud and sliding as far as the slimy, improvised shoot would take him. Visitors who showed up during breaks could hear jubilant cheers as far away as the parking lot as player after player flung himself into the mud-slide. Although Froggy and Craig Cox gave him a run for his money, and the big linemen splattered more mud, Scott Jordan became the undisputed mud-slide champion of Canal Winchester, in 1975.

Scott hadn't come out for football until his senior year, but certainly had the right mentality for the game. A natural athlete he excelled at basketball and dominated in track and field. In fact, his State pole-vault record stood for nearly 25 years at Canal Winchester. And pole-vaulters, notoriously not quite right in the head, have to possess a certain degree of reckless physical courage in order to engage in such a hazardous sport.

Scott Jordan, senior, starting punter and backup QB

Charging a pit (lined with nothing but loose bags of foam in 1975) at top speed while carrying a 14-foot pole, planting it into a narrow plastic box with sufficient force to bend it backwards, launching themselves over ten feet in the air and then kicking their legs over a metal bar while descending nearly upside down is not for the timid. Scott Floyd Jordan stood six-feet tall, had a lean, athletic build; straight, jet black hair and dark brown eyes. The oldest of seven he was responsible, serious and absolutely fearless when racing toward the ribbon of mud behind the bleachers.

There was added excitement when Scott's turn approached, the yelps and cheers of teammates rose to a crescendo. Nicknamed after his father, chants of *"Floyd, Floyd; Floyd!"* followed his mad dash to mud-slide immortality. Diving head-first he lifted his head, threw his shoulders back, raised both legs behind him and slid on his belly faster and farther than any Indian before or since.

A long whistle-blast broke up the fun and the last hour of practice was dedicated to scrimmaging – offense verses defense. When the varsity worked on defense, the junior-varsity ran offensive plays against them, and when the varsity worked on offense, the junior-varsity played defense, doing their best to stop the first-team. Without Jeff Black CW didn't have a starting quarterback that summer; the offense, therefore, initially received the lion's share of attention. Two contenders fought for the starting quarterback position, junior, Gregg Wright and senior, Scott Jordan.

Gregg Wright had just transferred from Hamilton Township; unlike his older adversary for the job, he had experience playing football – and quarterback – since Pop Warner. Born December 12, 1958 Gregg was part of another sizable family; his mom and dad – Kaye & Lou – had five children: Gregg, Cindy, Mark, Joy and Brad. After six years in the Hamilton school district, the Wrights moved to Canal Winchester, creating competition for the vacant QB slot.

Gregg Wright, junior, starting quarterback.

Both signal-callers had good throwing arms, though there was considerable doubt that either would be called upon to use them. Offensively, Dad ran the winged-T, a ball-control system. He did so because at a small school like CW he never knew whether he'd have stand-out players at the skilled positions. And though his math skills were not as strong as those of his brother's, he clearly understood that throwing the football had just three possible outcomes – two of which were bad.

So quarterbacks handed-off, executed play-action fakes, ran sweeps, naked bootlegs, quarterback draws and protected the football. Indeed, every quarterback, running back and receiver from junior high on up knew that protecting the football was paramount in the Canal Winchester football program; to fumble was to risk the wrath of my father at his most unhinged.

Ball control became the Holy Grail during Dad's tenure; he concurred wholeheartedly with Georgia Tech Football Coach John Heisman, who once told his players, "*Gentlemen, it is better to have died a small boy than to fumble this football.*" Only on rare occasions would his teams throw. During the preceding 1974 campaign, for instance, Jeff Black threw just 27 passes throughout the entire ten-game season, or 2.7 pass-plays per game. According to Coach Dave Lewis – '*The Lew-I*' - Dad was "*very, very run-oriented.*"

"*I mean he made Woody Hayes look like he ran a wide-open offense.*" He said laughing, adding; "*But he was patient with it. It was his philosophy and he stuck with it. A lot of coaches, even in college, I can't tell you how many coaches in college; they come out and they run their best play two or three times. You stop it and they never come back to it; not Mike, his teams worked at running the football.*" So while Gregg and Scott took snaps from Mark Hartman, they worked on memorizing plays, handing the ball off cleanly, executing fakes and staying out of the ball-carriers' way.

LINEMEN:

On either side of center Mark Hartman (#52) - were left-guard Bill Griffith (#65), and right guards Bill Willison (#71) and Brett Van Meter (#66) – who alternated running plays in from the sidelines. Captain '*Buffalo-Bill*' Allen (#75) started at left tackle, and his counterpart on the right side of the line was Mark '*Baby Hays*' (#74). Next to '*Baby Hays*' at right tight end was senior Rick Ross (#88) and his bookend-opposite on the left, junior Neal Seymour (#80), completed the front seven.

Mark Alan Hartman, AKA '*Box-Car,*' the starting center, was as hard-hitting a football player as ever suited up at Canal Winchester. Mark and Matt William Hartman were twins whom Coach Lewis enjoyed ribbing because they looked nothing alike: "*Twins my ass!*" were his exact words in our interview. "*They're the only twins I've ever seen that look absolutely nothing alike.*" Mark stood six-feet two inches tall, had broad shoulders, muscular legs and was the quiet brother.

Mark Hartman, senior captain, center and defensive lineman.

Not much of a 'rah rah' type, or screamer, Mark led by example. His taciturnity made him all the more intimidating; both at practice and on the field. The psychology is comparable to the fear Wellington's silent Red Coats engendered in Napoleon's Armies, who sang at the top of their lungs as they marched in column, bearing down on their British adversaries. Conversely, soldiers of the UK, crouching in line, uttered not a word. After Bonaparte's demise his soldiers acknowledged that nothing unnerved them more than the eerie, foreboding silence of the British lines before the first muskets rang out.

Mark Hartman, with surly intensity and a punishing hitting style similarly rattled his opponents; so much so teammates voted him captain. When he did speak, however, it was with quiet confidence and authority. As one of his teammates recalled: *"Mark was the one who challenged us. He was the one who'd say we could do better, that we had to rely on each other, that we were a team."* Though a man of few words when he spoke it mattered; Mark was the anchor of the group and one of two team-captains on the offensive line.

Because most coaches are right-handed, Dad observed they had a tendency to place their best athletes on the right side of the offensive line and run the majority of their plays in that direction. He therefore decided to place his best blockers on the left side of the offensive-line and run more plays to the left. The differences between right and left tackle, or right and left guard were not necessarily pronounced, but there were differences, and no more glaring example of that difference could be found than at left guard. Lining up next to Mark Hartman was Bill Griffith – 'Billy-B' – all five-foot-10-inches and 170 pounds of him; the smallest offensive linemen on the team. William Scott Griffith was born September 11, 1957, and grew up outside of CW on the farm that the Griffith family had worked since 1933. Unlike his classmates Bill Griffith had left town after finishing 3rd grade to attend the Columbus Boy Choir School in Princeton, New Jersey. Though he remained at large for five years, the *Times* ran periodic stories charting his progress in Princeton, featuring smiling photographs of the blond, handsome young man who had left the small town for the big city.

Bill Griffith, senior, left guard and linebacker.

Returning in the 9th grade to attend high school Bill found himself odd man out. All those summers he had not played baseball in town and the unwanted attention in the *Times* didn't sit well with former classmates. "*It was obvious,*" he recalled, "*that I was no longer one of the guys. In some instances the resentment was so thick you could cut it with a knife.*" Football, therefore, became the vehicle allowing his re-entry into the life he had left behind. "*It was,*" he says, "*a way to become part of the group again, as much as possible in high school.*"

Of course, being 'part of the group' is relative; senior Gary Cox, for example, thought "'*Billy-B' was 'weird,' he was different. He was a farmer; a real life farmer who was always complaining about his back. He was always trying to stretch it or crack it and he was the only guy on the team who wore those white forearm pads that went from your wrist to your elbow. He was puny for a guard and linebacker, but he was tough.*"

As gridiron assets go *toughness* trumped everything else on the Canal Winchester football team. And it compensated for the myriad individual idiosyncrasies particular to each player. For despite his 'weirdness' Gary Cox and the rest of Bill Griffith's teammates respected his play, though they did their best to get a rise out of him. "*I remember,*" Gary continued, "*he drove an old, brown, Ford Mustang and one time when we were watching films 'somebody' popped his hood and stole his coil wire. He was hot when his car wouldn't start. 'Bill-B' was getting really steamed and then we showed him the wire. We all laughed, even 'Billy-B' and then we returned it to him.*"

Despite his size – he looked nothing like the other burly offensive linemen – 'Billy-B' earned the starting guard spot, on the left side of the offensive line, because, unbeknownst to teammates, he played with a huge chip on his shoulders. Next to Bill Griffith at left offensive tackle was captain '*Buffalo Bill*' Allen. A former running back, Bill Douglas Allen blew out his knee during his sophomore year; the injury was so severe it looked as if organized sports, especially running down field carrying a football while eluding tacklers, would no longer be an option for him.

"*Buffalo Bill Allen,*" Coach Lewis recalled, "*was potentially a MAC-type fullback (Mid American Conference). But he just destroyed his knee back-peddling in the old gym during a basketball game. There was water on the floor, and Bam! Down he went, Anterior-Cruciate-Ligament.*" In 1973, repairing that type of injury was anything but routine; nor were surgeries anywhere near as refined as today. *"Back then,"* Coach Lewis continued, *"that was a career ending type injury. Basically it ruined his baseball season the following spring and he ended up missing his entire junior year."*

Bill Allen, senior captain, left offensive tackle

Bill Allen went from being one of the finest athletes in his class to walking about on crutches, wearing an awkward knee brace and getting used to the idea that the camaraderie - the highs and lows of athletic competition - the butterflies experienced before football and baseball games, were no longer going to be part of his world. He became a spectator; but a good one as it turned out. Bill attended every game. He also attended every practice; hobbling up and down the sidelines on crutches, carrying water bottles, helmets and equipment for coaches and teammates; shouting encouragement and support.

He lifted weights and worked hard on rehabilitating his mangled knee. Despite missing his junior year of athletics, Bill became an inspirational figure to teammates and they voted him captain after the 1974 football season. *"He was a big enough kid,"* Coach Lewis continued, *"that even though he could no longer play fullback he could play on the offensive line. He was just a great kid, from a great family; great work ethic. He couldn't play much defense but he gave it everything he had on the O-line."*

On the opposite side of the O-line, right guard Bill Willison didn't join in commiserating over 'Buffalo Bill's' damaged knee. Indeed, Bill Shawn 'Wee-Willie' Willison had a shattered knee of his own requiring weekly Cortisone injections and the draining of built-up fluids. Dad taped his knee before practices and games and as a result, Mr. Willison wasn't overly sympathetic to 'Buffalo Bill's' problems. Once during summer conditioning, after a workout had concluded, a group of my friends approached 'Wee-Willie' near the water spigot.

Bill Willison, senior, right offensive guard.

Although we hadn't yet started 7th grade, Bill Willison's reputation preceded him - and we were well aware of it. To put it mildly, he was colorful – I thought he was crazy at the time – there was something dangerous about him; a volatility, an aggression more pronounced than in his teammates. 'Wee-Willie' was not 'Wee' in the slightest. He was a big man; beefy, broad-shouldered and thick. He walked jauntily, with some sort of weird spring in his step; and his dark brown eyes seemed to protrude nearly out of his skull when animated – which was often. Bill's family moved to CW in 1963; his father, a Columbus firefighter and Korean War veteran, enhanced his eldest son's extensive vocabulary of profane verbiage, and Bill was always more than willing to share it.

Anyway, we approached Bill Willison, and noticing his taped knee asked, *"Why don't you wear a brace like Bill Allen?"* BILL WILLSION: *"Because I'm not a fucking pussy!"* He replied smiling. For added emphasis, immediately after the word 'pussy' rolled off his tongue he drew an enormous mucous-projectile and spat upon the green grass of Weiser Field. He was a great spitter; spitting often and with dramatic flair, each salivic collage seemingly communicating an ever-changing emotional state: nonchalance, disgust, anger and at times, derision.

When Coach Lewis reminisced about 'Wee-Willie' he confirmed my youthful impressions: *"He was"* - the 'Lewi' paused for a moment before finishing the thought - *"I mean, he was a little different; Bill Willison heard the beat of a different drummer."* An ironic statement given Bill played drums in the CW band. In fact, the decision to play football rather than handle percussion had been difficult. *"The hardest choice I ever made was whether to play football or be in the band. I played as hard for the band and 'Bakes'"* (Mr. Baker) *"as I did for Coach Locke and the team."*

Fortunately for the team he opted for football. And though he did march to the beat of a different drummer, Bill Willison shared the work-ethic common to the team. *"I'll tell you,"* Coach Lewis remarked, *"He was one of those kids when he was a freshman he was not a very good athlete. He wasn't particularly strong, wasn't particularly quick, but he was one of those success stories that when you get a kid in the weight room and get him in a program and he's willing to work hard then you end up with a good football player. He worked his butt off and ended up really having a great senior year."*

It would have been tragic had he put in all that hard work and never been able to play, but it nearly turned out that way. Teammate Rick Ross recalled that Bill nearly gave up the ghost during two-a-days that summer. (Predictably, this only added to his reputation) *"One morning,"* Rick began, *"Bill Willison arrived at practice and said he'd forgotten his football cleats. So he was going to drive back home and get them. It seemed like forever before he returned,"* Rick said shaking his head. *"In fact it was at the end of practice. Come to find out while driving home Bill got hit by a train* on Gender Road – and he lived! We tortured him pretty heavily afterwards. Needless to say his car wasn't in the best of shape."

Junior running back Steve Crist, likewise remembered Mr. Willison's showdown with the speeding locomotive: "*During morning two-a-day calisthenics Coach Locke notices Bill Willison is missing and starts to pace and squint and asks a couple guys where Willison's at. In Coach Locke's program he expected seniors to lead by example and as time ticked by we all held our breath figuring we were going to be in for a long, tough practice. Then, toward the end of the work-out Bill comes screeching into the parking lot, runs into the locker room and emerges a few minutes later.*"

"*Willison's jogging up the hill and Coach Locke said, 'Where in the hell have you been Willison?' And he looks right at coach and calmly replied, 'I got hit by a train.*" Steve laughed at the memory before concluding, "*If you knew Bill you'd understand, we all just rolled, so did Coach Locke, Coach Roth and Coach Jones. That was Bill Willison; he was the guy who kept the team loose. You never knew what he was going to do.*"

By the time two-a-day practices began in August 1975, he stood 6-feet, two-inches tall; weighed 235 pounds, and was an intimidating package. "*This guy scared me,*" recalled one respectful junior. "*I always thought he was going to pick a fight with me. He'd pick a fight for any reason, at any time. And he was always making wisecracks about crabs. One day during practice,*" his teammate went on, "*Kristy 'V' walked by with another male student and Bill Willison shouts out: 'Hey, you like seafood? She's got crabs!' He was fucking crazy.*" Right on cue, however, came the trump card - Toughness – in 'Wee Willie's' defense. "*On the field he was tougher than hell. He just quietly smashed his opponents.*"

Bill Willison ran plays in from the sideline, sharing time with Brett Van Meter. Van Meter didn't look like the typical linemen, but more closely resembled a brawny bodybuilder. A junior, born in 1959, Brett Van Meter had curly blond hair; dressed suavely in white slacks and button-down shirts, and wore a fashionable necklace made of small seashells. His good looks, snazzy attire and easy-going smile masked his ferocity on the gridiron. Brett probably had less than 5% body fat.

Brett Van Meter, junior, right offensive guard, defensive middle guard.

Van Meter wore skin-colored, rubber forearm pads that began practices and football games stiff and dry, but ended drenched in sweat. Like the majority of his teammates he played both ways – offensive and defensive linemen in his case. When playing defensive middle guard, he would swing his meat-cleaver forearm to decapitate opposing centers. Perhaps the finest compliments Brett ever received came from a pair of seniors: *"We had some hitters,"* fullback/linebacker Matt Hartman remembered, *"And let me tell you, Brett Van Meter could 'pop' you. I mean he could hit!"* Tight end/defensive end Rick Ross concurred, smiling when asked about Brett Van Meter, and then opining, *"Van Meter was a wild man. He could hurt you!"*

Indeed, nearly every player interviewed for this book made a point of mentioning Mr. Van Meter's penchant for laying the wood to erstwhile opponents. Gary Cox certainly shared the sentiment, remarking, *"Brett was a guy who did not take shit from anyone. At middle guard he had a funny stance. He always seemed to be looking up like his butt was always lower than his head and that he was seemingly getting ready to run up a hill. It was a weird stance. But no one ever teased him about it."*

The team's youngest linemen, fittingly known as 'Baby' Hays, played beside Brett and Bill at right tackle. Mark Hays wasn't handsome, blond and chiseled like his older brother - John. He certainly wasn't bad looking; his face was softer than his brother's; resembling that of a kindly dairy farmer. He had a broad forehead, cheeky jowls and thick, brown wavy hair. Mark did share his older brother's smile, and certainly his size. Despite being the youngest starter on the team he was nevertheless its biggest; as a junior he stood six-feet, 3-inches tall and weighed in at 245 pounds.

Mark Hays, junior, right offensive tackle, defensive lineman.

Senior cornerback Gary Cox (#42) was impressed with 'Baby's' size: *"He was absolutely the biggest guy on the team and we went at it pretty good during two-a-days – and once was enough for me. I always remember him,"* Gary went on, *"looking down at me, like he was a giant; looking at me with that baby face through his big, bushy eyebrows."*

The youngest starter on offense, Mark wasn't as vocal as his older teammates, not nearly as demonstrative as Bill Willison, for example; but like Bill Griffith, he had a sizable chip on his shoulder, playing as he did in the shadow of his big brother's stellar reputation. Running the Winged-T meant a lot of two tight-end sets, which fitted Dad's philosophy that running the football, and keeping it out of opponents' hands while killing the clock, was key to winning. As a result both offensive tight ends were used primarily for run-blocking.

On the left junior Neal Seymour, (#80) was starting for the third straight year. In fact, Neal Seymour was one of the few CW football players to start every game since beginning as a fourteen year-old freshman. At the football banquet following Neal's senior year in the autumn of 1976, Dad would call him *"The greatest athlete I've ever coached; and I've coached a lot of them."* Weighing 205 pounds, fast and extremely strong, Neal was the team's leading receiver when circumstances left no choice but to throw.

Neal Seymour, junior, left tight end, defensive end.

Neal's teammates concurred with Dad's assessment. One upper classman remarked, *"Neal Seymour was the stud of the team. Like Froggy, everything that he did seemed to be effortless. Neal could block, catch any pass thrown at him, run great routes and he hit really hard on defense. When Neal ran he seemed to glide, it was such a smooth, effortless motion, like Froggy."*

At right end was (#88), senior Rick Ross. Rick's family had moved to Canal Winchester in 1969. Like fellow linemen Bill Willison, Rick's father also served on the Columbus Fire Department. And like his position opposite, Neal Seymour, Rick started at both tight end and defensive end, rarely coming off the field. Rick – Richard Lee Ross II – to family, stood six-feet, 1-inches tall; was lean, blond, charismatic and loved playing football for CW. Though his parents had lovingly bestowed upon their eldest son the full name of 'Richard Lee Roth II,' his teammates weren't anywhere near as contemplative when bequeathing the seemingly mandatory nickname.

Rick Ross, senior, right tight end, defensive end.

"We called him 'Dog' Gary Cox recalled (though he never explained why). "'Dog' was unbelievably strong," continued his profoundly sensitive classmate, "He was as strong as a horse. During senior day at the end of the school year he and I wrestled in the pond at Old Man's Cave and he literally picked me up and tossed me – splash! 'Dog' was tough, let me tell you"

"We were obsessed with winning," Rick remembered, "It was an obsession, and every game the stands and the end zone were always jammed with spectators. People who didn't even like football still came on Friday nights; it was the place to be." And it was; but the attention bestowed upon players under the Friday night lights was still weeks away as they scrimmaged behind the bleachers in stifling August heat. The ubiquitous use of nicknames –'Froggy,' 'Box-Car,' 'The Bionic Man,' 'Wee-Willie,' and 'Roller-Ball' - is aptly American and has a long pedigree. In 1882, for example, Private Sam Watkins of the First Tennessee remarked of his Civil War regiment, "*Almost every soldier in the army . . . had a nickname;*

and I almost believe that had the war continued ten years, we would have forgotten our proper names."

Gary Griffith, senior captain, aloft. Halfback, punt return and safety.

That held true at Canal Winchester High School in 1975: In the offensive backfield Scott *'Mud-Slide'* Jordan (#10) and Gregg *'Joe-Willie'* Wright (#12) alternated at quarterback; handing the football to fullback Matt *'Roller Ball'* Hartman (#33); halfback Gary *'Froggy'* Griffith (#21), or halfback Steve *'The Bionic Man'* Christ (#44). Once the handoff was secured they watched the running backs charge into the maelstrom that was the line of scrimmage.

And it was a maelstrom: opposing linemen crouched in three and four-point stances less than a foot apart, eyes focused intently on the football. The slightest change in Mark Hartman's grip would send defenders crashing into the offensive line, their teeth biting down hard clenching slimy, plastic mouthpieces. When the ball was snapped would-be tacklers shot into blockers, swinging forearms against the chests and throats and helmets of those daring to attempt to move them. Blockers grunted after launching violently into defenders, driving their legs as taught on the two-man sled, straining every muscle. With the burst of Dad's whistle seven intense battles came to an abrupt halt. The maelstrom parted, both sides turning from the other; regrouping for the next play, and repeating the process until the coaches were satisfied.

By 9:30 am the crisp morning air and dewy grass had been burned away by an unforgiving August sun. When the offense finished scrimmaging Dad blew his whistle and work began on the kicking game. *"Punt team line up!"* barked Coach Jones; and Scott 'Mud-Slide' Jordan prepared to take long-snaps from Mark Hartman. The JV defense lined up opposite punt formation with the goal of blocking the punts; and another struggle commenced on the line of scrimmage.

When Scott punted, blockers sprinted down field to cover (annihilate, actually) the return man. This accomplished, the tacklers huddled up where the ball-carrier had been dropped to punt back the other way, and so it went, over and over again until they got it right. Once punt practice was over everyone raced down the hill, across the cinder track, and lined up to practice kickoffs, kickoff returns and extra-points. Dad often remarked that the kicking game could not be emphasized enough.

"We were constantly practicing kickoffs, punts, returns and field goals," Craig Cox recalled with a groan. *"The field-goal team would line up on one side and the **entire** rest of the team would line up on the other. We practiced kickoffs until we would almost pass out. And if we had an extra-point blocked, or a punt blocked, or if the return man beat the coverage we'd have to run a lap around the track, then run back to the huddle and try to do it again."*

The young man selected to replace Jeff Black on kickoffs and extra-points was junior, Steve Crist – AKA 'The Bionic Man.' That autumn of 1975 Steve Crist would score more touchdowns than any running back in all of Franklin County. He was one of the two or three finest running backs ever to suit up at Canal Winchester, and his nickname was right on the money.

Steve Crist, junior. Halfback and defensive monster back

Lee Major's television series *The Six-Million Dollar Man* was hugely popular in 1975 – it wasn't uncommon to see guys throwing one another about in horseplay while chanting 'Nah, nah, nah, nah, nah;" or moving in faux slow-motion to similar sound effects from the show. Canal's junior halfback seemed to possess his TV namesake's uncanny physical abilities. 'The Bionic Man' stood six-feet tall, weighed just over 200 pounds, and carried not more than 4 or 5 ounces of body fat. He had dark brown hair, brown eyes and a compact, solid frame.

Born March 30, 1959 Steve was raised in Canal Winchester. His grandfather, Roy Crist, served as CW's Superintendent of Water and Streets, and had installed Canal's first water and sewer lines. Steve's father worked for AT&T and was CW's fire chief. His mom worked at JC Penny's, a position she felt she had to keep in order to pay her son's ever-more expensive food bill, explaining that by the time Steve started his junior year in high school he was drinking at least one gallon of milk every day.

Handsome, built like a Mack truck, quiet and an unbelievably hard runner, the 'Bionic Man' became the work-horse for the Indian's ground attack. *"He always had that little boy mustache,"* Gary Cox remarked, adding, *"Steve was a pure football player. The 'Bionic Man was our power back who got the majority of carries. He ran hard, hit hard and when tackled Steve always 'bounced' on the ground. It was weird but he ran so hard he would hit the ground on his belly and 'bounce.'"* When not running over opponents or bouncing off the ground Steve had inadvertently stepped on an upperclassman's toes.

In 1974 Matt Hartman had started on defense at monster back, a position which guaranteed numerous opportunities to make tackles; and offensively at halfback, which ensured numerous opportunities to carry the pumpkin. With the emergence of Steve Crist, however, Matt was unceremoniously moved from monster back to linebacker, thereby diminishing his tackles, and from halfback to fullback, diminishing his opportunities to score. During our interview I asked Matt, "What was the worst thing about football?"

"That's easy for me, personally," he began. *"It was going from being an all-league monster back to linebacker so Steve Crist could play monster back. On offense I went from the guy who carries the ball to the guy who blocks for the guy carrying the ball."* Matt paused, remembering the sting of losing his spots. *"I will never forget the practice that I found out. I knew I wasn't going to play monster back and then Jerry Jones put me in the down position on the 6-2 defense. And nobody had ever talked to me about it.*

"I was pissed. I was pissed for the rest of practice and I'll never forget Coach Locke calling me into his office, telling me I was a cry baby and that I wasn't a team player. What pissed me off was nobody called me in to say, 'listen this is what we're going to do.' I don't think it was handled well. But what are you going to do when you have a Steve Crist? You're going to make room for him; unfortunately both positions where room was made for him were mine." Then Matt added, *"But Steve Crist was absolutely a stud."*

Matt's situation was by no means unique. Dan Dierdorf once remarked *"Football is an emotional game played by emotional people."* And powerful emotions came into play, consuming both players and coaches from the first snap of two-a-days until the season ended three months later. Nothing hurt more than giving everything to a program, only to get beat out by another athlete. And every starter had outperformed someone to win his job.

On the other hand, winning depended on intense competition for playing time. Every student-athlete who came out for football knew from day one there were no guarantees he would ever see the field. It was a system based on merit, not seniority, and gave added prestige to those who won jobs. An alumni familiar with the system recalled, "*Coach Locke put the best players on the field regardless of whether they were seniors or freshman year-in and year-out. That meant moving some players from position to position each and every year based on team needs, but there were no safe spots.*"

The athletic meritocracy worked for the good of the team but also created intense battles for positions. To get an idea of that intensity, consider the struggle for cornerback between Junior, Craig Cox (#34) and Senior, Kurt Swiger (#83). When two-a-days began the Cox brothers were unknown commodities, having lived in Canal Winchester only a few months.

Gary Cox, a senior, (#42) quickly won a starting spot at defensive cornerback; earning the unique distinction of being weirdly fast in reverse. As Dad put it, "*Gary Cox could run faster backwards than any human being I've ever seen in my life.*" This is a potent skill for someone seeking to play defensive corner. Craig Cox, on the other hand, though one of the fastest men on the team, was a year younger, smaller and virtually unknown to the coaching staff. So despite excellent speed he began the season playing on the junior-varsity and had to watch the first few games of the year from the sidelines.

The individual occupying Craig's desired position was senior Kurt Swiger. Lean, cerebral and hard-working, Kurt's father was a professor at Ohio State University and his mother an elementary school teacher. During four years in the program Kurt had played several different positions - offensive and defensive line, receiver and cornerback. Bleach-blond, Kurt wore a round, salad-bowl haircut to keep his locks in place. His demeanor being what one might expect from the son of two academics: quiet, thoughtful and well-versed in the responsibilities and assignments of nearly every position on the team.

When the season began Kurt started at cornerback opposite Gary Cox, playing mostly man-to-man coverage as '*wide as the wide and as deep as the deepest.*' Craig Cox didn't know that Kurt's parents were teachers, nor that he had given four years to the program, nor that starting meant the world to him. All Craig knew for sure was that Kurt Swiger held down the only position that might possibly lead to playing time for him. *"I learned to hate Kurt Swiger,"* Craig recalled of their competition, *"even though I didn't really know him. He had my position."*

"One day in practice Kurt had the ball on a sweep and I came up and hit him as hard as I could. I flattened him and jarred the ball loose. He had what I wanted, so I hated him. I eventually got what I wanted. It's too bad because he was a really good guy and we got along well; nothing personal - strictly business." Every starter represented another ball player who'd been beaten out; guaranteeing two-a-days were both intense and emotional.

Finally, after a warm-up lap, calisthenics, snake drill, two-and seven-man sled drills, tackling practice, a review of plays, water-break, the mud-slide competition, full-contact scrimmaging, punt team, kickoff team, kickoff-return team and practicing extra-points, Dad blew his whistle, raising four fingers in the air. The gesture was mimicked by players and coaches; fifty or so mud-splattered, winded, tired and very sore young men raised their arms high above the sea of helmets, brought their collective thumbs into their palms, often displaying taped and bloodied digits, and began chanting in unison: *"Fourth-Quarter-Drill! Fourth-Quarter-Drill! Fourth Quarter Drill"*

Despite the enthusiasm with which 'Fourth Quarter Drills' were announced, they were at heart tests of will, stamina and character. Whistles shrieked from all three coaches and jumbled lines formed facing the big sled. Tri captains were out front, followed by seniors, juniors, sophomores, and ending, once more, with the lowly freshman. Every player clapped and chanted in unison, *"4th Quarter drill! 4th Quarter drill!"* Once the throng reached a crescendo Froggy charged the seven-man-sled, leaving his feet, hurtling into the first pad.

With contact the din morphed into a grunting, primitive cacophony. Often the impact was violent enough to move the entire sled. Froggy immediately spun, ran back from whence he started, turned and charged the third pad. That shot signaled Buffalo Bill, who likewise raced to the first pad, hit it as hard as he could, spun and continued down the length of the sled; followed by Mark Hartman and eventually by every player on the team. Coach Locke, Jones and Roth stood atop the long wooden plank behind and at the base of the sled, easily adding an additional 500 pounds to its weight.

Different techniques were used during 4th Quarter drill on the 7-man-sled. These included stiff arming the upper pads, forearming the upper pads, monkey rolls between shots, and attempts to buckle the steel frames supporting the pads. When a metal rib snapped – as it did from time-to-time – the hard-hitting Indian was awarded a hero's reception from the mob behind him. Finally, the first-team offensive line approached the sled; a football was placed in front of the middle pad and Gregg Wright bellowed, *"Set, Oklahoma, Hut!"*

With that the starting linemen shot into the sled, their shoulders pressing the pads, heads tilted back, looking up at the coaches who were bellowing from above; legs driving and driving and driving until the whistle finally blew. If linemen anticipated the snap-count or jumped off sides, Dad blew his whistle, barking, *"Take a lap! If you can't count then you'll run!"* With starters disengaging from the sled and running down the hill toward the track, the junior-varsity quickly lined up in their stead, driving the sled while the starters grumbled at one another on their quarter-mile lap.

A second long whistle brought 7-man-sled drills to a close; the entire team then raced back down the hill, across the cinder track, and lined up at the north end of Weiser Field. Players were spent, bone-tired, and looked it. Usually about this time Dad would bark *"I wonder if Pick-town's players are tired this morning? I wonder what they're doing at Bloom Carroll right now. Let's go! Suck up your guts!"* 4th-quarter-drill continued with fifty-five yard wind-sprints from sideline to sideline, down and back and back again.

The workout even sapped the strength of the Bionic Man; *"Fourth quarter drill,"* Steve Crist remembered, *"always consisted of finishing practice with a minimum of ten 55-yard sprints – the length of the field from side-to-side – and depending on Coach Locke's mood another 10 on top of that as hard as we could before he huddled us up and brought practice to a close."* Fellow junior Neal Seymour put it a bit more succinctly; *"Fourth quarter drill,"* he said, *"was a matter of survival."*

"Canal Winchester will not be out-hustled on the football field," Dad bellowed as his Indians raced back and forth across Weiser Field. *"Canal Winchester football players will not be out-worked! Let's go! Suck it up! Suck up your guts!"* With the final wind-sprint Dad blew his whistle, the team huddled up and coaches spoke for a few minutes before ending practice.

Now past 10:00 am - the sun busily baking sweat streaks onto their bodies, the morning practice was finally over.

Then something amazing happened, because it wasn't required or even suggested by the coaching staff. The seniors led the team off Weiser Field onto the track; mimicking the men who had just put them through hell, captains yelling; *"Let's go! Suck it up; Time for Gassers!"* Without helmets and shoulder pads - they ran in groups as fast as they could down the track's straight-aways, weary 100-yard-dashes; slowing down, jogging the arching turns, recovering, catching their breath, and then sprinting once more; repeating the 'gassers' until they had circled the cinder track four times.

With that the first of the day's two practices was over. The team walked slowly back to the school, descended the cement stairwell leading to the great metal door and reentered the locker room. When the big door swung open an aromatic bouquet of liniments, rubbing alcohol, Aquavelva, dried blood, sweaty socks and jock-straps; practice jerseys; shower mildew, Old Spice and the pungent odor of old cleats, urinals and commodes combined in one vast vaporous cloud; welcoming them back.

Opposite the metal door was a long green chalkboard where Dad drew up plays and opposing defensive schemes; and where one of the seniors would have written the words, "THINK ABOUT IT!" across the top of the board. Those words were never fully defined but were tacitly understood among CW's Indians – never really needing to be spoken of or expanded upon.

Teammates repeatedly said 'THINK ABOUT IT' to one another; using it to end less than serious antics at practice; keeping it to themselves as language appropriate only for the team. It wasn't something said to girlfriends, parents or members of the marching band. All encompassing, it related to the amount of work required to win; the responsibility they carried as varsity football players; the example they were supposed to set for younger kids coming up in the program; and as a simple reminder that like their head coach, many would rather die than lose.

One thing constantly on their minds, as Neal Seymour indelicately put it, was that *"Two-a-days sucked! When we got to August we knew summer was over."* Indeed, those who'd lolled about at the pool for most of the summer no longer frequented that establishment – or any other.

Food and sleep were uppermost in everyone's mind now, and players working part-time jobs sought massive quantities of chow, and as much rest as they could get before returning to the locker room at 6:00 pm to go through the entire ordeal again.

"*Oh my God,*" remarked an upperclassmen's sister who wished to remain anonymous, "*my brother would come home, drop his gym bag on the floor, head to the kitchen and stuff himself. He'd eat like a pig! It was disgusting. He'd just sit there with his head down, shoveling food into his mouth; then he'd go upstairs and sleep. He was always tired and always hungry. I never knew why he was so hungry.*"

Teammates who were contributing to increased sales at both *Super-Duper* and *Conrad's Market* during August certainly understood. Bear Bryant, Alabama's legendary football coach, once remarked, "*I make practices real hard because if a player is a quitter, I want him to quit in practice, not a game.*" Canal Winchester, with a senior enrollment of under 100 students, male and female, could not so easily afford to lose football players; but Bear's maxim was philosophically correct. Two-a-days gave coaches an opportunity to find out who gave up during conditioning drills, quit on blocks, didn't finish sprints, or stopped driving their legs when tackling.

Two-a-days were the hardest ordeal student-athletes faced at CWHS, and were intentionally designed that way. And though Dad mostly agreed with Bear Bryant, he completely agreed with an Ohio coaching legend closer to home – Wayne Woodrow Hayes – who liked to say, "*There's nothing that cleanses your soul like getting the hell kicked out of you.*" Heading home to eat and recover before evening practice, the Mighty Indians of '75 felt exceedingly cleansed.

By 5:30 pm the coaches had gathered in Dad's office to discuss evening practice, apply copious amounts of *Deep-Woods-Off* to keep the usual plague of mosquitoes at bay (adding to the olfactory cloud discussed above), tape the walking-wounded and greet players entering the locker room. Music blared from an AM/FM radio sitting beside the chalkboard despite the lousy reception in the dungeon-like confines of the cinderblock cellar.

1975's top five pop songs emanating from the speakers were: 1. The Captain & Tennille's *Love Will Keep Us Together*; 2. Glen Campbell's *Rhinestone Cowboy*; 3. Elton John's *Philadelphia Freedom*; 4. Freddy

Fender's *Before the Next Teardrop Falls*; and 5. Frankie Valli's *My Eyes Adored You*. And the most popular songs of August 1975 were: Eagles, *One of These Nights*; Bee Gees, *Jive Talkin*; Hamilton, Joe Frank and Reynold's *Fallin' in Love*; and KC & the Sunshine Band's '*Get Down Tonight*.

A few players washed their practice jerseys and pants between practices, but most did not, making suiting up a less than agreeable experience. The first item of protective gear – besides the jock strap – to be put on was the girdle. It resembled a pair of gray, geriatric diapers and housed two hip-pads and one tail-pad. After the first week of two-a-days many girdles could stand up on their own - having been repeatedly drenched in sweat and then left to dry at the bottom of metal lockers. Once the crusty girdle had been pulled over the jock football pants were pulled over the girdle.

Practice pants had the texture and feel of old burlap bags. Two large thigh pads protected the quadriceps and two, thin, foam kneepads covered, but did not protect the knees. Despite the heat, T-shirts were absolutely imperative as they prevented shoulder-pad straps from rubbing the armpits raw. Linemen wore massive shoulder-pads; running backs hoisted somewhat smaller pairs, while receivers and quarterbacks wore the smallest shoulder pads of all.

With girdle, pants, T-Shirt and shoulder pads in place, players donned practice jerseys, torn, mesh rags that had seen far too many two-a-days, and sat down to put on their cleats. Cleats were put on last due to the slick, cement floor. Many a young man busted his ass going in and out of the locker room, always to resounding cheers from sensitive teammates. With that lockers slammed shut and players carefully stepped over to the big steel door, usually giving it an arm-shiver to free it from its mooring.

As they approached Weiser Field players walked past CW's concession stand; its lower-half of cinder blocks painted deep maroon; the upper, wooden frame painted white and adorned with images of feathered Indian warriors. Across the cinder track the eastern end zone of CW's gridiron beckoned as the team instinctively collected in groups determined once more by class ranking.

"*Evening practice was tougher than morning practice,*" a senior commented, "*but at least we were awake when it began.*" By 6 pm, the wet grass, early-morning haze and empty bleachers were distant memories. The air was hot and humid, the grass was bone dry, and swarms of mosquitoes replaced the morning haze. Parents who'd been at work during the morning workout already lined the top rows of the bleachers to watch their sons.

Despite the late hour, the structure of practice was identical to that of the morning sessions. Seniors, sensing the tick of the clock, began donning helmets, buttoning chin-straps and inserting their rigid, plastic mouthpieces. Coaches emerged from the locker room, chatter subsided and the team slowly moved onto the track. Dad gave a long blast on his whistle and the Indians took off on their evening warm-up lap.

After that Froggy, Buffalo Bill and Mark Hartman led calisthenics, doing their best to make it interesting. *"Froggy was great at keeping things light,"* Craig Cox fondly recalled. *"He knew when to get serious, but he liked to have fun too."* And apparently jumping jacks fell into the latter category. *"When he would lead jumping jacks,"* Craig continued, *"sometimes he would bring his hands out in front of him, up and down, like he was jacking off a giant penis, while yelling in cadence, 'Horst, Horst.'"* (Mrs. Horst was Canal Winchester's high school guidance counselor).

Snake-drill followed calisthenics, then tackling practice, blocking practice; driving the sleds; reviewing plays; water break and mud-sliding when the ground permitted. The one significant difference between the two practices was the presence of the aforementioned spectators – parents, and especially young women. While football players beat the hell out of each other behind the bleachers, Mr. Baker's marching band rehearsed in an empty pasture beyond Weiser Field; and the varsity cheerleaders practiced routines in front of the elementary school.

By the time scrimmaging commenced, cheerleaders – firm of body and long of hair – band members, girlfriends and the inquisitive had ascended the bleacher steps to observe the unfolding drama below. And if competition, heat, pain and glowering coaches did not suffice to raise the level of intensity; testosterone – pulsing now through adolescent veins – did.

Parents with younger kids congregated on a cul-de-sac abutting the rear of the practice field. When the evening scrimmage, kicking practice, fourth-quarter drill and gassers were finally completed, it was well after 8 pm. The team, completely spent, had managed to mark off another two-a-day. Parents stood about in clusters talking to one another and to Coach Jones, Roth and Locke, as tired players trudged to the locker room to pry sweat-laden uniforms from their bodies and shower.

Finishing evening practice was far more rewarding than finishing the morning one. Another two-a-day had been conquered, or simply 'survived' as Neal Seymour put it, and large dinners, an evening of television and a full-night's sleep beckoned.

The atmosphere at evening practice was different as well. Rather than fast-approaching mid-day heat and another grueling practice looming just a few hours away, tranquil twilight was settling in. Fireflies flashed along the wood-line behind the baseball diamonds and in the meadows beyond Weiser Field. And loud, olive colored crickets, though out of site, throbbed discordant music in unison. During August katydids reserve their symphonies to afternoon hours, but evenings and nights belong to crickets. As the team abandoned the field they did so to a growing entomological chorus.

Though short-lived idylls, they were nonetheless part of the two-a-day experience. Another experience was the wrath incurred when some unfortunate football player had the temerity to miss practice. Absence from practice, whether excused or otherwise; was an unconscionable sin during my father's tenure. His stint in the Marine Corps had made him unable to bear tardiness or absences for nearly any reason.

He was a kindred spirit in this regard to Notre Dame's Frank Leahy, who once informed his 'Fighting Irish football team,' *"Lads, you're not to miss practice unless your parents died or you died."* Players christened it 'LOCKE-TIME' and learned, often the hard way, that to be an 'Indian' meant being on time. *"He just left players if they weren't on time,"* a still surprised junior recalled thirty years later. *"I remember one year we had a scrimmage at Columbus Academy and the bus was set to leave at 7:45 AM. I can't remember who it was but I think a couple starters hadn't made it to the parking lot. Coach looks at his watch and says, 'We're ready bus driver.' And I said, 'Coach John and Dave aren't here yet, I think they're on the way.' Locke just looked at me silently for a moment then looked back at the bus driver and said, 'let's go.' And we left them behind. I tell you what; everyone showed up early after that!"*

Banishment:
"And God looked down in anger
For disobeying he did shout
Admonished and banished forever . . .
To the four winds cast them out . . ."

(Tomas O Carthaigh –The Banishment from the Garden)

Grueling as two-a-days were, they mercifully concluded in less than three full weeks, just before classes began. As much scrimmaging as the team had done against one-another, there was no way to get a feel for the strengths and weaknesses of the squad until it faced comparable outside competition. Nearly every senior played both ways, leaving mostly underclassmen opposite them during practice. This would not be the case when Groveport came to scrimmage at Weiser Field, or when the team traveled to scrimmage Columbus Academy.

At high school football scrimmages both squads place their best players on the field in a controlled, teaching situation where coaches stand only a few feet from their teams. *"I got banished in my first scrimmage against Columbus Academy,"* senior quarterback Scott Jordan recalled laughing. As with his rigidity on punctuality, my father was monumentally intolerant of players not doing what he had instructed. He never bawled out players if they simply couldn't handle opponents; or if his kids gave it everything they had but couldn't outrun or outhit better athletes. But if - after teaching and coaching day after day, week after week, repetitiously drilling assignments into player's heads – a young man opted, for whatever reason, to dismiss his instructions: Katie bar the door.

Junior Neal Seymour described it eloquently, *"We all thought he was crazy. I remember one scrimmage,"* he explained, *"when I was in the 7th or 8th grade, in 1971 or 1972, I was watching from the sidelines and they (the opponent) ran a play and picked up about 5-yards. And Coach Locke just went off on someone. They ran the same play and gained a couple yards. Again he went off on the same kid. They ran it again and gained maybe 5-inches and he went off again!"*

Neal then summed up the lesson, *"He went off again only this time it was to praise the same kid for giving an all-out effort. That made a huge impression on me. Give it your all or get your ass chewed out. And every year without fail Coach banished someone to the sideline during a scrimmage. In 1974 Tom Delong and I actually bet on who'd get banished. The very first play of our very first scrimmage Tom gets banished and when he got to the sideline he's just about going crazy with rage and I'm dying with laughter."*

Though Neal enjoyed his compatriot's discomfort and Scott Jordan recalled his banishment with laughter, it was neither pleasant nor funny at the time. According to Scott Jordan his own exile resulted from disobeying explicit instructions on the proper way to run a quarterback sweep. Once past the offensive end, with the defense pursuing via angles to intercept him, Scott was to cut it up inside, back against the grain, taking advantage of defensive over-pursuit.

When they ran 'Quicky-8' and Quicky-9' during morning and evening practices Dad had taught his quarterbacks - over and over and over again - to turn it up inside after breaking containment – and they did. Now, in the first scrimmage of his life; with an entire playbook to remember, his teammates looking at him for the play, all three of his coach's just feet away and the entire varsity Columbus Academy defense poised to stop him; Scott knelt down in the huddle and said, *'Quicky-9 on one, Quicky 9 on one' ready-break!'*

At that all eleven Indians clapped hands, spun out of the huddle and ran to the line of scrimmage. Scott placed his hands under Mark Hartman and barked, *'Set, Ohio, Hut!'* Box Car snapped the ball, the weak side of the line fired out, sealing off backside pursuit while the left (strong) side attempted to drive their defenders backward and to the right – away from the 9-hole. *"I was supposed to cut it up inside on that sweep, but I just kept running outside and I got banished,"* Scott recalled. *"Get off the field! Get off the Goddamn field! How many times did we run it? How many times did we run it! Get him off the field!"*

It was a humiliating and humbling experience for the lone exile jogging towards the sidelines, all eyes following him. As gridiron seasons slipped past year by year, Dad mellowed somewhat with age and his players became more vocal about their disdain for the practice of banishment, and within a few years of Scott's experience, the wrathful exile of players to the sidelines ceased to be part of the football program at Canal Winchester. When Scott ran off the field in 1975, however, it was alive and well. He stood quietly in exile, watching the scrimmage, wondering if he'd get back in the game.

And that was the point. Dad believed practicing and scrimmaging should be pressure-packed, intense, mentally and physically stressful experiences – and they were. As Matt Hartman remembered, "*Coach Locke never relaxed and he never relaxed on us, in the film room, during scrimmages and especially at practice.*" So when the ten-game schedule began, some players were surprised to find games easier than the grind they'd already experienced. Most – though certainly not all – games turned out to be far less stressful than practice.

On the other hand; tumultuous, adult-adolescent interactions are certainly a two-way street given the rapidity with which my father and those sharing his profession at the time accumulated gray hair. Indeed, the young men in his charge never ceased to surprise and amaze him. No matter the number of repetitions, explanations, film-instructions and scrimmages that took place under his tutelage, seventeen and eighteen year-olds possess a breathtaking capacity to disregard coaching.

One example in particular occurred during an actual game. Since arriving in CW in 1967, Dad taught the same snap count. Quarterbacks barked, '*SET*,' which put linemen and backs into their three-point stances; *STATE* – which could be any of fifty, several of which (Texas, Ohio) were audibles, and finally '*HUT*.' So if the QB called "*Counter 5, on two, on two, ready break*" He'd say, "*SET, OKLAHOMA; HUT! HUT!*" the snap coming on the second '*HUT*.'

It never changed or fluctuated in any way during his 25-year tenure at the helm. Nevertheless that mundane, almost involuntary set of verbal commands – in the hands of high school football players – added several white hairs to his graying mane. "*We're on the five yard-line,*" he began, still sporting a look of disbelief thirty years later. "*We're in scoring position, so I call Goal-Line Right.*" (Goal-line right/left calls for an unbalanced line by moving the weak-side-tackle next to the strong-side-tackle). "*The huddle breaks and the kids line up,*" he continued, shaking his head. "*They get down in their stances and then all-of-a-sudden my starting right-tackle, who was a straight-A student and went on to become an airline pilot, bolts out of his stance and points at the quarterback.*"

"*Bam! We get hit with a five-yard false-start penalty and of course I'm pissed. They're backing up, reforming the huddle and I can see from the sidelines the quarterback and tackle are still jawing at one another. I call another play but they don't break the huddle because they're arguing. I'm* thinking, 'What in God's name is going on?' And by this time we're about to get hit with a delay-of-game penalty; so I call time-out and jog onto the field to find out what in the hell is going on."

"I get into the huddle and ask, 'What's up? What's the matter?' And my senior tackle says incredulously, 'Coach he said Tallahassee! Tallahassee isn't a state is it?' And the QB says, 'It is too and even if it isn't he should have run the play! Tallahassee's a state isn't it coach?' And about half the kids in the huddle were arguing for, and the other half against, Tallahassee statehood in the middle of the fucking ball game." (Laughter) The discipline, repetition, film-study, long practices and attempts to keep things simple, therefore, were an integral part of the program for good reason.

Canal Winchester played two scrimmages that summer to determine its starting lineup; once those contests were over - the banishments endured and position battles decided - two-a-days at last came to an end. Classes began Tuesday September 2, 1975 and while most students grumbled about the end of summer vacation; members of the football squad relished wearing clean, dry clothing rather than sweat-soaked uniforms.

They savored sitting comfortably in the auditorium listening to Mr. McCann; and sitting comfortably in class listening to their teachers - instead of running, blocking, tackling, standing in line or knocking the hell out of one another on the hill. They also appreciated being *asked* politely to do things instead of getting yelled at, ordered to 'take a lap,' being unceremoniously banished or having whistles ring in their ears. Compared to what they'd been through, school was an oasis of peace and tranquility, and their tired bodies welcomed what others did not.

Yet memories of two-a-days stayed with them the rest of their lives and like most memories, are especially strong when triggered by smell, as Matt Hartman explained. "*That hill! We used to practice on that hill and it was always so hot. Within a few days it was covered with mud and sweat and had that peculiar smell. When I smell that today, no matter where I'm at, I think of two-a-days: that weird combination of sweat and water and mold.*" Matt stopped for a moment before considering the bright side, concluding, "*But we used to have some great mud-sliding contests down that hill!*"

Chapter XIV:

THE REGULAR SEASON

With two-a-days behind them the team adopted an entirely different schedule for the ten game regular season. Practice began at 3:00 pm – less than 25-minutes after 9th-period bell rang the school day to a close. **Mondays** the JVs played a game - either at an opponent's school or on Weiser Field - meaning that underclassmen weren't available at practice. The varsity, therefore, with no-one to hit on Mondays, spent much of the time watching game-films - both of the previous contest and of the next opponent. Afterwards offensive and defensive formations were reviewed, followed by light running and stretching.

Tuesdays meant full-pads and full-contact. The toughest practice of the week, it was far enough removed from the previous game to allow for recovery, and far enough ahead of the next to realistically prepare. It was a bruising ordeal; as Kurt Swiger put it, *"Tuesday was the monster practice, long, intense and physical;"* followed by films. **Wednesday** night focused solely on defense and was tougher on the JVs than on the varsity.

The life of JV football players, "the scout team," is grueling. On Mondays the JVs had played four, full quarters of football and on Tuesdays, despite any residual soreness, had defended against the varsity offense. Wednesday nights the JVs not only faced their older, stronger teammates on the first-team defense, but did so while running plays and formations with which they were thoroughly unfamiliar. They paid for it in pain.

Thursday's practice, the lightest of the week, was referred to affectionately as '*Sock & Jocks.*' The squad wore practice jerseys, shorts or sweatpants, cleats and helmets. The workout took place on Weiser Field rather than the hill, there was no hitting or running. **Friday** night was game night, the consummation of all their hard work; preceded briefly by film-study.

Perhaps 'film' and 'study' are not the right combination of words to describe what went on in that darkened recess across the hall from the locker room. "*Film instruction' from on-high*" would be a better description. The film room was a narrow, rectangular space of white cinderblock walls – a once joyous destination while in elementary school. Trips to that locale during the halcyon, K-6-wonder-years meant deliverance from classroom instruction. Classes filed through double doors, sat in two sections of metal-folding chairs, and partook of Franklin County's finest educational, cinematic offerings.

But when Dad announced; "*Film room! Let's go!*" it wasn't nearly as pleasant an experience. For starters the folding chairs were stacked at the end of the room, leaving only two or three to sit upon, and these went to the coaching staff. Players sat to either side of the projector and on wrestling mats; atop tables, on old desks – wherever they could find a spot. When film sessions ended it usually took several minutes of disentangling before the team could exit the cramped little space.

The supreme evaluator of gridiron performances Dad began sessions by threading the 16mm projector with film of upcoming opponents or previous games; shouted, "*Get the lights,*" and gripped the dreaded control panel that allowed him to run plays forwards and backwards, over and over and over, until he had made his point.

When studying opposing football teams, the varsity starters were keenly interested in their competition. Each player was especially anxious to gauge the size, strength and speed of the man who would be playing opposite him. During Canal Winchester game-films players watched with rapt attention to see how they performed on any given play. And more importantly whether the coaching staff noticed their successes or mistakes. It wasn't only coaches noticing mistakes either, ever so supportive teammates cued in on poor performances as well.

Rick Ross: "*Oh man, if you screwed up in films, everybody tortured you. We never wanted to mess up because we'd get it from Locke and our buddies* too. *I never wanted to mess up because I didn't want to listen to it,"* Being singled out left players feeling like stunned deer in the headlights. *"What the hell are you doing Cox? What are you supposed to do on slant 6? Is that what we worked on this week?"* It certainly wasn't all negative; coaches were quick to praise when someone threw a good block, made a shoestring tackle, broke a long run or completed a (rare) pass.

Unfortunately for the Mighty Indians of 1975 – and every team before and since – football players possess an uncanny ability to remember the exact quarter, series, down and play-call that resulted in their getting beat or blowing an assignment. That memory-capacity kept them focused and silent in the film room, patiently waiting for the hammer to fall. *"You would always remember where you screwed up in a game,"* junior Neal Seymour lamented, *"and you just hoped Coach Locke wouldn't catch it. Of course he caught everyone and then would run it on the projector, back and forth about 1,000 times."*

Well, perhaps not one-thousand times, but it certainly felt like 1,000 when the focus was solely on one player. Upper classmen, those who'd weathered many rugged campaigns and the film studies accompanying them, had no thicker skins than their younger protégés – even captains; as Craig Cox recalled. *"We were watching films one day after practice,"* Craig began with a grin, *"and I noticed Froggy out of the corner of my eye sliding off this old desk. He started crawling out of the room. As he crawled past me I whispered 'Froggy, where you going?' He said, 'Watch the next play,' and kept moving across the floor."*

"I looked back up at the screen, Froggy had the ball and must of seen a ghost because he gave this juke move and tries to fake someone out – but there was no one there. He tripped and fell out of bounds. The whole room busted out laughing. Coach Locke said, 'Where's Froggy?' Locke looks around and there he was crawling out into the hallway."

Film instruction was first and foremost a teaching tool and an opportunity to study opponents. *"In watching films with Locke,"* Coach Lewis recalled, *"one of the things he always did - sure we always looked to what their best plays were and all that – but he looked for particular players that we could pick on. And once he found it he stayed with it, exploited it mercilessly – countered off it, play-action-passed off it and made them stop it. If they did then he'd try to figure how they did it."*

Coach Lewis, who would spend twenty years coaching in the collegiate ranks concluded, *"Locke studied film to exploit weaknesses – all coaches do that – but where a lot of coaches will go in and change their whole offense to try to take advantage of some weakness, that's one thing a lot of young coaches I've worked with over the years and even some veteran college coaches I worked with didn't understand: get your offense/defensive philosophy, whatever it is, put it in, and then as your looking at your opponents, stay within the framework of your own offense and defense to exploit what they're doing. Locke was doing that when I started working for him in 1971,"*

WEEK I:

BEXLEY

(September 4, 1975 - Home)

Bexley, Ohio is located east of Columbus along the banks of Alum Creek, and straddles Broadway Avenue, a section of the old east-west corridor Route 40. Incorporated in 1908, Bexley lies just 12-miles north of CW, but was in many ways Canal Winchester's antithesis in 1975. A semi-urban, cosmopolitan college town and home to Capital University. Students at Bexley High School consistently finished in the top 5% nationally in scholastic aptitude testing, and the district had just hired a new football coach.

In 1970 Bexley replaced the Mifflin Punchers as the Indian's first non-league, opening game gridiron opponent. This had turned out to be a fairly even match; in their previous five meetings Dad's teams won three games and Bexley two. Impatient with mediocrity, the Bexley Lions lured Earl Focht from Hamilton Township after the 1974 season.

It was during the 1974 season, when Jeff Black led Canal to the Mid-State League crown - that Earl Focht guided Hamilton Township to the Metro League championship. Coach Focht, therefore, was a proven winner who inherited 15 returning lettermen when he took the reins at Bexley. Aware of Canal's reputation as a ball-control offense and Dad's statistically verifiable aversion to throwing the football, Coach Focht prepared his Lions to crowd the line-of-scrimmage in order to stop the run.

Because Bexley, Ohio is home to a sizeable Jewish community both schools agreed to play the season opener on a Thursday night so that Bexley's Jewish students could observe Rash Hashanah. As a result the September 4th opener was the first high school football game played in the State of Ohio in 1975. Not only would football fans attend, but coaches from programs the Lions and Indians would face later that year planned to send their staffs as well.

Game day at Canal Winchester High School was a loud, multi-colored, celebratory spectacle that grew steadily in size and scope until the final whistle ended the football game later that night. Players arrived at school wearing game jerseys – white for home-games, maroon for away-games – and nearly the entire staff displayed their support by wearing maroon and white apparel of one kind or another: ties, slacks, scarves, blouses and jackets, and even maroon and white socks.

Adding to the pageantry was an important element in local dating customs: that of football players bequeathing their non-game jerseys to girlfriends. Said jerseys served as symbols of solidarity in vanquishing the opponent and, equally important, as symbols of romantic possession, ensuring hallways, gymnasium, classrooms and Canal's cafeteria were virtual seas of maroon & white when the school day commenced Thursday, September 4, 1975.

Additional flashes of Canal's colors came compliments of the varsity cheerleaders (Melissa Black, Lori Hardwick, Peggy Fox, Debbie Crist, Jamie Padgett and Cindi Hunter) who arrived at school wearing maroon & white skirts, maroon knee-high stockings and white turtleneck sweaters. The sweaters - sporting a large **_W_** across the chest, duly enhanced these young lady's shapely forms and forever seared **_W_** into the psyches of every red-blooded, American male in the building. After reciting the Pledge of Allegiance over the school-wide PA system, Mr. McCann reminded students of kickoff-time and where tickets would be sold during lunch-hour.

Varsity Cheerleaders, Peggy Fox, Melissa Black, Debbie Crist Lori Harwick, Jami Padgett and Cindi Hunter.

The season's first game, last game, homecoming, and games with CW's two biggest rivals, Bloom Carroll and Pickerington, also warranted pep rallies. These were raucous affairs attended by every student in grades 9-12, support staff, faculty and administrators. Cheerleaders performed skits in which that night's opponent suffered some indignity at the hands of the Mighty Indians. With Bexley, an unfortunate stuffed lion ended the rally with a noose about its neck – hung in effigy - to the cheers of the roaring throng.

Football players sat - and at times stood - across the edge of the gymnasium stage facing the student-body. At the first pep rally Dad introduced the offensive and defensive starters, spoke briefly about the team, and reminded students how important their support would be to the Indians. Several times during the extravaganza a segment of Mr. Baker's band cranked out *"Long-Train Running"* and *"Celebrate"* by the Doobie Brothers; and the *"Bugler's Dream"* to the delight of the crowd.

A raucous pep rally.

Bill Willison enjoyed the best of both worlds during pep-rallies; sometimes leaving the stage and sitting in with the band. *"Pep rallies were great fun,"* he recalled, *"sometimes I sat with the team and sometimes with the band. When that auditorium was jam packed and 'Bakes' turned us loose it was awesome. I bet the sound was amplified fifty times. Everyone in the place could feel the adrenaline."*

Fellow senior Gary Cox agreed, *"I loved game day."* He recalled three decades later. *"Wearing the jersey to school made me feel proud. I also felt like a stud. Not cocky or boastful but extremely confident. I knew I was part of something great. The pep rallies were great; it was like we were on display – being honored – like 'here's your stud football team.'"*

The 'Bionic Man' concurred, though according to junior halfback Steve Crist, the school day couldn't end soon enough for most team members. *"Game day at school was like, everyone watched the clock – more so than usual – and could not wait for school to be over so we could play the game. After the pep rally we usually watched about a half hour of film, which was pretty much the only thing players were able to concentrate on during game day."* When the rallies ended the auditorium emptied in record-time, students boarded school buses or exited the building through its front double doors to walk home; leaving only players and coaches behind to watch films before heading home themselves.

Coach Locke didn't organize team dinners during his tenure at Canal Winchester. He felt players - having sat in school all day surrounded by the hoopla - needed a few hours to decompress before game-time. Rather, they were reminded to eat at least two hours before kickoff, which left the span between films and returning to school to dress for the game to the individual athlete.

Dad, who never spoke after the workday unless he had to, arrived home, sat on his couch and ate silently while reading. More often than not he hadn't slept much the previous evening and after his meal sat quietly, occasionally looking up from his book to check his wrist watch. Players did the same: they ate, watched some television, took short naps, and kept an eye on the clock.

Some players did partake of a shared meal, however, and this became an important tradition. *"We had a ritual of going to Ponderosa Steak House,"* Steve Crist recalled. *"We went there to eat before every game; me, Froggy, Matt and Mark Hartman and Buffalo Bill Allen. We went every Friday about 3:30 or 4:00 to Hamilton Road to eat steak."* Afterwards, they too parted ways, going home and lying down before returning to school later that evening. That Thursday, after eating and resting, the young men began filtering into the eerily quiet locker room.

For all the hell raised over the course of two-a-days: grunting, straining, bone-jarring collisions and blaring whistles; and the game-day cacophony of slamming lockers, classroom bells; the rhythmic cadences of the band, rousing cheers and the roar of the crowd at pep rallies, the pregame locker room sounded more like a Shaolin Temple. When anyone did pipe up they were liable to have a senior simply say, *"Think about it."* Dad wrote scouting reports for players and mimeographed them during his free period. These outlined the opposing team's offensive and defensive formations, enumerated certain important plays and tendencies, and concluded with *"Remember, play pretty for the people!"*

While the team dressed and reviewed the scouting report Dad busied himself taping knees, ankles, hamstrings and wrists; Coach Jones and Coach Roth walked through the locker room patting shoulder pads and shaking hands - speaking softly in hushed tones to various players. Although Coach Roth worked primarily with linemen his humor and compassion were greatly appreciated by the entire team, especially when pregame 'butterflies' were churning.

251

"*Coach Roth kept the pulse of the team,*" the 'Bionic Man' remembered gratefully. "*He was the one you could talk to if you weren't having a good day; he's the one who'd console you after screwing up or getting chewed out and he was an excellent motivator and source of calm before the storm during pregame.*" Outside that solemn locker room, the atmosphere was anything but calm.

Parking lots on both sides of the school were full by 7:00 pm. While long lines of spectators shuffled slowly but deliberately through the gates and past the ticket booth, little kids dashed about throwing miniature plastic footballs sold just beyond the gate by the Canal Winchester Boosters Club. Clusters of people milled about on the cinder track; and members of the CW Fire Department stood near their emergency vehicles at the Eastern end of Weiser Field, sipping *Coca Cola*, eating hotdogs and munching popcorn from red & white bags.

Weiser Field looked nothing like it had during two-a-days when the team ran 55-yard wind sprints and worked on the kicking game. The freshly cut grass gave off the faint smell of ripe summer watermelon, hash-marks and line-numbers were trimmed in snow-white lime powder, and bright orange pylons marked both end-zones. Lights that would later bathe the field in misty luminescence after sunset, were already glowing in the twilight of dusk.

The concession stand did a brisk business, with five cashiers, three facing forward and one on each side window, busily selling candy, hot dogs, Coca-Cola; hot chocolate, popcorn, peanuts and soft pretzels to ravenous fans. Cheerleaders practiced their routines. Members of the PTA sold maroon & white carnations. The Kiwanis Club, Lions Club, FFA and 4-H Club members strolled about in uniform jackets and shirts, talking earnestly about their organizations and the prospects for the 1975' Indians.

Both bands could be heard playing in the distance. Chief Miller's police cruiser sat next to the emergency squad. Fans stood along the fence-line surrounding Weiser Field as the Bexley Lions, already lined up in neat rows in their blue and white uniforms, were noisily barking out their calisthenics count. The scoreboard, painted pine-green and held aloft by two sturdy telephone poles, sat dark 47 weeks of the year but on game nights it resembled a great, square Christmas tree at the Western end of Weiser Field, with bright red lights forming four sets of zeroes above the words *Visitor* and *Home*.

When the Indians left the locker room and emerged at the top of the cement stairwell, family members as well as fans unknown to them began clapping, cheering and yelling, *"Let's go Indians!"* Like an accordion the commotion drew the focus of the multitudes onto the 35 young men clad in maroon & white. One upperclassman remembered walking from the locker room to the field as *"being like a rock star. I was never a rock star, but when we walked to the field everyone just stared and began screaming and clapping. We were so jacked up, the lights, the noise, the pent up adrenaline, it was hard to keep it together."*

During pregame, the two teams warmed up on opposite ends of the football field, doing calisthenics, a few agility drills and reviewing offensive and defensive formations; occasionally stealing furtive glances to size up the opponent. As with his penchant for doing the opposite, Dad rejected the standard shouting matches between teams while warming up.

On nearly every football field across Ohio it had become customary for opposing squads to 'count-off' in loud, macho shouts. Not so at Canal Winchester. Tapping into psychology for an edge, Dad surmised it might be more unnerving to opponents to remain absolutely silent while warming up – like the British at Waterloo. And the silent treatment seemed to work because the team garnered far more attention with mute calisthenics than did their barking opponents.

"It was almost eerie," remembered Roger Hanners. *"They'd come out, run the snake drill and then do their jumping jacks, push-ups, you know the whole thing and you never heard a sound. There was some sort of intimidation factor about it you couldn't quite put your finger on and it was effective."* Mr. McCann agreed; at Dad's retirement banquet almost twenty years later in 1993, he fondly recalled the novelty of the Nija-esque Indians. *"Locke,* Mr. McCann began from the podium, *"you had the highest IQ of any teacher on staff and nobody knew it because of the way you act and dress. (Laughter) Hell, I remember the way your teams warmed up without making a sound; it was amazing – like Gary Cooper in High Noon – now who thinks up something like that?"*

Warm-ups concluded, both squads returned to their respective locker rooms. They had only a few minutes to visit the can, strap up helmets and steel their nerves before launching the 1975 football season. For some the tension became unbearable: *"Jeff Damron used to slam the lockers with his forearms and his head,"* a fellow senior recalled. Adding, *"Bill Griffith used to stretch his back anyway he could, asking other linemen to pick him up and 'crack' it; and Bill Willison, that fucker was crazy, he'd start spitting, in his own hands or between his feet on the cement floor – over and over, I don't think he was even aware he was doing it."*

Dad, though a ham at times, didn't act in front of the team. His pregame speeches were short and forthright, honest no-nonsense assessments of what would need to be done by his no-nonsense young men. Standing in front of the team, he would announce whether they'd kick or receive, and then say, *"Kickoff team, raise your hands!"* He'd count the hands aloud, and when he reached the correct number, eleven, the locker room would explode in cheers and guttural bursts. *"Receiving team, raise your hands!"* Again eleven men on the receiving team, and eleven raised hands, and the concluding explosion. *"Punt team, raise your hands!"* Once more the count, eleven raised hands and the emotional release.

At that point Dad spoke a few words, players listened earnestly and then the entire team rose and exited the locker room to face the Bexley Lions. Steve Crist remembered that Thursday evening. *"There was so much tension,"* he began. *"This was the day we had waited for. A chance to find out if we were as good as everyone thought we were; if all the hard work would pay off. The one thing Coach Locke said to us in the locker room – and I'll never forget it – he told us we had worked hard and to have fun and concentrate on the things we'd already accomplished together. And then, right before we left the locker room he said, 'The eyes of Ohio are on you. Have a good game and show them what Canal Winchester Football is all about.'"*

Back on the field one last ritual remained before kickoff. Dad removed and folded his glasses, placing them in his front right breast pocket, and then yelled two words: *"Now Varsity!"* At that the silent Indians were silent no more. They erupted spontaneously, raced toward their coach and began jumping on him. Those reaching him first provided a protective bear hug while those racing down the sidelines leapt into the air, landing somewhere into the jumble of heaving Indians.

Newcomer Gary Cox was somewhat taken aback by the unexpected violence of the whole thing. *"The pregame ritual 'Now Varsity' was weird for me the first time I experienced it. We went from quiet, serious contemplation* to this frenzy engulfing coach." Senior Matt Hartman on the other hand, who came up in the system, loved 'Now Varsity.' "*Coach Locke would take off his glasses,*" Matt remembered, "*and then put them in his pocket or handed them to somebody, right before kickoff. At that moment we would all pile on top of him. I always tried to be the last one; to jump into the middle of the pile. And then it was time to turn it on baby!*" On the sidelines I watched my father emerge from the pack looking disheveled and slightly beaten – which he was – appearing even more forlorn without his glasses.

Now Varsity!

Interestingly, both the '*silent count*' and '*Now Varsity!*' pregame rituals traced back to a single evening in 1971. Dad's fifth year as head coach opened with a drubbing at the hands of Bexley, 24-0. The previous 1970 CW team had gone 10-0 and to say the defeat was somewhat shocking to Indian fans is an understatement. After the Bexley loss they won the next three games, only to lose 24-14 to Fisher Catholic midway through the season. With a record of 3-2, the Indians next faced Millersport, who hadn't lost or been scored upon thus far that year.

"*I didn't know what to do,*" Dad recalled years later. "*So I told them not a word on the bus. Millersport was just tougher than hell and we had to play them at their place. We were huge underdogs going in and the kids knew it. I kept them quiet on the bus ride over and when we got into the locker room I didn't let them speak. I wanted their adrenaline to build. I turned off the lights and told them to think about it. I was just winging it man, let me tell you,"* he admitted.

"I told them not to look at Millersport's team, their players, during warm-ups; that only one captain would lead calisthenics – we had never done that before. And it was weird because our fans didn't know what was going on and started yelling, 'Come on coach! Get them up! Let's go Indians! What's the matter? Pick it up!' They didn't know I told them to be quiet and thought something was wrong. It was really kind of eerie."

"Finally, maybe a minute before kickoff – and this just came to me, I hadn't planned it – I took off my glasses and yelled 'NOW!' And all that pent up energy, the silent bus ride, the quiet locker room, not saying a word in pregame - they just exploded and damn near knocked me out." Just as players can recall every misstep during football games, coaches are renowned for their ability to recall the most minute details from past gridiron contests.

"It was 0-to-0 and we had to punt because we were on our own 19-yard line. I called punt and my senior captain, John Gardner, came to the sidelines with tears in his eyes and said, 'Coach we can make it! We shouldn't punt. If you let us go for it we'll get it!' So I said OK. And if we hadn't of got it we would have gotten our ass beat – but we got it and beat them 32-0. Being as superstitious as I am, we continued the silent count and 'Now Varsity' from that game on."

And now, four years later, September 4, 1975, the Indians performed the silent count and jumped once again upon their coach, pummeling him, releasing pent up emotions, celebrating the game's arrival. When the frenzy abated the kickoff return team ran onto Weiser Field; the 1975 high school football opener was at last underway.

Coach Focht had done his homework to prepare for the opener against Canal Winchester; when Mark Hartman bent down to snap the ball eight Lion defenders were on, or near the line of scrimmage to stuff the run. Despite Bexley's defensive formation Dad would not alter Canal's running attack unless Bexley proved they could stop it. He continued to call Steve Crist's number, running him off-tackle between Bill Allen and Neal Seymour. After 12 plays the Indians *'matriculated-the-ball-down-the-*

field' to Bexley's 7-yardline. Dad then sent in 'Quickie-9,' which called for Gregg Wright (who had won the quarterback competition) to run where Froggy, Matt Hartman and Steve Crist had been running, – to the left and around the end.

When Gregg crossed the goal line untouched, teammates quickly surrounded and bear hugged him, linemen picked him up and patted his helmet. Fans on Winchester's side of the field cheered wildly; the CW marching band stood in the bleachers playing 'Celebrate,' and cheerleaders on the cinder track shook their collective pom-poms. A triumphant Gregg Wright jogged back to the sideline with the football tucked under his right arm and tossed it playfully to statistician Sandy Hays, who blushed, giggled and then smiled broadly as fellow 'Super-Stats' Ellen Bohl, Sue Longo and Debbie Hunter embraced her.

Statisticians Sandy Hays, Ellen Bohl, Sue Longo and Debbie Hunter
watch the action from CW's sideline.

Unfortunately, in the hubbub, the extra-point team missed the point-after kick, despite having practiced it morning after morning, night after night for nearly three weeks. Dad, needless to say, was not pleased, loudly making his displeasure known to the extra-point team and anyone else within a six-mile radius. Despite the precise and methodical nature of their first drive CW was unable to score again in the first half.

After receiving the kickoff Bexley completed four passes in a row before Brett Van Meter intercepted quarterback Jim Betz's fifth pass; returning it 19 yards before getting tackled from behind. It was the game's first big break. With Bexley continuing to crowd the line of scrimmage, Dad – against his better judgment – called a pass play. Unfortunately, Gregg Wright returned Jim Betz's favor, throwing his first interception of the year at 9:29 of the 1st quarter.

That was the game's second big momentum shift. Despite having won the QB competition, Gregg Wright threw two interceptions that night. At half-time the score read 6-0 Canal Winchester. It had been a hard-fought first half - and having beaten Bexley the previous year by the slim score of 22-20, Dad knew it was going to be a battle until the final whistle.

In the locker room, while bands marched across Weiser Field, he explained that so many Bexley defenders crowding the line of scrimmage meant Canal's running backs would find plenty of open ground if they could just breach that initial three-yard area – the maelstrom. And that's what they did in the second half. Because his philosophy dictated that if something worked it should be adhered to until stopped, he adhered to calling Steve Crist's number off tackle - over and over and over again.

The persistence paid off; Bexley's down linemen eventually tired; Canal's O-line took heart and with Matt Hartman barreling through the line as lead blocker, the Bionic Man scored from four yards out in the third quarter. He scored another TD after a 19-yard run in the 4th quarter - ending the game with 117 rushing yards – five more than Bexley's entire offensive ground game.

Even with the majority of carries, the Bionic Man was not alone grinding out yardage. Matt Hartman carried twelve times for 98 yards and Gary 'Froggy' Griffith ran it thirteen times for 93 yards, for a running back total of 308 rushing yards, not including the running of quarterbacks Gregg Wright and Scott Jordan. With the lead well in hand, the starting punter and backup QB, Scott Jordan, entered the game. Moments later he threw a beautiful 19-yard touchdown pass to Rick Ross.

Fellow Ohioan William Tecumseh Sherman once remarked being famous meant getting killed on the battlefield and having your name misspelled in the newspapers. And for Scott Jordan - despite excellent punting and being the only quarterback on either team to throw a touchdown pass - the General's words proved prophetic. *The Lancaster Eagle Gazette* christened him 'Mike Jordan' in the following day's sports edition.

Scott also pinned Bexley deep in its own territory in the 4th quarter with a booming 52-yard punt. Trailing 27-0 the Lions began throwing on almost every down; steadily moving the football - until Froggy intercepted another Jim Betz pass to kill the drive. Defense wins championships, and Canal's 5-3 and 6-2 schemes smothered the Lions allowing just 92 rushing yards, and only 20 through the air.

Defensively, Dad believed in attacking. Stunting down linemen, blitzing corners, safeties, and linebackers, angling his defenders one way or another, and as with the offense, position discipline. Defensive ends were taught not to allow anyone outside. Linebackers were to read offensive guards, and when they sniffed out a pass, were to bark "Pass! Pass!" and quickly drop into hook and curl coverage while keeping wary eyes on backs out-of-the-backfield. Down-linemen were taught to use their hands, and especially forearms.

Neal Seymour and Rick Ross anchored either end of the defensive line. Mark 'Baby' Hays, Bret Van Meter and Mark Hartman held the defensive tackle, middle guard and defensive tackle positions respectively. Matt 'Roller-Ball' Hartman and 'Billy-B' Griffith filled the linebacker spots. Steve Crist roamed the field at 'monster back.' Kurt Swiger and Gary Cox played tenacious man-on-man coverage at the corners, and Froggy rounded out the top-11 at free safety. When the final whistle ended the game Bexley had thrown two interceptions, given up five sacks and had managed only 112 yards of total offense.

"We're not that good," Dad was quoted in the next day's edition of the *Times, "but we're getting better. The boys were as scared as I was."* The game's leading rusher would never forget the sizable crowd, and how many fans remained behind when the game ended. *"There was a huge crowd and it was somewhat intimidating; even after the game ended, they lined that fence, milled about the ball diamond and near the entrance. I had never seen that many people at a CW football game before. The first person I saw after the game was my Dad who congratulated me. I would see him first after every game that followed – that's a nice memory for me."*

Despite the lopsided outcome it had been a physical, hard hitting football game. Winning momentarily masked the cuts, bumps, bruises and trauma resulting from bone-jarring hits while the victory bell rang. It would be a different story the following morning. And it wasn't just physical aches and pains. The mental strain, nervous tension and pregame 'butterflies' also took their toll.

"It was a hard-hitting game," Gary Cox remembered. *"I knocked a guy out. I was playing man-to-man coverage at corner and Bexley's flanker ran a quick slant. I read it and hit him as hard as I could across the bow and knocked him out. That guy I knocked out, I can still see him. It remains vivid in my memory to this day. We were all pretty sore the next morning."* Because the game remained close into the third quarter second-teamers had remained on the sidelines.

Gary Cox, senior cornerback

Junior Craig Cox, for example, never once stepped foot on Weiser Field, which was fine with his mother, Janet. According to Steve Blake, who helped out with the football program and lived across the street from Lt. Colonel David Cox and his family, notwithstanding Gary's fondness for hitting and Craig's desire to play, Mrs. Cox would have preferred that they both stay out of harm's way. *"I couldn't believe it,"* Steve Blake recalled dismayingly. *"I'd never seen anyone do that before; but Jan worried they'd get hurt and when the hitting started there'd she be; she's standing up in the stands yelling, 'Get Gary out of there! Get my boy out of there!'"*

Although Gary and Craig appreciated their mother's concern neither shared it. *"I wanted in there so bad,"* Craig lamented. *"But I was a complete rookie and knew I wouldn't play much. I was hoping for a blowout so I could get in; I ended up standing there talking to Gary every time he came off the field. It's harder to watch than play, let me tell you."* Fortunately for everyone involved in the program – sans Janet Cox - the following game would provide the blowout Craig and his fellow underclassmen desired.

WEEK II:

FISHER CATHOLIC

═══════════════════════════

(September 12, 1975 – Home)

Though Mid State League champs in 1974, the scheduling gods clearly smiled upon Canal Winchester their first two contests of the 1975 season. These were home games which gave the Indians a decided edge. And having played the first nonconference game on a Thursday, they had an extra day to prepare for the MSL opener against Fisher Catholic. While it is true Dad admired hard work and athletic competition, he held an almost visceral dislike for Catholic football programs. He was not anti-Catholic, being an equal-opportunity-skeptic where religion is concerned. Rather, the ability of Catholic programs to recruit struck him as an unfair advantage. He felt that Catholic teams should compete in all-catholic leagues.

The Ohio High School Athletic Association did not subscribe to that view; and Fisher Catholic was already on the schedule when Dad took the CW job in 1967. Actually, it wasn't known as Fisher Catholic then, but as Bishop Fenwick; and prior to that, Saint Mary High School. Founded in 1891 in Lancaster, Ohio - Saint-Mary/Bishop-Fenwick/ William V. Fisher-Catholic High School – like most schools in small Ohio towns - took its football seriously. In their eight previous meetings, however – to the disgust of Irish fans everywhere - Canal Winchester had won six games to Fisher's two.

Fisher Catholic teams were well coached, fast and like CW, had a loyal fan base. In 1974 the Indians managed to squeak by 13 to 6; the 1975 Fisher squad was reputed to have excellent overall team speed. The Irish's head coach, Hank Leckrone, and his staff had scouted CW's opener against Bexley. Two days later, Saturday September 6, 1975, Coach Locke, Jones and Roth returned the favor by attending the Fisher Catholic, Zanesville Rosecrans Football game.

Fisher won that game 14 to 6 against a larger opponent. According to the ever-so-slightly biased *Lancaster Eagle Gazette*, the Irish victory over Rosecrans mirrored David's triumph over Goliath: *"Saturday night the Irish of Hank Leckrone proved that size is not everything as they beat big Zanesville Rosecrans, 14-6 in the season lid-lifter. Rosecrans outweighed Fisher by an average of 40-pounds per man but FC made up for the size deficit in speed and pride."* Where and how the *"40-pounds per man"* stat was arrived at is anybody's guess; but Canal's coaching staff was impressed with Fisher's speed.

On Monday – again with the JVs playing at 5:00 pm – the varsity stretched, went through calisthenics, did some light running and then listened as Dad explained Fisher's offensive and defensive formations on Weiser Filed. Afterwards they went into the film room to watch both their win over Bexley and the Fisher-Rosecrans game films. Though Canal Winchester was – in Dad's mind – a better football team, he didn't dare tell his players that. He had coached long enough to know, in his words: *"Kids just can't believe a weaker team can beat them. They have to find out the hard way that any team can beat your ass if they want it badly enough."*

So throughout film instruction Dad emphasized Fisher's blazing team speed, impressed upon them that FC had won its opener against a larger team, and reminded them how close last year's game between Canal and Fisher had been. It would also be important to play disciplined ball as Coach Leckrone was known to gamble. All three coaches repeatedly warned against fake punts, onside kicks, flee flickers and the occasional reverse. During the Rosecrans game, for example, Coach Leckrone called a *double* reverse – on 4th and nine. The Indians watched that play over and over again.

Fisher Catholic played a 6-2 defense. Their down linemen positioned themselves in the gaps between opposing offensive linemen. When center

Mark Hartman snapped the football Friday night there would not be a middle guard directly in front of him, but rather two down linemen to his immediate left and right. The same would be true for offensive guards and tackles. Every program in the MSL put a premium on stopping the run, and Fisher Catholic didn't buck the trend. At Tuesday's practice, therefore, Coach Jones lined up the beleaguered JV defense in the 6-2; placing down-linemen in the gaps, mimicking Fisher's D.

Wednesday's defensive practice emphasized position discipline. Neal Seymour and Rick Ross were warned not to let Fisher's runners beat them outside, and to watch for reverses. Linebackers Matt Hartman and Bill Griffith practiced tackling backs catching swing passes out of the backfield, and monster back Steve Crist prepared to key on Fisher's quarterback, Chris Henry. Defensive backs Gary Cox, Kurt Swiger, Craig Cox and Froggy readied for Fisher's senior offensive end, Bill Motter, whom they expected to get a lot of touches. It was Motter who had scored Fisher's first TD against Rosecrans by catching a 29 yard pass from Henry; and Bill Motter who had gained the first down on the double-reverse.

The twelfth of September turned out to be a fine evening for playing football in 1975. Though the days were still relatively hot, by evening temperatures had dropped and dusk arrived much earlier than it had just three weeks before. Both teams looked forward to playing football in 68 degree weather under clear Ohio skies. Fans shuffled through the entryway; the concession stand sold its goodies, and the Indians practiced their peculiar style of psychological warfare by going through calisthenics using a silent count.

Unfortunately for Fisher Catholic their spirited pregame warm-up proved to be the evening's only excitement on the visitor's side of the field. The Indians were bigger - and faster as it turned out - than their Irish opponents and by half time the score was 34-0. As in their matchup against Bexley, Dad discovered the Irish couldn't stop Steve Crist. So he ran the Bionic Man over and over again behind Bill Allen. Well prepared for Fisher's 6-2 defense, the line blocked well; Steve Crist scored twice – the second time after 'Baby' Hays recovered a fumble on Fisher's 30-yard line. And for the second week in a row the Bionic Man passed the century-mark, gaining 115 yards in the first half alone.

The Irish found themselves in a hole almost from the moment they stepped on the field. Having won the coin toss they went three and out on the first offensive series, and prepared to punt from their 36 yard line. Quarterback Chris Henry also handled Fisher Catholic's punting duties – which made the probability of a fake much higher. His first punt didn't go well, as even the *Lancaster Eagle Gazette* acknowledged, "*Henry took too much time handling the snap on an attempted punt and Winchester successfully blocked it at the 32 yard line.*" Three plays later Steve Crist scored his first touchdown. After the game Coach Leckrone would claim that the blocked punt had "*a demoralizing effect . . . and once down it was difficult to return.*"

Trailing 14-0 Fisher moved even more defenders toward the line of scrimmage, and Dad – against his better judgment – went to the passing game. Unlike the previous week, however, when Gregg Wright threw two interceptions and zero TD passes; he demonstrated why he'd won the quarterback competition by throwing two long spirals that went for scores, one of 25 yards and the other of 35, both to Junior, Neal Seymour.

Defensively Bill Motter was kept in check; QB Chris Henry was harried, sacked and chased in his own backfield much of the night and the Irish were held to 54-total offensive yards – ten of which came through the air. As one newspaper account put it, "*The Indians did a rowdy job of chasing Henry around the backfield each time the FC quarterback attempted to pass. Tackle Mark Hartman and end Neal Seymour helped the defensive line sack Henry several times.*"

Leading 28-0, with only four minutes left in the half Canal forced Fisher Catholic into another punting situation. Froggy waited alone on the 25 yard line to receive the punt; the football went aloft into the dark blue sky spinning end-over-end beneath the field lights; Gary positioned himself to catch it, momentarily vulnerable while looking up at the pumpkin descending to earth, caught the ball, and raced 75 yards down the sideline behind the Indian's punt-return team. It was 34-0. And Dad wanted it to stay that way.

Having coached four years at Richwood and nine at Canal Winchester Dad had seen plenty of coaches run up the score on beaten teams. It not only demoralized the losing side but, in his opinion, was poor sportsmanship. He had no intention of leaving the Mid State League any time soon; and no desire to create long lists of coaching enemies. Understanding that running up the score led to hard feelings, he brought the varsity offense out of the game - leaving only the starting defense in place to prevent Fisher from making a game of it. Despite the lopsided score it was – according to Craig Cox - another hard hitting affair.

"*I was on the kickoff team,*" Craig recalled sheepishly. "*I was running down field as fast as I could run. The ball went to the opposite side and I was turning toward it when I saw a guy standing there in a blocking position. I thought, 'I've got momentum! I'll run him over and show him what CW football is all about.' I hit him running at full speed with my head down. He came up swinging both forearms and hit me under the chin. I reeled backward, the wrong way, and green slime started coming out of my nose and running down my face. Wow! Hello! Talk about a wake-up call.*" In the distance, somewhere in the middle of CW's stands, Janet Cox's voice could be heard demanding that Craig be taken out of the game.

His older brother Gary had a similar experience, but in his case he dealt the blow rather than received it. "*I blindsided this poor schmuck on a return,*" Gary recalled with evident satisfaction. "*And when I got to the sidelines everyone was crediting Neal Seymour with the hit. I thought, 'Cool, Neal got one also.' It was only later, the following week when we were watching films that Coach Locke said, 'Hey that's not Neal, that's Cox! Way to go Animal. From that point on Coach Locke always called me Animal.*" It wasn't, however, all milk & honey for CW, as one unfortunate second half episode demonstrated.

Leading 34-0 the starting defense remained on the field to preserve the shutout. During the third quarter Steve Crist was called for 'spearing' – hitting an opposing player with the helmet – and thrown out of the game. Roger Hanners, WHOK's play-by-play man, saw the whole thing. "*The kid from Fisher Catholic was already tackled but Steve was closing in so fast he couldn't stop and made the hit. Steve Crist would never intentionally spear somebody but the ref threw him out of the game.*" Roger paused for a moment and then added, "*I remember seeing tears in his eyes because he couldn't play. He was a great football player.*" Standing on the sideline when Steve came out of the game - the fans on Canal's sideline booing the call – I watched in amazement as tears rolled down Steve Crist's face. Boys my age looked up to high school football players, who seemed larger than life.

And at the moment a very large Steve Crist stood in front of me; one of the most important players on the team, christened the 'Bionic Man' by teammates, six-feet tall, chiseled, incredibly strong and powerful, the leading tackler on an imposing defense and leading scorer in Franklin County, and he was crying because he couldn't play football. His teammates patted him on the rear, hugged him, hit his shoulder pads, telling him it was OK. Football really is an emotional game played by emotional people.

"I'll never forget that night," Steve recalled. *"What I remember most about the Fisher Catholic game was getting thrown out in the third quarter. I was devastated. I had never been thrown out of anything before in my life – not baseball, football or basketball, never; they had put in a new rule that if tacklers used their helmets it was an automatic ejection. I hadn't done it on purpose but they threw me out. After a while Coach Locke told me not to worry about it and that he was going to take me out anyway."*

In the first two games of the 1975 season Canal Winchester had scored 61 points and given up 0. And despite Dad's best efforts at not running up the score it didn't sway Fisher Catholic's hometown newspaper. As Neal Seymour recalled. *"It was 34-0 at halftime, our offense never went back on the field and the Lancaster paper said that Fisher Catholic's defense held us scoreless in the second half: that was the headline!"* Besides CW, two other MSL football teams, the Pickerington Tigers, and Bloom Carroll Bulldogs, remained undefeated as the 1975 campaign got underway.

Notwithstanding Canal Winchester's two opening victories, Dad was quick to remind *Times'* reporters that *"though I'm pleased with the defense it hasn't yet faced a 'good offense."* This was not a dig at Bexley or Fisher Catholic, but rather an attempt to remind his players that they weren't necessarily as good as everyone in town was telling them they were.

INTERLUDE:

For CW residents uninterested in high school football, or those who enjoyed staying home Friday evenings, TV choices for September 12, 1975 between 7:00 and 11:00 pm were limited. Blockbuster Video wouldn't be founded for another ten years; no one in town had Cable TV or owned a computer; and so the three networks were pretty much the only non-football game in town. WCMH Channel 4 (NBC) aired

Truth or Consequences at 7:00 pm; *Sanford & Son* and *Chico and the Man* between 8:00 and 9:00 pm; *The Rockford Files* with James Garner at 9:00 and *Police Woman* starring Angie Dickinson at 10:00 pm.

WSYX channel 6 (ABC) ran *Bowling for Dollars* at 7:00; *Mobile One* at 8:00; and the *ABC Movie of the Week* between 9:00 and 11:00 pm. WBNS channel 10 (CBS) aired *Eyewitness-90* at 7:00 pm; *Big Eddie* from 8:00 to 8:30; and *M*A*S*H* featuring Wayne Rogers, Alan Alda and McClain Stevenson between 8:30 and 9:00 pm. *Hawaii Five-O;* starring Jack Lord and his immaculately quaffed do, aired from 9:00 to 10:00 pm. The lineup certainly goes a long ways towards explaining the popularity of small town athletics in the 1970s.

Football players usually took about an hour to clear the locker room after games; what with the band serenading the team; the ringing of the victory bell and the time it took to peel off uniforms, jam shoulder pads and helmets into lockers, shower, dry off and change. Fortunately, by the time they got home, Channel 10's Friday night *Chiller Theater* was on deck at 11:30 pm. Spent from another week of school and football, most settled in with friends or dates to watch *Chiller's* black & white horror classics.

Hosted by Columbus' very own 'Fritz-the-Nite-Owl,' AKA Frederick C. Peerenboom, *Chiller Theater* aired old monster movies. Every Friday night central Ohioans looked on as Frankenstein, Count Dracula, werewolves, vampires, Godzilla, ancient mummies and radioactively enhanced super bugs from 1950s cinema paraded across flickering television screens. *The Blob; Attack of the Fifty-Foot Woman; The Bride of Frankenstein, The Thing* and *Mothra Vs. Godzilla* all made appearances - and at every commercial break viewers could count on 'Fritz-the-Nite-Owl' - wearing large owl glasses - to make humorous remarks at the expense of the film.

Once the locker room had cleared Dad stopped home to give Mom a hug before driving to King Arthur's Steak House located along Route 33 on the outskirts of town. He had befriended the owner, Ralph Lockett; and like his father Norman, he enjoyed sitting in darkened bars, eating an occasional Hero sandwich, drinking cold beer with his coaches and unwinding after the long week. It was fortunate he was a successful coach, for not everyone in the community approved. *"My parents didn't like the fact that Coach Locke went out to King Arthur's and drank,"* Matt

Hartman recalled. *"They didn't like that at all,"* he continued. *"Small town, you know. It didn't bother me or any of the other players. I was the first to stick up for him. But you know my parents were probably much more conservative in the way they were brought up."*

My father awoke at 5:55 am every day of his coaching career. It was not until long after retirement that he managed to stay in bed until 6:30-7:00 am. Saturday mornings following football games he rolled out of bed at 6:00, descended the staircase, made a cup of *Taster's Choice* instant coffee, sliced a banana to place atop toast and began reading the morning newspaper. The previous night's game films were dropped downtown at CW's Police/Fire Department just inside the front door. By 7:30 am either he or one of his coaches had picked up the films and were busily dissecting the team's play in the film room.

Dad gave the team Saturday and Sunday off with no expectation that anyone show up for films, but over the years players had learned that the staff reviewed game film Saturday mornings, and so began filtering in two and three at a time. Wearing shorts, old blue jeans, sweat pants and T-shirts they arrived with hot coffee purchased from Parker's Sohio or 'The Woods' gas station just outside of town. Without a word they sat down on either side of the projector and, along with the coaches, began rating their performances; afterwards drifting off to enjoy the hard earned free time.

The Ohio State football Buckeyes played on Saturday afternoons and after the usual, frenetic morning rush on Conrad's Market and Super Duper, Huntington Bank, Bolenbaugh's Hardware, the Wigwam, Shade's Restaurant and Canal View Pharmacy, the town emptied nearly as quickly as it had filled up. By kickoff time most streets were deserted and the bustling little village of just a few hours before resembled something of a ghost town.

In 1975 Cornelius Green quarterbacked the Buckeyes and Archie Griffin was rushing his way toward a second Heisman Trophy. In the unlikely event an Ohioan was not a Buckeye football fan, Kings Island Amusement Park was hosting daredevil Evel Knieval that Saturday afternoon; September 13, 1975. Evel, wearing his trademark red, white and blue sequined outfit - complete with cape - planned` to entertain the multitudes by jumping his motorcycle over several buses.

Jaws was still in movies theaters that weekend, but nearly everyone had seen it by September. *Rollerball*, starring Paul Newman; *Shampoo*, starring Warren Beatty; *The Longest Yard*, starring Burt Reynolds; *Serpico*, starring Al Pacino, and *Death Wish*, starring Charles Bronson all made their debuts that autumn. The previous Tuesday, September 9th 1975, ABC premiered *Welcome Back Kotter* with Gabe Kaplan as prodigal son returning to Brooklyn to teach his beloved 'Sweat hogs,' led by newcomer John Travolta. The following evening; Wednesday, September 10th ABC debuted *Starsky and Hutch* with Paul Michael Glaser as 'Dave Starsky,' and David Soul as 'Ken Hutchinson' - along with the star of the show - their red and white Ford Gran Torino.

Outside Canal Winchester the larger world did what it always does, writhed in turmoil. The nation had witnessed the first presidential resignation in August 1974; the following spring, during April 1975, it lost its first war. In the interim the country's only unelected president became the target of several bungled assassination attempts. The day before Canal and Fisher Catholic squared off to play football, Lynette 'Squeaky' Fromme – a deranged spawn of the Manson Clan - had been arraigned for the attempted assassination of Gerald Ford.

Reflecting the inanity of her times she warned the presiding judge, *"There is an army of young people and children who want to clean up the earth . . . The gun is pointed, your honor, the gun is pointed. Whether it goes off is up to you."* Union leader Jimmy Hoffa was still missing since his disappearance in July; and Patricia Hearst - abducted in February 1974 – had joined her kidnappers, the 'Symbionese Liberation Army' and was busy holding up banks. It was, by any barometer, a tumultuous time of uncertainty and accelerated change – both socially and politically.

In our rural Ohio community that outside world did occasionally impact residents directly: as with the 1973 Mideast oil embargo, but also indirectly, slowly, with sufficient time to absorb and consider the various changes swirling about us. It wouldn't always be thus, but before the information revolution swept insularity aside it was still possible to grow up in a small town feeling distinct and apart from larger societal trends that appeared absurd, even alien from life at home – Canal Winchester, Ohio.

WEEK III:

MILLERSPORT

<hr>

(September 19, 1975 - Away)

*"Twenty-two men . . .
Chasing a pigskin' ball . . .
The generals . . .
waging . . . athletic war.
And . . . the words they use,
Never amount to more than four . . ."*

(Tom Zart – Football)

Millersport, Ohio had much in common with Canal Winchester. Like CW it was a small, rural farming community in 1975; also like CW it owed its origins to the Ohio/Erie Canal. Millersport began as a trade port on the waterway, and still boasts well preserved remnants of the canal that ran through the center of town. Millersport, founded in 1825 by Mathias Miller, lay just West of Buckeye Lake, a former swamp known locally as the 'Buffalo Licks' that locals had cleared and turned it into a reservoir supplying water to the canal.

The twenty-five mile bus ride to Millersport was long and bumpy. The teams had first squared off in 1957, a home game for Canal Winchester and also the occasion for the official dedication of A.B. Weiser Field.

Despite the solemn ceremony the new rivals played to a 0-0 tie. In sixteen subsequent gridiron meetings - they did not play each other in 1964 and 1965 – Canal won 8 games, Millersport won six, and they tied twice. Since Dad had taken over the program his teams had won six of eight contests.

In 1975 Millersport's head coach was Ken Keener. Though his Lakers won their second ballgame against Fairfield Union 6-0, they got off to a rough start in the season opener, losing to perennial powerhouse Newark Catholic 60-0. In Canal's first away game of the year the Indians could count on playing in front of a hostile crowd, on unfamiliar turf and far from home; very far from home according to the Cox brothers.

Indeed, while twenty-five mile trips are manageable hops in one's own automobile; on back country roads aboard elongated school buses the distance seemed to double. *"We came from Nebraska,"* Gary Cox remembered, *"but I had never seen anything like this before. We kept going and going and as we were driving on the bus I was thinking, 'Jesus Christ, where in the hell are we?' I swear it looked like the football field was in the middle of a cornfield."*

Though Gary had been an Indian long enough to know he was supposed to 'Think about it,' before gridiron contests, his mind wandered as he and his teammates sped ever onward into the darkness. *"Literally, I had no idea where we were going on that bus. It was pitch black on these lonely, back-country roads and there's nothing but cornfields everywhere. We finally made it to Millersport High School and the only thing I could see was the football field lit up and absolutely surrounded by cornfields. It was like something out of the Twilight Zone."*

Younger brother Craig concurred. *"On the bus ride to Millersport I was thinking 'Where the hell are we going?' That ride seemed like it took four hours. We got off the bus and I'm thinking 'Talk about being in the middle of nowhere'"* The Lakers football team, though down in 1975, became the first to host CW, and the first to score on them. But despite the cornfield maze separating the towns and being far from home, the visitor stands were full of Indian fans that night, and they would have a lot to cheer about.

Canal scored five touchdowns at Millersport, holding the Lakers scoreless well into the fourth quarter. Steve Crist ran for two scores; Froggy ran for one; Steve Potter another and even fullback Matt Hartman plunged across the goal line on a one-yard dive. It was not offensive production, however, that players remembered about the Millersport game – it was getting scored upon. The following day's *Lancaster Eagle Gazette's* first sentence on the contest remarked, *"Winchester's goal line was dented for the first time this season at Millersport."*

It was a cold, damp night and both teams were fairly splattered with mud by halftime. Canal had dominated all four quarters. Unfortunately, with another defensive shutout within their grasp, mental lapses led to a score. And when it did those standing on Winchester's sidelines would have thought the Indians were losing 50-0. When the Lakers' Joe Guyselman crossed the goal line Millersport fans rose to their feet cheering; across the field all hell broke loose as my father began speaking loudly in tongues – very loudly. "It was *classic,*" Neal Seymour later recalled. *"Locke's going crazy after we let them score. He's stalking up and down the sideline and players, the stat-girls, coaches – everyone's avoiding him like the plague when he comes their way."*

'Where in the hell is my defense?' He's barking and nobody's answering. 'Where in the hell is my defense? Coach Jones, have you seen my defense? Coach Roth, have you seen our defense?' Where in the hell is my defense?' Ah, man," Neal recalled smiling, *"It was absolutely classic Locke."* Though remembered with humor it wasn't nearly so funny Friday the 19th of September 1975.

Defensive coordinator Jerry Jones and Head Coach Mike Locke watch the action from the sidelines.

As the *Lancaster Eagle Gazette* recorded in the following day's paper, *"Guyselman scored Millersport's touchdown with 24-seconds left in the MSL tilt."* Twenty-four seconds shy of their third shutout, Canal surrendered a score in 'garbage time,' clearly rankling the head coach that they had scored at all. So he stomped up and down the sideline bellowing about his lost defense; when the game ended the Indians boarded the school bus for the long ride home - despite the win - with a sour taste in their mouths.

Those unfamiliar with the sport of football might reasonably ask what difference it possibly made whether Canal won by 26 points or 32 points. They handily defeated their opponent, keeping them scoreless for 59-minutes and 36-seconds, and won the third straight game of the season; why erupt, asking where one's defense had gone? Millersport had, after all, prepared for an entire week to find ways to score against Canal Winchester. The answer is twofold. The first part can best be explained by reading the following exchange between *ESPN* Sports Center host Chris Berman and former All-Pro offensive guard, and football analyst Mark Schlereth; as it perfectly captures the coaching mentality and the way in which players view coaches.

CHRIS BERMAN: *"I don't understand coaches. Why, why do coaches do some of these things we've seen week-in and week-out this season? I mean its 43 to 3 with less than 10-seconds left and Marvin Lewis calls time out on the 5-yard line so they can try to score? Why do they do that? Why not just let the clock run out? I mean the game's not even close even if they scored four touchdowns."* Schlereth, who started four years at the University of Idaho; played 13 seasons in the NFL, winning three Super Bowls – two of which while blocking for Hall-of-Famer John Elway – had been around long enough to give a succinct and definitive answer. MARK SCHLERETH: *"Because coaches are crazy."*

As the son of a coach I can confirm Mr. Schlereth's insightful analysis. The primary reason behind Dad's eruption, however, is more complex. He was, as mentioned earlier, hyper-competitive; detested halfhearted effort in anything and everything; and could not abide players losing focus and allowing weaker teams get the better of them. To give up scores to faster, stronger, more physical teams was an acceptable part of the sport – to relax after once getting the lead - unpardonable.

His ranting also had something to do with his understanding of the Indian's schedule in 1975. Although Dad would never let his team hear him say it, he knew that, at least on paper and barring injury, they should win their first four or five football games. He wasn't sure how they'd fare in the last five. So while a letdown against Millersport wouldn't hurt that night; it could cost the MSL Crown against Bloom Carroll or Pickerington. A single loss would also eliminate any chance – however slim – that Canal Winchester had of making the Ohio High School football playoffs.

For Canal Winchester, making those playoffs had proved a tough nut to crack. A statewide panel of sports writers, broadcasters and football 'experts' reveled in citing statistics to determine the best football team in each of Ohio's three divisions. Statistics figuring in their calculations included total team rushing yards, passing yards, combined total offense, rush defense, pass defense, total team defense, points surrendered per game, points scored per game and level of competition. But it didn't seem to matter.

In 1970, for example, Canal Winchester won 10 games, scored 302 points and gave up only 41, yet did not make the playoffs. In 1974 Canal Winchester proved that their previous undefeated campaign had been no fluke by winning ten games for a second time, scored 225 points, surrendered just 47 and again missed the playoffs, despite impressive statistics and the acclaim of the sports writers who compiled them. Unfortunately for the Canal Winchester Indians, sports writers didn't select playoff teams, a computer did.

Today there are six different football divisions, and soon to be seven, in the State of Ohio. The largest schools make up Division I, the small schools Division VI, and almost any team with a decent record gets a shot at the playoffs. Each division is represented by 32 teams from four regions with the top _eight_ in each region qualifying for the postseason. Programs with 8-2; 7-3 and even 6-4 records routinely compete in the playoffs. When Canal played Millersport in 1975, this was not the case.

In the 1970s Ohio's school districts were divided into three divisions, Single-A (A), Double-A (AA), and Triple-A (AAA); and again four regions. But only _one_ Class-A, Class-AA and Class-AAA, team advanced from each region to the playoffs. Amazingly, in a state with 88 counties and over 1,000 school districts, just four Single-A teams qualified for a two-game postseason playoff to determine the Class-A champs.

According to the computer formula used to select those four finalists, football teams amassed points three different ways. (1) Points were awarded for winning. (2) Additional points were awarded based on the record of each opponent; defeating a team with 7 wins, for example, was worth more than beating a team with five. (3) Points were awarded for beating teams in a higher division. If Class-A Canal Winchester beat Class-AA Dublin, CW would receive more points than if they had defeated another Class-A program.

For Canal Winchester, the problem was twofold. First, there were a number of excellent football programs throughout the state in Class-A, including perennial powers Newark Catholic and Middletown Fenwick in their region. Second, with only one nonleague game, the remaining nine programs in the MSL played each other week-in and week-out; making it difficult if not impossible to beat a higher division team having more than four or five wins. This was not the case for programs with greater scheduling flexibility.

Playing hard, staying focused and winning games were the only things Dad's team actually controlled in their drive to make the postseason. And so he endeavored to control the hell out of it. Having twice won every football game during the regular season without being allowed to compete with the computer's choice of best Class-A program in his region, had left a bitter taste in my father's mouth. Not only was he deprived of a chance to win the State Championship, but his players – in his mind - were cheated. In 1975, he intended to do everything in his power to see that his Indians advanced to the playoffs - which helps explain his stalking up and down the sideline loudly demanding to know whither his defense had gone.

After the third week of the 1975 season, nine of ten top-ranked, Class-A teams in Region 12:1 were undefeated.

1. Middletown Fenwick, 3-0; (149 computer points)
2. Newark Catholic, 3-0; (127 computer points)
3. Canal Winchester, 3-0; (95 computer-points)
4. Salineville Southern, 3-0; (39 computer points)
5. Jamestown Greeneview, 2-1; (38 computer points)
6. Carey, 3-0; (32 computer points)

7. Monroeville, 3-0; (32 computer points)
8. North Lima, 3-0; (32 computer points)
9. Minister, 3-0; (32 computer points)
10. Sidney Lehman, 3-0; (30 computer points).

WEEK IV:

BERNE UNION

==========

(September 26, 1975)
Parent's Night

As there were no rewards for finishing third in the computer rankings the Indians understood they were in for a long, hard week of practice come Monday. If the interview their coach gave the *Lancaster Eagle Gazette* following the victory over Millersport was any indication, the Indians were definitely in for hard sledding. *"Extra work,"* the quote began in the Gazette story, *"is what Canal Coach Mike Locke has in store for his team this week. Locke was extremely upset with his team's 32-7 conquest of Millersport last Friday. 'We didn't execute well, especially on defense,' said the Indian boss. 'I am very disappointed with our showing against Millersport,' he commented."*

Most players, especially upper classmen, followed league play in the local papers, and Dad's words were recognized for what they meant: difficult days ahead. As one senior commented after reading of his coach's disappointment, *"I got an awful feeling in my gut when I read the Gazette. We all knew it was going to be a rough week. Coach Locke wasn't a big talker, so when he said he was disappointed and he planned to work us, we knew he meant it. He was pretty upset"*

How upset is a matter of conjecture because their next opponent, Berne Union, hadn't scored a touchdown during its first two games, managed only one score in week three and had yet to win a football game in 1975. With local papers and nearly everyone in town telling Canal's football players how good they were, much of Dad's purported angst over their lackluster Millersport performance was designed to counter all the 'atta-boys,' and keep the team focused on continually improving.

In fact, two newspapers had recently used terms such as *'weak-sisters,' 'extremely young,'* and *'also-rans'* in describing the 1975 Berne Union Rockets. The same night Canal beat Millersport; the Rockets played Fairfield Union, losing for a third straight time, 13 to 6. Head Coach Bob Winningham had been forced to start a freshman quarterback – fourteen-year-old Greg Holland – against Fairfield Union when his starting QB announced he couldn't play because of a painful blood blister.

Without an imposing opponent on the immediate horizon to focus his team's attention, Mike Locke assumed the role of chief obstacle; keeping the squad's minds – and bodies – fully occupied on their shortcomings. *"Ah, he dogged us,"* remembered Rick Ross. *"It was really quiet in films on Monday and at Wednesday night's defensive practice he announced, 'I want the starting defense that was on the field when we quit against Millersport out here right now!'*

"You could've heard a pin drop, Rick continued.*"He started running us and yelling things like, 'Canal Winchester's Defense doesn't quit on the football field!' 'Canal Winchester's Defense doesn't lose focus!' 'Canal Winchester's Defense doesn't stop playing hard because we're winning the God Damn football game!'Canal Winchester's defense doesn't quit God damn it!' And all the while he's running us ragged; sprint after sprint after sprint. It was intense. But you know what? It worked because we never let down again the rest of that year."*

Berne Union High School is located in neighboring Fairfield County in the village of Sugar Grove. Berne Union was, if anything, even smaller than Millersport. Indeed, according to the US Census Bureau, Sugar Grove's population in the year 2,000 numbered a mere 448 souls. The town was - and is still - a small, rural farming community approximately twenty-seven miles east of Canal Winchester. Fortunately for the Cox brothers, the matchup in 1975 was a home game for CW and so they were spared another arduous bus trip into 'no-man's land.'

Parent's Night was always special; while Homecoming is for players, students and a few alumni, Parent's Night celebrated families. After silent warm-up and the coin toss, every varsity football player lined up in the eastern end of Weiser Field with their folks. The parental presence reduced profane language among the young men – even Bill Willison - and it was a proud moment for both players and their guardians.

Speaking of 'Wee-Willie' Willison, Parents Night had perhaps more meaning for him than most that evening. Bill's grandfather was bedridden; had been so for a long time, and his illness had denied him the opportunity to watch Bill play football. Bill Willison, being a senior, knew it would be the last Parent's Night he'd take part in, so he approached Captain Ronnie Cook of the CW Fire Department for a favor. Along with the gaggle of parents in the end zone before the Berne Union game got underway that night; was the CW emergency squad. Inside the squad with its bay doors opened wide was Bill's grandpa.

For all the stories of Bill Willison's wild behavior – grappling with speeding locomotives comes to mind – he tenderly loved his grandpa as much as anyone ever loved a grandpa; the old man's presence deeply affected Bill that night, and he played with great intensity and emotion. As Bill remembered years later, *"Ronnie Cook brought my grandpa to that game. It was his one and only chance to ever see me play . . ."* After trailing off, Bill simply said, *"Thanks Ronnie."*

After grinding practices on Tuesday and Wednesday and the pageantry of Parent's Night, the game itself was rather anticlimactic; when the fourth quarter mercifully ended the scoreboard read Canal Winchester, 56; Berne Union, 0. The following day's *Columbus Dispatch* tactfully headlined its article on the mismatch, *"Crist, Griffith Have Big Night for Winchester."* The *Lancaster Eagle Gazette* on the other hand, perhaps frustrated with Fairfield County teams faring so poorly against Canal, headlined its article, *"Indians Kill BU,"* later referring to the outcome as an *"Indian Massacre."*

As for Dad's policy of not running up the score on defeated foes, two Indian touchdowns were compliments of Gary Griffith's punt returns – one for 53 yards, the other 63 – and an interception return. Minus those non-offensive touchdowns the game would have ended 35-0. In fact, Canal's varsity offense never took the field after halftime. Even victorious Indians got tired of the 'massacre.' Gary Cox, for example, remarked,

"*What a total smear. I remember thinking at one point, 'God, please let this game end. This is embarrassing.'*" After the drubbing Canal's defense took during practice that week they played inspired ball; limiting the Rockets to eighty-two rushing yards and just 50 in the air.

Steve Crist scored two TDs; converted 3 extra-points and kicked a 36-yard field goal; Froggy scored three times, the two punt-returns mentioned above and a forty-one yard run from scrimmage. Both Steve Crist and Gary Griffith rushed for more than one-hundred yards. Fullback Matt Hartman scored one TD, adding another 80 rushing yards; and quarterback Gregg Wright scored a 2-point conversion. The interception return came from an underclassman trying desperately to crack the Indian's defensive lineup – Craig Cox.

Despite the lopsided contest and the desire of some varsity players to see it come to an end, such blowouts were golden opportunities for JV players. Notwithstanding his speed, hard work on special-teams and doing everything in his power to get the coaches' attention, Craig Cox hadn't been able to beat out Kurt Swiger for the starting cornerback position opposite his brother. While Canal's starting defenders went through hell during the week Craig spent his time formulating strategies to acquire playing time. "*I knew I had the chance to play a lot,*" he remembered. "*We all knew Berne's record; they were one of the worst teams in the league that year. So once Gary and I walked our folks to the sideline I made a point to stand as close to Coach Locke as I could.*"

"*I followed him up and down the sideline, his shadow, until sometime in the third quarter when he turned to me and said, 'Get ready, you and Swartz can start alternating at corner once the 4th quarter begins.' I couldn't wait til the fourth quarter,*" Craig recalled. "*Finally, as the fourth quarter started, coach sent me in, but right before I ran on the field he said, and I'll never forget this, he said, 'If you're going to play you might as well intercept one!' I laughed but a couple plays later they threw to my side.*"

"*My receiver was doing a long down & out; he made the cut, the football is in the air spiraling toward the sidelines, just hanging there. I thought, 'I can knock this down.' I got closer – 'Maybe I can catch this.' It's hanging, we're both moving toward the sideline – jump – I got it!*" At this point in Craig's story he accelerates the delivery. "*Come down, stay in bounds, duck under the official – watch the feet – OK run down the sidelines; I got tackled as I planted my left foot over the goal line. I rolled over, got up and* was immediately smothered by teammates. I ran to the sidelines and coach ran up to me, grabbed the front of my jersey and said, 'See, I told you so!' The crowd was going crazy, God, what a memory."

Nothing went right for the Rockets that night and nothing seemed to go wrong for the Indians, with one glaring exception – for one particular Indian. Despite leading Franklin County in scoring; and leading Canal's defense in tackles, the 'Bionic Man' was shown no favoritism from on-high. During the second quarter Steve Crist had the unmitigated gall to run outside instead of inside on 'Slant-6' after being coached – since two-a-days - to run the play inside. "*I finally learned how to run 'Slant-6' that night*," Steve began his tale of woe.

"*The play came in from Van Meter and we ran it from our own 30-yardline. I decided to break it wide around the end. When I got tackled out of bounds I looked up and there was Coach Locke, red faced and screaming at me, 'Where the hell are you going? Hit the hole off tackle!' His blood was definitely up because he proceeded to call 'Slant-6' eight consecutive times. We'd huddle up and waited for Van Meter or Willison, and every time they came in to the huddle they said, 'Slant-6,' and so we kept running it. We finally got down to the three-yard line where coach changed the play and Froggy ran it in.*" Steve shook his head, concluding, "*I never ran 'Slant-6' outside the end again.*"

Both the Pickerington Tigers, (22-6 over Fisher Catholic) and Bloom Carroll Bulldogs (20-12 over Millersport) won their games that night, keeping pace with CW and remaining undefeated in the Mid State League. The Indian's road grew steeper the further they moved into the season; once Canal played Fairfield Union the following week their final five opponents – unlike their first five – all had winning records. Fortunately for his weary Indians Dad was quoted in the local press as "*pleased*" with the offense's execution and defensive effort against Berne Union. Keeping in line with Matt Hartman's observation that he never let up, however, Dad remarked to the *Times'* reporter that "*We let down some in the second half though.*"

The Mighty Indians cheer their number-one ranking in the state of Ohio

INTERLUDE:

The win over Berne Union marked the final football game of September 1975. Friday's upcoming contest would be the 3rd of October. The calendar's tenth month is traditionally the time of year Ohioans most associate with football. The weather is crisp and cool in the evenings, days are mild and night descends quickly, meaning that evening football practices often concluded in the waning half light of dusk. Autumn colors in Canal Winchester, as nearly everywhere else in the Midwest, are spectacular; yellow, violet and purple leaves adorn the trees, orange pumpkins and ruby red windfall apples - bathed in brilliant sunlight - are set against soft blue Midwestern skies. At night stars twinkle closer to earth in the darkness and the Big Dipper hangs lower in the night sky. It is beyond doubt that God Almighty Himself created October weather for the game of football.

On Saturdays, Dad attended Fisher Catholic football games, scouting the Indian's future MSL opponents. Sunday mornings, however, we usually did something together as a family. Occasionally Mom packed sandwiches and we'd drive towards Lancaster until Dad espied an especially inviting pond and disembarked to fish. We'd usually spend two or three hours angling for bass, blue-gills, crappie and sunfish before heading home.

We also frequented local orchards beginning in October. Freshly pressed, tangy cider and big bags of ripe, red apples were worth the trips; and we made an outing of it nearly every weekend. Sunday nights at home were somber – at least for me. Television before bedtime offered

60-Minutes; Hee-Haw and the *Lawrence Welk Show* – not exactly programs of interest to twelve-year-old boys. NBC, Channel-4 did air weekly Disney movies; but it was pretty much a crapshoot as to what they'd run. It was difficult - after being home with your guard down; spending time together as a family - to jump back into the melodramatic world of Jr. High School. But that's the way it was for everybody.

With the halfway point of the 1975 season just a week away, media attention began to grow; and it grew not only for Dad, but also for Coach Jones, Coach Roth, the players, and the entire town. Whereas the Indians were assured coverage in the *Times* and *Lancaster Eagle Gazette* no matter what their record, the team's fourteenth straight victory led to additional, incremental attention in both the *Columbus Citizen Journal* and *Columbus Dispatch*. Though denied an opportunity to compete in the playoffs after the 1974 campaign, Canal Winchester had nevertheless remained undefeated over nearly a season and a half.

The victory over Berne Union caught local sports writer's attention. It was somewhat unusual for small town, non-Catholic football programs to stay unbeaten over the course of two seasons. Following their first undefeated season in 1970, for example, the 1971 Indians went 8-2; a respectable record, but not perfect. And to their credit, most sports writers recognized how difficult it was to win ten games in a row – let alone extend the streak into the following season. Consequently, when the prognosticators and broadcasters published rankings following the Berne Union win, Canal Winchester was United Press International's number one, Class-A football team in the state of Ohio.

Dad had remarked on the topic of remaining perfect during our interview; *"Ah, man,"* he began shaking his head. *"People outside the sport have no idea how hard it is to put together an unbeaten season in football. One holding call can lose a football game; a single interception or fumble can lose a football game. Not to mention the dirty, cheating convict bastards!"* (My father's colorful reference to referees)

"The convicts can cost you a game, let me tell you. And even good coaches blow games – gambling on fake punts, onsides kicks or going for it on fourth down. And I don't just mean at Canal, it's amazing how good, well-coached and lucky you have to be to win all your games." Four games into the 1975 season the Indians continued to win and along with the added attention and victories came increasing pressure; each contest becoming bigger

than the one preceding it. With the next matchup - against Fairfield Union - set to mark the start of October football Dad assured the *Times* —and through it his players - that the Falcons would be *"The first test of the team's capabilities."*

WEEK V:

FAIRFIELD UNION

==

(October 3, 1975 - Away)

Fairfield Union High School – like Fisher Catholic, Millersport and Berne Union – makes its home east of Canal Winchester in Fairfield County. A consolidated school district, it serves students from three rural communities, Pleasantville, Rushville and Breman, Ohio. From 1818 – when formal classroom instruction began - until the 1920s, students from each community received schooling in their respective hometowns. Some consolidation occurred during the 'Roaring Twenties' but Fairfield Union didn't come to life until 1957 when the Ohio Department of Education conducted a statewide survey determining how best to consolidate Ohio's smaller school districts.

Pleasantville and Rushville amalgamated in 1957 and Breman joined the pair in 1959. By May 1961, construction had begun on new school buildings which would accommodate kids from all three towns. These new buildings had been completed when classes began in September 1962. The football field was laid out in 1965, though home games had to wait until boosters raised sufficient funds for field lights. Canal Winchester first met the Fairfield Union Falcons on Weiser Field in 1963; Canal won the game 20 to 14.

Dad's record against the Falcon's stood at six wins and two losses prior to their meeting in 1975. The two losses were back-to-back in 1968-

286

1969, the first being a 52-6 drubbing, one of the worst defeats Canal ever suffered in Dad's entire career. Since the 69' season, however, the Indians had won five straight against the Falcons. And despite Dad's usual warnings in the papers, they were expected to extend their winning streak to six in 1975. Fairfield's gridiron was remote and seemed abandoned and forlorn amid the campus' one hundred and thirty sprawling acres of open fields until football fans assembled and brought it to life on game nights.

From CW it's an eighteen mile straight shot down Route 33 to Fairfield Union, located due east of Lancaster. Despite playing in front of a home crowd, enjoying the role of underdog, and having the opposing coach lauding their abilities, Fairfield Union operated at the decided disadvantage of having lost five in a row to Canal Winchester. Moreover, in the first four games of the '75 season the Falcons' had managed only one win under their new head coach. Canal's veteran head coach was in his ninth season at the same school, while the Falcon's head coach had led his squad in just four games. And in the week of this contest the UPI ranked Canal Winchester the best Class-A football team in the state and the AP had ranked them second.

Nevertheless, first year Falcon Coach Joe Dimotrovich, as would any good coach, insisted the opposite in the days leading up to the game. *"We feel honored to be playing against somebody who is rated as high as Canal,"* he informed the *Lancaster Eagle Gazette*. We're looking forward *"to having the opportunity to knock them off. We're going to throw 16 to 25 times this week,"* he continued. *"We will try to loosen them up with the pass."* Notwithstanding Coach Dimotrovich's optimism the *Gazette* wasn't convinced, referring to Canal as *"The Mighty Indians"* and singing their praises.

"To upset the Mighty Indians Fairfield Union will have to stop Canal's running attack," the *Gazette* sports editor informed readers. And *"that would be a minor miracle since the Winchester backfield has been chewing up Jaws type yardage on the ground this year."* In the same article the editor managed to peg Dad's offensive philosophy to a Tee. *"It's never been and never will be a secret what Canal will do offensively,"* he observed *—"run."*

Back at CW High School, press attention combined with the UPI and AP rankings were big news. That Friday, October 3[rd,] Indian football players arrived sporting maroon (away) jerseys for only the second time that year; girlfriends, potential girlfriends and sisters wore white jerseys; the cheerleaders and 'Bakes" musicians planned a monster pep rally at the end of 9th period and both faculty and students bestrode the hallways in a blur of maroon & white apparel. *"It was reaching a fever pitch,"* Steve Crist remembered. *"Not only at school but in town, everyone stopped to congratulate us being ranked number one."* Ironically, "a fever pitch" had also been reached that Friday afternoon at Fairfield Union High School.

DATELINE: Friday, October 3, 1975. *Lancaster Eagle Gazette; FALCON COACH RELEASED.* Unbeknownst to Canal's coaching staff, that day's *Gazette* reported Fairfield Union had fired its head coach. *"An official source told the Gazette late Thursday,"* the article began, *"that first year Fairfield Union football coach Joe Dimotrovich has been relieved of his coaching duties. Dimotrovich confirmed the report early this morning and said he would appeal his suspension at an October 13th board meeting. According to the source, the Falcons' boss was removed from the coaching ranks Wednesday as a result of 'deteriorating conditions on the football team'."*

The one-win Falcons, now thrown in turmoil, would be led against the state's number-one ranked Class-A football team by three assistant coaches; identified in the paper as Tom Muchler, Dale Ferbrache and Terry Markwood. Besides the obvious advantage the termination dealt to Canal Winchester; it also illustrates how precarious is the position of head coach. A poor won-loss record, disgruntled players and dissatisfied parents did not - and does not - translate into long term job security in Ohio, especially in October.

The *Gazette* immediately contacted CWHS for Dad's reaction. Predictably, he used the opportunity to warn of possible new dangers. *"Canal coach Mike Locke, upon hearing of the Fairfield Union situation, said that he thinks the Falcons will be sky high for tonight's Mid State contest."* No matter who coached the Falcons in 1975, the Indians respected Fairfield Union. Indeed, nearly every Indian football player remarked on Fairfield's annual team size. *"Fairfield Union was a big team and was always hard-hitting,"* remembered one CW football veteran.

"They had a huge fullback," Craig Cox recalled. *"He ran to my side – my guy had blocked Rick Ross – and the FB got through. I ran up, lowered my head and he ran me over like I was a feather."* (Perhaps Mrs. Cox was right

to fear for her sons). Notwithstanding their size and punishing style of play, and the occasional scamper beyond the line of scrimmage, Fairfield Union, like Bexley, Fisher and Berne Union before them, could not score against the Indians. Four quarters of football yielded just 139 yards of total offense for the Falcons. Besides stuffing Fairfield's running game Canal also intercepted two passes. Brett Van Meter came down with a deflected ball, stopping a drive, and for the second week in a row Craig Cox made a pick and returned it for a touchdown; unfortunately the TD was nullified by a clipping penalty.

Canal's offense made good the *Lancaster Eagle Gazette's* prediction of an attack focused almost exclusively on the run. Dad called only four passing plays that night. The 'Bionic Man' scored three rushing TDs; kicked four extra points and ran for 174 yards on thirteen carries. Captain Gary Griffith scored two TDs, one a thirty-four yard run from scrimmage and the other a long punt return. There were only two sour notes that evening for Canal Winchester. The first occurring shortly after Gregg Wright threw a 27-yard TD pass to Neal Seymour. Gregg injured his right knee, left the game midway through the second quarter and was unable to return.

The other discordant note occurred on special teams. Emphasizing the kicking game had paid dividends. Not only had the defense surrendered just six points in its first five games, but the kickoff and punt teams hadn't given up a cheap score. With the scoreboard reading 27-0 in the first half against Fairfield, Dad agreed to let Steve Crist attempt a fifty-yard field goal. Gut-instinct told him to punt and bury the Falcons in their own territory; but the continued success of his defense and earnest pleas of players swayed him otherwise. According to the 'Bionic Man' the fifty-yard-field-goal attempt didn't turn out to be such a good idea.

"We were ahead by so much in the first half," Steve began earnestly, "that we talked coach into letting me try a 50-yard field goal just before the end of the 2nd quarter. Coach called timeout and sent the field goal team onto the field. I was so pumped up, had my head down, great snap and then bang! I kicked it so hard it ended up going 50-yards – fifty yards straight up in the air. I'm serious, Steve concluded laughing. That field goal went 57 yards, seven yards past the line of scrimmage and fifty yards into the air. I never lived it down." During the second half, with Gregg Wright out of the game, Senior Scott Jordan came off the bench and did a nice job running the offense. Scott threw two completions to Rick Ross and scored on a naked bootleg – though like Craig Cox's interception, it too was nullified by a holding penalty.

Scott 'mud-slide' Jordan's first year of organized football was going well. Though he lost out to Gregg Wright in the quarterback competition, he had won the respect of his teammates. The lopsided nature of Canal's first five contests ensured he saw plenty of duty as the backup. On Parent's Night, Scott even played some fullback. He had won the punting job outright, though thus far in the season the Indians offense had been so successful that they seldom needed to punt.

In every game but one the Indians had scored on their first offensive possession; and with this evenings' forty point victory Canal was averaging 37.8 points a game at the midpoint of the season. Consequently, the Mighty Indians just didn't punt that much; which worked to Scott's advantage. The luxury of punting only two or three times a game enabled 'Mud-Slide' to give it everything he had and then some when the occasion arose. The results were booming punts that denied opponents' almost any chance at decent field position.

Unfortunately, neither his steady hand in relief nor excellent punting stopped the *Lancaster Eagle Gazette* from referring to Scott as "Mike" Jordan. Speaking of the Fourth Estate, their coverage of Canal's fifth straight win was extravagant. The *Time's* headline read '*The defending league champs poured it on in the first half to whip Fairfield Union 40-0*'; the *Columbus Citizen Journal*'s story was entitled, '*Canal Winchester hangs a 40-0 shiner on defenseless F.U.*"

All four local papers, the *Columbus Dispatch, Citizen Journal, Lancaster Eagle Gazette* and *CW Times*, devoted nearly as much attention to Canal's winning streak and rankings in the press and computer polls, as they did to the game itself. Revealingly, when queried about the stellar rankings by *Gazette* reporters, Dad commented, "*It's a good thing we're rated high in the press because we don't have a chance in the computer rankings.*" He made a point in the *Times* interview, however, to single out Brett Van Meter for "*outstanding play on defense along with Gary and Craig Cox.*" Elsewhere in the Mid State League that night both Bloom Carroll and Pickerington continued to keep pace with Canal, winning their games to also remain undefeated; Pickerington decisively so, beating Millersport 56-6.

With the season half over, Steve Crist put the prevailing attitude of his team into perspective. *"At this point we knew we had something special,"* he recalled. *"We had destroyed everyone we played; hadn't lost a game since 1973; and only given up 6 points after five games. We knew we had the hardest part of our schedule ahead and you could tell the coaches believed it was going to get a lot tougher. But we believed. It's hard to put into words, but we knew we were special. It didn't matter that Carroll and Pick-town were undefeated, we just couldn't believe anyone could beat us, ever."*

WEEK VI:

LOGAN ELM

═══════════════════════════════════

(October 10, 1975 - Away)

The casual reader has no doubt recognized that after each game my father would warn his team that the following opponent was at last the real deal — attested to not only by his dire warnings; but also by Steve Crist's comment that the team *"knew we had the hardest part of our schedule ahead and you could tell the coaches believed it was going to get a lot tougher."* Though it's part of a coach's job description, indeed his primary responsibility, to ready his team for each and every game no matter how weak or tough the next opponent; at this point in the season his warnings truly reflected the relative strength of the remaining schedule.

Although Canal Winchester was 5-0; both Bloom Carroll and Pickerington also remained undefeated, Amanda Clearcreek had but one loss and the Indian's next opponent, Logan Elm, had won its last two ball games. Not only would the Indians be playing on Logan Elm's home turf, but the game was to be Logan Elm's Homecoming. The 'Braves' were always big, physical and hard-hitting - as Canal's veterans well knew; and the Indians found themselves in agreement with their coach's comments in that weeks' *Times*, "It's time to go," he said. *"So far we don't know how tough we are, but from now on we'll be playing the stronger teams. We're going to find out if we're as tough as we think we are."*

Logan Elm, like Fairfield Union, arose out of the 1957, Statewide consolidation of Ohio's smallest school districts. Prior to then Pickaway, Washington and Saltcreek had educated their own. Logan Elm High School, built in 1960, accommodated students from all three towns; twelve years later in 1972 a fourth school, Laureville, joined the district. With athletes from four different communities to draw upon, Logan Elm had become a formidable opponent in the Mid State League. CW and Logan Elm first met in 1965, and the Braves beat the Indians 28-6. It must have been an unsettling loss for Canal because the teams didn't meet again until 1973 when Canal won 28-13; and again the following year – 1974 – when Dad went to 2-0 against the Braves, beating them 21-0.

The name 'Logan Elm' derived from the American Elm Tree under which *Logan*, the famous Mingo Indian Chief, delivered his '*lament*' in 1774 following the Yellow Creek Massacre. This Elm tree stood close to the area selected for the new school. Though the tree died in 1964 it had stood well over 100 feet tall and the site upon which it grew is still considered an important Ohio landmark. Unfortunately for Canal's football fans – and to the utter dismay of the Cox brothers – Logan Elm's location meant another journey deep into Ohio's hinterlands. Nearly a straight shot south from CW, the primary artery leading to Logan Elm was known locally as the 'Widow-Maker,' the much dreaded Route 674.

From CWHS, buses carrying the marching band, cheerleaders and football team need only turn right and drive south on Franklin Street, which became Route 674 on the outskirts of town, and then follow the meandering road until it ended a mile from Logan Elm's football field. Nearly everyone understood that Route 674 was dangerous. Hilly, edged by trees and intermittent corn fields; continuously bisected by east/west thoroughfares and abutting a never ending line of hidden drives, over the years it had been the scene of multiple accidents and several fatalities. Traveling too fast on the 'Widow Maker' momentarily launched automobiles airborne when traversing its hills, and whether traveling north or south drivers knew to take it slow. Nearly everyone that is, except Mable Long.

Bus driver Mable Long, fourth from left.

Mable Long was hard core. She drove school buses for the CW school district and when students, athletes or musicians boarded buses piloted by Mable, they knew instinctively to hang on to their collective asses. Mable stood approximately 5-feet, six' tall, was solidly built, had short brown hair, a ruddy complexion and was absolutely fearless. Her husband, Frank, also worked for the district, handling building maintenance. The Longs had a daughter, Monica, but they also raised three boys – one of whom was my classmate, Kent.

And Mable knew how to handle rowdy boys. It didn't matter who you were, if Mable Long thought you were out of line she'd get up in your grill – and nobody talked back. She once commented on the affection shown her husband, Frank, by the teaching staff, *"Ah, hell,"* she inveighed. *"I've worked here longer than Frank and I do more than he does. But you'd never know it because teachers around here talk about Frank like his shit don't stink!"* As the Indians climbed aboard the big black & yellow school bus Friday October 10th 1975, carrying their helmets and shoulder pads, nearly every one of them said a silent prayer upon spotting Mable behind the wheel.

With nightfall coming earlier every day the physical, hardnosed Winchester football team, along with every other passenger on the bus sans Mable, were tossed, bumped, battered and scared straight on a hell raising ride through the gathering October twilight. *"Man, I couldn't believe it,"* remembered one underclassman. *"I thought we were going to die on that fucking road. Nothing scares Mable Long but she scared the hell out of me! Of course, we made good time though."*

The Brave's head coach, Perry Griffith, had warned that week that his team *"Planned to give Canal Winchester all they can handle and then some."* As complimentary toward the Indians as Dad was toward other teams in the league prior to playing them, Logan Elm's head coach remarked, *"The Indians are super, well-coached and make very few mistakes."* Unfortunately for Canal, Coach Griffith's magnanimity was not shared by their fan base. *"Their fans were real mouthy,"* remembered Senior Rick Ross. *"When we walked from the visitor's locker room out onto the field their fans spit on us."*

And the fan base was enormous; the Fairfield County Fair held its second-to-last day of activities October 10th and a quirk in the schedule left only the Indians and Braves playing football that night. The *Lancaster Eagle Gazette* reported, *"Winchester–Braves Only Friday Mid-State Contest: Thousands of Fairfield County residents are expected at the Fairfield County Fair and Logan Elm football game tonight, but you can bet all 10 of the MSL coaches will skip the fair and attend the CW v. LE matchup. Two will coach and eight others will watch very intently from the stands."* It was a toxic brew – literally – as hundreds of fans spent the day enjoying the Fair and more than a few adult beverages. After which they descended on Logan Elm High School to root for their Braves and rail against the hated Indians.

Having recovered from the unsettling bus ride the Indians now found themselves deep in enemy territory, surrounded by an extremely hostile crowd and facing a solid, well-coached football team whose season would be made by knocking off the champs. Bill Willison succinctly echoed Rick Ross and their teammate's assessment of Logan Elm when he said: *"Rude fans, bad refs, rotten field."* Adversity, however, is a powerful mistress; she can draw teams closer together when they unite to overcome her, and amid the spittle and cacophony of derisive fans, the Indians intended to do just that.

When Captains Bill Allen, Gary Griffith and Mark Hartman returned from the coin toss they reported bad news: Logan Elm had won the flip and elected to receive the kickoff. As it happened, the fortuitous toss in the Brave's favor turned out to be their only real break that night. The Indians, wearing their visiting team maroon jerseys, took the field after 'Now Varsity' and lined up to kick off. Steve Crist had a unique kickoff style: placing the football horizontally on the tee, he would kick squibs with his powerful leg, usually denying return-men a clean shot at the ball. Dad called these 'worm-burners,' and though they looked ugly it was effective in keeping the football out of the hands of an opponents' fastest' athlete.

On this night the 'Bionic Man' kicked it so hard that the pigskin actually got quite a bit of air under it. Rotating weirdly and at odd angles the football sailed towards Logan Elm's best running back, Jeff Reichelderfer, but when he tried to catch it in the air it bounced off his body, fell to the gridiron and tumbled end-over-end across the turf. Unsecured 'pumpkins' were the "Holiest of Holies" to CW football players and within seconds the ball was smothered by a pile of Indians at the Brave's 22 yard line. This mistake, on the very first play of the ballgame, took the air out of the home team, and, more important, out of their fans. Seven plays later and just two minutes after the opening kickoff the score read Canal Winchester 7, Logan Elm, 0.

In that first, two-minute drive Dad called fullback Matt Hartman's number and *'Roller Ball'* responded by pounding it up the gut on several short running plays. Once these inside-runs had lured the Brave's defenders into crowding the line of scrimmage, Dad changed up by calling quickie-8 on Logan Elm's 7-yard line. This was a quarterback keeper designed to go outside. Logan Elm bit on the fake inside handoff, and CW struck pay-dirt. It was fitting that Matt Hartman led the way on that first drive because he had approached Dad prior to kickoff and asked permission to address the team.

"I asked coach if I could say a few words to the team before the game," Matt began. *"I had gotten a letter from my older brother Craig from Marietta, Ohio."* (Craig Hartman had been an athletic all-star at Canal Winchester, All State in baseball and most valuable player on the football team in 1973) *"Now here's a guy that walks out on the football field his senior year and is the MVP. And he was a 10-times better baseball player than he was*

a football player," Matt explained. *"In his letter he wrote that he'd just been cut from Marietta's baseball team."*

Matt continued. *"And so I just told the guys, 'We have to leave it all here. You guys know my brother and know what a stud he was; what an athlete he is and he no longer plays college ball at Marietta. Very few people in this room will play college football so we have to leave it all right here.'"* The speech must have worked because Canal remained unfazed by the hostile crowd and had been unstoppable on the opening drive; scoring on their first possession and keeping the Brave's defenders on their heels. On defense the Indians shut down Logan Elm quarterback Bob Sargent and kept the Brave's most explosive running back, Jeff Reichelderfer, hemmed in.

After forcing Logan Elm to punt Canal began another methodical, time-consuming drive that culminated with an eight-yard touchdown run by Gary Griffith. So potent was the Winchester offense that punter Scott Jordan kicked only twice that night. Logan Elm, on the other hand, punted after every offensive series, and thus became the fifth of six opponents to remain scoreless against CW. Just before the first half ended the 'Bionic Man' scored on a three-yard run. Rather than kick the extra-point Dad called a two-point play; Gregg Wright connected with Rick Ross in the back of the end zone for the conversion and CW ended the half with a three touchdown lead.

"We felt great, man," remembered one fired-up senior. *"We let our play on the field do the talking. But when we ran to the locker room their fans really let us have it; called us every name in the book. But then I couldn't believe what happened next."* What happened next threw senior captain and normally unflappable Mark Hartman into paroxysms of rage; which subsided only after he had destroyed part of a cement retaining wall. Halftimes are fairly short in high school football – usually no more than 20-minutes, just time enough to get restroom breaks, address injuries and make offensive and defensive adjustments.

Coaches Locke, Jones and Roth met briefly before sitting players down, asking questions and then drawing up plays and formations on the chalkboard. Having spoken to the team, and with only five or six minutes left in the break, the Indians were about to return to the gridiron when someone discovered that several wallets were missing. Actually, every wallet left behind in the locker room had been stolen outright or emptied. At that point, while players did quick inventories of their possessions, the visitor's locker room exploded in a fit of colorful invective that would make any Marine Corps DI proud. "*Someone broke in,*" Gary Cox recalled, "*and not only stole our wallets but all our valuables.*"

Though no one on the team could match Bill Willison's fluency in the realm of the profane, both Brett Van Meter and a suddenly enraged Mark Hartman gave it a go. "*When Mark discovered his wallet stolen,*" Gary continued, "*he was as angry as any of us had ever seen him. I mean he was pissed. He put his helmet on and with all his equipment rammed into an inside, cinderblock half-wall until it cracked and part of it just tumbled down. I actually felt sorry for whoever had to line up opposite him in the second half because he was pissed!*"

It had been a tough night: the bus ride from hell, jeering and spitting fans, and then having what little money they kept in their wallets stolen. An unexpected comical respite fortunately brought the Indians back to an even kilter before leaving the locker room. "*Coach got us settled down and we were about to run out on the field when this huge sigh caught everyone's attention,*" recalled an amused junior.

"*It was Van Meter. He's pissed like everyone else and is slamming his locker and cursing. His wallet was still there - unlike a lot of the guys who had theirs stolen outright. Brett still had his but it was empty. He was rifling through his wallet when he sighed this huge sigh of relief. We all turned around and he was smiling ear-to-ear - because his condom was still in there.*" When asked about the incident thirty years later, Mr. Van Meter said only: "*What can I tell you? It was the 1970s.*"

The Indians emerged from the locker room in a hitting mood, which was fortunate because the Braves were also ready to strap-it-up. Aware that the entire league's coaching staffs were on hand watching their performance; and that Canal Winchester was in the process of ruining their homecoming, Logan Elm intended to lay the wood to the Indians in the second half. And according to Matt Hartman, the Braves did kick it up a notch during the third and fourth quarters. "*They were a decent team. They had some horses down at Logan Elm, let me tell you,*" remembered that night's motivational speaker. "*All them farm boys, they weren't bad that year and man, they could hit.*"

A sentiment fellow senior Gary Cox agreed with completely. "*That was a hard-hitting game,*" the cornerback recalled. "*For the second straight week, while making a tackle on kickoff return, I got an elbow in the nose. It didn't bleed and it wasn't broken but it hurt like a mother-fucker. I had two black eyes and all the next week at school I had to walk up and down the hallways looking like a damn raccoon."* Gary paused, *"I asked Coach Locke if I could get a facemask with a vertical bar from top to bottom. He made sure I got one and my eyes and nose were thankful."*

For Gary's younger brother Craig, the sixth game of the season marked his ascension to first team defense. *"Coach Locke told me to practice with the starting defense the day before the game,"* Craig recalled proudly. *"But Coach never really told me I was a starter. I was confused. 'Is he just getting me ready?' When the game started and the defense ran out, I just stood there, looking up at him. He said, 'Cox, get in there!' and pointed to the field. I ran like hell to the huddle. Coach probably thought I was an idiot. The funny thing is, I was so sky high and so nervous at the same time I don't remember anything from that game, except we beat the hell out of each other."*

Despite physical play from both teams, Logan Elm couldn't move the football against Canal's defense, and in the third quarter the Indians broke the game wide open. In fact, due to a single running play, the third quarter at Logan Elm is still remembered fondly as a momentous watershed for the Indians. Dad took Gregg Wright out of the game for a series, replacing him with punter and backup QB Scott Jordan. 'Mud Slide' looked to the sideline, awaiting 'Wee Willie' and the play. Moments later Bill Willison ran into the huddle and blurted out 'Quickie 9' to his teammates.

Scott took the snap, broke contain and raced around the left end untouched by Logan Elm defenders for five yards, then 15, and a few seconds later, thirty. Logan Elm's fans grew quieter with every hash-mark Scott sped past. At last, just before striking pay dirt, Scott was shocked to see Canal's husky and not so fleet-footed fullback, Matt 'Roller Ball' Hartman, take out the last defender. *"It was awesome,"* Matt said smiling thirty years later. *"We still talk about that when we run into each other. Scott was like the second or third fastest man on the team and he had his hand on my shoulder almost the whole way. Let me tell you I was huffing and puffing."*

"But I was out there, baby" Matt remembered proudly, *"and Scott ran in my hip pocket a good 25 yards. We raced all the way to the goal line and I threw the last block before he scored."* The watershed event was not Matt's

hustle, Dad referred to Matt Hartman in interviews as '*The Heart and Soul of the Team*,' but rather that the following day's *Lancaster Eagle Gazette* not only recorded the 34 yard TD run, but referred to 'Scott' Jordan as '<u>Scott</u>' Jordan for the first time that year.

Not long after Scott's TD jaunt, Froggy intercepted a Bob Sargent pass ending Logan Elm's last shot at crossing the goal line. Canal's final score came when Steve Crist kicked a 34-yard field goal that thankfully went straight through the goalposts, as opposed to just straight up. When the fourth quarter ended Canal had scored 30 points, gained nineteen first downs, had five different offensive players score, rushed for 370 total yards and not only kept Logan Elm from crossing the goal line but limited their entire offensive output to 163 total yards – or no more than 41 yards per quarter both running and passing.

From the stands Head Coach John Roller of Bloom Carroll and Jack Johnson of Pickerington agreed that the 1975 Canal Winchester Indians were as complete a football team as either had ever seen. Paying homage to both his Indians and Logan Elm's Braves Dad remarked in the *Times*, "*We played a fine ballgame. It was the first time we've been really tested all season. Our offensive line play was outstanding and Matt Hartman had an excellent game.*" And in the *Gazette* he said of the Braves, "*They had splendid personnel, a good reason to be worried before the game. Logan Elm is no weak sister in this league. They will give several other schools a rough game.*" Logan's Coach Griffith went straight to the point about the outcome: "*They were just a better team,*" he said. "*They dominated the game. We played 11 on 11 out there and they bested us.*"

Interlude:

Despite Mable's searing pace north to Canal Winchester, the team didn't make it home until well after *Chiller Theater* began at 11:30 pm that Friday. The following night, Saturday October 11, 1975, a new TV show called *Saturday Night Live* debuted on NBC. Its first guest host, comedian George Carlin, would later acknowledge being stoned on cocaine that evening, but despite Mr. Carlin's altered state *SNL* quickly surpassed even '*Chiller Theater*' in popularity for Canal's youthful late-night television audience. The premiere of *SNL* was one of many important milestones dating to October 1975 - both in American pop culture and in the world of sports.

1975's tenth month literally began with a punch when Muhammad Ali fought Joe Frazier in an epic rubber match in Manila, Philippines. Christened '*The Thrilla in Manila*' by the flamboyant former champion, Ali and Frazier went 14 of 15 rounds before '*Smokin Joe's*' trainer, Eddie Futch, threw in the towel. Seven days later the Boston Red Sox beat the Oakland Athletics 5-3, winning the American League Pennant; and the Cincinnati Reds beat the Pittsburgh Pirates 5-3, winning the National League Pennant. Both clubs swept their opponents in three straight games, winning with identical scores in the third. It looked as if the Word Series would be something special in 1975.

The same day *SNL* premiered on NBC the Red Sox crushed Cincinnati in Boston 6-0 to win the Series opener. The next day, Sunday, the Reds bounced back, defeating the Sox 2-1. Tuesday, Wednesday and Thursday evening games the following week ensured that most Indian football players, as well as CW's faculty and staff, would arrive at school somewhat sleep-deprived. In the collegiate football ranks Woody Hayes' Ohio State Buckeyes - having defeated UCLA 41-20 the week before - were ranked number one in the nation, followed by Oklahoma, USC, Nebraska and Texas rounding out the top five.

That week, while the Reds and Red Sox battled and the Indians prepared to face their seventh opponent, the number one pop song in heavy rotation was '*Bad Blood*' by Neil Sedaka; the number one Country tune was Charlie Pride's '*Hope your feelin' me (Like I'm feelin' you)*'; and the number one pop album in the United States was Pink Floyd's '*Dark Side of the Moon*.' In Canal Winchester audible reception came primarily via the AM dial, which didn't play much '*Dark Side of the Moon*.' Diehard Pink Floyd fans had to drive to Eastland Mall, about 15-minutes from downtown Canal, and then patronize 'Record Land' to purchase vinyl 45s, 78s, or 8-track tapes.

With Ohio's very own Cincinnati Reds playing in the World Series and its Buckeyes atop the college rankings one wouldn't expect sports editors to make much room for high school football. But Au contraire. The late, great *Columbus Citizen Journal*, impressed with Canal's winning streak, sent a photographer and *CCJ* sports writer, Bob Whitman, to CWHS on assignment. Whitman spent the day interviewing players, coaches, faculty and students; observed practice and profiled the team in a lengthy story. His article, entitled, *Winchester rolls to 6-0*, is a portrait of the Indians at mid-season and worth quoting.

In October 1975, less than a year remained before the nation would celebrate its 200th birthday and Whitman began by describing Canal's head coach with that in mind. *"That's a Bicentennial beard that Coach Mike Locke has growing wildly on his face and it's a regular revolution he's been coaching through six weeks of this season."* The accompanying photo shows Dad in a short-sleeved shirt standing beside captains Mark Hartman, Gary Griffith and Bill Allen. *"What he has turned out down in Canal Winchester,"* Whitman's write-up continues, *"is a team to rival the best of the teams Locke's coached in the nine years he's built a 69-15-1 record."*

Further along, discussing Canal's talent, Dad is quoted saying humbly, *"When you have the No. 1, and No. 2, scorers in Franklin County, you've got something going. All I have to do is stand on the sideline and worry."* To which Whitman expanded, writing *"And Winchester certainly has something going. Steve Crist and Gary Griffith - Froggy to you - have been the rage of the County scoring list to date."* Like reporters from the *Times* and *Gazette*, Mr. Whitman was well aware of Dad's run-oriented philosophy. Referring to the Indians as a *'High-scoring machine'* he pointed out that in six games the offense had scored 219 points and accumulated *"1,931 total yards, 1,718 of which are rushing yards as Locke is not the greatest exponent of the forward pass."*

For his part my father took the opportunity to remind players and fans that Canal's final four games would be their toughest. Mr. Whitman provided a lot of detail in discussing offensive and defensive personnel; listing the heights and weights of starters, and referring to the Indian's O-line as *'Big and rugged.'* When questioned about their tremendous size Dad still managed to find dark clouds in the silver lining. *"This is the biggest team I've had,"* he said, *"but not the deepest. The problem is that we can't afford to get anyone hurt."*

After spending the day with Dad, Mr. Whitman was struck – as most people were –by my father's wardrobe. Dad wore white belts and white shoes because *"good guys wore white"*, and the article suggested his beard couldn't be used as a disguise because *"Locke's white coaching shoes are dead giveaways."* Mr. Whitman concluded his article by pointing out that both Bloom Carroll and Pickerington, the Indians' next two opponents, were undefeated in the MSL.

WEEK VII:

BLOOM CARROLL

(October 17, 1975)
Homecoming

After losing their nonconference opener to Johnstown, the 1975 Bloom Carroll Bulldogs had proceeded to defeat five MSL opponents. Led by John Roller, the Bulldogs were well coached, physical and mirrored Canal Winchester with an emphasis on running the football and playing disciplined, hardnosed defense. Because of its close proximity to CW - about ten miles - Bloom Carroll was traditionally the Indians' biggest rival. Indeed, several players from Canal and Carroll were next-door neighbors whose choice of school district had been determined merely by the jurisdictional line separating Franklin and Fairfield Counties.

Bloom Carroll's and Canal Winchester's sons were well acquainted with one another through Millersport's Sweet Corn Festival, CW's Labor Day parade, pick-up baseball games and on local outdoor basketball courts. The two schools competed year-round in football, basketball, baseball and track. During summers little league baseball and swimming also brought them together. Cyclists routinely made the trip between towns. Earlier that summer a young man from Bloom Carroll stopped his bike in front of our house after spotting Dad strumming his guitar on the porch swing. From atop his bike he yelled, *"Are you Coach Locke?"*

When Dad answered that he was, in fact, Coach Locke, the cyclist dismounted, walked onto our front porch and introduced himself. His name was Dave Cotner, Bloom Carroll's starting quarterback, and the chance encounter led to a lifelong friendship between the two men. Once the gridiron season got underway, however, mutual admiration went out the window; both squads kept a close eye on the other's record while looking forward to their annual showdown. As senior Rick Ross put it, *"We were friends around town. But when it came time to playing Carroll we felt we had to beat the shit out of them. Otherwise we'd never hear the end of it – from them - for a whole year."*

Besides abutting one another Canal and Carroll were similar in other respects. Like CW, Carroll owed its origins to the Ohio/ Erie Canal. Built around the junction of the Ohio/Erie and Hocking Canals the town had been plotted as early as 1829; though not officially recognized under State charter until 1858. Its first large buildings were warehouses constructed to store crops before they shipped to market on the ubiquitous canal boats. Agricultural and small, Carroll remained that way – with a population of less than 1,500 people as of the 2,000 Census.

Bloom Carroll didn't host annual sweet corn festivals as did Millersport, pumpkin shows like those of Circleville or Labor Day parades like Canal Winchester. What it did have were two exceedingly popular native sons of whom the town was justifiably proud. On April 15, 1875 James J. Jeffries was born on a farm in Bloom Carroll, Ohio. Twenty-four years later Jeffries became heavy weight boxing champion of the world. Known as 'The Boilermaker,' he ruled his division for six years before retiring in 1905. Likewise, Lon Chaney, 'The man of 1,000 faces' lived for a time in Carroll, Ohio and visitors to the tiny hamlet were made aware of the fact – whether they wanted to learn of it or not.

Of course football players didn't care one whit about prominent citizens from the dark recesses of their communal past. Like other small towns in the MSL, Bloom Carroll and Canal Winchester were farming communities whose athletes were interested in competing for local bragging rights. The teams had first met in 1958; a game Canal won 30-0. Dad's record against Bloom Carroll was 6-2, his losses coming back-to-back in 1972 and 1973. Carroll's new coach, John Roller, would become quite the nemeses for Dad over the years. An excellent tactician and motivator Coach Roller had already managed to rack up five wins his first year as head coach.

Homecoming

Homecoming at Canal Winchester saw alumni returning to familiar stomping grounds, catching up with old friends, teachers and coaches, taking in the football game and reminiscing. Some alumni even attended the formal dance, which, for the vast majority of students, was the social highlight of the first half of the school year. Freshman through seniors attended, and most students were consumed with summoning the courage to ask someone to homecoming, getting the perfect dress for that grand occasion, ordering corsages, arranging for reliable transportation, talking about homecoming and decorating for homecoming.

Homecoming Queen, Melissa Black

A student vote determined which young ladies made up 'Queen and Court' — an enormous honor - and another homecoming topic generating intense debate as the election neared. One week prior to the big dance, the Student Council tallied votes in utmost secrecy, announcing the winners at the homecoming pep rally. In 1975 the Football Homecoming Queen was Melissa Black. Her senior attendant was Becky Detty, her junior attendant, Cindi Hunter (surprise, surprise), her sophomore attendant, Amy Bauer and her freshman attendant, Belinda Haynes. The reading of these names during the rally made for great theater: suspenseful, eagerly anticipated, full of import and high drama.

Freshamn attendant, Belinda Haynes.

Sophomore attendant, Amy Bauer.

Junior attendant, Cindi Hunter.

Senior attendant, Becky Detty

When Melissa Black's name was finally called she placed her head in her hands and wept. Fellow varsity cheerleaders thronged about her, as did her attendants; students thunderously applauded and the band struck up *Hang on Sloopy* to the delight of the swaying crowd. Their triumph, however, did not conclude the drama, for now 'Queen and Court' had to select official 'escorts' from the hormonally deranged male population of CWHS.

Fortunately, Melissa Black, younger sister of local sports hero Jeff Black, was already dating *Buffalo Bill* Allen. And what a pair they made. Melissa, a 'ginger,' had red hair, light skin, dark eyes and a face full of freckles. She was absolutely darling, with a gorgeous smile, and her cheerleading uniform fit her wonderfully. Bill Allen, whom Gary Cox once compared to a sword-wielding Viking, also sported wavy red hair, and the couple could have blended unnoticed nowhere save in the Irish countryside.

When it came to selecting escorts, attendants were class-bound. Freshman Belinda Haynes had to choose a freshman escort; sophomore Amy Bauer had to select a sophomore, etc. They were photographed for the *Year Book* and at halftime of the homecoming game, each young lady and her escort were announced over the static PA system before being solemnly led to the center of Weiser Field. At the dance the following evening Queen and Court occupied a place of honor in the best seats in the house. Besides the formalities, there was also an unofficial rite connected to Homecoming that created sexual tension, sometimes caused embarrassment, and focused everyone's attention on something other than football.

It was traditional for the queen's official escort, the king, to kiss her at halftime when she was crowned. No one is quite certain how this annual tradition got its start but it had been around as long as CWHS celebrated homecomings. In years when kings and queens were mere friends, the kiss would be but a peck on the mouth, but when the participants were truly enamored of each other, things would get more interesting. The crowd would watch in silence, then coo approvingly, and finally cheer lustily when the puckered duo relinquished their passionate embrace, and the longer the kiss the greater would be the crowd reaction. So there was a suspenseful anticipation on the sidelines and in the stands when Melissa Black and Bill Allen stood before Canal's fans on the fifty yard line.

A likely antecedent of the Homecoming kiss may be found in George Bareis's **_History of Madison Township._** In it the author describes an amorous custom practiced by Winchester's earliest residents. "*The long evenings of the fall,*" Mr. Bareis begins, "*brought the apple cuttings preparatory to making apple butter, and the corn husking; forty, fifty or more would gather at a neighbor's at evening; the corn was placed on a huge pile, the men and boys would gather about it, and as the work went on they threw the husks behind them, when the girls would take them away, some with rakes, others in their arms. The boy who found a red ear of corn had the privilege to take a kiss. The girls understood this and as soon as a red ear was brought to light the lucky finder would break for the girl.*" (And like the crowd about Weiser Field over a century later) Mr. Bareis concluded, "*To the great merriment of all present.*"

When the Indians made their way to school on game day that Friday, none imagined that nearly every rite of passage associated with the annual homecoming football game would come to naught. By ninth period, while the students busily celebrated another raucous pep rally, it began to sprinkle; a light, gentle misting from an iron gray sky. But since the elements had thus far been relatively benign, no one paid much attention. While the opening game weather had been hot, the next five games saw one damp outing (Millersport) and four crisp, autumnal evenings under twinkling stars and low-hanging moons.

Surely the gridiron gods wouldn't spoil homecoming for the Indians by raining on their parade. It was inconceivable. But light drizzle turned to steady rain, the temperature dropped and cold northerly winds began to blow in gusts, pelting those in its wake with splinters of watery ice. It looked as if homecoming festivities would take a back seat to staying dry.

My father understood – intellectually - that there were large swaths of life beyond his control, such as death, taxes, the weather, and uncooperative mechanical contrivances. Indeed he often referred to himself as a *'mechanical moron,'* knowing deep in his soul that he couldn't repair a broken furnace or start a stalled automobile. This grudging acknowledgement certainly didn't mean he like it. On the contrary, Dad resented it, and over time developed a tendency to anthropomorphize inanimate objects that crossed him. Once, when our car broke down, for example, his reaction was something along the lines of: *'God Damn dirty son-of-a-bitch!' He hates me! That's what it is! The son-of-a-bitch hates me!'* Whereupon he kicked the idle station wagon before storming off barking, *"I can't stand it! The son-of-a-bitch hates me!"*

Similarly, he took inconvenient weather patterns as a personal affront. Dad routinely looked to the skies when getting drenched at practice, saying, *"Ah, come on Thor! God damn it lay off!"* In 1971, after several weeks of rain-soaked Friday night football games, he went so far as to have his assistant coaches join him in paying ritualistic homage to a decrepit shoe; a colorful but vain effort to alter the weather by appeasing the 'rain gods.' So the four of them, educators all, lit their votive cleat at the eastern end of Weiser Field and sacrificed the old shoe to the rain gods. Dad insisting the ritual really ought to persuade *'Mighty Thor'* to stop *"Drowning our asses!"* On homecoming night 1975, therefore, the mist that turned to drizzle; and then steady rain, and at last a raging tempest by kickoff, was interpreted in Canal's locker room as an intentional, perfidious affront to my father and his football team. Alas, it became an absolute downpour; the fountains of the great deep opening up and unleashing rains of biblical proportions.

In the locker room just before taking the field Dad approached senior fullback Matt Hartman, pulling him aside. *"I remember it to this day and it's amazing I didn't take it personally,"* Matt recalled, laughing at the memory. *"I hadn't fumbled in two years; when it's that wet and slick and muddy turnovers can be a huge factor. So Coach Locke says, 'Matt you're going to get the pumpkin tonight. Everybody else out there is down on your level; no speed, no moves.'* (Laughter) *And he was right, no speed, no moves, but buddy I was a mudder and I was jacked up because I knew I'd be getting the ball."*

When the locker room's big steel door opened and the Indians ascended the concrete stairwell, the temperature read 37' Fahrenheit, and by the time the game ended three hours later had dropped to 33', just a tick above freezing. Such temperatures are nowhere near too cold for Midwesterners, but combined with howling winds and drenching rain, it felt much colder than 33' degrees. Despite his enthusiasm about that night's game plan to call his number more frequently than usual, Matt Hartman winced at the biting wind and leaned forward into the pelting rain like the rest of his teammates making their way to Weiser Field.

"It was absolutely driving rain," Matt remembered. *"I mean it couldn't have been more than 35' degrees; it was freezing and absolutely cold and wet."* The Cheerleaders, clad in heavy woolen sweaters, donned see-through rain slickers and sheltered beneath maroon and white umbrellas as the cinder track turned to black, slimy goo. Consequently, for the cheerleading squad and the fans they sought to inspire, homecoming devolved into a miserable test of endurance.

The home crowd was larger than expected considering the elements; the visitor's stands on the other hand contained only loving – extremely loving – parents. Of the four newspapers that routinely covered Canal Winchester football, three abstained, leaving only the *Times* to record the event for posterity. The hearty Cox family, an intrepid, martial clan, was well represented that night, rain be damned. Gary and Craig were on the field and their youngest brother, Denis, a seventh grader like myself, was the official ball-boy that night. Their parents, Janet, Dave and the boys' grandfather were hunkered down in the stands beneath umbrellas and blankets, Dave and Grandpa to watch their boys play, Jan to plead that they be taken off the field.

Craig Cox occasionally looked up through sheets of rain to locate his grandpa, but couldn't manage to find him. *"I nearly froze,"* he recalled. *"At halftime when I went into the locker room; my hands were curled up and locked. I ran them under warm water."* As for grandpa, after the game the family patriarch explained what it was like in the *"God-forsaken"* stands. Craig said, *"My grandpa was 63 years old at the time and he stayed for the entire game. When it was over I asked how he was doing and he said: 'Shivering like a dog shitting bones, boy! Shivering like a dog shitting bones!' Grandpa liked to say that and we repeated it for years – every time we got caught in the rain"*

Matt Hartman did indeed get the pumpkin eighteen times that night and ran for 80 yards in the muck and mud. Ever the selfless player, 'Roller Ball' regretted that *"We had a lot of weapons that weren't able to come out that night and it's a shame."* Contrarily, Matt's peers didn't see it that way. Several teammates remarked on his gritty performance; how many carries Matt had and how hard he ran. Kurt Swiger said, *"That was Matt Hartman's type of field. He had a super game at fullback and we just ran all over them."* An underclassman watching from the sidelines, and only slightly given to exaggeration, nicely summed up 'Roller-ball's contribution: *"Matt Hartman ran the ball unbelievably hard against Bloom Carroll; in the rain and cold and mud. He must have had 100 carries."*

Perhaps the only thing Dad enjoyed about the horrendous conditions that cold, rainy night was that it gave him yet one more reason to follow his instincts by having his team refrain from throwing the ball. In four quarters of football CW's QB Gregg Wright threw exactly zero forward passes, though he did run eight times, gaining 42 yards. Steve Crist scored three touchdowns; carried the ball twenty-three times and gained 123 yards. Because of the wind and rain TDs were followed by two-point conversion plays. The Indians scored 8-points in the first quarter; 8-points in the second quarter; and 16 points in the fourth.

Steve' Crist's final TD impressed the *Times* reporter, who wrote that the Bionic Man had *"Amazed the crowd by keeping his feet after getting hit behind the line and bulled his way into the end zone."* Defensively the Indians keyed on the Bulldogs best running back, Greg Storts. Dad assigned Steve Crist, his 'Monster back,' to hit Storts on every play, whether he had the ball or not; despite all that attention Mr. Storts managed to gain 94 rushing yards. The rest of Carroll's offense gained just thirty-eight additional yards. Dave Cotner, whom Matt Hartman referred to as *"An absolute stud,"* played well but threw two costly interceptions in the rain squalls.

Afterwards Coach Roller remarked, *"We didn't slow them down much. They ran with power off tackle. We did all we could but couldn't stop them."* Being the competitor that he is, however, Coach Roller concluded, *"I think we might have given them a better game on a dry field."* Dad praised Matt Hartmann and the offensive line. *"We played a super game. Our line blocked real well."* And then issued his weekly warning that the toughest test still lay ahead; this time at undefeated Pickerington.

Having defeated Carroll, Bill Willison and Steve Crist relished their newly minted license to boast: *"It was cold, wet and freezing that night,"* recalled 'Wee-Willie.' *"But I managed to break Carroll's running back's arm, Greg Storts; He was a good friend of mine and I planned to remind him of it."* The Bionic Man remarked, *"The game was full of turnovers, but the best part for me was intercepting Dave Cotner for the second year in a row. It gave me another year of picking at him!"*

The homecoming dance the following night was a much dryer – and warmer - affair. Young men wore jackets, ties and boutonnieres; young ladies sported skirts, high heel shoes and corsages of every variety and color. The multipurpose room, where clanging flatware, banging plastic trays, screaming adolescents and the commands of exasperated teachers filled the air Monday through Friday, had been converted into a dimly lit dance hall.

Tables were covered with snow white cloths and adorned with colorful arrangements of mums. Stacks of hay bales supported Jack O' Lanterns and scarecrows clad in bib overalls, serving as makeshift sculptures. Streamers floated down to the dance floor from the ceiling above. The hired disc jockey played dance tunes on his turntable: KC and the Sunshine Band's *Get Down Tonight* and *That's the Way (I Like It)*; the Bee Gees' *Jive Talkin* and *Nights on Broadway*; Van McCoy's *The Hustle*; ABBA's *SOS*; and ZZ Top's *Tush*. Most couples were reluctant to *'let it all hang out'* in front of their peers; but once two or three brave souls took to the dance floor the rest soon followed, letting down their guards and enjoying the music.

And no one could resist dancing to slow, romantic ballads. Once the DJ announced *"We're going to slow it up a bit,"* placing the stereophonic needle atop Joe Cocker's *You are so Beautiful*; Judy Collins' *Send in the Clowns*; or Frankie Valli's *My Eyes Adored You*; the floor of the multipurpose room was crowded with love-struck couples holding each other closely; turning round and round in tight amorous circles. The slow dance was essentially a prolonged, rotating hug, a rare opportunity to publically embrace one's sweetheart.

Melissa Black wore her favorite brown blazer over a v-neck sweater, a long plaid skirt, knee high boots, a scarf about her neck, an enormous corsage on her lapel, and the tiara traditionally bequeathed to Homecoming Queens. When the dance ended at 11:00 pm Juniors and seniors who could drive went out to dinner; leaving the warm, crowded multipurpose room to walk outside in the cool, black October night. In the year book under Homecoming '75 are the words: *"Mounting excitement, thundering pep rallies, voting for nominees, announcing attendants, glittering mums and finally . . . the night . . . the game . . . the queen . . . the dance."* And so it was.

Week VIII:

PICKERINGTON:

(October 24, 1975-Away)
'The Game'

"In thy faint slumbers I by thee have watch'd
and heard thee murmur tales of iron wars . . ."

(Shakespeare –Henry IV)

The showdown was set. The Indian's next opponent, the Pickerington Tigers, were also undefeated; statistically better on defense; had home-field advantage; were extremely confident and would play for the MSL crown on Pickerington High School's Homecoming. The Tiger's head coach, Jack Johnson, was a big bear of a man and had been a tremendous athlete in his own playing days. Standing over six-feet, Jack had brown hair, broad shoulders; dark, intense eyes and a thick black beard and mustache that obscured most of his face. As the big game approached Coach Johnson let it be known that his Tigers weren't intimidated by Ohio's number one Class-A football team. On the contrary, he looked forward to whipping them.

With two unbeaten teams playing for the MSL title so late in the season, press coverage began the moment Canal beat Carroll and

Pickerington shut out Fairfield Union on October 17th. The *Times* first mention of the showdown included the following exchange between reporter David Davies and Coach Johnson immediately following Pickerington's 19-0 win over the Falcons:

"When asked what he plans to do with Canal Winchester next week Johnson's answer was simple: 'We plan to beat em . . . right now we're leading the Mid-State League in defense, and we hope to keep it that way.'"

As an intense week of preparation began for the clubs, *WSYX ABC News; WHOK Radio; The Columbus Dispatch; The Columbus Citizen Journal; The Lancaster Eagle Gazette* and the *CW Times* ran stories on the Pickerington/Canal Winchester football game, descending on one or both schools seemingly every day for interviews.

If the word 'showdown' rings overly dramatic or smacks of hyperbole, consider the terms used to describe the impending contest by journalists at the time: *'The biggest game of the Mid-State League season and possibly the most exciting confrontation between two teams this year.' "The Game of the Year;' 'Canal at Pickerington Top Tilt in MSL,' 'Titanic Clash;' 'Epic showdown;' 'Classic Gridiron confrontation;' 'The Game;' 'A Gridiron Duel between two Heavyweights'* and on and on it went throughout the week, building to fever pitch.

"It was all anyone could talk about," remembered Steve Crist. It was certainly the biggest event in either community, endlessly discussed, eagerly anticipated and fretted upon during that late October week in 1975. Indeed, in both face-to-face interviews and written questionnaires conducted in researching this book, several players, especially underclassmen, couldn't always recall events from other games that year. When Pickerington was brought up, however, every athlete, coach, radio announcer, cheerleader and fan recalled the game in great detail. On several questionnaires players' required additional space to tell their recollections of 'The Game.'

When the *Columbus Dispatch* published its interview with Coach Johnson that week, entitled, *Confident Pickerington Ready For 'Big Game' With Winchester,* the article was quickly posted on the Indians' locker room bulletin board. Coach Johnson had informed reporter Bob Hunter that *"We began pointing to this game back in August when we started two-a-days. We felt then that we'd have a league contender along with Canal Winchester. Now we know that we do. We honestly feel that we can beat them."* Warming to his subject the Tiger's mentor pointed to his dominant defense. *"We lead the Mid-State in defense; in fact we may lead the entire state . . . They (Canal Winchester) have an excellent offense, so its gonna be their offense against our defense."*

Back in Canal Dad was careful not to offend, praising both Coach Johnson and his football team. *"I just think it will be a great game all the way around,"* he told sports writer Bob Hunter, keeping his commentary to a minimum. This wasn't just diplomacy; Dad genuinely believed Coach Johnson had done a marvelous job at Pickerington, especially so considering that the Tigers didn't establish an organized football program or field a team until 1965, just a decade prior to 'The Game.'

Starting from scratch in 1965, without Pop Warner or junior high feeder programs, and having only three seniors on their twenty-six man roster, their plunge into gridiron competition was an uphill battle. The Tigers, under their first coach, Buddy Epperson, lost all nine games during their inaugural season, including a 35-0 shellacking from CW, but improved as the campaign wore on. The following season Pickerington finished 2-8. Interestingly enough the first victory in Tiger football history came at the expense of Canal Winchester on September 17, 1966 when Pickerington QB Tom Rider scored in the waning seconds of the fourth quarter. The final score was Pickerington-8, Canal Winchester-0.

Pickerington is located along Sycamore Creek in northwest Fairfield County and is part of Violet Township, so named for the profusion of vibrant purple violets growing along the meandering banks of the creek. Like CW, the town was settled by Virginians. When originally chartered in 1815, citizens along Sycamore Creek christened it 'Jacksonville' to commemorate Old Hickory's victory at the Battle of New Orleans. Twenty-two years later, though, Ohio's Jacksonians petitioned the State legislature to change the name in honor of its founding father, Abraham Pickering.

Pickerington remained relatively small until the mid-1960s but had surpassed CW in size by the time the two schools faced off in the 1970s. An article in the *Lancaster Eagle Gazette* appearing the week of 'The Game' pointed this out; citing it as a factor in the rise of the Tiger football program. *"The community's growth rate,"* Gazette journalist Mike Dawson wrote, *"has played a big part in its up and coming football program. Pickerington,"* he continued, *"has grown quickly from a class-A school in athletics to AA, and in no time at all the northern Fairfield County school will be headed for the AAA ranks."* Prescient he was, for by 1991 the 'town' formally became a 'city' and according to the census boasted a population of 13,573 as of 2006.

All that of course lay in the future; back in 1975 the Canal Winchester and Pickerington school districts were relatively comparable, and their respective football teams appeared evenly matched. In some respects, uncannily evenly-matched. After six MSL games, for example, CW had scored 224 points, (38 per game) and Pickerington - 222 points, (37 per game). CW had thrown for 233 total-yards, Pickerington for 224. CW had given up one TD, Pickerington had surrendered two. But these same statistics also bore out Coach Johnson's boast of having the *"best defense in the state."* The Tigers had held opponents to 277 total rushing yards, while CW had given up 522. Pickerington's pass defense had yielded 145 yards, CW had surrendered 256, and Pickerington had held its opponents to just 1,432 total yards in 1975, while CW had allowed 1,778.

On Tuesday afternoon, October 21st, as the Indians practiced offense behind the bleachers on the hill next to Wesier Field, an animated Steve Blake arrived on the scene clutching the *Lancaster Eagle Gazette* in one hand, and a can of *Coca-Cola* in the other. Mr. Blake – 36-years-old, prematurely gray, wide around the middle and obsessively devoted to CWHS football - had just finished work for the day. Upon reading the *Gazette's* sports page he drove straight to Canal's practice and handed the offending article to Coach Jerry Jones.

Having run their final wind sprint the Indians made their way to the locker room and crowded around Coach Jones, who was waiting for them just inside the big steel doorway. Jones read aloud from the paper while the team listened intently to Pickerington Coach Jack Johnson's remarks, and no speaker ever had a more rapt audience. *"Is Canal better this year than last year?' Johnson doesn't think so pointing out the graduation loss of Jeff Black. 'Jeff Black is one of the finer athletes ever to come out of this league. He could make anybody a winner.'"* Mordecai, who was usually prone to melodrama, on this occasion played it just right by making no comment. Neither did any of the players, though teammates made a point to pat Gregg Wright on the shoulder pads or give him a hug before entering the film room.

Interestingly, that bit of fan-initiated "bulletin-board material" was the only anomaly in their routine during four days of preparation. *"You know what I remember about the week leading up to Pickerington,"* Matt Hartman recalled. *"I remember we didn't do anything different. That's what I remember. We all knew it was a big game, we knew it was huge. But we didn't practice any different, we didn't prepare any different and by the end of the week we felt like we were going to go over there and kick some butt."* After pausing for a moment he added, *"I'll tell you what, though; when we watched Pick-town in films we knew they were tough. They hit people. I mean they had one lineman who was huge and playing at their place on homecoming, we understood it was going to be tough."*

That's not to say the comments in the newspapers didn't bother some players and provide added fuel to an already smoldering fire. To the contrary; left guard Bill Griffith found Coach Johnson's characterization of the game being decided by *"his defense against our offense,"* especially annoying. *"It was the biggest game of the '75 season,"* the senior offensive lineman remembered, *"and then Jack Johnson made all kinds of unwise statements in the papers about us – how we weren't as good as last year's team and how his defense was the best in the state. We couldn't wait to play that game."*

On Friday October 24th, while Pickerington's students prepared for homecoming, the Indians were idle, and the long wait became an excruciating ordeal. Though parent-teacher conferences gave Canal's students that day off, Craig Cox was unable to stay home. *"I was all hyped up,"* he recalled. *"I mean, I couldn't relax. Time was moving too slow. It's tough enough when we were at school all day, going to the pep rally, watching films, having some distractions; but at home all day on the biggest game of the year – I couldn't take it so I went to school and sat in the whirlpool."*

Canal's whirlpool in 1975 was a mobile stainless steel tub, resembling - and not much larger than - a spittoon. Maddeningly for Dad, one never could be quite sure where it was located for coaches from different sports rolled it away whenever one of their athletes needed to soak an aching appendage. The tub was equipped with what looked like an outboard motor, and because it was capable of achieving cauldron-like temperatures, Dad repeatedly warned users not to overstay rehab in its bubbling waters.

Craig Cox, alone in the bowels of CWHS that day, managed to find it. *"I was sitting in the whirlpool,"* he continued, *"trying to relax and take my mind off the game when Coach Locke walked into the locker room. And coach got pissed when he saw me sitting there. He said, 'Cox! What do you think you're doing? Get the Hell out of there right now!' I guess he thought it would drain all the energy out of me or something. Man; that was the longest day waiting to play that game."*

Crowded as Pickerington would become that Friday evening Canal Winchester would become inversely empty as a ghost town. Band members and their parents; band directors and spouses, cheerleaders and parents, coaches and wives (except for Mom), football players and their parents, grandparents, and extended families, the teaching staff, administrators, significant others, and every fan in town made their way to Pickerington for 'The Game.' In Canal's locker room before leaving Dad reminded his team to focus, telling them how best to approach the big showdown.

Two years before, the Indians had played Bloom Carroll for the 1973 MSL crown, but had lost the game. Reflecting on the loss, Dad realized his team had played *not* to lose. They had been tentative, afraid of making mistakes. And *'we got our ass beat,"* he recalled years later. It became a valuable lesson, one he imparted to players two years later before boarding the bus to Pickerington. Having advised his team to focus, he then urged that they play with reckless abandon by attacking, being aggressive; playing the game to win, picking each other up. And most importantly, that they not play to keep from getting beat.

"It was so quiet on that bus ride," Craig Cox recalled. *"I mean, it was always quiet but on the way to Pickerington you could have heard a pin drop. When we started out there were some whispers but when we crossed Route 33 the Captains yelled, 'Think About It!' as they did on every bus ride, and it became absolutely still inside that bus."* The Indians were heeding Dad's advice to focus, but fortunately for the stressed young men, an unanticipated and completely unexpected moment of levity broke the tension.

"It had been such a long wait; the pressure of continuing the win-streak; all the hype that week. We were pretty tense," Craig explained. *"And then, after we crossed 33, I heard Coach Locke and Coach Jones laughing; we all looked up and out the windows and there was this huge sign that said, '**TIGERS**

EAT SHIT AND HOWL AT THE MOON!' Everyone broke up. It was great. To this day I don't know who made the sign but it worked. It really took the edge off.

The sight greeting the Indians at Pickerington High School brought the tension back immediately. Attendance estimates varied from newspaper to newspaper the following week -5,000, 6,000 and 10,000 were all cited - but no player on either team had ever seen such crowds before. "*I thought I'd been nervous on the way over,*" Steve Crist remembered. *'But I have never seen that many people at a high school football game before in my life; there were so many people they were stacked three, four, and five-deep around the football field.*" Senior Rick Ross was similarly taken aback.

"*There must have been over 5,000 people there to watch that game and then we found out Ohio State Coach Woody Hayes was there. He was standing in the end zone watching when we came out for warm-ups. Woody fucking Hayes in the end zone! I just about shit myself.*" The hype, the presence of local sports celebrities, and the excitement didn't adversely affect every player. Senior Gary Cox, the Nebraska move-in who had thought himself lost in the Twilight Zone on previous road trips, had gained an unshakable confidence by the eighth game of the season. "*By this time,*" he recalled, "*when the bus started taking off on those lonely country roads, heading into cornfield country and God only knew where; I didn't care where we were going because I was on the biggest, baddest high school football team there ever was.*"

Nor did the enormous crowd seem to bother Gary's younger brother, Craig. The junior Cox had been so focused on the game and his assignments he had forgotten it was Pickerington's homecoming until the bus pulled through Picktown's gates. *When we got to the game I saw all these floats; I'd completely forgotten it was Picktown's homecoming; but that fired us up even more – kick their ass on homecoming! Hell Yes!*" Nothing quite stirs a young man's blood as the opportunity to ruin an opponent's homecoming.

Despite the Tigers having home field advantage, Canal's huge (have-son-will-travel) fan base – if not negating, certainly checked Pickerington's edge in attendance and volubility. So when the Indians emerged from the visitor's locker room and jogged onto the field for silent warm-ups they were simultaneously cheered and jeered, lustily, and in equal measure. Across the way the Tigers barked cadences with bravado during calisthenics. The pregame psychological warfare had begun.

Canal's defenders knew it wouldn't be easy to stop Pickerington's wishbone triple option, even after having spent a week preparing for it. Quarterbacks in the wishbone had the 'option' to hand off to the fullback, either halfback, or keep it themselves on every play. Sophomore Keith Kristoff ran the system for the Tigers and enjoyed the luxury of having one of the MSL's best running backs behind him. Halfback John Barr had gained over 700 yards in six MSL contests and scored 11 TDs. A physical, punishing runner, Mr. Barr trailed only Steve Crist in touchdowns that year. Beside him in the backfield were fullback Brian McClaskie and halfbacks Tom Hellman and Bob Stansberry.

Like Canal Winchester, Tiger athletes played on both sides of the ball. And one dual-purpose lineman in particular, Jack Neal, had drawn the attention of those who regularly fought it out in the pits. Mr. Neal played both offensive and defensive tackle. Quick off the ball, strong and extremely athletic, Jack appeared especially large in game films. Indeed it was his size that first drew the eyes of so many Indian linemen as they sat quietly watching Pickerington's football team on flickering, black & white 16-MM film. Though he was listed at 6-foot, 4-inches tall and weighing 250 pounds, most Indians believed Jack Neal to be much bigger than advertised. "*Jack Neal,*" recalled Bill Willison, "*was the biggest guy I ever played against; he must have weighed 320 pounds.*" Whatever his weight, Mr. Neal was a force to be reckoned with down in the trenches where football games are ultimately decided.

At last the undefeated foes faced one another across the gridiron, the Indians wearing maroon away-jerseys, maroon pants and white helmets adorned with a single maroon stripe running front to back. The Tigers sporting their white home-jerseys, white pants and purple helmets with the letter **P** stamped in white on either side. Roger Hanners and the WHOK sports crew, having built a custom booth on the back of a pickup truck towering over the crowd, were already describing the scene on the airwaves.

The Game, the Indians kick off to the Tigers, October 24, 1975.

As Pickerington's Marching Band played the National Anthem; thousands of fans in the stands and infield stood and sang; young men on both sidelines held their hands across their hearts trying to keep them from bursting: *"For the land of the free . . . and the home . . . of the . . . Brave!"* As the word 'brave' departed the lips of the multitudes an unearthly, ground-shaking roar rocked the stadium; Canal's kickoff team ran onto the field to boot the ball and the Tigers set up to receive it; 'The Game' had begun.

In one of Jack Johnson's pregame interviews he had said, *"If we can play mistake-free football we have a good shot at winning."* And he was right. The most damaging football mistakes are turnovers - interceptions and fumbles - that kill drives, waste scoring opportunities, and demoralize defenses by placing them in untenable situations. And while most teams can overcome the occasional holding call, clip and off-sides penalty, *they cannot win* by giving their opponent 'the pumpkin.'

Unfortunately for Dad it was his Indians who made the first mistake. After a squib kick by Steve Crist to start the game Canal held Pickerington to a three-and-out. Defensively, middle guard Bret Van Meter keyed on fullback Brian McClaskie; fought off blocks and hit him every play. Likewise, the Bionic Man zeroed in on John Barr, shadowed his every move and attempted to pop him every down. Defensive ends Neal Seymour and Rick Ross 'stayed home,' forcing everything that came their way up inside; while down linemen shot gaps, swung club-like forearms and bottled up the interior line. In the secondary both Cox brothers, and Gary Griffith played physical man-to-man coverage, stopping Pickerington's first drive cold.

On fourth down the Tigers punted to Froggy who stood alone on the 25 yard line. As the pigskin descended end-over-end he moved forward to make the catch, but the football bounced off his shoulder pads. Canal's senior captain fumbled, Pickerington's Kevin Boggs recovered, and the turnover handed the Tigers both the early edge and excellent field position, the first break of the game.

Picktown's fans, discouraged when forced to punt after failing to convert on third down, were now suddenly delirious. Their band and sidelines were going absolutely nuts. Canal's fans, who just moments before had been cheering the Indian's defensive stand, were stunned, as were its players. The fumble instantly advanced Pickerington 35 yards, forced the Indian's defense back on the field, and put their backs to the wall on their own 31 yard line. If the old gridiron adage *'defense wins championships'* is true, then this sudden reversal of fortunes represented an ideal opportunity to prove it.

To that end Dad raised his fist and began barking, *'Let's go Defense! Get out there and show em what CW football is all about! Let's go Defense! Suck it up! They haven't scored yet! Let's go!'* In the huddle Mark Hartman admonished teammates to calm down and do their jobs, and put out the fire now raging on Pickerington's sidelines. And they did. Starting on Canal's 31 yard line Pickerington managed to move the ball just three yards to the 28. Three plays, three yards. The fire that only moments before had been an emotional conflagration dwindled away. Rather than attempt a field goal, the Tigers decided to pin CW deep in its own territory and play for field position. The punt sailed out of bounds at the 15 yard line, and for the first time Canal's offense took the field.

Pickerington's defense proved as good as advertised. Canal in turn struggled to move the ball. Punter Scott Jordan was therefore placed in the unusual position of being forced to punt. In their first seven ball games the Indians had scored 251 points and given up seven. When Scott actually punted it occurred when CW already had a substantial lead. His legs were fresh because he never kicked more than two, or three times a game, and the only pressure had come from his desire to improve his punting average. Tonight, however, with Canal and Pickerington locked in a defensive struggle and the scoreboard reading 0-0 it was a different story.

Scott ran onto the field, joined the huddle and said, '*Punt on one. Punt on one. Ready; break!*' He Lined up 17 yards behind Mark Hartman and barked, "*Set, Oklahoma; hut!*" Mark shot the football back in a tight spiral; Scott took one step and booted the ball. And like Steve Crist's 50 yard field goal attempt against Fairfield Union the football sailed fifty yards into the air – straight up into the October night - and damn near straight down. An audible groan issued forth from the visitor's stands and Canal's defense again faced another series on their side of the field.

Back and forth it went for most of the first quarter. Canal would gain a first down and then three plays later be forced to punt. Pickerington would gain a first down, sometimes even two first downs, and they'd be forced to punt. And every time Froggy prepared to receive one of those punts tension and nervous strain grew because of that first fumble.

On the other hand, Gary Griffith was not voted captain by his teammates for nothing. Whipcord tough he came from a big family full of boisterous brothers; had endured his parents' divorce and watched his siblings scatter and move away. He had stood by his youngest brother, Tony, after his car accident, and lived not with his mom or dad, but rather with an older couple whom he barely knew. Not much rattled him, not even fumbling in the biggest game of the year.

With 4:17 remaining in the first quarter the scoreboard read 0-0. As Pickerington prepared to punt after another stalled drive, and Froggy once more stood alone thirty yards downfield; the strain in the visitor's stands was palpable. All eyes focused on number 21. The booming punt drove Froggy back to the 20-yard line where the ball hit the ground and began to roll out of bounds. Gary Picked it up, made the first tackler miss and then raced down Pickerington's sideline behind Canal's 'picket-fence.' Eighty yards later he crossed the goal line and Canal led 6-0. Indian fans stacked three and four deep about the field as well as the throng in the stands were in a state of utter euphoria; screaming, cheering, high-fiving and hugging one another while singing Mr. Griffith's praises.

And with good cause: punt and kickoff returns have a beauty all their own. A lot of open field separates players; greater speed is achieved by defenders covering kicks, and the gridiron grows incredibly congested at the point of impact where return men are usually downed. Had cameras focused on Canal's stands, as opposed to the action on the field, they would have recorded fans following the arc of the football, exhaling in relief once the pigskin was safely secured, craning their necks to locate the ball carrier amongst the jumbled confusion, and then rising with their hearts in their throats as Froggy broke free from the pack. Had Gary been tackled after an initial, hopeful burst an enormous "Ahhhhhhhhhhh" would have rose in unison.

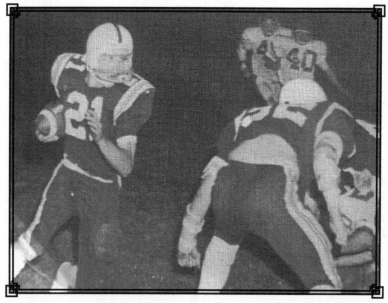

Gary Griffith, races down the Pickerington sideline to score the TD of the game.

When ball carriers elude would-be tacklers, however, the return is one of the most exciting and electrifying plays in football. And Froggy was not tackled. After a week of intense media coverage and then watching an Indian team that averaged nearly 40-points a game struggle without so much as a field goal, Gary Griffith's punt-return absolutely jolted Canal's sidelines into an exhilarating, unbridled fit of pigskin pandemonium. WHOK's Roger Hanners did his best to call the return without bias for listeners but found it impossible. *"I remember it was 0-0 at the time,"* he began. *"They punted to Gary and he took it back all the way for the TD.*

And I was broadcasting this, you know, 'He's at the 20, he's at the 30' and so on like any broadcaster would; but I couldn't help being partial because it was Froggy that was doing it. I lived with him, he was a son to me and I knew how much it meant to him." Roger shook his head before concluding, "And you know what? That just turned the game. That was the game breaker right there."*

Actually, Mr. Hanners' contention that Froggy's TD was a 'game-breaker' is further proof that understandable bias got the best of him. Other than the punt return Canal had generated almost no offense against Pickerington, and when Steve Crist lined up to kick the extra point, Picktown's Jack Neal and Mark Samborsky, having by now become familiar with CW's snap count, shot through the line and blocked the kick. Perhaps they had grown *too* familiar because the block was nullified by an off-sides penalty. Rather than kick again Dad called a roll-out pass; Froggy emerged wide open in the back of the end zone but Gregg Wright's pass sailed over his head and the score remained 6-0.

The CW punt-return for a touchdown hardly broke the game wide open. Pickerington responded by denying CW the PAT and starting a methodical drive as the first quarter wound to a close. Faking to fullback Brian McClaskie, QB Keith Kristoff alternately kept the ball or handed off to John Barr, driving his Tigers to Canal's 24-yard line. As had happened after Froggy's fumble, however, the Indian defense rose to the occasion when it mattered most and Pickerington's drive stalled. After CW stopped the Tigers in what looked to be another three-and-out, Coach Johnson decided to go for it on fourth down. He called Kristoff's number on an end sweep, hoping to gain yardage on the edge but their QB was met unceremoniously by both Steve Crist and Gary Cox whose tackle ended the threat.

Coaches aren't the most patient people in the world and football coaches in particular have noticeably limited powers of forbearance; and my father had none at all. As my sister was fond of saying, *"Dad's a great guy; he just doesn't have a fuse."* And as six points does not a margin of victory make, Canal's coach had reached the end of his tether. Having observed the earlier sky-high Scott Jordan punts, and later having watched Pickerington drive nearly the length of the field, Dad exhorted his offense to get in the game and make a contribution to winning. He also silently admonished himself for being too conservative in his play calling. With CW starting on its own 27 yard line, seventy-three yards to cover before reaching the end zone, Dad made up his mind to pass.

But before doing so he meant to draw Pickerington's defenders closer to the line of scrimmage. For six straight plays Canal lined up in run formation - using both tight-ends - and ran Steve Crist off tackle or Matt Hartman up the gut. Two first downs later on their 47-yard line, Dad could see Pickerington's linebackers edging up to the line; keying on the Bionic Man. Right Guard Brett Van Meter stood beside him waiting for the call; '*Counter-5, deep-down-the-middle-pass.*' Van Meter smiled; then raced to the huddle to tell his quarterback.

Wright's eyes widened when he got the play. He crouched down in the huddle and looked up at his teammates, spit out his mouthpiece and said, "*Listen up; Counter-5, DDM-Pass; Counter-5 DDMP. Listen up! We have to sell it; remember line, fire out like it's a run; Steve let's make it a good ball fake; On one - on one - Ready Break!*" Counter-5, DDM P was a play-action pass. The QB pivoted and faked the handoff to the halfback. The linemen fired out as if to run block - freezing the linebackers. The tight end initially hit the man opposite him, 'selling' the run, before releasing and running his pass pattern.

Considering the Indians only got to throw three or four times a game they broke the huddle more enthusiastically than usual. Gregg barked the snap count, center Mark Hartman hiked the pigskin, right guard Brett Van Meter pulled, making it look like he was heading into the 5-hole to block. Halfback Gary Griffith stayed home to pick up pass rushers off the end - as did Matt Hartman - while Steve Crist charged toward the 5-hole as if he had the pigskin yet again. Tight end Neal Seymour hit his man and then released, running down field waving his left arm. He was wide open when Gregg heaved the football. Thirty-nine yards later Neal hauled it in and raced toward the goal line before being dragged down at Pickerington's 10-yard line.

Canal's sidelines were going crazy. This was more like what the fans were used to seeing when the offense took the field. Coach Johnson clapped his hands and prepared his team for a goal line stand. On first and ten Matt Hartman got the ball, running behind his brother Mark and Left Guard Bill Griffith. Rollerball gained two yards in a cloud of dust. On second down Matt Hartman ran for three more tough yards behind his brother Mark and Right Guard Bill Willison ('*hey-diddle-right-up-the-middle*'). On third down, with just five yards separating

Canal's offense from its first offensive TD, Dad went to his bread-and-butter play and called Steve Crist's number off-tackle behind the left side of the line. Left Tackle, *'Buffalo Bill'* Allen and Left Guard Bill Griffith double teamed Jack Neal, fullback and lead blocker Matt Hartman hit the linebacker, and the Bionic Man, Steve Crist, shot through the hole and into the end zone to give the Indians a 12-0 lead.

From the sidelines the TD made it look as if CW had finally taken control of the line of scrimmage, and because CW had failed to covert after its first TD, Dad decided to go for two. This would have made the score 14-0, but the Tiger's staunch defense stuffed the running play and the score remained 12-0. It had been a tough, hard-fought game to that point; a defensive struggle reflected in the score. And Pickerington was about to get the football back with almost four minutes of time remaining before the first half came to an end. After the game Coach Johnson, asked if his team went flat after Gary Griffith's punt return, insisted that it had not. And he was right. Nothing Canal did in that game came easily, neither before nor after the punt return.

For the third time since the game began Canal lined up to kickoff. Steve Crist booted a nearly un-field-able worm-burner and the Tigers offense took the field. Keith Kristoff and John Barr went back to work, but with less than three minutes to go on their final drive of the half they found themselves fighting not only Canal's defense but the play clock as well. The Tigers, however, had lost none of their fight, and they also caught two huge breaks. On a third down option play Canal was called for face-masking, a 15-yard penalty that gave Pickerington an automatic first, and kept the drive alive.

With time winding down the Tigers reached Canal's 35 yard line. The Indians responded by stuffing the run on first and second downs for no yardage. On third down, Coach Johnson called a pass play. When Kristoff was sacked for a loss Canal's fans let out a huge sigh of relief. But a yellow flag, unnoticed at first, lay upon the gridiron. This time the Indians were called for roughing the passer; another 15-yard penalty, another automatic first down. Dad, as might have been expected, at last blew his stack, venting mightily to no one in particular.

"You God Damn convict sons-a-bitches! Quit trying to cheat us! God damn dirty convict bastards! God damn home job! Quit cheating us!" Red of face, glasses fogged by steam emanating from his ears, he stormed up

and down the sideline letting it out. On the field Canal's defense stood on their own 20-yard line waiting for the Tigers to break their huddle. Fans on both sides of the stadium rose to their feet in suspense. The game clock read less than a minute to go.

On first down Canal smothered John Barr at the line of scrimmage and a tremendous roar went up from Winchester's fans. Coach Johnson, as had his opponent across the field earlier in the game, now sought to take advantage of the Indians' keying the run. On second down, with just 49-seconds left, he called a halfback pass. The Tigers set up in run-formation. QB Keith Kristoff pivoted and flipped the ball to running back John Barr exactly as he had all game; Barr took the pigskin and ran two or three strides to sell the run, then pulled up and fired a tight spiral towards the end zone. Seconds later it was caught on the 5-yard-line by a fast moving blur wearing jersey number 21.

CW's Froggy Griffith. The captain of the Indian's ship had not only scored the first TD of the game but had prevented Picktown from scoring the last TD in the half. Canal's offense ran on the field, the QB took the snap and knelt down to run out the clock. The score remained Home: 0 Visitors: 12. For fans the matchup had thus far lived up to all expectations. The two teams were knocking the living hell out of each other and the game was far from being decided.

"There was a lot of tough hitting out there," recalled Craig Cox, *"it was an incredibly physical football game."* Just minutes before the half ended Pickerington had run a reverse. Well coached, Craig had refused to take the bait and stayed where he was supposed to be on defense. *"For some reason,"* he said, *"I stayed home and sure enough the play came back to me."*

"I wasn't faked out," he continued, *"and tackled the ball carrier running him out of bounds. I took him down hard and he landed on his stomach. His right leg was bent back at the knee and the spikes of his cleats were sticking up right into my ribs – on the left side of my chest. The wind went right out of me. I couldn't breathe, I couldn't move and just laid there for a second. I thought about staying down but remembered my mom was in the stands and would be worried. So I got up, ran all the way across the field without any oxygen and took myself out of the game."* Young Mr. Cox was a fine football player and a good son who knew his mother well; after the game Doc Burrier examined Craig and found fractured ribs.

Canal's defense smothers a Pickerington running back,
shutting out another opponent

Pickerington HS sat atop a hill overlooking the football field, which left both teams no choice other than to jog side-by-side, silently, up its blacktop path to their respective locker rooms. In the locker room Dad told his team - especially the defense - that they had played a strong first half, but went on to remind them that one half does not a football game make, and that Pickerington was well-coached and could be expected to do some things right in the second half. He urged his players to keep up the pressure, and assured them that another CW score would take Pickerington out of its game plan and put the contest out of reach.

In Pickerington's locker room the Tigers, though down 12 points, were encouraged. CW may have won 17 straight games, but they weren't dominating tonight. The score proved that, along with the blocked PAT, and both failed CW attempts to run for two-point conversions. Coach Johnson told his Tigers they need only keep the game close to have a shot at coming out on top.

On the gridiron below the Tiger Marching band took the field, followed shortly thereafter by Pickerington's Homecoming Queen and her court. Pickerington's track (unlike the cinder track surrounding Weiser Field) was all-weather and absolutely inundated with humanity. Lines for hot chocolate, Coca-Cola, popcorn and hot dogs stretched all the way back to the infield. Picktown's fans cheered their homecoming queen while little kids flitted in and out of the crowd, and on Canal's side of the field grave men huddled to discuss the Indian's precarious lead.

Sue Thomas, aka 'Teach', descended from the thin air of the crow's nest, where she had filmed the first half, and walked about to stretch her legs. On WHOK Radio Roger Hanners did his best to come across even-handed in his reportage. The station's tower, located on Route 33 in Lancaster, broadcast at 1320 on the AM dial and reached sports fans as far away as Columbus, Circleville, Canal Winchester and all across Fairfield County. It wasn't simply journalistic standards, however, that pushed Roger toward pained impartiality. *"I was in the sporting goods business at that time,"* he recalled. *"So I called on all these other schools to do business; and I knew all the coaches and had to be very careful about what I said because it would always get back to them."*

Unfortunately for Pickerington the third and fourth quarters were nearly identical to the first and second. Both clubs continued to hammer away at the other in a physical defensive struggle. Pickerington mounted several drives into CW territory only to see the Indian defense stiffen in the red zone; Canal moved the ball methodically into Tiger territory only to have Picktown's number-one ranked defense rise to the occasion. And Senior Scott Jordan continued to punt the football straight up into the dark October skies only to watch it fall straight back to earth.

Pickerington's last real offensive threat came late in the third quarter after *"a poor kick gave the Tigers good field position on the Indian's 39 yard line"* as the *Lancaster Eagle Gazette's* Mike Staton would report the next day. Still very much in the game and with plenty of time to go, Picktown's Keith Kristoff and John Barr alternately carried the pigskin to the 26-yard line. On second and 7, however, John Barr fumbled after a terrific collision, Canal recovered and the threat was over. Before the game Coach Johnson had said if his team played mistake-free they had a good chance at winning.

He was certainly right about that: a 12-7 football game, for example, would have gone down to the wire before the outcome was decided. But the Tigers had made mistakes. No football team can be mistake free, and in Picktown's case, on both of its most promising drives, they turned the football over: late in the first half when Kristoff was intercepted by Froggy, and in the waning moments of the third quarter when John Barr fumbled and Canal recovered. As the fourth quarter ticked away and it appeared CW would emerge victorious, the Tigers redoubled their efforts. *"It was smash-mouthed, hard-hitting football,"* remembered Bill Willison. *"In fact, it was the only game that year that we really had to give it everything we had all four quarters to come out on top. I mean, we just beat the shit out of each other until the very last play"*

Canal's offense had the football on the game's final possession, and as the scoreboard's game clock wound down Indian fans belted out the final countdown in uproarious unison: "six . . . five . . . four . . . three . . . two . . . one!" When the game ended young men removed their helmets and shook each other's mangled hands, and Coach Johnson and Coach Locke met at midfield to exchange pleasantries. Pickerington's players were understandably dejected after coming so close in such a hard-fought ball game. The Tiger cheerleaders wept as did several member of the queen's court.

At that moment it is safe to say – despite good sportsmanship displayed by both teams and their respective schools – that every resident, student, faculty member, coach and athlete within Pickerington's community limits was sick to death of the Canal Winchester Indians; sick of their team, their coaches, their raucous fans and their damned winning streak. *"Some of the girls on those floats,"* Gary Cox remembered, *"were crying their eyes out after the game."* The defeat was a bitter pill to swallow, especially on homecoming. As dejected, disappointed and low as the Tigers were with the loss, Canal Winchester was equally delirious with their win.

"The whole town was on the field after the game," Steve Crist recalled, *"and it was at that point, standing on Pickerington's field with almost everyone you'd ever known - that we knew we were part of something really special. It's hard to put into words; we were on top of the world, we were on cloud nine and the entire town was on cloud nine with us. We hadn't lost in almost two years and we didn't think anyone could beat us – not ever. It was something."*

Dad praised the Tigers to reporters swarming about him, singling out Pickerington's Bill Sergakis, Dave Noble and Jack Neal for having played outstanding defense. Though he didn't show it – and would never have admitted it - Canal's head coach was fairly exhausted himself. He rarely slept much the night before football games, and had known Pickerington V. Canal Winchester 1975 would be one hell of a football game.

Guarded with his words to reporters; careful not to demean opponents and perpetually worried that his team might start believing no one could beat them, Dad spent the entire football season walking a reticent, circumspect tightrope. Now, however, caught up in the moment, he at last lowered his guard. *Times* reporter Robert O'Callaghan, who had been standing just a few feet away taking notes, would describe the scene in the following week's edition. *"For the past eight weeks,"* Mr.

O'Callaghan began his column, "*CWHS football coach Mike Locke has been most cautious about his team's chances of repeating as MSL champions. He has repeatedly said he wasn't sure if the key to his squad's success this season has been due to talent on the Indian's squad, or rather to the weakness of the teams CW has dueled.*"

"*Locke knew the answer Friday night. Amidst the blaring of brass and wind instruments played by an exuberant CW band and surrounded by well-wishers after the Indians hard-fought 12-0 win over a tough Pickerington team, Locke raised his arm, pointed a finger into the cold night air and shouted, 'We're number one!'*"

Coach Johnson was gracious in defeat when discussing the game with reporters. Of the long pass from Gregg Wright to Neal Seymour that had set up Canal's only TD drive, he said, "*We broke down on our pass defense. They're a fine team.*" Calling the matchup '*ideal*' Coach Johnson likened their central Ohio showdown to the Boston Red Sox V. Cincinnati Reds World Series. "*The fans,*" he concluded, "*got their money's worth.*"

Indeed they did. Notwithstanding the euphoria of belonging to such a special group, winning the big game, continuing their unbeaten streak and keeping their playoff hopes alive, the Mighty Indians of '75 were - at the end of the day - comprised of young, hormonally-unbalanced, testosterone-laden adolescent males; as Gary Cox demonstrated immediately following the contest. "*I distinctly remember,*" he recalled, "*one beautiful babe from Pickerington. I mean, she was a knockout - blonde hair, absolutely gorgeous girl, sobbing after they lost. She was crying so I figured; what the hell, why not try to 'console' her. 'I'm sorry; there, there: cry on my shoulder. That's it. By the way, what's your name? Can I get your phone number so I can call you later?' My timing wasn't the best in those days and needless to say she looked up at me and turned away, but I had to give it a shot.*"

On the bus ride home Matt Hartmann led teammates in a cheer peculiar to the Indians. Like their silent pregame warm-ups the ovation was quiet and understated, reflecting the values preached by their head coach. Since his arrival in 1967 Dad had stressed to his charges the importance of playing with 'Class' - not talking trash, taking cheap-shots or running up the score on opponents; picking up those they'd knocked down, dressing neatly and letting their play speak for them.

That Matt Hartman took it upon himself to create this cheer was a bit surprising in light of 'Roller Ball's' oft-expressed low opinion of huzzahs and pep rallies. When asked for this book about Friday rallies, for example, his response was less than enthusiastic. *"Pep rallies? Ah, you know, rah, rah – cheer, cheer. The team sat across the front of the stage in the old stadium. Then we left."* But as it turned out, it was Matt 'rah-rah' Hartman himself who approached Dad his junior year to ask if he could lead the team in a cheer he'd written. He did so at the next pep rally, and the cheer differed strikingly from others chanted that afternoon. It wasn't bellowed, screamed or even yelled but rather whispered, faintly, forcing those in attendance to fall silent.

*"Give me a **C**,"* he whispered looking down at his teammates sitting across the stage, and a team *"**C**,"* echoed back in low whispers. *"Give me an **L**,"* and in chorus the young men whispered, **L**, *"Give me an **A**,"* Matt continued; and the letter **A** arose in one low voice. At this point cheerleaders, faculty and staff joined in, murmuring each letter in turn as Matt directed. *"Give me an **S**,"* and the **S** returned from 400 whispering students; *"Give me another **S**,"* and it too issued forth. *"What does it spell?"* Matt intoned as an understated CLASS emitted from the crowd. *"Say it again."* "CLASS" *"What do we have?"* CLASS. *"One more time;"* CLASS. With that he sat down and the place went wild. Dad liked it so much he added an acronym: **C**ourage-**L**eadership-**A**ttitude-**S**pirit-**S**portsmanship and used it the rest of his coaching career. The week after Matt's cheer made its debuted during the 1974 season, as the Indians prepared to storm through a giant banner on Weiser Field, Dad noticed the cheerleaders had inscribed the word CLASS atop the mast.

Now, as the bus rumbled south to Canal Winchester, an intangible moment of togetherness, victory and satisfaction prompted 'Roller Ball' to whisper, *"Give me a C."* The long yellow vehicle, thus far noisy and boisterous on the celebratory return trip, at once grew quiet up front as upperclassmen responded with a whispered, *"C."* That cued the rear of the bus to fall silent, its occupants listening earnestly in the dark for Matt's voice and the next letter. *"Give me an L,"* and the cheer continued. Twenty minutes later the bus pulled into the parking lot, idling next to the FFA's green house and Mr. Baker's band room, the hinged door swung open, and the young men exited into the darkness. They were 8-0.

WEEK IX:

AMANDA CLEARCREEK

===============================

(October 31, 1975–Home)
Halloween

Dad being Dad, he immediately considered the haunting prospect of losing the game following 'The Game' - and not unreasonably. Hard-fought, emotionally draining showdowns between unbeaten teams, where so much energy is expended by players and coaches alike, often leave both teams flat. So rather than bask in the victory over Pickerington, Canal's coach earnestly embarked on a campaign emphasizing the pitfalls of complacency.

The next opponent, Amanda Clearcreek, had lost only once that year; any letdown against such a dangerous foe could jeopardize everything they'd worked for since August. It was important for his team to understand that if they didn't focus and play hard they could lose; or as Dad put it so eloquently to his players, *"Just because we beat Picktown doesn't mean Amanda can't come to our place and kick our ass."* Fullback Matt Hartman's observation is once again apropos; *"Coach Locke never relaxed and never relaxed on us."* It was ever thus.

Senior Kurt Swiger agreed, explaining *"We were all beat up pretty good after playing Pickerington. On the following Monday we did some light running and watched the game film; but after that it was back to the grind. We had too much at stake for a letdown and the coaches really stayed on top of us."* Though not necessarily appreciated at the time the hard work appeared sensible in hindsight.

"Coach Locke," Roller Ball recalled 30-years later, *"he pushed us. I mean, there was no let up; but in retrospect it's probably one of the greatest coaching jobs ever. Not the wins but the attitude; because when you take a bunch of kids who have won 18 games in a row, to keep their heads from getting so big that they can't fit through the door; I mean you're talking about sixteen, seventeen and eighteen-year olds here, you know; and we knew we were good. How could we not? But Locke never let us believe we were too good to get beat."*

During those long afternoon practices in 1975 Coach Locke's unrelenting pressure wasn't nearly as appreciated by his football team as it would be in the future. Craig Cox had a hairline fracture in one of his ribs, Steve Crist suffered from a pinched nerve, both of Matt Hartman's forearms were black and blue; Bill Willison's knee was swollen and leaking more fluid than usual, Bill Allen's reconstructed knee was swollen and aching more than usual, Gregg Wright could barely turn his head more than a few inches without excruciating pain, and Scott Jordan was nursing a bruised ego. Nonetheless, every one of them practiced with the rest of the team.

Matt Hartman's point about inflated egos was not a figment of his imagination but rather a distinct possibility considering the circumstances, and something that needed to be monitored and held in check. Not that the Indians who made up the team were self-absorbed megalomaniacs. On the contrary: as Roger Hanners remarked, *"I've never seen any group of competitive athletes more selfless; or who meshed together quite the way they did."* The head coach concurred, remarking in that week's *Lancaster Eagle Gazette* that he was 'surprised,' *"At the high level of attitude . . . maintained this year. I knew the attitude would be good but it has been great."*

It was also true, despite team chemistry, positive attitude and selfless play, that they were decidedly human; a celebrated group of young men on a wildly popular and successful football team in the midst of a two-year winning streak in a small, sports-crazed Midwestern town. Whether they were walking the school's hallways, strolling through town or sitting in Zeke's barber chair, they were sure to receive compliments, pats on the back, 'attaboys!' and car horns blaring their praises. It isn't hard to grasp their susceptibility to an inflated sense of self.

The tribal totem identifying owners as members of the Mighty Indians of '75 was the coveted varsity letter-jacket. Maroon (of course) with white stripes down its sleeves; CANAL WINCHESTER stitched across the back and the letter *W* sewn on the breast, it bestowed upon the wearer great dignity and drew much-appreciated attention from members of the fairer sex. These jackets, worn by athletes from every sport, proliferated in classrooms and hallways in the waning days of October. The football players not only displayed the letter *W*, but proudly sported two football-shaped patches unique to their jackets. One read "*1970 MSL Football Champs, 10-0*", the other "*1974 MSL Football Champs, 10-0*". And the 1975 Indians hungered for a third.

Amanda, Ohio, yet another small town in neighboring Fairfield County, lies about twenty-four miles south and slightly east of Canal Winchester. Amanda has remained small through the years; the 2000 census recorded just 3,411 residents in the township. Their football program, however, has long remained disproportional to the size of the community. The team qualifies for the state playoffs nearly every year and in 1999 won the Division V State Football Championship. The Aces and Indians first met in 1958 in a game CW won 16-0. Dad's record since taking over in 1967 was 7-1; after losing the opener, his Indians had gone on to post wins over Amanda for seven consecutive seasons.

Amanda's losing streak to CW didn't help their coach, Tal Gulbis, who left after the 1973 season. Though Dad's relationship with the MSL's coaching fraternity was good; that had not been the case with Tal Gulbis. After CW beat Amanda 34-0 in 1972, Coach Gulbis accused CW of running up the score. "*I told Tal after the game that I'd never run up the score*," Dad explained, "*I put in our reserves in the third quarter, but Tal didn't believe me and said they'd 'get even' next year. How in the hell do you stop reserves from scoring?*" he asked three decades later, still somewhat miffed at the accusation.

The very next year, 1973, Coach Gulbis' final season, Canal led Amanda 48-0 at half. "*Tal said he'd 'get even' but it didn't work out that way*," Dad said smiling. "*The funny thing was,*" he continued, "*Tal really thought we ran up the score in 72; and like I said, How do you keep reserves from scoring! So we punted on first down the entire second half in '73.*" What do you mean you punted on first down? *"We punted on first down. Our defense stuffed them on their first drive of the third quarter; they lined up and punted; after the return I sent our punt team out and punted right back to them on first down. He couldn't accuse us of running up the score that year by God!"*

So every time Amanda punted Canal lined up and punted it back? *"Yea; and our fans were going nuts; absolutely ape shit. 'What the hell is he doing? Why not put in the reserves? Locke's lost his mind! What in the hell is going on?' They were giving me hell but we were up 48-0 and if I'd put in the reserves and they scored Tal would've accused me of running up the score again - so we played it that way."* Pausing for a moment he smiled and then added, *"It was great man."* The streak continued in 1974 when Canal won 29-0. Fortunately, Amanda's first year Coach, Jeff Ardnt, did not think Dad had run up the score and the relationship improved. Indeed, according to the *Lancaster Eagle Gazette*, the Ace's new head coach was quite impressed with Canal Winchester.

In an article written the week of their game Coach Ardnt was said to be *"in awe of the Indians."* Which isn't to say he liked Canal Winchester all that much; to the contrary. *"They (CW) don't belong in our league,"* he complained. *"Why don't they go play somebody their own size like Ohio State or someone? They are really big and really good."* As Coach Arndt's upset-minded Aces rumbled north to face the scourge of the MSL that Halloween the Indians understood they had a lot to lose.

Should both CW and Pickerington win that night (Pickerington was playing Bloom Carroll) the possibility of CW and Picktown ending the season tied for the crown would remain, and the title not decided until the last game of the year. A CW loss and Pickerington win would tie it up that week; and CW, were they to drop their final two games, might conceivably finish second. Only a CW win against Amanda combined with a Picktown loss to Bloom Carroll would clinch another MSL championship that night.

Coach Arndt's admiration for the Indians hadn't stopped his Aces from winning seven-games (six by shutouts). They had lost only once in 1975, and like every team playing Canal, the matchup was an opportunity to dethrone the reigning champs. Beating Canal Winchester would make their season. And as it turned out, Amanda would score in a way no other team managed that season. Another overflowing crowd surrounded Weiser Field; seniors were playing their final home game, and the contest quickly validated Dad's obsession about a letdown. *"They were a tough opponent,"* Steve Crist explained. *"They were sky high and we were lethargic – still feeling the effects of last week's game. Coach wasn't happy with us at half and neither were the seniors."*

Hoping to take the air out of the Aces early, Canal drove the ball the length of the field by running the Bionic Man off tackle; Matt Hartman up the middle and Froggy around the edges. From Amanda's seven yard line Steve Crist ran once more behind Bill Griffith and Bill Allen to score the first TD of the game, then kicked the extra point, and just like that it was 7-0. So much for lethargy. On the other hand, the ease of that first drive may have led to overconfidence.

When the Aces received the kick they systematically and methodically moved the ball down the field. With their quarterback, Dave Daugherty, handing off to running backs Tom Hinton and Mark Marshall, Amanda piled up one first down after another until the Indians found themselves on the 3-yard line with their backs to the end zone. Coach Arndt, sticking with what worked, called Hinton's number from three yards out and the Ace's powerful back crossed the goal line. Daugherty had not thrown a single pass during the drive.

Indian defenders were stunned when Tom Hinton strolled into their end zone. They had given up only one TD all year. Linebacker Matt Hartman, as confused as were his teammates, was also 'ticked' – as he put it. *"They were tough,"* he remembered. *"I mean they really did – on that drive – stuff it down our throats and we couldn't stop em. And that was the only time all year, I mean, Millersport was a fluke. Amanda's was not a fluke. They shoved it down our throats."* Amanda's TD shocked Canal's defense back to life; when the Aces went for two the Indians stopped them short; the score read CW 7; Visitors 6.

The second quarter began with CW nursing a one-point lead and the Amanda Aces believing they had a good shot at upsetting the Indians. Having emerged from their funk CW's defense kept the Aces out of the end zone for the remainder of the first half. To shake up his offense as the second quarter got underway, Dad called a pass play. Gregg Wright faked the handoff to Steve Crist, and then heaved a forty-five yard bomb to Neal Seymour, who caught it on the run and was finally dragged down from behind at the Amanda 16-yard line. CW's crowd was delirious and celebrating, cheerleaders were jumping up and down on the cinder track, while players on Canal's sideline ran toward the opposite end of the field to get a better view of the action.

Then the crowd grew strangely quiet. Fans continued on their feet but had stopped celebrating, their arms and hands at their sides as they looked intently toward the gridiron. Cheerleaders tried to find out what had happened beyond the wall of people surrounding Weiser Field, the band had stopped playing, and Dad was jogging onto the field with Coach Jones and Doc Burrier. Neal Seymour lay crumpled on the ground holding his left knee writing in agony. Neal had started since his freshman year in 1973, an unusual accomplishment, and tonight's matchup might have marked his 29th consecutive game without injury had he not been tackled on the 16 yard line.

"I remember 'Box Car' (Mark Hartman) *holding my hand as I flopped around on the turf,"* Neal recalled. *"It wasn't so much the tackle that wrenched my knee though,"* he said wryly. *"I was running full stride and then my left foot came down in a depression – like a wide divot - in the old field. I was getting dragged down at the same time when it just buckled on me."* Neal eventually sat up while Doc Burrier examined the knee; players on both teams watched in silence as did everyone else in the stadium. At last he made it to his feet, placed his arms about Dad and Coach Jones and limped gingerly to the sidelines.

When Neal stood the crowd exploded in thunderous applause. His two brothers were already making their way towards the sideline to meet him while his mom, Darlene, conspicuous in Neal's number 80 Jersey, watched silently, her right hand covering her mouth, and his little sister, Becky, cried as only seventh grade girls can cry. *"I'd never been hurt before; thankfully it didn't have to be operated on,"* Neal recalled, *"but it was sprained, swollen and sore. The following week I think I only made it on the field for three plays before having to sit down."* Senior Kurt Swiger replaced Neal at tight end and four plays later - with the ball on Amanda's one-yard-line - Gregg Wright ran it in behind right end Rick Ross for the score.

At halftime the scoreboard read, CW 14 Visitors 6. Steve Crist described the ensuing locker room chat as less than pleasant. *"We were ahead, but hadn't played well at all. Everyone was angry about giving up that TD and then Neal went down. Coach Locke was not happy and let us know* it" After making several halftime adjustments – including assigning the Bionic Man to key on Tom Hinton, the Aces best running back – Dad reminded the team that this was the senior's last home game and every underclassman owed that group his best performance. Besides the Ace's TD and Neal's injury something else gnawed at the Indians that night: they were worried about their chances of making the playoffs. Corner Gary Cox recalled the intense desire to aid their postseason cause by winning handily.

"We were so eager to make the playoffs. We wanted to show everybody in the State of Ohio that we had the best A-team anywhere. And that didn't include giving up touchdowns." The angst expressed by players and coaches over Amanda's lone TD is an illuminating barometer of team standards that year. As Kurt Swiger put it – looking back a quarter century later -*"Amanda had the only truly deserved TD on us all year. They marched down the field with no penalties to help them. It was legitimate and just set us off. They didn't score again. When you think about it though that's pretty amazing,"* he offered proudly. *"Pretty amazing isn't it? One good drive in 10 games; we had an awesome defense!"*

The Indians emerged from their halftime locker room fired up and anxious to make amends for their lackluster first half performance. They drove the length of the field on their first, third quarter possession and Gregg Wright scored once again, though a bad snap resulted in a missed extra point. But the Indians now led 20-6 and Canal's defense kept Tom Hinton and Mark Marshall out of the end zone the rest of the game. Another long, methodical CW drive in the fourth quarter put the contest out of reach when Steve Crist scored his 137th point of the season, increasing the margin to 27-6.

The Bionic Man, whom the papers described as a *'fleet, stalwart, and powerful runner,'* ran for 126 yards on twenty-four attempts against Amanda. Steve Crist averaged 5.25 yards a rush in 1975, and broke the 1,000 yard mark that Halloween night, having gained 1,011 yards in just nine games. Jimmy Crum, the bespectacled, toe-headed, loud-jacket-wearing sports editor for WCMH TV channel 4 remarked on air that night – *"I think Woody Hayes might want to speak to that young man."* When the game ended the mood on Canal's sidelines had much improved since halftime. Asked by the *Times* beat reporter to talk about his 1975 squad Dad remarked, *"This might be the best team I've ever had.*

Our offense executed well, much better than it has for a while. But we worked hard on it all week."

Coach Locke liked to joke that Canal's winning football program was due to *"All coaching and no athletes."* Actually he understood better than most that no team, no matter who's coaching, wins consistently without athletes – or as Woody Hayes entitled his manifesto for Ohio's coaching fraternity, **You Win With People**. Coach Arndt alluded to it earlier in the week when he suggested that Canal ought *"to play someone their own size – like Ohio State."* The Indians were indeed loaded. Standing on Weiser Field, basking in the warmth of 19 straight wins, Dad began rattling off the 'people' he was winning with to reporters; *"Bill Griffith, Brett Van Meter and Gary Griffith had outstanding games;"* he said. *"And Mark Hays, he played a super game and Junior Ricky Gates did real well, too."*

Dad's obsession over a possible letdown after the physical struggle against Pickerington proved well founded. That same night, less than ten miles from Weiser Field, Bloom Carroll, who had struggled mightily against Logan Elm the week before, handed the Pickerington Tigers their second straight defeat. Picktown; third in the league in total offense and first in defense, had expected to move the ball easily against BC. It didn't turn out that way. Carroll quarterback Dave Cotner scored with time running out in the second quarter; and the Bulldogs held on to upset the Tigers 6-0. The Canal Winchester Indians were Mid State League Champs for the second year in a row.

Interlude

Defeating Amanda, a team with a winning record and six shutouts, had helped Canal in the playoff computer polls. Both Middletown Fenwick and Canal Winchester competed in Region Twelve-One. Fenwick had won the Single-A State Championship in 1974 and despite an early loss in 1975, had led most of the year in the computer rankings. The week CW had defeated Amanda, however, Fenwick had beaten a team with a poor record, so despite both programs having won their respective contests, Canal had narrowed the gap on the strength of Amanda's overall record.

What's more, though CW was heavily favored over its final MSL opponent, Liberty Union, who had won just 3 games in 1975, Middletown Fenwick's final regular season game was against Hamilton

Ross; an undefeated team sporting an 8-0-1 record. If the Indians were to win their 20th straight football game and Fenwick were to lose its final game of the year, there was a very good chance Canal Winchester would advance to the playoffs for the first time in school history to face Newark Catholic the following week.

"If" of course, is the middle word in *life*; the only thing Canal could do was prepare for Liberty Union; keeping their collective fingers crossed while they did so. Weiser Field, in the final week of regular season practice, looked much different than it had in August, September or October. The verdant greens of summer were gone and the vibrant oranges, reds and purples of mid-October had given way to sere browns. Trees stood bare. The once soft blue skies overhead were now slate gray and players had taken to wearing heavy, long-sleeved shirts beneath their shoulder pads and jerseys.

That Tuesday, November 4th, their parents stood patiently in long lines to vote in off-year elections. Gerald Ford, in office just over a year, was serving as the nation's first unelected President, Governor James Rhodes was leading the Buckeye State, and Tom Moody was running for a second term as mayor of Columbus that week. Canal Winchester's citizens and fellow Ohioans, as it turned out, were not in a giving mood that autumn. They voted down tax breaks for industry, a transportation bond issue, tax-free bonds to boost housing construction and an urban improvement bond. The stagnant US economy, which had not fully recovered from the 1973 Arab oil embargo, ensured the vast majority of Ohioans were less than eager to increase their tax burden. John Lennon won his case against US Immigration November 7th, allowing him to remain in the United States; and the USMC celebrated its 200th birthday November 10th 1975.

In the sporting world Woody Hayes's Buckeyes were still ranked first in the country as November got underway. Of Ohio's two NFL football franchises, Ken Anderson quarterbacked Coach Paul Brown's Cincinnati Bengals; and Brian Sipe quarterbacked Coach Forrest Gregg's Cleveland Browns. Racing champion Jimmy Caruthers had just died of cancer at age thirty in Tustin, California; Pete Rose was named MVP of the 1975 World Series; and the Reds' Sparky Anderson won National League Manager of the Year.

Sparky's counterpart, Boston's Darrell Johnson, won American League manager of the Year. Georges Carpentier, who had waged war against Jack Dempsey for the 1921 heavyweight championship of the world, died that week. Howard Cosell, Don Meredith and Frank Gifford manned Monday Night Football's broadcasting booth; Baltimore's Jim Palmer won the American League's Cy Young Award, and New York Met Tom Seaver won his third Cy Young in the National League.

But most importantly of all, in the eyes of Canal Winchester's sports-minded-citizens, the Mighty Indians of '75 were busy on the hill behind the bleachers across from the cinder track next to Weiser Field, preparing for their final regular season football game against Liberty Union-Thurston High School.

WEEK X:

LIBERTY UNION

═══════════════════════════════════

(November 7, 1975 Away)

Liberty Union, located along Walnut Creek in Baltimore, Ohio, about 15 miles northeast of CW, shared a long gridiron history with Canal Winchester. Indeed, the first meeting of the Lions and the Indians was a season opener in 1921, during President Warren G. Harding's first year in the oval-office.

Like so many small towns in the area, Baltimore owed its initial growth to the Ohio Canal. And like CW, and several other towns in the MSL, it had changed its name over the years. In fact, Baltimore, Ohio developed somewhat schizophrenically: In 1825, settlers of Swiss origin on the western edge of what is now Baltimore christened their village *"Basil"* in honor of Basel, Switzerland. On that very same day, Virginians from the Old Dominion living on the east side rejected 'Basil' in favor of *'New Market'* – which they changed to *Baltimore* eight years later. The Swiss, however, held fast to Basil, and the little town endured a century with its split personality intact.

Paper manufacturing developed in Basil/Baltimore and provided an economic foundation for its Swiss/Virginian residents. Mills with wooden waterwheels sprang up along Walnut Creek splashing its choppy waters, driving the engine of growth. Nearing its centennial; during the 1919/1920 academic year, the local school adopted the name *'Liberty'* after the township; and '*Union*,' to celebrate the unification of Baltimore and Basil into – 'Baltimore.' Forty years later Liberty union consolidated with nearby Thurston, Ohio to create the Liberty Union-Thurston School District.

Starting in 1967, Dad had won six meetings with LU. In 1973, however, the Lions had denied CW a share of the MSL crown by beating them 19-0 in the last game of the year. CW had avenged that loss the following year, winning 9-0 to end its 1974 season undefeated. As with every team in the league, knocking off CW in 1975 would make the Lion's season; but the Liberty Union Lions had additional motivation. Head Coach Max Beougher had announced that he was stepping down to concentrate on his duties as junior high school principal. He would be coaching his last football game against the hated Indians.

Coach Beougher, part and parcel of Liberty Union's athletic program, had coached in the district in one capacity or another since 1958. After four years at the helm of the Lion's football program the well-liked and well-respected skipper had decided to hang up his whistle. "*If you stay in coaching long enough*," Coach Beougher was quoted in the *Lancaster Eagle Gazette*, "*you pay your dues.*" His players, having watched him pay those dues over the last four years, were determined to send him out a winner.

Coach Beougher was a class act, and his assessment of his final gridiron opponent was lofty: "*Best Class-A team in the state; better than last's,*" he remarked on Canal Winchester; because of "*their outstanding line and backfield plus a defense that won't let you score.*" Dad reciprocated, praising the Lion's defense, their offensive capabilities and insisting that "*We are going to have to play tough to win.*"

All the warnings in the world about '*playing tough to win*' didn't much register with the Indians that week. They were 19-0 over two years; had just beaten the MSL's four toughest teams and their final opponent was only 3-6. The Indian's minds were elsewhere that week, as were those of their coaches, despite their pregame rhetoric. "*Going into this game,*" Senior Gary Cox recalled, "*we kept thinking that we would have to blow them away to get in the playoffs and that Middletown Fenwick would have to lose. We knew Fenwick had more computer points than we did.*"

The Indians definitely had Fenwick on the brain while watching film of Liberty Union that week. Aware of their own accomplishments – a 9-0 record with seven shutouts – the very real possibility of playing on the largest football stage in Ohio was so tangible they could almost reach out and grab it. *"We were number one in the UPI poll,"* another senior added. *"We averaged 32 points a game and had given up only two touchdowns. If Hamilton Ross could just beat Middletown we'd finally have a chance to show what we could do."* None of that, of course, would mean anything if the Lions succeeded in sending Coach Beougher out with a victory.

Friday November 7, 1975 dawned cold and rainy, nothing like the downpour of the CW Homecoming, but light rain fell most of the day. Football players arrived at school that morning wearing maroon (away) jerseys while girlfriends donned white jerseys not needed by the team that night. Kickoffs were scheduled at 8:00 pm in the 1960s and 1970s, and the early sunsets of late autumn made it seem much later. By the time Mable Long pulled the bus away from CWHS, darkness completely enveloped the team.

Captains Mark Hartman and Bill Allen briefly reminded teammates what was at stake, and when they finished Captain Gary Griffith added, *'Think about it.'* The squad grew still as the young men rode in self-imposed silence in the darkness of the bus. Mable steered west out of town, north onto Gender Road, and then east toward Baltimore on Ohio-256. A half hour later the Indians disembarked, shook off the terror of the careening night ride, walked purposefully into the visitor's locker room and at length proceeded to the field for silent calisthenics.

The night got off to a good start when Froggy, Buffalo Bill and Boxcar returned to the locker room and announced that they had won the opening coin toss. Upon receiving the 8:00 pm kickoff Canal Winchester went to work, and despite slimy grass, cold weather and a wet football, the opening drive went off without a hitch. When CW had reached the Lion's 30-yard line, Dad not surprisingly called Steve Crist's number and running to his left behind Guard Bill Griffith, Tackle Bill Allen and Tight End Kurt Swiger, the Bionic man scampered untouched into the end zone.

Canal's band struck up in celebration and moments later Quarterback Gregg Wright ran in for the two-point conversion. Before Coach Beougher's offense had stepped on the field the scoreboard read LU-0: Visitors-8. *"We started out well,"* Junior Steve Crist remembered, *"but everyone had their minds on Middletown. We kind of walked through that night as we waited word on the Fenwick game."* The Lion's confirmed this. Recovering nicely after CW's first drive LU played inspired defense.

In fact, the score stood 8-0 until just twenty seconds remained before halftime when Steve Crist scored the Indian's second TD by again running off-tackle. Gregg Wright then hit Rick Ross in the back of the end zone for another two-point conversion, and the scoreboard read LU-0, Visitors-16, as both squads made their way to the locker rooms. As he Jogged off the field celebrating his catch, Rick Ross had noticed that Canal's fans appeared distracted. *"Everyone was bundled up but it looked like a lot of folks had their heads down,"* Rick recalled. *"Then I realized our fans were listening to other State-ranked teams while they were watching us."*

Actually, a slew of portable transistor radios squawked static in the visitor's stands that night. The question on everyone's mind and what so many half-muffled ears were straining to hear was, who's winning, Middletown Fenwick or Hamilton Ross? *"The emotion that night was incredible,"* Senior Kurt Swiger recalled. *"Everyone knew if we won and Middletown Fenwick lost Canal Winchester was going to the playoffs."* Yet the emotion Kurt spoke of was not enthusiasm or eager expectation, but rather deep concern, an edginess and indescribable angst over something the Indians and their fans could not control.

Liberty Union began the second half fired up but was unable to move the ball against Canal's stingy defense. On the other side of the ball the Lion's defense proved just as stingy, denying the Indians another score. Though not pleased with his offense Dad recognized that LU was overmatched and began substituting reserves and underclassmen into the game. *"I remember Coach Locke calling a bomb pass to me in the fourth quarter,"* recalled Kurt Swiger. *"He was trying to get me a touchdown. The pass was underthrown, however, and knocked down. But I always appreciated him trying for me."*

The final MSL gridiron contest of 1975 concluded rather anticlimactically, at least for CW, with the scoreboard still reading: LU-0, Visitors-16 as the fourth quarter drew to a close. Liberty Union's Head Coach was thrilled with his Lion's play. *"It was the best effort of my coaching career,"* an emotional Max Beougher remarked after the game. Despite the somewhat lackluster performance of its offense, CW had held LU to 80 total yards, 76 of which came on the ground, recorded its eighth shutout, and finished the season 10-0.

Indian fans poured out of the stands and converged on the field, proudly surrounding their team beside cheerleaders, the marching band and most of CWHS's student body. Unlike the victory celebrations following wins over Pickerington and Amanda, however, the emotional edginess lingered. Ty Zerby, a USAF Captain then stationed at Rickenbacker, and whose sophomore son, Mike, played for the JV's, approached Dad at the fifty yard line to vigorously shake his hand. Afterwards, recounting the brief exchange to his wife – Connie - he said, *"I could feel the tension in Mike when we shook hands. He seemed to be there but not there. Man is he wound up! I could feel the strain in him. He wants it so bad for his kids, but I tell you, he's wound up like a snare drum."*

"The elation of winning that final game – all the games, really" Kurt Swiger recalled, *"was quickly dampened when news that Middletown had won reached the field."* Fenwick had prevailed over previously unbeaten Hamilton Ross 21-0. The five measly points separating Canal and Middletown in the computer rankings might as well have been 1,000. Reporters immediately surrounded Dad seeking his reaction: *"Sure, we're kind of down,"* he began. *"We scored 306 points and gave up only 13 and have won 20 ballgames in a row."*

Taking a deep breath he seemed to sigh; *"We've done all that we could do."* When asked why a team that stood number-one in the UPI poll, and number-two in the AP could not advance, he said, *"The thing that kills us is the fact that we're in a 10-team league, and because of that half our teams have to lose every week. That's the only thing I think is unfair about the system. It discourages league play and I don't think that's right."* Having gotten it off his chest he collected himself, adding, *"We don't want to sound bitter. We're not. Fenwick did it when it had to."*

The victory over their twentieth consecutive opponent and their eighth shutout of the year suddenly took on the feeling of a loss, which in one sense it was: the loss of a shining goal that they had imagined, worked hard for and fought to achieve. *"The seniors took it hard,"* Steve Crist remembered. *"Just like that the season was over; our seniors knew they'd just played their final game and we wouldn't get a chance to show the rest of the State how good we were."* Buffalo Bill Allen - All Mid-State

League Offensive Tackle; All District; 3ʳᵈ Team A.P. All Ohio - walked dejectedly toward the locker room unable to speak.

The massive Senior Captain who reminded Gary Cox of a plundering Viking with his disheveled red mane, who had played the entire year in pain with a swollen knee - left the field in silence, tears streaming down his face. In the visitor's locker room; sitting motionlessly on a long wooden bench; staring blankly at the wall of lockers, Buffalo Bill slowly pulled off his wet, sweat-stained shoulder pads. They hit the concrete floor with a thud. His teammates, equally withdrawn, seemed not to notice. Finally, in an almost inaudible voice he muttered, *"I'm never going to wash this jersey again."*

Fellow Senior Gary Cox, who had heard the big lineman, remarked later, *"Bill's sentiments echoed everyone's on the team."* Gary's sentiments also echoed those of the entire team when he summed up their failure to advance to the postseason: *"I didn't understand it,"* he recalled. *"We shutout eight teams in 10 games, scored 306 points, gave up only 13 and hadn't lost since 1973? We didn't make it to the playoffs for whatever reason, but we knew in our hearts we were the best team on any football field in Class-A."*

Steve Crist recalled their ride back to Canal Winchester; *"The distance between Baltimore and Canal isn't far at all but that was a long, quiet ride home, let me tell you."* There wasn't much to say. 'Roller Ball' didn't feel like reciting his cheer. Coach Locke, Coach Jones and Coach Roth sat mute at the front of the bus, feeling their kids had been wronged; the athletes quietly sifted through a wide range of conflicting emotions: their ho-hum performance in the win that night over LU, the streak, their second consecutive MSL Championship and the stark finality of it all.

Then something remarkable happened to transform the mood of every passenger on Mable's bus and give the Mighty Indians of '75 a memory they would never forget. Several players used the term 'unbelievable' in describing the site awaiting their sore eyes as they at last reached the outskirts of town. In an extraordinary moment not seen in Canal Winchester in over thirteen centuries, Mable Long slowed to a crawl as a kaleidoscope of unearthly light flooded her bus. There on the streets lining Canal Winchester were hundreds, if not thousands of residents waiting patiently in the cold, damp night air to welcome their team home.

"*It was just unbelievable*," remembered Senior Rick Ross. "*It seemed like the entire town was out; I mean the town was just cranked! Chief Miller's police cruisers were in the middle of the road flashing their lights and sounding their sirens; the fire trucks were there and it was lit up like you wouldn't believe.*" Mable slowly crept east on Waterloo Street; cheers, whistles and screeching sirens pulsating through the bus's walls, reverberating amongst its occupants.

After pulling into CWHS the Indians poured out of the bus to be greeted as conquering heroes. The lights surrounding Weiser Field were on, illuminating the night sky; Mr. Baker quickly assembled his marching band and led them stepping in unison down the length of the field. "*We marched down the field with the band that night,*" remembered cheerleader Peggy Fox three decades later. "*They were playing Long Train Running and when we reached the end of the field we kept right on going through town for the victory march. I marched with my best friends (then and now) Sandy Hicks and Neal Seymour.*"

Disappointment over missing the playoffs gave way to feelings of joy and pride as the young men marched triumphantly down the streets of their hometown. CW's mayor, police chief, fire chief, teachers, businessmen, alumni, former athletes and residents of all ages formed almost uninterrupted receiving lines on both sides of the streets, through which the band, cheerleaders, coaches and victorious Indians proceeded. Looking like the torch-lit parades that once wended through cobblestone-paved hamlets in medieval Europe the procession happily soaked up the cheers and adulation.

"*It was just unbelievable,*" remembered Steve Crist. "*The bus ride had been so long and so quiet until we hit the edge of town. And then there was the band, fire trucks, police cars and I know it had to be over half the town out there,*" he said smiling. "*We all piled out and away we went celebrating.*" Not everyone partook. For Craig Cox, always thoughtful and sensitive, the evening was still fraught with overwhelming emotion. Very much like the afternoon of the Pickerington game when he couldn't relax and had headed off to the high school; the scene into which he was thrust proved too much for him.

"*I didn't go,*" he lamented thirty years later. "*To me, all that celebrating just meant it was over and I didn't want it to be over, so I went home. When I got home I thought about going back but decided not to. I just couldn't believe it was over.*" The initial excitement of the welcome lifted the team's spirits when the parade began; but as they marched on through the crowds tears began welling up and rolling once more. Bill Willison recalled the deep emotion the parade engendered that night.

"*Next to the birth of my daughter,*" Wee Willie said long afterwards, "*that was the best. I marched with the band; somebody handed me a drum, I took off my shoulder pads, strapped on the drums and marched through town in my football uniform playing with the band. Man, I loved it.*" He concluded, "*We knew we were the best even if they didn't give us a shot. Mike Locke had balls! He would have scheduled Cincinnati Mohler if he could have - and we would have wanted him to.*"

Kurt Swiger, perceptively, put the victory march into context. "*I walked with Bill Allen,*" he remembered. "*Bill was crying and I was trying not to. It really sunk in as we walked through town that I had played my last football game ever. We had a lot of mixed emotions. We had just won our twentieth game in a row and were kind of in awe over the accomplishment. We marched and cried at the same time. There were tears of joy, disappointment and realization that it was over. That victory march was real special, it made us feel important and gave us some closure to the season.*"

For my father the triumph was bittersweet. He had built an excellent football program at Canal Winchester. In nine seasons he'd won four league titles, went undefeated three times; compiled a 73-15-1 record (Winning 82% of his games) and had never finished lower than third in the MSL. When the game ended earlier that night he was asked if his 1975 squad was the best he'd ever coached. "You *better believe it,*" he responded without hesitation. "*It's the best team I've ever coached. Santa Claus could have coached this team to an unbeaten season.*" Even so, the opportunity to advance had been denied.

Ironically, amid the cacophony of sirens, brass instruments and cheering fans, my father was alone that night amongst the throng. His mom and dad, Leora and Norman, had been dead then for nearly fifteen years. His only brother, Phil, lived 1,000 miles away in Bangor, Maine. His wife of almost twenty years couldn't bring herself to attend games, and his children, home in bed by this time, were too young to truly appreciate his accomplishment. While the assistant coaches were friends, at bottom they were co-workers and employees, and his players were young men for whom he was responsible.

And so he too marched through the maze, shaking hands, accepting pats on the back, taking long strides clad in his white bucks, maroon pants, wide white belt, maroon and white shirt and even wider maroon and white tie. Later that night, after celebrating, relaxing with friends and well-wishers at King Arthur's Steak House, Canal's head coach walked through the front door at 106 East Waterloo Street, positioned himself on his couch next to the lamp, adjusted his heavy plastic glasses and began reading alone in the quiet living room of the Locke Clan's little Sears Home.

Across town Weiser Field lay dark and silent. The Mighty Indians of '75 who poured out so much emotion beneath its lights, were already receding into the shadow world of memory. Canal's streets, so boisterous just a few hours before, were empty and still. The locker room where his team had so diligently '*thought about it*' sat dark and deserted, littered with discarded mouth pieces, chin straps, torn practice jerseys, sweat-stained elbow pads and the general debris of male adolescence. Above the coach, in his room across from the stairway, Mike Locke's only son, 'Little Locke', lay awake, unable to sleep.

EPILOGUE:

When the dust settled the MSL's 1975 final standings read:

(1) Canal Winchester 9-0 (6) Liberty Union 3-7
(2) Bloom Carroll 7-2 (7) Millersport 3-5-1
(3) Logan Elm 7-2 (8) Fairfield Union 2-7
(4) Pickerington 6-3 (9) Fisher Catholic 2-6-1
(5) Amanda Clearcreek 6-3 (10) Berne Union 0-9

Pickerington never recovered from its epic showdown with the Indians and dropped its final two games that year. The honors and acclaim for Canal Winchester, however, began rolling in. Seven Indians were named to the MSL's First Team Roster (Steve Crist, Matt Hartman, Mark Hartman, Gary Griffith, Bill Allen, Mark Hays and Neal Seymour). Mike Locke was named Coach of the Year. The final polls, in which CW stood first in the UPI, second in the AP, and third in the OHSAA, were stellar achievements but absent an expanded playoff, the best 1975 Class-A team would remain forever undetermined.

Of course there is something comforting in "what-might-have-been." One can never prove a negative and as Canal's season ended on November 7th 1975 players and coaches could make the argument that victory was probable had they only been given the opportunity. The truth is that no one will ever know how Canal Winchester might have fared in the playoffs. It is interesting to note that Middletown Fenwick, Region 12-1's representative, was defeated 11-0 the following week by J.D. Graham's Newark Catholic squad.

Fenwick's loss prompted several local sports writers to surmise CW would "*Not have allowed 11 points and certainly wouldn't have been shut out.*" A moot point by then of course. A week after the season ended veteran *Times* Sports Editor Robert O'Callaghan attempted to describe what he'd witnessed that autumn on Weiser Field. Beginning with a disclaimer he wrote, "*It might appear to be prejudice, but this particular column is giving credit where credit is due. This writer has seen many high school football teams in the past and in many parts of the country, but this CW team is the finest I've ever seen perform on a football field.*"

Prior to Canal's annual high school football banquet the *Times* issued a special supplement honoring the MSL Champs. Twenty-nine local businesses purchased advertising space for the twelve page pullout. Coaches, graduating seniors and starters were interviewed under the banner: *A Tribute To The Canal Winchester Indians 1975 Mid-State League Football Champions.* Beneath the ledger appeared the team's group photo. The lengthy addition included straight reporting, opinions, photos of individual players and one-on-one interviews.

So euphoric were Canal's fans that one writer went so far as to compare the Indians to that year's undefeated, Division-I, Ohio State Buckeyes. "*Matt Hartman,*" the comparisons began, "*the pile-driving fullback who plays a mean defense reminds us a little of Pete Johnson . . . Steve Crist, a versatile halfback who can turn on the speed, make the cuts, block and catch passes of Archie Griffin.*" Gregg Wright compared favorably to Cornelius Greene, Froggy to Brian Baschnagel and my father, though mentioned elsewhere in the supplement as "*A lanky absent-minded professor,*" to the Buckeyes venerable Woody Hayes.

The addendum's advertising reflected Canal Winchester's pride in their team as the following three examples attest: "*Jack Helm Ford INC. 'The Indians Rode the Opposition Just Like They Were Mustangs.' 1975 Mustang II Clearance Sale.*" The local bowling alleys' read: "*Canal Lanes Bowling: 'Coach Mike Locke's Indians Have Rolled Two Straight Strikes In The Mid-State League, and with Room to Spare.'*" And local State Farm Insurance agent James Bright's ad said, "*Like A Good Neighbor, The Indians Are There (At The Top Of The MSL).*"

The banquet, held at 6:30 Monday evening, November 24, 1975 in the multipurpose room, was a potluck affair for which attendees were assured a '*covered-dish supper, salad and dessert.*' The long aqua-green cafeteria tables, lined up in three sections across the multipurpose room, filled quickly that evening. At the front of the cafeteria three additional tables, covered with white table cloths, served as assembly area for the casseroles, Johnny Marzetti, macaroni salads, meatballs, fried chicken and potatoes. Mounds of brownies, cookies and cakes loaded the dessert table.

Several chests full of soda and two large urns, one containing hot coffee, the other cold cider, provided liquid refreshment to the team and its well-wishers. C.A. Miller, beaming from ear-to-ear, said a few words before inviting the multitudes to partake and lines quickly formed about the ample provender. The dining accommodations in the multipurpose room rapidly became standing-room-only, proving once again that success really does have a thousand fathers.

Mr. Brisker, Mr. McCann and C.A. Miller huddled to find a solution to the sudden overcrowding dilemma. After walking in and out of the multipurpose room several times C.A. announced that the ceremonies would move to the auditorium following the meal. That turned out to be a wise decision because the after-dinner crowd filled every seat in the auditorium. Team, coaches and cheerleaders sat in the first couple rows while Mr. McCann, Mr. Brisker and C.A. sat together on stage. The cheerleaders were immaculately dressed in long skirts, boots and high heels, blouses and vests. The football players and coaches wore slacks, dress shoes, jackets and ties.

The ceremony followed the same pattern year after year. First, each cheerleader was introduced by her adviser, who spoke fondly of the young lady before she was called forth to the proscenium. This was capped off by the captain briefly addressing the audience, thanking the advisor, presenting her with a gift, and breaking into tears while the audience applauded. Mr. Brisker, the athletic director, then introduced the cheerleaders' advisers and coaches, adding funny details or brief stories about the student-athletes before ceding the microphone.

Next up, junior varsity coaches, Jerry Jones and Jim Roth introduced the JV athletes, beginning with players who made up the reserves' starting offense and defense. Assistant coaches work extremely closely with their charges and both Coach Jones and Coach Roth relayed funny anecdotes or unknown attributes for every freshman, sophomore and junior called to the stage. After being introduced each nervous young man walked before the assembled masses, carefully negotiated the steps leading to the stage, approached the coaches, shook their hands and received his certificate, letter and small gold football pin.

Each quiet, self-conscious football player then took his place standing behind the coaches in a slowly forming convex line until the last Indian had received his due. For parents of freshman and sophomores the JV ceremony was every bit as important as what was to follow. Nevertheless, as the evening wore on and C.A. Miller, Sue Thomas, Mr. McCann, Mr. Brisker, Coach Jones and Coach Roth all had their say, the tension and anticipation built toward the main event of the evening.

When the JV's exited the stage the excitement and electricity were palpable. Mr. Brisker approached the microphone and began his introduction: citing the head coach's 73-15-1 record, his 82 winning percentage, four MSL titles, three undefeated seasons, including two back-to-back 10-0 campaigns, four MSL Coach of the Year Awards, his selection to coach in the following spring's Ohio High School All Star game and the titanic clash at Pickerington on October 24th. At last he leaned forward and said, *"Ladies and gentlemen, I present to you the Head Coach of the Mid-State-League Champion Canal Winchester Indians – Mike Locke."*

Dad stood from his seat and ascended the stairs as the audience arose in unison to give him a thunderous standing ovation. Arriving at the podium Dad smiled, nodded his head in recognition, and politely asked everyone to be seated. But the audience just clapped and whistled and cheered and stomped and nobody sat down. Dad looked back at his bosses, and again at the crowd, but the ovation went on like that for two or three minutes nearly bringing down the house. When the tumult had finally subsided, Dad began to introduce the Mighty Indians of '75, giving special attention to graduating seniors.

Scott Jordan, he said, is a *"fine punter and backup quarterback and excellent mud-slider"* who, Dad wished, would have come out for football a year earlier. Likewise, Jeff Damron is *"the type of player that I really hate to lose; I wish he'd come out a year earlier as well. He's a real good athlete and he made us better."* Bill Willison, "Wee Willie" the team comic, played in pain and kept everyone loose. Captain Bill Allen also played with a *"bum knee, earning All MSL Offensive Tackle, All District, 3rd Team A.P. All-Ohio honors."*

Bill Griffith, the team's smallest offensive lineman, had won *"All League 'Honorable Mention'"* but in the head coach's opinion that was less than he deserved, which was also true for Rick Ross who earned *"All League Honorable Mention"* at defensive end, to which Dad objected, saying *"I don't understand Rick not receiving All League honors, he's as good as any defensive end in the MSL."*

Captain Mark Hartman ascended the stage and shook his coach's hand. Dad informed the audience that his graduating center had earned *"All League, All District; Most Valuable Lineman. UPI 1ˢᵗ and A.P. Honorable Mention All-Ohio;"* Matt Hartman, following his brother Mark, was introduced as an *"All-League Fullback and 2ⁿᵈ Team All-District linebacker."* Captain Gary Griffith had two sets of parents in attendance that night, all four beaming proudly as the head coach rattled off Froggy's accomplishments: *"All Mid-State League Defensive Halfback; All District 1ˢᵗ Team Defensive Halfback; Honorable Mention A.P. All-Ohio and Hickle Award Winner."*

Gary Cox was lauded for being *"an excellent tackler who obviously learned solid fundamentals while playing football in Nebraska."* Kurt Swiger was complimented for *"selfless play, positive attitude and never missing a single practice."* And on Dad went down the list singing the praises of each young man, thanking him for his hard work, shaking hands and attempting to convey to the audience how truly special they all were. Juniors Brett Van Meter, Rick Gates, Mark Hays, Gregg Wright, Neal Seymour and Craig Cox followed the seniors. Sitting in the audience that night, Janet Cox could finally enjoy seeing her sons with the rest of the team.

When Steve Crist came on stage Dad referred to him as *"Our own Bionic Man,"* spoke of his excellent attitude and took the time to list his many gridiron exploits: 20 TDs, 3 two-point conversions, 11 extra points and two field goals totaling 143 points for the season – first in Franklin County. *"The only time I ever really worried about Steve was during the Bloom Carroll game when he hurt his bionic shoulder. I was afraid he'd gotten short-circuited in all that rain."*

When the last Indian took his place at the end of the line, Dad asked that they walk forward to the edge of the stage. Standing proudly before family and fans Dad said *"Take a good long look at this group of young men. Teams like this come around maybe every fifteen to twenty years or so;*

so take a good, long last look." Darlene Seymour, clad in Neal's number-80 football jersey, stood to applaud and the rest of the congregation joined in. The auditorium soon convulsed in one long rapturous final salute. Mark Hartman, having located his mom and dad in the audience, turned toward the stairs and the Indians descended the proscenium to sustained, rhythmic clapping, whistles, cheers and tears.

At that point Dad announced a special guest, Woodrow Roach. Within moments Mr. Roach stood next to Dad on stage. Canal's citizens quickly realized the invited guest was the only African American in the building. An observation Mr. Roach made as well. *"There aren't too many black folk around these parts are there?"* he asked rhetorically scanning the crowd. Dad began his introduction: *"Woodrow Roach was one of the most heavily recruited running backs in the State of Ohio. He arrived at Ohio State on full scholarship; lifted weights, learned the playbook and in four years never once missed practice."*

"And yet," Dad continued as he revealed the significance of Mr. Roach's appearance, *"Woodrow never saw the playing field. He wanted to play, prepared to play but didn't because he backed up a young man by the name of Archie Griffin."* At that the audience let out a gasp of comprehension. *"There's a lesson in that for our underclassmen,"* Dad concluded as many in the auditorium nodded their heads in agreement. *"Woodrow Roach ran every wind- sprint, worked on the scout teams and kept a positive attitude; he never griped or complained. Woodrow Roach did everything he could to help his team; he put his team first. And come spring he'll graduate from Ohio State University."*

With that Woodrow Roach said a few words about hard work and perseverance, the crowd gave one last round of applause and the 1975 football banquet drew to a close. One of the first to reach the stage after the lights came up was Bishop Ready Head Coach Dave Lewis. The 'Lew-I' approached his old associates, shaking hands and congratulating them on a job well done. Former players were happy to see him, but Sue Thomas couldn't help giving him a dig: *"Well hello there Coach Lewis,"* she said with a broad grin. *"I hate to have to say that we did it without you. But we did it without you!"*

Dad had never claimed that teams like his undefeated 1970 or 1974 squads came around only once every fifteen or twenty years, and his insistence that the 'Mighty Indians of '75 were somehow unique turned out to be quite prescient. As of this writing no Canal Winchester football team has gone undefeated in the 36 seasons that followed the 1975 run. Liberty Union Coach Max Beougher's observation that, *"If you stay in coaching long enough you're going to pay your dues"* also proved prescient in my father's case. In the *Times* supplement several underclassmen spoke confidently of going 10-0 in 1976, and that *"You get used to winning around here."*

Though no one on stage that November 24th would have believed it, the following season would begin with a 32-0 shutout of Canal Winchester. The Indians lost nine starting seniors to graduation that November 24th: Matt and Mark Hartman, Rick Ross, Gary Griffith, Bill Griffith, Bill Allen, Bill Willison, Gary Cox, and punter Scott Jordan. Moreover, Neal Seymour began the '76 campaign struggling with a bad knee, Steve Crist sprained an ankle and Gregg Wright did not return for his senior year.

Nor had Craig Cox, whose Air Force family had relocated once more, this time to Alaska. Consequently, the 1976 Indians lined up for their opening game against Bexley without two of the previous season's guards, one of its halfbacks, its center, fullback, left tackle, left guard, right tight end, quarterback, cornerback and punter. When the game mercifully ended the winning Lions and their fans rushed onto the field in celebration. Canal's long winning streak was over.

Canal Winchester struggled to win five games in 1976, much to the delight of the rest of the Mid State League and those in CW who resented Dad's success. The 1977 season also ended with a 5-5 record, and in 1978 Dad had his first losing season when Canal finished 3-7. Those three seasons marked the nadir of my father's coaching career. Nonetheless, in many ways the 1976, 1977 and 1978 seasons represented his finest, most determined efforts in the coaching profession. When your record is 73-15-1 and you've beaten all-comers two years running it's not hard to coach football in a small Ohio town. That's not the case when your record reads 13-17 over three seasons.

The same people who wanted to make Dad mayor and thought he could coach at OSU suddenly knew more football than he did. My best friend's older brother, for example – who had played on the 1975 squad - provided ample, unsolicited advice, apparently expecting me to pass it along, insisting, *"Your Dad's got to change his playbook man!"* At that point his mother chimed-in to second her son and offer additional advice on offensive and defensive schemes.

That sort of thing was widespread in town during that period and it had to hurt. My father's coaching profession was his identity. He never introduced himself, for example, as a teacher, but rather as the *"Head Football Coach at CW."* Nevertheless, despite losing athletes to graduation and injury, and the slow creep of the drug culture into high school in the late 1970s, he made no excuses, did not seek employment elsewhere, or turn his back on the program he'd built. Rather, he continued to scout, watch film, attend clinics, oversee the weight lifting program and prepare his teams as best he could to win.

Starting in the autumn of 1979 it paid off. Canal turned things around by winning at least seven games that year and again in 1980, 1981, and 1982; and in 1983 they finished 9-1, losing only to archrival Bloom Carroll. A few years later, in 1988, the Indians nearly achieved another perfect season. CW was 9-0 going into the final game, but came up short against Fairfield Union, losing 31-21. The 1975 Indians, therefore, stand out as the last undefeated team Mike Locke ever coached.

Eventually OHAA expanded the playoff system and in 1984 CW advanced, only to lose to Newark Catholic 34-14. Four years later they made the playoffs again but lost to Portsmouth Notre Dame 10-6. To this day Dad believes that Canal would have advanced at least eight or nine times had the system been altered earlier, and that the best team he ever coached had been denied their shot.

When he finally hung up the whistle following the 1991 season his coaching record read: 173 wins, 74 losses, 3-ties. He had won 70% of his games during a quarter century at the helm, posted just two losing seasons and won seven league titles. The height of that success undoubtedly came during the autumn of 1975 when he mentored the last undefeated and the mightiest of his teams.

In the *Times* supplement that fall of 1975, varsity athletes were questioned about their futures. **Steve Crist** thought he might like to play college football and major in mathematics. After graduating from CWHS in the spring of 1977 Steve enrolled at Muskingum College where he played football for two seasons. The Bionic Man earned a degree in accounting, married his high school sweetheart, varsity cheerleader Jamie Padget, raised three children in CW and became Director of

Planning and Controller for the Nationwide Insurance Company in Columbus, Ohio.

Gregg Wright explained to the *Times* that "*I was just determined to put forth the best effort I could,*" at quarterback, and that being an Indian "*meant a lot to me because it's the first championship team I ever played for.*" Dad remarked of Gregg Wright, "*He's going to be one of the best QBs in the league next year.*" As it turned out, Gregg didn't play for CW, or anywhere else in the MSL in the autumn of 1976. Always a free spirit, and just a half-credit shy of graduating, Gregg took a summer course and finished high school early.

He got married early as well, and followed his wife to Winston Salem, North Carolina. The marriage did not last long and after his divorce Gregg moved to Florida where he became a professional barber and "*spent as much time as I could lying on the beach in the sun.*" Today he is remarried and a proud father who lives in Texas, and works as Service Manager for a large Denton car dealership. When asked about his time at CW, Gregg remarked, "*It was wonderful. We were a great team. Coach Locke was a great guy. I have nothing but respect for that man.*"

Neal Seymour told *Times* reporters he enjoyed rock music, especially the Eagles, and that he'd like to earn an education degree and teach English. He Attended Ohio University in Athens, lettered in football all four years, and was voted captain of the 1980 Bobcat squad. Now married with children, Neal teaches English at Teays Valley High School. His experience as an assistant football coach and head wrestling coach there gave Neal the following perspective: "*I used to think Locke was crazy,*" he said smiling – "*until I became a coach myself.*"

'Box Car' - AKA, **Mark Hartman** - indicated he'd like to attend a MAC conference school, play football and major in business or physical therapy. And Mark did indeed play football at Otterbein, later becoming a teacher and successful football coach in his own right. Married, he and his wife, Susan, have two children, Ashley and Derek. Mark became Athletic Director in one of Ohio's largest school districts before retiring to enter private business.

Matt 'Roller Ball' Hartman had once entertained the idea of entering the ministry, but later changed his mind. After graduating in the spring of 1976 Matt enrolled at Ohio State University and graduated four years later. Matt and his wife Leisa have one son, Jeremy. They have now been married for thirty years, and today Matt is Sales Engineer at Tyco Electronics, a business establishment where no one other than Matt knows his true identity is 'Roller Ball.'

Bill 'Buffalo Bill' Allen attended Muskingum College in New Concord, Ohio where he played football until his knee finally gave out. Married since 1982, Bill has three children and makes his home in Florida where he is plant manager of an electronic manufacturing facility. His eldest son, Brad, played college football for Vanderbilt University. His two daughters, Jennie and Jillian Allen, are also athletic like their father. The two excel in volleyball, among other sports. Of his time with the Mighty Indians of '75, Bill says, *"I was lucky to have Mike Locke as a coach, he taught me about hard work. He was a true winner"*

Scott 'Mud-slide' Jordan graduated in the spring of 1976, and enrolled at Franklin College in Columbus, Ohio. Later, Scott took over Dysart Corporation upon the death of his father and today runs the family business with his brothers and sisters. **Gary 'Froggy' Griffith**, AKA *'The Game-breaker'* went on to university as Roger Hanners had hoped, graduated with honors and became a successful businessman living – nearly unforgivably – in the State of Michigan. **Bill Willison** expressed an interest in *"baseball and mechanical work, especially on cars and motorcycles."* Fittingly, as the only earth-dweller other than Superman to assault an on-coming train and live to tell the tale, Bill bought a jeep after high school and immediately entered the work force. After ten years working construction he followed in his father's footsteps to become a firefighter. The following year his daughter was born, *"the greatest day"* of his life. Now divorced, Bill is a lieutenant for the Columbus Division of Fire and lives with his daughter four miles outside Canal Winchester.

In 1975 **Kurt Swiger's** passions were *"tennis, baseball and golf."* He also admitted to a fascination with mystery novels, particularly those of Agatha Christie. Kurt planned to enroll at OSU and perhaps attend law school. In the autumn of 1976 he went to Ohio State, and graduated in 1980. He Became a manager at Wendy's and then followed his fiancée, Carolyn, to Charlotte, North Carolina. In 1988 he began a new career as an accounting manager with Allstate Insurance Company where he continues to work. Kurt and Carolyn Swiger have been married for more than twenty-five years and have three children, Daniel, Jessica and Meghan.

Cheerleader **_Peggy Fox_** moved to Florida after graduating, where she worked as a bartender before taking a position with Battelle Memorial Institute. Peggy worked at Battelle for thirteen years before leaving to become a fulltime homemaker. She's been happily married for 25 years.

Rick Ross, who endeared himself to my father after once taking a particularly vicious hit by saying; *"Don't sweat it coach, it's only pain,"* told reporters he *"hated to sit still"* in 1975. He thought he might like to go into law enforcement or *"some physical job."* Rick attended and played football at Oberlin College but later transferred to Franklin University where he earned his degree in business. His profession as manager of Dave Gill Pontiac has kept him on the go for over 25 years. On the home-front, Rick "robbed the cradle" to marry CW Class of 1977 graduate Debbie Mullins. The Ross's live just outside town at 'The Villages at Winchester' where they've raised three sons - Jeremy, Justin and Josh.

The Cox brothers, Senior **_Gary Cox_** and Junior **_Craig Cox_**, departed Canal Winchester in the summer of 1976 as abruptly as they had descended upon it the previous fall. Their father, Lieutenant Colonel David Cox, had been transferred to Alaska and the family packed up lock, stock & barrel and headed north to the future. Craig played his final year of high school football for yet another new team. Eventually, both Gary and Craig enrolled at Ohio State University. After graduating Gary entered Capital University Law School and today is as Assistant Attorney General for the EPA. Now divorced, Gary has two children and lives in Columbus, Ohio. Craig became an engineer, prompting his father to quip, *"Gary puts em in jail and Craig builds the jails."* Married and with multiple offspring, Craig lives in Mansfield, Ohio and is still the thoughtful, sensitive builder he was back in 1975.

Brett Van Meter graduated from CWHS in 1977. He briefly attended college, but his work for Ohio Auto Auctions induced him to leave school and dedicate himself full time to business. Today Brett is the manager at Ohio Auto Auctions and has worked for the company for more than twenty-five years. The young lady whom Gregg Wright was once so sweet on, Sandy Hays, fell in love with Brett and they married in 1988. Together they had a daughter, Brittany, and divorced in 2009.

Bill Griffith, had expressed an interest in ROTC and biological science when interviewed in 1975. Bill believed his most likely avenue to higher education would run *"Either through Ohio State or Miami of Ohio,"* and prescient he was. He began his studies at Miami University and after one year there transferred to Ohio State. Bill later took over the family farm, married Ellen Bohl and raised two sons, Brad and Tyler Griffith. He stays busy planting, weeding, stacking hay, laying drainage tiles, repairing farm equipment, vaccinating livestock and going to night school. Indeed, in his spare time Bill has earned a second Bachelor of Science degree and was busy working on an MBA as of this writing.

Junior **Mark "Baby" Hays** had spoken in 1975 of *"Working on cars, especially a jeep that he's fixing up."* Mark graduated in the spring of 1977 and entered the workforce, staying in shape on a construction crew. Like Rick Ross, Mark robbed the cradle to marry 1980 Canal grad Mary Meinhart. Today Mark is Sales Manager at Saturn Southeast's car dealership. He and Mary have been together more than twenty-five years and have two beautiful daughters, Anna and Devin-Marie.

Coach **Jim Roth**, AKA Fidel Castro's look-alike, left Canal Winchester the same year Mark Hays graduated. *"The Teays Valley School District paid higher salaries for teachers and so I really couldn't afford to stay,"* he recalled. Jim taught wood shop and coached at Teays Valley until his retirement in 2000. Today Jim is back where he began his teaching career, living in Canal Winchester with wife Vicki. He occasionally gets together with Dad over beers at a local watering hole where they solve all the world's problems. Jim's son, Brian, makes his home in Arizona and Brian's two children have made Coach Roth a doting grandfather.

Mrs. **Sue Thomas**, AKA, "Teach," taught and coached at Canal Winchester from 1969 through 1978. Wanting to spend more time with her son, she approached C.A. about reducing her coaching load. When they couldn't come to an accord she tendered her resignation. She married William Willis in 1979 and they started their own business, *WW Cabinets*, that operated for 29 years before a deep recession forced them to close its doors. Today, Mrs. Willis is the proud mother of two sons, Nick and John Willis, and seven grandkids. 'Teach' continues to make her home in Canal Winchester and is still a big supporter of girls' athletics and all things Indian.

Mary Matyac graduated from Canal Winchester in the spring of 1976 and enrolled at Ohio State University where she studied business and psychology. Mary met her husband, Ken Sigman, at Ohio State and they've been married for more than thirty years. They live in Montgomery, Alabama with their two children by birth, Kyle and Heather, and an adopted son, Jeff. *"Through the years we have taken in troubled teenagers to help them over the hump. We have two of our own children and the last boy that we helped through high school stayed and became a part of the family. He has been with us for eighteen years now."* Despite residing in the south, Mary insists that *"Canal Winchester, Ohio is still my home."*

Jerry 'Mordecai' Jones left Canal Winchester in 1979. The low period in Dad's coaching career, 1976, 1977, 1978, had strained their relationship; both personally and professionally. Dad felt Mordecai had lost the kids' respect, and replaced him as defensive coordinator. Mr. Jones felt Dad was losing and therefore using him as scapegoat. At an away game during the autumn of 1976, when CW had just given up a score, longtime Indian football fan John Delong yelled from the stands, *"Hey Locke! Who's going to be your defensive coordinator next year?"* Coach Jones lost it, spun around, raised both arms in the air and bellowed back, *"Shut the hell up you old goat! You dirty . . ."* before Dad could calm him down.

When Mr. Jones left the district he took a job with Pickerington where he coached against Dad as Jack Johnson's assistant for three years before leaving secondary education for good. Jerry and Jenny Jones practiced *'open marriage'* for a time while still living in CW, but inevitably divorced. Mordecai left the Buckeye State, earned his Ph.D., and today teaches at a university in New Orleans. One afternoon, twenty years after leaving Canal, he showed up on our doorstep. He and Dad had a long visit. Old wounds had healed and fences were mended. They periodically touch base over the phone and Jerry stops past the house when in town.

Judy Haffey, Canal Winchester's beautiful, trumpet-player attended Tennessee Temple University in Chattanooga. She and her husband, Jay Jackson, have been married for thirty years and have two sons, Chad and Kyle. The Jacksons make their home in Springfield, Ohio where Judy works as a medical office manager. She still enjoys making the trip to Canal Winchester on Labor Day to *"walk down memory lane."*

Dave Lewis, *"The Lew-I"* - was head football coach at Bishop Ready HS from 1975-1979, before entering the college ranks. That coaching journey saw him travel to St. Norbert College in De Pere, Wisconsin;

West Virginia Wesleyan College; the University of Indianapolis where he became defensive coordinator, and back once more to the Buckeye State when he became defensive coordinator at Muskingum College in New Concord, Ohio. Coach Lewis returned to the HS ranks as head coach of the New Albany Eagles, served as athletic director for Reynoldsburg HS, and today teaches Health and Physical Education at Eastland-Fairfield & Technical Schools. Dave has been happily married for more than thirty years and attends Canal Winchester's annual Labor Day parade when he can get away from his responsibilities. He calls Dad every Christmas and they have remained friends going on five decades.

The Mighty Indians of 75 Team Photo

Shadow and Memory

The Mighty Indians who battled as if their very lives depended on winning, once fleet of foot and strong of limb, are now in their fifties. Indeed, their own children are older than they were when, as young men, they won the MSL in 1975, and finished first in the UPI State Poll. Though unimaginable in 1975, CWHS no longer has any memory of the team or their magical run. Superintendent C.A. Miller, Principal William McCann, English teachers Isabelle Woodward and

Sally Duus, Latin teacher Ruth Sievert, Secretaries Ginny Hartman and Betty Ferber, bus driver Mable Long, and WHOK sportscaster Roger Hanners are long since dead.

Librarian Jim Butts and teachers Jerry Jones, Kathy Hurt, Howard Siegrist, Elisa Zanner, Linda Ralph, Bill Lake, Sue Thomas, David Chesnut, Jim Roth, Kevin Peters, David Baker, Gretchen Gelbach and Mike Locke are all retired. As are Athletic Director Dan Brisker, and Guidance Counselor Rosetta Horst.

The town too - at least parts of it - has also passed away. Cellar Lumber, Canal Kitchen Pizzeria, Canal View Pharmacy, Parker's Sohio, Conrad's Market, Super Duper Grocery, Canal Lanes Bowling, Meuser Farm Sausage and Winchester Laundry & Dry Cleaning are no longer in business; they have been replaced on the outskirts of town, where the fields once seemed to stretch on forever, by tract-housing, shopping centers and fast food restaurants. Today, assistant coaches Jerry Jones and Jim Roth are in their sixties, and the intense, 36-year-old, brown-haired, blue-eyed Head Coach who prowled the Indians' sidelines for 25 years is in his seventies.

Dad's dark curly hair is now cotton white and a surgically replaced knee has shortened his once elongated strides. The volcanic temper responsible for 'banishing' offending athletes has mellowed, tempered by years and medication taken for his heart. When he walks through town he is no longer recognized as once was the case in the Halcyon Days of Yore. But across the fruited plain his former players remember. They can still hear the echo of his whistle, the shrill commands readying the team for fourth quarter drill, the cadences of calisthenics: "*One, two, three — one; One, two, three - two; One, two, three -three.*" The emphasis on responsibility, hard work and discipline, and the memory of how much Coach Locke cared. "*I would have crawled over broken glass for him,*" Matt Hartman remarked in our interview. "*I don't know why. It's not because he was a cheer leader and got us up for games or even because we won. It was his, it was his . . . aura. It was what he did day in and day out as a coach and a teacher.*"

When the Canal Winchester School District constructed its new football stadium in the early 1990s the powers-that-be christened the new Victory Bell in honor of Mike Locke. The small plaque reads: "*Head Coach Mike Locke, 1967-1991.*" Fans no longer walk through town to take in games at the new stadium as they did at Weiser Field. Now they drive, park their cars and walk past the bell without giving it much notice. Yet, if future generations could somehow travel back in time - before the information revolution and computer age, 500-channel TV, cell phones, I-Pods, DVDs, Twitter, Blackberries, Instant Replay, ESPN, the *'tuck rule'* and the advent of the World Wide Web – sports-minded travelers would do well to select the autumn of 1975, and Canal Winchester High School. Stepping from their time-machine, they would soon hear the wild shouts of young men celebrating an especially lengthy mud slide on a hill behind rusted, paint chipped bleachers across from an empty football field. Above the din of whistles, the rhythms of calisthenics and the sounds of clashing pads would also be heard the distinct voice of a confident young football coach, busily and single-mindedly preparing his Indians for battle.

Coach Locke, 35 years after his Mighty Indians finished 1st in the State of Ohio at Mike Locke Stadium.

POSTSCRIPT

As I wrote in the introduction, Dad passed away just prior to **_Little_ _Locke_** going to press. Seven months after I completed the first draft of this manuscript, however, and eighteen years since Dad last walked the sidelines, Canal Winchester High School celebrated its football centennial. The 2009 season opener with Bexley coincided with a reunion of classes dating back to the 1950s. Coaches, players and cheerleaders, young and old, returned to their alma mater to commemorate the milestone. Three weeks prior, I received a call from Christopher Jones, president of the Touchdown Club, informing me that the stadium would be named for Dad, and that it was to be a surprise. Now 70 years old and walking with a cane, Dad was called to the 50-yard line just before kickoff.

"I thought they wanted me to oversee the coin toss," he admitted later. At that the PA announcer asked his family to join him at midfield. Mom, Laura, Little Locke, my wife Linda, and our two daughters stood beside Dad. A huge banner was unfurled behind him as Mr. Jones listed his accomplishments. When the announcement ended hundreds of his former players, standing before him on the track, cheered their approval. Dad dropped his head into his hands and wept. There wasn't a dry eye in Mike Locke Stadium.

Coach Mike Locke Ceremony

We direct your attention to the 50-yard line, and ask that Coach Mike Locke and his family; join Superintendent Kim Miller-Smith, and School Board President Stan Smith for a special presentation.

As we mark the 100th Anniversary of Canal Winchester Football, one person stands out among the many who have contributed to the "pride, spirit and tradition" that is Canal Winchester Football. Coach Mike Locke walked the sidelines for 25 of the 78 seasons Canal Winchester has played football, and compiled a record that is unparalleled in the history of football in our community. Tonight we recognize a special coach and a special person.

Although we are focused on football tonight, keep in mind that Coach Locke also coached track at Canal Winchester High School for 32 years, compiling an equally amazing record as head coach. During his 32 years as coach of the track program, Coach Locke's teams produced league championships, district titles, and individual champions too numerous to recount.

As the head football coach at Canal Winchester High School, Coach Locke is simply without peers. His record of accomplishment from the 1967 season through the 1991 season includes the following:

- His won-loss record of 173-74-3 represents 47.5% of the 364 wins in the history of Canal Winchester football. The next highest win total for a Canal Winchester football coach is 39.
- Of the 8 league titles won by Canal Winchester, Coach Locke's teams won 7 of them.
- He coached the first two playoff teams in school history. It would be another 19 years until Canal Winchester made the playoffs again.
- 16 of 24 First Team All-Ohio Football Players in school history were coached by Mike Locke.
- 71 of 143 First Team All-League Football Players (49.9%) in school history were coached by Mike Locke.
- 7 Times Mike Locke was named Coach of the Year
- His 1975 Team was voted Class A State Champions by UPI, and his 1970 Team was Third.

- **Between 1973 and 1975, he coached his team to 22 consecutive victories, still a school record.**

Even though Coach Locke retired from coaching after the 1991 season, he can still be found on a Fall Friday night sitting in the stands watching the Indians. And, in 2007, when the Indians returned to the State Playoffs for the first time since Coach Locke's 1988 team, it was Coach Locke who spoke to the team after their pregame meal on Thursday night.

For his unparalleled contributions during his 25 years as head football coach, and his 32 years as head track coach at Canal Winchester High School, it was the unanimous decision of the Canal Winchester School Board that from this day forward, the Student Activities Center at Canal Winchester High School shall be known as Mike Locke Stadium.

Congratulations Coach Locke.

Mike Locke Stadium.

ACKNOWLEDGEMENTS:

It is amazing how much time, effort and help is required in writing a book, even light nostalgia such as this. Three works in particular were invaluable to the project. Though I have never met or spoken to two of the authors, all three books were immensely helpful. George F. Bareis's *History of Madison Township: Canal Winchester and Groveport, Ohio* provided a wealth of anecdotal and general information on Winchester's development. Likewise, Lillian M. Carroll and Francis S. Steube's *Canal Winchester Ohio: The Second Ninety Years* is a treasure trove of facts, locations and dates on 20th century town history.

Scott Stiteler's *A History of Canal Winchester High School Football: 1909-2001* is an impressive compendium of statistics and information, everything from scores, to 'Most wins by a Coach,' overall records, group photos, etc. I only wish I had known of it *prior* to spending seven months in the Ohio Historical Center's Archive/Library poring over microfilm! Once discovered, however, Scott's book was extremely helpful as a factual barometer and statistical resource. None of these authors, however, are in anyway responsible for my interpretations, oversights or mistakes.

Speaking of the Ohio Historical Center; fellow curators Cheryl Lugg Straker and Sean Pickard read the entire manuscript, offering invaluable suggestions and 'tough love.' Indeed, a former director once remarked in a staff meeting at OHS, *"If you ask Steve what time it is, he'll give you the history of the watch."* My writing suffers the same shortcoming. Cheryl and Sean were tactful, but forceful, in recommending I pare it down – considerably. I am indebted to them both. I would like to thank Herff-

Jones Publishing for allowing the use of their images found in Canal Winchester's 1974 and 1975 yearbooks - *The Pepenaus.*

No one spent more time on the manuscript, checking for grammatical errors and poor sentence structure than University of Maine professor emeritus Phil Locke. It was a labor of love, for nothing else could explain the considerable time he spent making **_Little Locke and the Mighty Indians of '75_** a much better book than it otherwise would have been. I would also like to thank Christopher Brookhouse for allowing the use of his poem, **"For Stephen,"** it its entirety; as well as everyone who sat for an interview, filled out questionnaires, endured repeated phone calls and email solicitations, or simply provided photos for the book:

Mike and Patricia Locke, Laura Locke, David Lewis, Roger Hanners, Matt Hartman, Neal Seymour, Becky Seymour Shaw, Steve Crist, Jim Will, Kurt Swiger, Elliot Swiger, Susan Willis, Bill Willison, Bill Griffith, Mark Hays, Judy Haffey Jackson, Gary Cox, Craig Cox, Denis and Karen Cox, John Hunley, Peggy Fox, Rick Ross, Dale Burrier, Colleene Fagan Weiser, Dale Burrier, Rick Shirk, Pat Zerby, Scott Jordan, Dr. Phillip Locke, Valerie Getreu-Yonnotti, Coach John Roller, Gregg Wright, Joy Wright, Letta Riddell, Edward Riddell, Jeff Damron, Gary Griffith, Lynne Helfrich and Coach Jim Tressel. Judy Fleming of the Canal Winchester Area Historical Society was especially helpful, and generous, in tracking down images, and for sage advice. Likewise, Lynne Helfrich's collection of town photos was of immense help.

I would especially like to thank my daughters, Emily and Ruby Locke, for 'being quiet while Daddy is writing,' and for their patience when Mom & Dad were reviewing the manuscript. Last, but certainly not least, I want to thank my wife, Linda Joan Locke. God was having a good day when he made her. However slight and inconsequential this book, it would not exist at all without Linda. Thank you. And thank you for rubbing my feet and legs after the spinal cord injury.

Steven P. Locke
Granville, Ohio 2012

Made in the USA
Middletown, DE
17 March 2018